GO FOR THE GOLD!

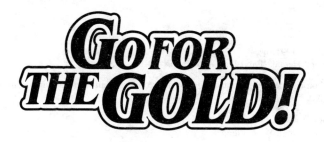

Go for the Gold!

A daily devotional for juniors

KAY D. RIZZO

Review and Herald® Publishing Association
Hagerstown, MD 21740

This book was
Edited by Richard W. Coffen
Designed by Helcio Deslandes
Cover photo by Bob Daemmrich Photos/Texas
Typeset: 10 pt Times Roman

PRINTED IN U.S.A.

96 95 94 93 92 91 10 9 8 7 6 5 4 3 2 1

R&H Cataloging Service
Rizzo, Kay D.
Go for the gold.

1. Devotional calendars—Seventh-day Adventists. 2. Adventists—Prayer—books and devotions—English. I. Title.
242

ISBN 0-8280-0613-X

MEET KAY RIZZO

"Of all the jobs I've tried, being a kid was the most difficult," Kay D. Rizzo admits. "And by the time I discovered how to play the kid game, someone changed the rules—I became an adult." Kay grew up in Troy, New York, and graduated from Union Springs Academy and later from Atlantic Union College with degrees in English and home economics. At the top of Kay's "best friends" list are Richard, her husband, and their two daughters, Rhonda and Kelli.

Kay considers herself a teacher first, a writer second. Since her first teaching assignment in a little desert church school at Sunnymead, California, Kay and her husband have taught at Shenandoah Valley Academy, Wisconsin Academy, Blue Mountain Academy, Sandia View Academy, and Milo Academy. The opportunity to live in so many exciting places and meet such interesting people supplied the background for many of the stories included in this book.

A Milo student's challenge and the invention of personal computers launched her writing career with *Guide* magazine. In 1984, Kay switched from classroom teaching to full-time writing, but will abandon her computer in an instant for the opportunity to tell children stories at camp meeting, or at Sabbath school or church, or to conduct a seminar for young writers.

Kay's insatiable curiosity sometimes gets her into trouble—such as the time she attempted to boil an egg in the microwave. Doesn't work, just makes a yucky mess to clean up!

"I'm glad that Jesus said we were to become as little children," Kay admits, "because it allows me to enjoy being the kid I always wanted to be."

DEDICATED

to my mother,
whose childlike curiosity taught me how
to really see the world around me.

WAY TO GO!

I will teach you the way you should go. Psalm 32:8, TEV.

Ready! Set! Go! The shot from the starting gun cracks through the morning air, and the race begins. The crowd cheers as the Olympic runners lunge off their starting blocks, immediately jostling for position. The course is long and hard. The runners will climb many hills and cross many valleys. "Pick 'em up 'n' put 'em down, pick 'em up 'n' put 'em down"—step after step, mile after mile they run until they finish the course.

Winning a long-distance race takes more than just being able to "pick 'em up 'n' put 'em down." To make it to the Olympics, a person must have inherent talent, personal determination, hours of practice, a balanced diet, even good sleep habits. However, the difference between the gold medal winner and the athlete who "also ran" is often owing more to the coach's ability than to that of the runner. Coaches don't teach runners how to run as much as they teach them how to win.

A runner and his or her coach analyze the runner's past races as well as the races of past Olympic winners. The coach devises a winning strategy for the runner—when to pace an opponent and when to leap ahead. The coach studies the opponent's style and behavior in order to tell his runner what to avoid. While it may look to the audience that the runner is out on the track all alone, he or she isn't. The coach is there every step of the way, sharing hints on the best way to win and shouting encouragement.

I am an Olympic runner—in the Heavenly Olympics—and I have a coach. My coach and I work on my "running" style. He helps me identify the flaws that slow me down and prescribes exercises necessary for me if I want to win. He outfits me in the best running gear available. He points out the strengths and weaknesses of past Olympic winners such as Moses, Daniel, and Sarah. He clues me in on my lying "opponent's" devious tactics. Coach has worked out a winning formula, custom-designed just for me. My coach is Jesus. He's your coach too. He can show you the way to go—and the way to win. We are guaranteed winners as long as we listen to our winner of a coach—Jesus.

Today, you and I stand on the starting block of a new year—January 1, 1992. We are training for the Heavenly Olympics. Our coach is calling out His instructions for winning the race.

Get ready! Get set! Let's go!

THE GAME PLAN

You guide me with your instruction and at the end you will receive me with honor. Psalm 73:24, TEV.

"I want to win! I want to win!" Jeff puffed his way around the track. He had to show his new coach just what he could do. Determined, he picked up and put down his left foot, then the right. And one after another, the other competitors in the race passed him, a few even lapping him, before he crossed the finish line. Jeff didn't understand it. When that starting gun sounded, he leaped from the starting block and within a few strides out-distanced even the fastest competitors. But he couldn't maintain his speed for the entire course. The same thing had happened at his last school, and now it was happening again at the academy.

Ashamed, Jeff hurried to the locker room, hoping he could shower, dress, and get away before his teammates returned from the field. And he almost succeeded. He slung his gym bag over his shoulder and turned to leave only to come face-to-face with the academy coach—the one person he wanted most to avoid. "Hey, Jeff." Coach Bentley placed his massive hand on the boy's slight shoulder. "I was impressed with your speed today."

"Impressed?" Jeff gasped, "with my speed? What speed? I was last to cross the finish line."

"True," the coach nodded. "But you sure do know how to get off that starting box."

"Great," Jeff muttered, "a lot of help that is. Within one lap I began falling behind."

The coach scowled, then said, "Do you know anything about sprinting?"

"Sprinting?"

"Yeah, sprinting," the coach repeated, looking Jeff up and down. "Body types and talents vary. Not everyone is designed for long-distance running. By the looks of you, I'd say you'd make a pretty speedy sprinter. Think about it."

"Hey," Jeff responded and broke into a big smile. "Maybe you're right. Maybe I've been trying out for the wrong sport all along. How'd you know?"

Coach Bentley grinned and tousled the boy's hair. "It's my job to know, son."

Your coach, Jesus, knows what's best for you too. It's His job to know. So just ask Him which way to go. He already knows the answer.

JANUARY 3

GO FOR THE GOLD

Peace be to you, fear not: your God, and the God of your father[s], hath given you treasure. Genesis 43:23.

There is more than one way to go for the gold. Imagine yourself browsing through your grandmother's attic. Sunlight filters through particles of dust as you push your great-great-grandfather's military trunk to one side. You've looked through the trunk so often, you've memorized its contents: his World War I uniform, his canteen and knapsack, his ribbons of valor for dying for his country—all smelling of mothballs.

On the spot where the trunk has been standing you notice a strand of red yarn caught between the floorboards. As you pull the yarn free, one of the boards moves. Beneath the board you find a moth-eaten, red-and-black-checkered work shirt. In the shirt pocket is a small, leather-bound book—your great-great-grandfather's diary.

Inside the front cover on the book is a folded sheet of paper, yellowed with age. Carefully you unfold it. It appears to be a map—a map to your great-great-grandfather's hidden treasure. Your heartbeat accelerates as you recall the family legends regarding your great-great-grandfather's buried treasure.

In one corner of the map, there is a drawing of a building. You recognize it as the line shack at the edge of "the old south forty." In the opposite corner is a drawing of what appears to be an outcropping of rocks. You remember climbing those rocks with your cousins last summer. At the base of the rocks is a red X. Your hands shake with excitement.

Could the map be real? Did your great-great-grandfather really hide his wealth before leaving for the war? Did he bury a chest of gold nuggets, of silver coins, of rare jewels?

This year you and I are going for the gold. In some cases, like that of the Olympics medals, the gold must be won. In others, like that of great-great-grandpa's gold, it's hidden and waiting to be found. The Bible is both a training guide for winners and a map for treasure seekers. As a map, it will lead us to the treasures of wisdom and truth. As a training guide, it will help us bring home the gold—heaven. So take your pick—training guide or treasure map—either way you win. For Jesus is true gold—gold beyond compare.

THE GOLD SEEKER

By faith Abraham, when called to go to a place he would later receive as his inheritance, obeyed and went, even though he did not know where he was going. Hebrews 11:8, NIV.

Five-year-old Ed Schieffelin's obsession for prospecting began the morning he arrived at his father's mining claim beside the Rogue River in southern Oregon. The water glittered with gold flecks. By noon he'd collected a teaspoonful of flecks. When he showed his treasure to his father, the man laughed. "That's only mica—fool's gold, son." Fool's gold or not, Ed knew he'd spend the rest of his life searching for treasure.

Many years later, in January of 1877, he struck it rich by discovering the fabulous silver ledges of Tombstone. After buying a home on San Francisco's Nob Hill for his parents, he married a young society woman. The excitement of the Tombstone strike faded quickly, and San Francisco's high society bored him. Ed longed to disappear into the backcountry once again.

After making out a will in which he left everything to his wife and his favorite nephew, the prospector headed north to Oregon. He built a cabin near the head of Days Creek, a tributary of the South Umpqua River. Whenever he needed supplies, Ed walked to the Days Creek Store.

When months passed and Ed didn't come into town for more supplies, the owner of the store decided to hike up to Ed's cabin. The grocer found Ed Schieffelin facedown on the ground outside his cabin. He'd died of a heart attack. A jar standing nearby contained samples of gold ore that later assayed at $2,000 a ton. In his diary Ed wrote that he'd found gold that would make the Tombstone mine look like a salt mine. Along with a set of general directions to the mine, he said he'd left a red woolen blanket there so that he could easily locate the spot.

When word of Ed's death reached San Francisco, his nephew traveled up from California and searched the rugged wilderness in vain. The young man returned to San Francisco empty-handed. And "the Red Blanket Mine" became a legend of the Pacific Northwest.

Like Ed Schieffelin, the man in this morning's text went out without knowing his destination—not because he felt restless and bored, but because God directed him to do so. Abraham traded the comforts of Ur for the discomforts of the wilderness, not because he wanted to find fabulous wealth, but because he was searching for a city of gold "whose builder and maker is God."

FAULTY MINE CLAIM

All the silver and gold of the world is mine. Haggai 2:8, TEV.

Each Sunday afternoon in September and October, Mark and Jeff, two academy sophomores, panned for gold at the base of Coffee Creek, where the stream flowed into the South Umpqua River. They filled four pill bottles with the small pebbles of gold they'd found.

In the academy library, the boys found a book on lost mines and hidden treasures. They read about Ed Schieffelin and the Red Blanket Mine. An honest-to-goodness gold mine near Coffee Creek—their creek? From that moment on, they dreamed of finding the fabled mine.

One particular Sunday, Mike and Jeff hiked up the rocky crags along Coffee Creek. After scrambling through a maze of blackberry bushes, they stepped into a clearing. The unexpected sound of a rifle bullet zinging over their heads caused Mike and Jeff to bite the dust.

A giant shadow loomed over them. "Get up!"

They obeyed. The sight of their grizzled assailant did little to inspire confidence. Mark eyed the wild-eyed stranger, then the rifle. Mark was scared! Glancing toward his friend, Mark could see the same terror reflected in Jeff's eyes.

The man aimed the gun at Jeff's forehead. "What ya' snoopin' around here for—my gold?"

"I-ah-well-uh—no, sir!" Jeff stammered.

"I'll use this rifle if I have to, to protect my claim." The man squinted his cold, beady eyes at Jeff. "The gold's mine—all mine! I'm only gonna' tell you boys once. Get out of here before I change my mind and decide to finish you off."

Terrified, Mike and Jeff took off like a shot in the direction the man indicated—stumbling and falling in their haste. The zing of a second bullet passing mere inches above their heads sent them sprawling into a patch of poison oak.

"And don't come back, ya' hear?" The man's last warning wasn't necessary.

When the boys reached the highway, they stopped to catch their breath. "I wonder if he's staked his claim yet?" Jeff asked.

"Hey, that rifle was all the mining claim I need. It's all his as far as I'm concerned."

However, Mark and the irate prospector were wrong. All the silver and gold is God's, not man's. Like so many other people in this world, the prospector will spend his life fighting to keep something that isn't his. And it's possible that he'll never gain the richest treasure of all—eternity.

JANUARY 6

HETTY'S TREASURE

For where your treasure is, there will your heart be also. Matthew 6:21.

The boy groaned as Hetty examined his inflamed leg. Ned's pain was excruciating. Overnight, his leg had swollen twice its normal size. The once minor infection had inched its way up the boy's calf and into his thigh.

Hetty shook her head sadly. "Only a doctor can help you now." Knowing how much the private hospitals of New York City charged for patient care, Hetty loaded her fever-racked son into the family carriage. They searched from one end of Manhattan to the other for a "free" clinic where the poor could be treated for very little money.

When she found one, Hetty rushed her son into the waiting room. The hospital receptionist summoned a physician immediately. One look at the boy's leg and the doctor shook his head sadly. "I'm sorry, ma'am, the infection has spread so far that all I can do is remove his leg. If only you had brought him in sooner."

Ned cried and pleaded, "No, don't take off my leg."

The doctor had no choice. The leg had to come off.

Frustrated, the physician pounded his fist on the operating table. "The poverty in this city," he shouted. "Will we ever win the battle against it? All for the lack of money, this boy will live out the rest of his live as an invalid!"

The good doctor didn't know that Henrietta "Hetty" Howland Robinson Green was far from poor. Instead, at the time of her son's injury, she was the world's richest woman—and the world's stingiest. When she died a few years later, she was worth $100 million. Her cash balance in one city bank alone was $31,400,000.

How could she do such a thing to her only son when there were hospitals and physicians close to her home who could have saved the boy's leg—all for a few pieces of silver? Where was her heart when her son cried out from the painful infection? Years later, as she watched her son hobble about on crutches, did she live to regret her actions?

Before she died, did Hetty discover what Jesus meant when He said, "For where your treasure is, there will your heart be also"?

OATMEAL AND ANSWERED PRAYER

In the same way the Spirit also comes to help us, weak as we are. For we do not know how we ought to pray. Romans 8:26, TEV.

I once heard a story about a missionary whom I'll call Sarah. Sarah's coworkers had already returned home to the United States on furlough. As her term of service at the small Southeast Asian mission neared its end, she began to experience severe pain in her side and stomach. To add to her misery, her paycheck from the mission board hadn't arrived.

Day after day Sarah went to the post office, hoping to find the much-needed money only to return to the mission compound empty-handed. As the pain in her stomach increased, her food supply dwindled, until all she had left was a large barrel of oatmeal—a food she detested. What could she do? Like any good Christian in an adverse situation, she prayed. Sarah asked that God heal her sickness and that the check from the mission board would arrive so she could afford a ticket home and buy something to eat other than oatmeal.

Weeks passed. Three times a day, every day, Sarah ate the hated oatmeal and watched for the letter from the United States. Slowly her health improved. Although God seemed to be answering her first request, He did nothing about her second. Finally the new missionaries arrived and with them her paycheck. After purchasing her ticket home, Sarah treated herself to a sumptuous meal in a local restaurant—not a dish of oatmeal in sight.

Immediately upon arriving in the States, she made an appointment to have a complete physical. She told the doctor about her illness and her unending diet of oatmeal.

He ordered medical tests so he could be certain Sarah's health had indeed returned. When he learned the results, the physician shook his head in disbelief. Sarah had recovered from a severe case of colitis. Had she been in the United States, the doctor would have performed surgery. He also told her that the hated diet of oatmeal had most likely healed her colon. Who would have guessed that the very thing Sarah hated the most was the answer to her prayer?

Like Sarah, you and I seldom know what is best for us, what we are really asking for when we pray. If we patiently trust God to do what is best for us, sooner or later we'll be glad He answered our prayers in His way and in His own time. Like Sarah, we'll discover that the King of the universe knew what He was doing all along.

JANUARY 8

VICTORY AMID THE JEERS

Let no man despise thee. Titus 2:15.

When he arrived in Munich, United States marathon runner Frank Shorter was returning to the city where he'd been born. He would be competing against his native countrymen in the 1972 Olympics. Once Frank began running the 26-mile marathon, all thoughts other than winning the race left his mind. He had maintained a good rhythm throughout the first 9 miles. Bored with the slow pace of the race, Frank accelerated, slowly pulling ahead of the other runners. From that moment on, he was never again challenged.

As he entered the stadium where the course ended, Frank expected to be greeted by cheers and applause. Instead, he emerged through the tunnel onto the track to booing and whistling. Confused, he wondered what he'd done wrong. He continued running in spite of the discouraging welcome.

What Frank didn't know was, just minutes before he arrived, one of the spectators had leaped from the stands and had run a full lap around the field before the security guards caught him and hustled him away. The shouts of censure were aimed at the spectator, not at Frank. Frank completed the race and won the gold medal for the United States.

It was natural for Frank to think the audience was booing him. No one else was around, or so he thought. However, despite the booing audience, Frank didn't give up. A real winner never does. For you see, "quitters never win, and winners never quit!" Have you ever tried to go for the gold, only to have other people boo you? It's discouraging, isn't it? It's tempting to give up, to quit running. I know. It's happened to me once in a while too. But God's Word advises us, "Let no man despise you." Refuse to be sidetracked by other people's opinions. Ignore the crowd's boos, hisses, and jeers. Go for the gold!

JANUARY 9

HECETA'S HAUNTED HOUSE

Put on all the armor that God gives you, so that you will be able to stand up against the Devil's evil tricks. For we are not fighting against human beings but against the wicked spiritual forces in the heavenly world. Ephesians 6:11, 12, TEV.

Ghosts and goblins? Do they really exist, or are they created by Hollywood scriptwriters? My Bible tells me that there is a very real world inhabited by Satan and his demons.

Whenever I hear about mysterious happenings that can't be logically explained, whenever I am tempted to be afraid of evil creatures lurking in the night, I remember a strip of beach along the Oregon coast called Heceta. Heceta is a small horseshoe-shaped alcove, a quiet eddy where I like to look for driftwood and to build sand castles. The rough hillside rising from the sandy beach is covered with evergreens that have been distorted by storms, tangled vines, and a scrub brush called Scotch Broom. Nestled in the curve of the cove, a sprawling four-story mansion looms high above the secluded beach. The owners of this stately home and its overnight visitors claim that the mansion is inhabited by a number of "playful ghosts."

The mansion's reputation for being haunted has lured tourists from all over the world. These seekers of the supernatural come to photograph the mansion, hoping to catch a glimpse of one of the resident ghosts.

The first time I saw the mansion and learned of its reputation, I felt chills run up and down my spine. I wanted to get away, to leave Heceta as quickly as possible. For I believe in keeping as far away from Satan's team of invisible tricksters as possible.

While I could get in my car and drive away from the haunted house of Heceta, sometimes there seems to be no way of escape from the devil and his evil buddies. In Ephesians 6, God tells us how to prepare for those times. He lists the armor we should use to avoid being injured by Satan's burning arrows or spears. Read Ephesians 6:11-18.

For fun, substitute the names of some of the modern soldier's equipment in the places for the old-time warriors' pieces of armor.

JANUARY 10

HECETA'S OTHER HOUSE

For I am convinced that neither death nor life, neither angels nor demons, neither the present nor the future, nor any powers, neither height nor depth, nor anything else in all creation, will be able to separate us from the love of God that is in Christ Jesus our Lord. Romans 8:38, 39, NIV.

If the haunted mansion were Heceta's only feature, I would never, ever return. But it's not. A building far more impressive draws me back again and again to this tiny stretch of sand. Each day when the evening shadows seep into the cove, filling each nook and crevice, the mysterious

Heceta Mansion disappears into the darkness of the night. Another structure, smaller and much less imposing, captures the visitors' attention. For perched higher up the hillside, on the northern rim of the cove, is a squatty runt of a lighthouse.

The light inside the white tower can be seen more than 30 miles out into the ocean's inky blackness. That powerful light saves hundreds of lives each year by faithfully sending a warning to the ships traveling along the jagged Pacific coastline. "Beware!" it says. "Dangerous rocks!" Fishing trawlers, pleasure boaters, freighters, and ocean liners depend on the light. After I've viewed the imposing mansion by day, at night the Heceta lighthouse puts everything back into perspective for me. Scary things do exist in this world. Whether they be ghosts or extraterrestrial beings or any of a hundred other strange occurrences that I can't always explain away logically, the Heceta lighthouse reassures me.

It reminds me that when unexplainable things happen, when it seems the "bad guys" are winning, I have today's promise that no matter how scary the world may get, or how frightened I may become, nothing—*nothing*—can separate me from Jesus and His love. No demons, no ghosts, no goblins, no little green spacemen, no forces of evil, can blot out Jesus and the light of truth He shines into my heart. No one can do that but me. I don't know how you feel about that promise, but I like it! It makes me even more determined than ever to keep as close to the Light as I possibly can—to let absolutely nothing come between me and God's love.

JANUARY 11

POWER IN SMALL PACKAGES

Kind words bring life, but cruel words crush your spirit. Proverbs 15:4, TEV.

If I told you that I have the most powerful and the most deadly weapon ever invented right here in my house, would you believe me? Probably not—but I'm telling the truth. It sits on the top shelf of my computer desk. It's a dictionary.

A dictionary? That's right, a dictionary. Not a nuclear energy plant, not a Peterbilt semi, not Mr. Body Builder of 1992, not a Russian-made, heat-sensing missile, but a plain, ordinary dictionary. Think about it for a moment. Simple words, strung together in just the right order, can change the world. Consider Adolf Hitler's book *Mein Kampf.*

Also, a few simple words, strung together in a totally different order, can bring freedom, peace, and happiness to the people of the earth.

Examples might be the Declaration of Independence, the United States Constitution, and Jesus' sermon on the mount. Have I convinced you yet of the power of words?

Read on. Did you know that the first hijacking of an airplane didn't occur at 37,000 feet in the air, but between the pages of a best-selling novel? Did you know that a middle-aged, balding man from the Midwest created a character in a book that affected an entire generation of young people? You've heard of Rambo, haven't you? And did you know that during the 1970s, a singing group called the Carpenters recorded "We've Only Just Begun," a song that convinced hundreds of people who had intended to commit suicide to choose life instead? The words of the song replaced with hope the discouragement these people felt.

Good or bad, words do change people. Whoever first said "Sticks and stones may break my bones, but names will never hurt me" didn't know what he or she was talking about. Broken bones heal much faster than broken hearts. And physical scars fade much sooner than scars left on the mind. Perhaps this is why the two saddest words in the English language are "too late." And the two most hopeful words—"I'm sorry."

So, do you ever feel weak and insignificant? Do you wish you had the power to change things, to make the world a little better? Through the gift of words, that power is already yours. You already possess the tools to change your home, your school, your church—and even your world. Through your choice of words, you can delight or destroy.

JANUARY 12

SET OUT TO WIN

Look straight ahead with honest confidence; don't hang your head in shame. Plan carefully what you do, and whatever you do will turn out right. Proverbs 4:25, 26, TEV.

So you want to be an Olympic winner? You want to bring gold medals home? You want to be the best runner, the best swimmer, the best pianist, the best student?

Jon Henricks, gold-medalist swimmer at the 1956 Melbourne Summer Olympics, gives this advice after his fifty-sixth straight win during a three-year period: "You see that pool there—well if you want to (be the best), dive in and start swimming. You do that for three, four, or five years, and every time you stop swimming, your coach bawls you out. . . . You get a crazy ear infection from the tropical waters, but you keep swimming. You shave your head and look like a zombie so that you can cut down on water resistance, and shave your legs for the same reason. You get invitations to parties and write back regrets. You are unable to accept due to a prior commitment—the pool. Up and down, up and down, then up and down again. You finish and it's time to do some weight lifting—or maybe go to sleep while your friends are out playing golf or fishing.'' Maybe then you can reach the top.

You have big dreams, goals for success? Perhaps you want to master the violin or the tennis court. Maybe you want to become a brain surgeon or an architectural engineer, or discover the cure for multiple sclerosis. Or your dream might be to be the next Sandi Patti.

Before you begin, consider the cost. What will you give up? Ask God to guide you in your choices. If your goal is worth reaching, it will take up both your time and your energy.

JANUARY 13

THE BEST WAY

Ask where the good way is, and walk in it, and you will find rest for your souls. Jeremiah 6:16, NIV.

Kevin just couldn't decide. Should he spend an extra hour after school working on his science project, or should he go down to the gym and shoot a few hoops? He could see nothing wrong with either of the activities. He'd get an A on his science project just as it was. But he also knew that if he spent a little more time on it, he could work out a few of the problems, and it would be spectacular. On the other hand, he'd been putting in long hours on the project, and shooting a few hoops with the guys would help him unwind.

That's when Kevin decided to ask his grandmother. Left penniless, the 15-year-old boy had come to live with his grandmother after his parents were killed in a car accident. During that time, he'd come to admire her wise counsel. He explained his dilemma to her.

Grandma listened, then explained that we don't always have to choose between good and evil. More often choices are between good and better. Sometimes there are no easy answers.

''I always make it a rule,'' Grandma explained, ''that if I have two possible choices and both seem right, I choose the hardest one to do. Almost always the hardest way is the best way.''

Kevin wasn't too certain about his grandmother's formula for success, but he decided to go along with it anyway. He worked on his science project and improved it. His teacher displayed Kevin's project at the state science competition, where he won first prize and a four-year scholarship to the college of his choice.

Do you have choices to make? If you want to be a winner like Kevin and Jon Henricks, the Olympic swimmer, it will take hard choices on your part. So how do you decide? When you read God's Word and you still don't know the answers, perhaps Kevin's grandmother's advice can help you choose the best part.

JANUARY 14

HOTDOGGING THE SUMMIT

Sometimes it takes a painful experience to make us change our ways. Proverbs 20:30, TEV.

Doug groaned in pain. He'd broken his leg, he just knew it. He couldn't believe his lousy luck. The first time on the mountain for the new skiing season, and now this.

It wasn't that Doug didn't know how to ski. The 11-year-old had been skiing almost since he had learned to walk. And the slopes—he knew every twist and turn of Mount Bachelor's ski runs, especially his favorite, the Summit.

"Remember to warm up on red before you try to ski the advanced runs," Mother had warned before driving out of the resort parking lot.

"Practically a bunny slope," Doug muttered as he stomped across the parking lot to the ski lifts. "Man, I think I know enough about skiing to choose which run I should begin on."

When he reached the ski lift area, Doug glanced toward the red lift and sighed. He'd been aching all fall to ski the Summit again. By just looking at the sign, he could almost feel himself sailing over the moguls. Then Doug made a decision—a decision that would remain with him for months to come. Minutes later Doug tried to move his right leg. The sharp pain brought tears to his eyes.

"Oh, no," he gasped, "I'll probably be grounded for the entire season. Where's the ski patrol when you want them, anyway?"

Before long, the ski patrol arrived, loaded Doug onto the toboggan, and transported him to the emergency station. Doug grimaced when the nurse asked him for his phone number.

"Does my mom have to know?" he asked sheepishly. *I hate it when she's right*, he thought.

The nurse laughed. "Don't you think she'll get suspicious when you show up at home with your leg in a cast? I'll have her meet you at the hospital."

Doug turned his head to the wall. *If only my ski binding hadn't jammed*, he thought. *If only that little kid hadn't appeared out of nowhere. If only I hadn't disobeyed Mom and tried to ski the Summit before doing a few runs on red first. If only . . . if only!*

JANUARY 15

A KERNEL OF FAITH

Now faith is being sure of what we hope for and certain of what we do not see. Hebrews 11:1, NIV.

Have you ever wondered what makes one popcorn kernel pop and another not? If you were to line up 10 kernels of corn in a row, could you tell in advance which of the kernels will pop and which won't? And why can't you place the unpopped kernels back in the popper and let them try again? You know, "If at first you don't succeed, try, try again." Think about it. Well, it makes sense to me, or at least, it did until I learned the secret of popping corn.

The secret to perfect popping lies within each kernel. Each kernel of corn either has a droplet of moisture hidden in its inner core or it doesn't. If the moisture is inside the kernel, the heat from your popper will turn the moisture to steam. And since steam takes more space than liquid, the pressure pushes against the inside of the kernel until it pops open. The result is a fluffy, white piece of popcorn. And if there is no moisture inside the kernel, it will just lie on the bottom of the popcorn popper and get hot. That's why a dead kernel won't pop if you try a second time. If there was no moisture within the kernel in the first place, there certainly won't be any the second time you heat it. Makes sense, huh?

Some types of corn have more moisture in them than others. Scientists crossbreed different strains of corn to create kernels that contain a larger moisture content. That's why Orville Redenbacher can claim that his corn is the "poppingest."

Now think about this fact: Whether your parents believe in God or not, when they go to the supermarket and buy a bag of unpopped popcorn, they probably don't question the grocer about the contents of the bag. They don't demand proof that the kernels in the bag contain the needed moisture in order to achieve the promised results. They most likely purchase the unpopped popcorn by faith—faith in the grocer, faith in the food distributor, faith in the farmer, and faith in the Creator.

Faith is such a little thing. As the text says: "Now faith is being sure of what we hope for [a bowl of hot, buttered popcorn] and certain of what we do not see [the droplet of moisture inside the kernel]." Why is it so easy for people to believe in a kernel of unpopped popcorn and so hard to believe in the Creator who placed the moisture inside the kernel in the first place?

JANUARY 16

A GREAT DAY FOR DREAMING

I run straight toward the goal in order to win the prize, which is God's call through Christ Jesus to the life above. Philippians 3:14, TEV.

"I'm going to enter the New York Marathon!" Linda declared.

"Come on, Linda, be serious," her friend replied.

For the average person, a 26-mile run is hardly more than a dream. For Linda Downs, it was an impossible dream. If she could not walk across her bedroom without the aid of crutches, how could she run a footrace?

Helen, a blind and deaf child, wanted the impossible also. She wanted to go to school.

Martin also dared to dream. He dreamed of a world devoid of prejudice—an impossible dream for a Black man. Like Linda and Helen, Martin did more than just dream. He turned his dream into a reality by working toward that goal.

And now, in 1992, history records the successes of these three dreamers. Linda Downs "ran" the 1982 New York City Marathon. Her time: 11 hours. Impressive for the first person ever to complete the 26-mile New York City Marathon on crutches. By crossing the finish line, Linda destroyed the mental and physical barriers for any person daring to dream beyond his supposed limitations.

And what about the deaf-blind woman? Helen Keller earned her Ph.D. Her accomplishment brought her the applause of presidents, prime ministers, and kings. Her writings and public speeches inspired thousands of impaired—and nonimpaired—individuals to go beyond, to break the mental and physical chains imprisoning them, to dare to attempt the impossible.

And while Martin Luther King, Jr., never saw his dream fulfilled, he did correct the nearsightedness of millions of people. He helped America see its citizens in beautiful, living, vibrant color instead of just black and white.

Linda, Helen, and Martin—three champions who dreamed three impossible dreams and won. What are your dreams today? Find out by doing the following exercise.

On a piece of notebook paper, write down one dream. Skip five lines, then write another dream, and so on until you run out of either paper or dreams. Across from each dream, list the things you'd need to do in order to turn that dream into reality. Discuss your dream list with God. Ask Him to help you choose the dreams that best fit His plans for you. Now for the fun part! Choose to do one thing today that will bring you closer to reaching one of the dreams on your list. This is how you begin turning a dream into a goal.

JANUARY 17

TURNING AWAY WRATH

A soft answer turns away wrath, but harsh words cause quarrels. Proverbs 15:1, TLB.

At the end of the service, the church's new preacher—fresh out of the seminary—stood at the door of the church to shake the parishioners' hands as they left. He had looked forward to this moment ever since the day in his sophomore year of high school that he'd decided to enter the ministry. Pleased with his morning message, the young pastor graciously thanked each member who complimented him on his sermon. One after another, the people introduced themselves to him, and he struggled to remember each of their names.

He had just shaken the hand of the head elder of the congregation when a matronly, middle-aged woman shook his outstretched hand and said, "I'm glad it's over."

The pastor bristled. *How dare she*, he thought. *She's glad my carefully prepared sermon is over? Did she find it that boring and difficult to sit through?*

The young man struggled to maintain his composure by giving the woman a sickly-sweet smile. "I beg your pardon," he replied.

The woman smiled pleasantly back at him and again said, "I'm glad it's over."

He couldn't believe his ears. Of all the nerve! Tempted to utter a sharp or sarcastic reply, the pastor swallowed hard and responded, "Well, maybe you'll enjoy next week's sermon more."

The woman eyed him curiously. "But I enjoyed this week's sermon, Pastor." By now, the head elder and a number of other church members were listening to the conversation.

The young minister scowled and cleared his throat. "Then, if you don't mind my asking, why did you say you were glad it was over?"

The woman and the nearby church members burst into laughter. The minister couldn't imagine what he'd said that was so funny.

When the woman managed to catch her breath, she explained. "Pastor, I was introducing myself. I said, 'I'm Gladys Over.' That's my name—Gladys Over."

The pastor reddened, cleared his throat again, and laughed along with the crowd, forever thankful he'd chosen a kind reply rather than the sarcastic one he first believed the woman deserved.

JANUARY 18

A BIBLE OF MY OWN

Thy word have I hid in mine heart, that I might not sin against thee. Psalm 119:11.

The little blue car bounced along the bumpy Los Angeles side street. From the middle of the backseat, Flora glanced at her two new friends. From the time Flora had met Alhandra, the two girls had asked her an endless barrage of questions. When Alhandra learned that Flora had Saturdays off from work, she invited Flora to attend church with her. Alhandra explained that the first part of the service was Bible study. "We all use our own Bibles and contribute to the discussion."

Flora's eyes narrowed. "Do you expect me to believe that you own a Bible, a Spanish Bible of your own?"

"Of course," Alhandra replied.

"You're making a joke, a very unkind joke." Flora drew her lips into a thin line.

"We're not joking, Flora," Noemi assured her new friend. "We have oodles of Spanish Bibles at our house."

"I don't believe you!"

"I'll prove it to you. I'll give you one to keep."

"Seriously?" Flora asked, her eyes wide and pleading.

"Yes."

Flora couldn't believe her good fortune. She would have her very own Bible. *Truly America is a land of great riches after all*, she thought. Before leaving El Salvador, Flora vowed she would not return home until she owned her own Bible. In El Salvador, Flora could never even hope to possess such a treasured item. The few pesos she earned barely supplied her with enough food to eat.

The young woman's appetite for God's Word had been whetted by a substitute teacher at the convent school she'd attended. The texts he secretly shared with his pupils only made Flora crave more. When she asked him for a Bible, he shook his head sadly. "I'm so sorry, muchacha, but Bibles are very expensive, and I haven't got that kind of money."

And now, years later and many miles from home, Flora was being offered a Bible of her very own.

Noemi and Alhandra kept their promise. Instead of taking Flora straight home, they detoured to Alhandra's place to pick up a Spanish Bible for Flora.

Flora could hardly wait to reach her studio apartment. Text by text, she discovered the treasures hidden between the black leather covers. Though she has read through the Scriptures many times since she received her first Bible, the promises she finds within those pages mean more to her with every passing year.

JANUARY 19

CRAMPED HIS STYLE

A good name is more desirable than great riches; to be esteemed is better than silver or gold. Proverbs 22:1, NIV.

Two competitors at the marathon championship Olympic games in 1904 were Felix Carvagal, a postman from Cuba, and Fred Lorz, of the United States. Though he'd never competed in an athletic event and had only a hazy idea of what a marathon race was, Felix hitchhiked his way to St. Louis. He showed up at the race wearing what spectators described as a nightshirt. The race had already started when a group of the American athletes found him some running gear.

Carvagal treated the entire event as a joke. He waved and shouted to the spectators as he ran. Occasionally he even stopped to chat with people along the way. After picking and eating a few peaches and a few apples from the trees along the route, Felix developed a stomachache and had to stop for a few minutes.

In spite of all the delays, he came in fourth. Officials believe that if Felix had taken the race seriously, he would have won the gold medal. He went down in Olympic history as "The Clown Prince of the Olympic Games."

Fred, on the other hand, took the marathon too seriously. He was first out of the stadium at the beginning of the race and first to break the finishing tape. Yet his name does not appear on the Olympic Roll of Honor. For, about nine miles into the race, Fred got a cramp and dropped out. He then accepted a lift in an automobile. A few miles from the stadium, the car broke down and Lorz ran the rest of the way. He received a tremendous ovation when he crossed the finish line. Just as Mrs. Roosevelt, the wife of the president, was about to pin the Olympic gold medal on him an official rushed onto the field and denounced Fred as the impostor he was. Lorz was suspended for life from participating in amateur sports.

Both men made names for themselves at the 1904 Olympics—one affectionately known as the clown prince, and the other as a disreputable impostor.

JANUARY 20

CLIMB THE HIGHEST MOUNTAIN

Jesus Christ is the same yesterday, today, and forever. Hebrews 13:8, TEV.

Mountaineer Edmund Hillary traveled from New Zealand to the Himalayan Mountains of Nepal, a small country north of India, in order to climb the highest mountain in the world—Mount Everest. He joined a team of climbers from Great Britain, along with a native guide named Tenzing Norgay.

Cold winds buffeted the team the higher they climbed up the rugged mountain. The air grew so thin that the hikers had to wear oxygen masks. One after another dropped out of the climb, until only Edmund and Tenzing were left. Almost out of oxygen, the two men decided to make one last push for the top. Up over a giant boulder and across a series of ridges, they discovered that they had nowhere else to climb. They'd conquered Mount Everest, the world's highest mountain.

Oops! Not quite. Poor Edmund and Tenzing. If they meant to climb the highest mountain on Planet Earth, some believe the team chose the wrong mountain. Mount Everest is the world's second highest mountain.

Now, wait a minute. If Mount Everest isn't the world's highest mountain, what is? Look on your map of the South American Andes for Mount Chimborazo. So who's right? Both, according to how you look at it. If you measure from sea level, then Mount Everest is 29,028 feet and Chimborazo only 20,561 feet high. However, if you measure by which mountain sticks out the farthest into space, then Mount Everest loses.

The earth is not round, you see. It bulges at the equator. At sea level, the ground surface of the earth is more than 15 miles farther from the center core of the earth at the equator than at the North Pole. Since Mount Chimborazo is 2 degrees from the equator and Mount Everest is 28 degrees, Chimborazo is approximately 2 miles higher than Everest. While the size of the two mountains hasn't changed much throughout history, science has revealed a different way of looking at them.

Don't you just hate it when you think you know the right answer and someone proves you wrong? Get used to it. In our high-tech world, what was true yesterday often proves untrue tomorrow. Nothing stays the same. You can count on it.

But God is the "same yesterday, today, and tomorrow." No sense worrying about the world's changes. The important things—like God's promises to His children—will always remain the same.

JANUARY 21

DOORS, DOORS, AND MORE DOORS

For the living know that they will die, but the dead know nothing. Ecclesiastes 9:5, NIV.

Why would anyone choose to design a house with doors that open onto solid brick walls or empty space? Why build stairs that lead nowhere? Why construct a 160-room mansion connected by miles of corridors—a six-acre crazy-quilt of a home? Fear, unreasonable fear.

Mrs. Sarah L. Winchester didn't set out to build such a bizarre house. In the 1880s, the widowed daughter-in-law of the manufacturer of the famous Winchester rifle, "the gun that won the West," moved from New England to San Jose, California, after the untimely death of her husband and two children. She bought a 17-room mansion under construction and assumed command of the 16 or more carpenters and artisans. While her orders made no sense to the experienced builders, she paid well, so they did as they were told.

Every weekday, for 38 years, the sound of sawing and hammering resounded through the rambling mansion. When she ran out of space to continue building, she bought the surrounding acreage and expanded farther.

The house became a gargantuan monstrosity of trapdoors, crooked halls, 40 stairways ascending and descending to nowhere, and more than 200 doors that open into unexpected places or no place at all. The reception room, where guests were never received, glittered with thousands of crystal prisms amid silver and gold leaf-covered carvings. The maple paneled ballroom, where no one ever entertained, housed a built-in pipe organ. The walls, floors, and ceiling in her bedroom were covered with imported white satin. Fear drove Mrs. Winchester to build the house. You see, the incredibly wealthy Mrs. Winchester was afraid of dying. When her husband and children died suddenly, she became convinced that the fortune she and her husband had inherited from her husband's father, Oliver Fisher Winchester, was cursed, tainted by the blood of all the people his guns killed. Frightened beyond reason, she turned to a spiritist medium for advice. The psychic told Sarah that as long as she kept building her house, she would not die.

In 1922 the hammering stopped. Mrs. Sarah Winchester had died. Too bad she wasted her entire fortune building doors in order to escape the guilt for sins already carried by Another. Too bad she didn't know that Jesus, God's Son, had willingly walked through the doors of death so she could live forever. Too bad Sarah Winchester did not know that when the Saviour rose from the grave, He broke down those doors of death for her. Too bad.

JANUARY 22

20/20 VISION

One thing I know, that, whereas I was blind, now I see. John 9:25.

The optometrist's assistant slipped the glasses onto Sam's nose. Instantly he felt a difference. He studied himself in the desktop three-way mirror. *Hmm*, he thought, *I need a haircut. I didn't realize I had gotten so shaggy. No wonder Mom has been hassling me about it.*

He turned toward his mother and grinned. For the first time, he noticed the little brown freckles across the bridge of her nose that Dad was always teasing her about.

As his mother paid the bill, Sam walked about the waiting room, picking up magazines, stopping to stare every time he passed a mirror. "So this is 20/20 vision," he muttered. "I like it."

During the drive home Sam marveled over everything he saw. "Have there always been three radio towers on that mountain?"

"Yes, son," Mom answered as she eased onto the interstate.

Sam kept up a running commentary on the passing scenery, reading every road sign. Suddenly he fell silent. When Sam finally spoke, he said, "Mom, I never realized you could see each individual leaf on a tree. I saw only a green blob before. Isn't that neat?"

A whole new world had opened for him. Colors were brighter. Objects stood out clearly and distinctly. Before he'd gotten the glasses, Sam hadn't realized just how much he'd been missing. At school Sam was surprised to be able to read the teacher's squiggles on the board, and at piano lessons he could see each individual note printed in his music book. Once in a while, he would slip his glasses off—just to remind himself of the difference they actually made.

Jesus speaks of people with poor spiritual eyesight—those who have eyes that cannot see and ears that cannot hear. These people think they can view spiritual truths with 20/20 vision, when actually their spiritual eyes had deteriorated much like Sam's physical eyes. And like Sam, they fail to be aware of the changes, of what they're missing.

Just as Sam's eyesight returned to a perfect 20/20 with corrective lenses, so also poor spiritual eyesight can be corrected by asking Jesus to give you spiritual glasses that will enable you to see the world through His eyes of love and understanding.

JANUARY 23

A NEW NAME

To him who overcomes, I will give some of the hidden manna. I will also give him a white stone with a new name written on it, known only to him who receives it. Revelation 2:17, NIV.

If you were planning a fancy dinner and had invited the following guests, how much food would you need to prepare? Your guest list includes: Martin Clifford, Harry Clifton, Clifford Clive, Sir Alan Cobham, Owen Conquest, Gordon Conway, Harry Dorian, Frank Drake, Freeman Fox, Hamilton Greening, Cecil Herber, Prosper Howard, Robert Jennings, Gillingham Jones, T. Harcourt Llewelyn, Clifford Owen, Ralph Redway, Ridley Redway, Frank Richards, Hilda Richards, Raleigh

Robbins, Robert Rogers, Eric Stanhope, Robert Stanley, Nigel Wallace, and Talbot Wynard. You'd go broke feeding all those people, right? Wrong! As strange as it may seem, all the names listed are the same person—Charles Harold St. John Hamilton. I don't know why Mr. Hamilton chose to use quite so many pen names for the more than 5,000 children's stories he wrote between 1906 and 1940.

There are a lot of reasons that writers choose to put names other than their own on a book. Sometimes they don't want people to know their true identity. Other times, their publisher is afraid too many books by one author will be published at one time. One author I have read about uses different pen names to make organizing his library shelves simpler—one name for his mysteries, another name on each of his biographies, and so on.

Most people think about changing their names at one time or another. Judy wishes she were a Jennifer. Rebecca imagines she'd be more glamorous if she were a Roxanne. Jason believes if his name were Jake, he'd be more macho. I once dreamed of becoming an Isabella, a character I read about in a book. While a few people, for reasons of their own, actually do go through the legal process of changing their names, most of us outgrow the urge in time.

Someday each of us, if we choose to be God's own child, will receive a new name. Our new name will fit us perfectly, since God will choose it for us.

JANUARY 24

A REAL FAILURE

Before his downfall a man's heart is proud, but humility comes before honor. Proverbs 18:12, NIV.

Honor and success result from hard work, from doing one's best, right? To a writer, it's a story in print. To an auto mechanic, it's a purring engine. To an optometrist, it's a customer with 20/20 vision. Would you consider the man I am about to describe as successful?

When he was 7 years old, he had to go to work to help support his family who had just been thrown out of their home onto the street. At age 9 this backward, shy little boy's mother died. At 22 he lost his job as a grocery store clerk. Though he wanted to go to law school, he couldn't afford it. At 23 he and a friend borrowed a great sum of money in order to buy a grocery store. Three years later his friend died, leaving him with a huge debt that took years to repay. At 28 he asked a lovely young woman to marry him; she refused. At 37, on his third try, he was elected to Congress. Two years later he ran again and lost the election. As a result he became ill from a nervous breakdown or job burnout.

At 41 his 4-year-old son, the product of an unhappy marriage, died. The next year he applied for and was rejected for the position of Land officer. Later he was defeated for the nomination for vice president of the United States. At 49 he ran for the U.S. Senate again . . . and lost again. Add to this a constant barrage of criticism, misunderstanding, rumors, and deep depression. At 51 he was elected president of the United States . . . but his second term was cut short by an assassin's bullet. He died in a tiny upstairs room across from where he'd been shot. By now you know I am speaking of one of the most highly regarded leaders in American history—Abraham Lincoln.

Abraham Lincoln failed miserably many times, yet he was a winner. Through his failures he learned to succeed by treating others more generously.

In the process of succeeding, do you make room for failures? When your teacher loses his cool, can you forgive him? When your best friend snubs you or when the class klutz drops a fly ball, how do you respond? What about Mom and Dad—do you make room for their occasional goofs? Do you allow yourself to fail without beating up on yourself? Allowing for failures—yours and others'—is the road to success. Remember, Abraham Lincoln learned the secret to success—humility comes before honor.

JANUARY 25

FRIENDS FOR LIFE

Iron sharpeneth iron; so a man sharpeneth the countenance of his friend. Proverbs 27:17.

Jesse Owens knew what the people in the stands thought as he walked out onto the track that day. This was Berlin—1936. Hitler, the country's dictator, was out to prove his theory of Aryan superiority to the world—the belief that all people not born blond and blue-eyed were inferior—especially Blacks and Jews.

With this in mind, Jesse, still in his sweatsuit, made a practice leap for the long jump, his best event. The judges counted it as his first jump. Rattled, he tried again and failed. He was one jump away from being eliminated in the tryouts when a tall, blue-eyed, blond German athlete strode up to him and introduced himself as Luz Long.

Uncertain what the German had in mind, Jesse shook hands. "Glad to meet you," he said. "How are you?"

"I'm fine," Long replied. "The question is How are you?"

"What do you mean?" Owens asked.

"Something must be eating you. You should be able to qualify with your eyes closed."

As the two men, the son of a Black sharecropper and the model of Nazi manhood talked, Long, who did not believe in the theory of Aryan superiority, gave Owens advice on how to be certain he'd qualify.

That afternoon Owens opened with an Olympic record jump. Luz Long matched it. On the final jump Owens broke the record by leaping 26 feet 5 3/8 inches, thus winning the gold medal. The first to congratulate Owens, in full view of Adolf Hitler, was Luz Long. The two men remained friends up until Luz's death in 1943. Jesse Owens admitted later, "You can melt down all the medals and cups I won, and they wouldn't be the plating on the 24-karat friendship I felt for Luz Long."

What is a test of true friendship? As in the case of Luz Long and Jesse Owens, true friends help and strengthen one another.

JANUARY 26

TOYS 'N' US

How great is the love the Father has lavished on us, that we should be called children of God! And that is what we are! 1 John 3:1, NIV.

Five-year-old Kelli believed that everything was alive—her toys, her stone collection, her shells, the furniture—everything. One Sabbath Mother invited guests home for dinner. Kelli was told to set the table while her mother changed clothes. When Mother returned, she heard Kelli talking to someone. Mother peeked around the corner in time to see her daughter talking to the everyday knives, forks, and spoons.

"Don't feel bad because we're using our good silverware today," Kelli soothed. "Mama's just giving you a day to rest, that's all. We still love you. We'll use you again tomorrow, I promise."

As Kelli grew older, she reached the Barbie and Ken doll stage of life. Kelli loved her miniature world and every doll in it. Each day, before Kelli put away her Barbies, she'd carefully dress and pose each doll in its townhouse. Though she would never admit it to anyone, she believed that when she left her bedroom, her dolls came alive. Hoping she could catch the dolls in action, more than once she crawled on her hands and knees down the hall and into her bedroom. When she saw that her doll family were posed exactly as she'd left them, Kelli decided her dolls were just too smart. They heard her coming.

One day it finally happened. The once alive and clever Barbies stopped being real to Kelli. They became toys again. The little girl with the vivid imagination had become a teenager who dreamed of someday meeting a real live "Ken" of her own.

When I am being forced to make a difficult decision, I remember Kelli and her dolls. It would be so much easier if God would move me about like Kelli did her dolls. But when God created people, He didn't want plastic Barbies and Kens, Skippers and Jasons. He didn't want mechanical toys that, when He pulled a little string would say, "I love You. I love You."

He wanted more from His created beings than Kelli received from her dolls. He wanted love. As much as Kelli loved her dolls and cared for them, not one ever showed her any love in return. That's why God didn't create a robotic Adam or a plastic Eve. He wanted real, live, mischievous, often cantankerous, sons and daughters who could appreciate the love He showered on them and could choose to love Him in return.

JANUARY 27

DIZZY, ANYONE?

For my thoughts are not your thoughts, neither are your ways my ways, saith the Lord. For as the heavens are higher than the earth, so are my ways higher than your ways, and my thoughts than your thoughts. Isaiah 55:8, 9.

Here's something to think about on this beautiful January morning. Imagine yourself standing motionless on the equator. What are you wearing? Can you feel your favorite T-shirt sticking to you because of the heat and humidity? Are there palm trees swaying in the breeze, or are you on board an anchored ocean liner? I have two questions for you. Even though you appear to be standing still, in how many directions are you traveling and at what speeds? Think about your answers.

You're automatically traveling at 1,000 miles per hour because of the rotation of the earth. At the same time, the earth circles the sun at 66,500 miles an hour. Simultaneously, the solar system (sun, earth, and other planets) is revolving around the hub of the galaxy, the Milky Way, at approximately 500,000 miles per hour.

Feeling dizzy yet? Your trip's not over. The Milky Way, in turn, is moving about the core of a cluster of galaxies at 1,350,000 miles an hour.

And, as Edward K. Conklin of Stanford University calculates, the Milky Way is moving outward from this core at a measly speed of 360,000 miles per hour.

So how many directions are you traveling at one time?

That's right. You're traveling in five different directions simultaneously. That's the easy part of the problem. Now for the difficult one—how many miles are you traveling each hour?

All right, don't waste too much lead and notepaper on this question. Also, save your calculator's battery. Even the most advanced mathematicians cannot calculate the speed achieved by combining these five sets of movements. And all this is happening while you are standing still somewhere along the equator.

The incredible greatness of the universe boggles the mind. Humans can't begin to understand the mathematical computations God used in order to create the universe. Imagine asking that enormous Intellect to explain just how He constructed the universe. It will take an eternity to understand the workings of such a Creator. And who knows, maybe you and I will be lucky enough to watch as He sets new worlds into motion!

JANUARY 28

ONE OF A KIND

You saw me before I was born. . . . [My] every day was recorded in your Book! Psalm 139:16, TLB.

Look in a mirror. What do you see? A thatch of brown hair? A shock of red? Golden curls or heavy black braids? Do you see brown eyes staring back at you? Blue? Hazel? Gray? Do freckles play dot-to-dot across your nose? Does a set of pointy ears ruin an otherwise reasonably well-put-together face? And those braces! Does the glint from all the metal in your mouth make you feel like an extraterrestrial being? Look closer, beyond the nose you believe is too long or too pugged, or just too, too __________ . (You fill in the blank.) Have you ever seen another face exactly like yours? Even if you are one of a matched set, your face is slightly different than your twin's.

On the day you were born, a nurse wrapped you in a blanket of either blue or pink, then carried you to the hospital nursery, where she placed you in a clear plastic bassinet alongside the other newborns. And if, when family members gathered beyond the glass partition to make strange faces at you, the nurse didn't point you out, they wouldn't have been able to identify which of the hairless, toothless, wrinkled creatures was actually theirs.

Fortunately, as days turned into weeks, and weeks into months, you got better looking. Your complexion softened. Your facial features molded along family lines until you became the lovely person you see in your mirror today—and you're not finished yet. The next 10, 20, 1,000 years will change you in ways you can't imagine.

However, your heavenly Father knows the changes that will take place. He has a personal interest in you, right from your very first moment of existence.

Before you were placed in the hospital nursery, before you uttered your first ear-splitting squall, before you emerged from your warm, little cocoon, your heavenly Father noted the tilt of your nose and smiled at your pixie-shaped ears. Once again, He saw His image reproduced. And He said, "That's good."

Now, look in your mirror again. Can you see the beautiful person God sees when He looks at you? The creature made in His own image? The one who would grow into the crown of His creation?

JANUARY 29

NOT EXACTLY KID STUFF

Do not let anyone look down on you because you are young, but be an example for the believers in your speech, your conduct, your love, faith, and purity. 1 Timothy 4:12, TEV.

"Teenagers today! What's this world coming to?"

Have you wondered what happens to a perfectly normal child when he turns 13? Does some strange, invisible force change him from a human to a monster? Does becoming a teenager scare you enough so that you wish you could leap directly to age 20? Before you try, you should meet a few special teenagers.

Louis Braille invented the Braille alphabet for the vision-impaired at the age of 15. Philo Farnsworth, 16, discovered the basic principles of television. God gave Ellen Harmon, age 17, her first vision of heaven. At age 13 Marjorie Gestring won an Olympic gold medal in springboard-diving. Georgia "Tiny" Thompson, age 15, became the first woman to parachute from an airplane. Fourteen-year-old Nadia Comaneci, of Romania, made world headlines when she scored seven perfect 10s at the

Olympics. Steveland Morris, born blind, wrote and recorded a solid gold hit by the age of 12. (Ever hear of Stevie Wonder?)

During the War Between the States, teenage boys, students at a military academy in Virginia, held off the Union Army until a regiment of Southern troops arrived, thus preventing the North from capturing the Shenandoah Valley. Kid stuff? No way! Every person I mentioned is a winner who just happened to be a kid.

You may not be athletic like Nadia, or scientific like Philo, or have the exceptional musical talents of Stevie Wonder. You may be nowhere near as brave as Tiny. That's OK. That's all the more reason to meet another remarkable teenager. No matter where your talents may lie, you can be a Timothy.

Timothy was a winner too. The apostle Paul told Timothy not to let people put him down because of his age—even though that was just what they were doing. Paul told his young friend to be an example in speech, conduct, love, faith, and purity to his church—talents any of us can receive through Jesus. Remember the text "I can do all things through Christ which strengtheneth me"? Like Timothy, your teenage years can be the very greatest if you choose to let Christ strengthen you.

How many winners can you name from the Bible and the early Seventh-day Adventist Church who also just happened to be in their teens?

JANUARY 30

CREATURE OF DEATH

What man is he that desireth life, and loveth many days, that he may see good? Psalm 34:12.

You are standing by the girls' locker room at school, waiting for the coach when you overhear the following conversation between two of your friends, Angie and Sandy. You recognize their voices immediately.

"Do you mean to tell me that Lynn got an A on the history final?" Angie snarls.

"That's right," Sandy replies. "She got not only an A but a perfect paper!"

"Hmmph! It's not hard to figure out how she did that," Angie suggests. "After all, she does correct papers for the History Department."

"You think she cheated? I never took Lynn for a cheat."

"Look, she sits alone in Mr. Singer's office, correcting papers, for three hours every day. Just how difficult would it be to peek into his test files just before an exam and . . ."

You know Angie's accusations are untrue because you are Lynn. How do you feel? Like you've been trampled by a crazed elephant or mauled by a rogue grizzly bear? As if your worst nightmare has come true—that the most bloodthirsty creature ever created has turned you into chopped liver? What beast do you think that might be? What animal causes human beings the most pain? Wolves? Lions? Crocodiles? Boa constrictors?

No, it is a tiny organism found on a mosquito. This creature spends part of its life cycle in a mosquito and part in a human (or other mammal) and is responsible for the most deadly scourge known to humanity—malaria. And since the mosquito lives on 70 percent of the world's land surface, this annoying little creature has, without a doubt, caused more suffering and deaths than all the wars combined. All because of that tiny, pesky mosquito. A little thing—such a little thing!

Like the human tongue—uncontrolled. Angie's sting hurts. And unless Angie learns to control her tongue better than the World Health Organization controls the mosquito, she'll be miserable the rest of her life. So will everyone around her. For while Angie can do little to control malaria, she can do a lot to control her tongue.

JANUARY 31

RICHES BEYOND IMAGINATION

They [the Bereans] received the word with all readiness of mind, and searched the scriptures daily, whether those things were so. Acts 17:11.

The senior archaeologist listened in disbelief to the deep-sea diver. "Sir, we found her. We really found the mother lode this time." The mother lode the young diver was excited about was the hull of *Atocha*, a Spanish galleon sunk off the coast of Key West, Florida, in 1622.

The divers uncovered riches beyond belief: bars of solid gold, chests filled with rare silver coins, copper ingots the size of manhole covers, gem-studded jewelry, and emeralds the size of Easter eggs. The value of the find? Priceless.

The sunken vessel should have been discovered much sooner than it was. For the wreck had settled a mere 20 to 30 feet beneath the surface of water at low tide. Throughout the years, debris accumulated atop the ship's hull. Before the divers could reach the treasure, they had to clear away layers of tangled fishing line, rusted hooks, and litter discarded by weekend fishermen. Imagine bobbing about in a little fishing boat only 20 feet above such an enormous treasure and never even knowing it!

Throughout time weekend scholars have obscured the truths of the Bible with layers of tangled lies and rusty snares. These casual "fishermen" often found themselves frustrated when their fishing lines hooked a snag—some text that just didn't seem to make any sense. By digging a little deeper, they would have uncovered unbelievable treasure.

The Bereans, a group of people from the city of Berea remembered for their serious study of the Bible, searched daily to uncover the deepest riches of God's Word. They refused to bob about only on the surface of God's Word, hoping to catch a promise here or a blessing there.

While only the best deep-sea divers were hired to dive for the *Atocha's* sunken treasure, you and I with the aid of the Holy Spirit can dive deeply into God's Word and discover His treasure chest for ourselves. Like the people of old Berea, we will grow rich on God's unending promises.

FEBRUARY 1

FROZEN FISH

Listen to what is wise and try to understand it. Yes, beg for knowledge; plead for insight. Look for it as hard as you would for silver or some hidden treasure. Proverbs 2:2-4, TEV.

Which is heavier, a bucket of ice or a bucket of water?

Since solid objects are heavier than liquids, the bucket of ice would be the heavier, right? Wrong. Water is different than most liquids because as it freezes, it becomes lighter.

So who cares? Fish, for one. If ice were heavier than water, a pond would freeze from the bottom up. This would cause the water plants to freeze and die. As the level of ice would rise, the fish would have to swim in shallower and shallower water, finally becoming frozen on the surface—not too cool for the fish population.

Instead, ice, being lighter than water, floats, allowing underwater plants and creatures to live year-round.

The world is full of interesting trivia that teach us about God. Our Creator overlooked no detail. If the tiny minnows in the lakes and the silver trout in the streams are important to Him, how much more concern must He have for you, His very own child?

Today's text advises you to "beg for knowledge; plead for insight. Look for it as hard as you would for silver or some hidden treasure." Nature's hidden treasures will help you understand your Creator better. In doing so, you will learn to love Him more.

So what's new with you today? What can you discover today about God's love for you?

FEBRUARY 2

MORE THAN A LITTLE LOVE

As a father has compassion on his children, so the Lord has compassion on those who fear him. Psalm 103:13, NIV.

Before the Vietnam War, wealthy Mr. Fong operated a prosperous umbrella factory in Saigon, South Vietnam. After the war, the Communists moved Mr. Fong and his wife, and their four daughters and 8-year-old son, Tu, into one small room of the original home they'd had before the North Vietnamese invasion. The government took charge of the umbrella factory and appointed Mr. Fong to manage the company. At the same time, the new government confiscated all the South Vietnamese people's fine art pieces, expensive jewelry, and gold and silver. While Mr. Fong obediently turned over the larger portion of his wealth to the government officials, he kept a small portion for emergencies.

Thankful just to be alive, the Fongs adjusted to the financial changes, to the enforced curfews, and to the other new laws inflicted on them. All laws except one. This one law disturbed them greatly. It required all males over the age of 12 to sign up for the draft. This law wasn't a problem for Mr. Fong. He was too old to be drafted into the army. However, their only son, Tu, was not.

Mr. and Mrs. Fong knew what happened to the younger boys when drafted. The smallest of the boys were ordered to crawl into holes in the ground, and through low, narrow tunnels, to find and defuse booby traps and land mines left behind by the American Army. If these young boys returned home at all after their military service, it was usually without a hand or an arm or a leg. The nightmare of such a tragedy crippling his number one son haunted Mr. Fong. As Tu approached the age when he'd be required to register, Mr. Fong's concern increased. The Buddhist father realized that he couldn't just stand by and do nothing. He had to do something—anything! But what?

When you see pictures of people from other cultures and countries, do you ever wonder if they feel the same things you feel? If they love as much as you love, or hurt as much as you hurt? The Fongs' story reminds us that concern for loved ones is universal. The loving Creator instilled in the hearts of human beings, whether Buddhist or Christian, Muslim or Hindu,

American or Chinese, French or Lebanese, the feeling of compassion for their children. Only sin can destroy this inherent love and compassion.

(Story to be continued tomorrow.)

FEBRUARY 3

MORE PRECIOUS THAN GOLD

The glory of children are their fathers. Proverbs 17:6.

Mr. Fong decided that no matter what it took, he would not stand by and watch the life of his number one son be destroyed. He devised a plan to prevent this terrible fate. When Tu reached his eleventh birthday, Mr. Fong contacted a member of the country's underground—a group of people who secretly opposed the new government and did all they could to destroy it. These adventurers agreed to smuggle the young boy out of the country—for a price. The price would be Mr. Fong's hidden collection of gold coins. Mr. Fong didn't hesitate. He and his wife would rather give up their hoarded wealth and possibly never see their son again than risk having Tu injured or killed by a land mine.

The father had no guarantee that the men of the underground would carry out their part of the bargain. He had no way of knowing if Tu and the other refugees would survive the boat trip to freedom. Even the risks of drowning in the South China Sea, of being discovered by the military, or of being killed by renegade pirates didn't stop the Fongs from paying the price to give their son the only chance that could save his life.

One moonless night Mr. Fong carried out the most difficult act of his entire life. Giving up his factory, his home, and his wealth was nothing in comparison. Mr. Fong took Tu to the appointed spot at the edge of the jungle, turned over his precious gold coins and his even more precious son to total strangers, and walked away.

Tu did escape from Vietnam. His adventure included all the horrors his father had imagined—and more. Tu survived to spend two years in a Philippine internment camp before he immigrated to the United States, where a Seventh-day Adventist minister and his wife adopted him. Through Tu's new family he learned to love God as his heavenly Father.

The memory of a loving Buddhist father who was willing to sacrifice everything in order to preserve the life of his son demonstrates to Tu just how far a father will go to save his children. If humans can love their children so much to sacrifice everything to save their lives, is it any wonder that God's love went all the way to the cross?

FEBRUARY 4

PUZZLED

Surely I would speak to the Almighty, and I desire to reason with God. Job 13:3.

Are you a puzzle freak? I am, and I especially enjoy word puzzles. I like crosswords, word finds, word scrambles, even those pesky word problems in your math book. I especially enjoy solving visual word puzzles. Here are a few of my favorites. Can you solve them?

1. *FUSS*
   0

2. i   i
   bag   bag

3. *WORKED*
   PAID

4. IMPROVEMENT   IMPROVEMENT

5. SODASODASODA
   SODASODASODA

6. COLLAR
   102 °

7. *STAND*
   TRY 2

8. 111111   another/another
   another/another
   another/another

Did you figure them all out? Would you like the answers? If I told you the answers were on page 265, but not to look ahead for them, would you wait?

If you're like me, you'd say, "It's my book. I can do as I choose."

What if I decided not to reveal the answers at all? Would you be irritated, frustrated, or not care?

If you're like me, you'd be irritated. You'd want the answers to the puzzles and you'd want them now, not a 100-plus pages later!

If only life were so simple. You and I face difficult problems that are more than mind teasers; some problems cause pain, loneliness, or tears—and have no easy answers.

Like Job in our text today wanted to talk with God, we ask God why these things happen. And we want His answer right away, not at the bottom of the page or on page 265, but now!

Sometimes God answers our questions through His Word, through wise counsel, or through a miracle—and we are satisfied. Other times He says, "Wait. In My time I make all things beautiful." Occasionally He says, "No. I have a much better solution for your problem—better than you can possibly imagine."

With each answer God says, "Trust Me. Have faith in My power and in My love for you." And when we do as He asks, we discover, as did Job, that God does know what is best for us. He does make all things beautiful in their time.

(Answers to the visual word puzzles: 1. fuss over nothing, 2. bags under the eyes, 3. overworked and underpaid, 4. room for improvement, 5. six-pack of soda, 6. hot under the collar, 7. try to understand, 8. six of one/half dozen of another.)

FEBRUARY 5

A WORRIED EWE

So do not worry about tomorrow; it will have enough worries of its own. There is no need to add to the troubles each day brings. Matthew 6:34, TEV.

One Sunday afternoon Pat and Ed Bailey sat in their home watching television. They lived high up in the Rocky Mountains of Colorado. They glanced up to see a female bighorn sheep staring at her reflection in their picture window. Ed grabbed a camera and took the ewe's picture, then tried to scare her away.

The Baileys returned to their televiewing.

Suddenly Pat and Ed heard a loud crack. Thinking someone must have shot the ewe, they dashed out of the house in time to see the ewe bounding up the hill as fast as she could go. She had not been shot, but had banged into the picture window.

"I guess she's learned her lesson," Ed chuckled as he and Pat went back inside.

Before closing the door, Pat glanced over her shoulder and screamed. The ewe was charging toward the house at top speed. Apparently the sheep had climbed the hill in order to get a running start.

The animal crashed through the glass and plunged into their parlor. The Baileys found the ewe lying stunned on the living room floor. Fortunately she had suffered only a bloody nose.

Since the Baileys didn't want the ewe to leave the house through a second window, they dragged the stunned animal outside. Once there, the sheep woke up and dashed off in a totally different direction.

The ewe's problem was stress. Upon seeing her own reflection, the sheep believed that a massive ewe on the other side of the glass was threatening her security.

At first the sheep fretted over the intruder, studying it carefully. Then she attacked. Still worrying over her potential problem, she chose to attack again. Her second collision must have convinced her that her efforts weren't worth the pain.

The ignorant ewe had never heard Jesus' words "So don't be anxious about tomorrow. God will take care of your tomorrow too. Live one day at a time" (TLB). Although she had enough real problems to solve that afternoon—her next meal, for one thing—she didn't really need to worry about the ewe behind the plate glass window.

Are you like the silly ewe? Are you a worrywart who frets about tomorrow's troubles? Do you worry that Sue might be more popular, Liz might be more talented, Ann might be more attractive, Hank might get better grades? Do you waste so much energy banging your head against imaginary problems that you have little time or energy left to become the person Jesus intended you to be?

FEBRUARY 6

MORE THAN A COVER GIRL GLOW

When Moses came down from Mount Sinai with the two tablets of the Testimony in his hands, he was not aware that his face was radiant because he had spoken with the Lord. Exodus 34:29, NIV.

Kelli, my youngest daughter, stood before me, garbed in yards of white satin—the satin I'd spent months fashioning for just this moment. The baby-fine veil over her face could not hide the glow of her eyes and the vibrant blush of her cheeks. It was as if a light were shining from inside her face. Her radiant shine didn't come from a bottle of makeup or from a compact of powder. Kelli stood before me, not as my little girl, but as a beautiful bride in love.

In a decade or less, you, like Kelli, will probably fall in love with a handsome young man or a vibrant young woman. As you approach your wedding day, your parents will get all soppy and sentimental, just as my husband and I did with Kelli. And if you and your sweetheart have conducted your courtship as Jesus intended, your parents will also detect in you the glow that comes from loving someone.

Every girl and every boy, if courageous enough to admit it, dreams of falling in love and marrying the perfect mate. This is good. This is the way God planned us to be. Unfortunately, if boys and girls spend all their time fantasizing about their dream partner's looks and how their dream partner can make them happy, they'll miss the most important task—the task of becoming the perfect partner who knows how to make others happy.

That's the hard part. It's much easier to expect a lot from another person and excuse your own nasty quirks. The best way I know to become a loving and lovable husband or wife is to fall in love with Jesus first. He is the best example of a perfect mate.

By getting to know Him, you'll become more and more like Him. You'll become gentler, kinder, more understanding. You'll look for ways to make the people around you happier. Your words will lose their cutting edge or their irritating whine. You'll love your family members and friends unselfishly. Believe it or not, this is the best way possible to make your dreams of a happy home come true. Become the loving person you would expect the perfect sweetheart to fall in love with.

FEBRUARY 7

A SPITTING COBRA

He has made everything beautiful in its time. Ecclesiastes 3:11, NIV.

Connie hates snakes. To her, snakes are evil, loathsome creatures, mutations of creation. She learned to hate snakes when her two cousins, Jim and Stub, chased her with garter snakes. With Connie, the only good snake is a dead snake. Even then, she'll have nightmares after looking at its dead body. She'll close her eyes if a snake is shown on television.

If Connie were walking in the desert and came upon a spitting cobra, her first reaction would be to kill it. After all, this cobra spits venom so powerful that it can blind a person. Even if she knew nothing about the spitting cobra's crippling venom, her fear would drive her to kill it.

Since Connie avoids even the mention of the word "snake," she doesn't know it, but recently scientists injected the spitting cobra venom into some mice that had cancer. The venom destroyed the cancer and didn't kill the mice. These scientists hope that one day soon, cobra venom will be used to help cure some kinds of human cancer.

Now, if Connie knew of the scientists' discovery regarding the cobra venom and if her own mother had a cancer that the cobra venom could cure, would Connie be so quick to kill the snake? Probably not. However, knowing my sister, she would still maintain a healthy distance from her hated foe.

The snake would not have changed. Only Connie would have changed. The new treatment that could save her mother's life would have changed her perspective. To Connie and her family, the formerly detestable creature would be considered beautiful, even a godsend.

If Connie had killed the spitting cobra before learning of its potential for good, she would have been ignorant. If she had killed the cobra after knowing it could save her mother's life, she would have been stupid.

When confronted with troubles, most people either react like Connie by aggressively attacking the enemy or by running in the opposite direction. Very few people look at the spitting cobras in their lives as an opportunity for God to turn evil into something beautiful. He promises to turn our adversities into blessings and our troubles into triumphs. God promises, in time, to make all things beautiful if only His people will believe.

FEBRUARY 8

PLAYING GAMES

Let us go forward according to the same rules we have followed until now. Philippians 3:16, TEV.

Coach Wyman blew the whistle. The freshman boys fell into line for PE class. "All right, guys," he began, "today we're going to play a new game called frefre. The object of the game is to get these sponge balls across the goal line at either end of the field. All right, ready to play?"

"Huh? Frefre?" Chip Hendricks raised his hand. "Do we pick teams?"

"It's up to you," the coach answered.

"You mean it's every man for himself?" David, the class computer whiz asked. "Won't that get kind of dangerous?"

The coach shrugged.

Chip scowled. "What are the rules?"

"There are none," Coach Wyman admitted.

"No rules?" Andy Kennedy screeched. "Ya' gotta have rules!"

The coach shrugged again.

"This is a dumb game," Andy grumbled.

"Yeah," Chip muttered. "What kind of game is it that has no rules, no teams, no nuthin'?"

The coach appeared not to have heard the boys' last comments, for he ordered them to begin. "Now I expect you all to do your best. Your quarter grade is depending on this activity."

"Our quarter grade? That's not fair!" Andy shouted. "We don't even know what you want us to do."

Without a word Coach Wyman tossed the two sponge balls into the air and walked off the field. A mad scramble ensued. When one of the sponge balls popped out of the pileup, Kurt, the class clown, grabbed it, charged down the field, and crossed the goal line.

"You get the A, Kurt," Coach Wyman announced.

"Hey," Andy angrily protested, brushing the grass stains off his knees, "that's not fair!"

The rest of the class voiced their complaints until the coach waved his hands to call them back to order. "Lately, whether we're playing basketball, soccer, volleyball, or whatever, you guys play as if breaking the rules were OK as long as you win the game. Today's demonstration shows you how rules add to the enjoyment of a sport," the coach explained. "Good grades are more pleasing if you play by the rules to get them. A home is happier when everyone plays by the rules. It is important to learn that a business, a career, even a marriage, can be destroyed if one doesn't play by the rules."

"OK, Coach," David interrupted. "I think we get the point. Can we go back to playing a real game now? One with rules?"

FEBRUARY 9

HISSING SNAKES

Test everything. Hold on to the good. Avoid every kind of evil. 1 Thessalonians 5:21, 22, NIV.

Gold has always been considered magical and linked by its color to the mythical powers of the sun, the giver of light. The people of ancient times referred to gold as "tears of the sun" or "sweat of the sun." Even the chemical symbol for gold—Au—comes from the name, Aurora, goddess of dawn. Because the metal was so rare and was supposed to possess mythical powers, people throughout time fought to possess it. The strongest bullies in each neighborhood soon owned the most gold. Before long, these bullies declared themselves kings and their neighborhoods, kingdoms. Somewhere along the way, these strong men claimed that their power and their right to do as they pleased had been given them by the gods. This policy was called the divine right of kings. And since gold was from the gods, all gold should be theirs. Thus kings and rulers everywhere measured their wealth and their power by how much gold they owned.

Before long, however, members of these royal families discovered a very practical purpose for part of their gold supply. Few kings died peacefully, since these individuals ruled by bullying instead of elections. The crowns changed hands only when a ruler died. If a monarch wasn't killed on a battlefield, he was killed by his greedy enemies at home, sometimes even by family members. Poison was the most popular way to rid a country of an unpopular king. The poison most often used? Arsenic.

Whether the kings of the ancient world discovered gold's protective power by accident or through the trickery of the court wizard, no one knows. Somewhere, somehow, they learned that when arsenic is placed in pale gold goblets, the gold warns of its presence by hissing like a snake and flashing like a rainbow. Magical powers from the gods? Hardly! Just simple chemistry any first-year chemistry student would know.

For you see, the pale gold goblets were made of electrum—an unrefined gold, a natural alloy of gold and silver. Since the kings' goblets were hammered into shape instead of refined in a fire, the basic silver along with other metals and natural impurities such as sulfides and arsenates remained. The poison arsenic released these impurities into the king's wine as hissing gasses. The traces of iron in the electrum became iron oxide, which produced the flash of rainbow colors. Many kings escaped being poisoned by just such a flash and a hiss.

The poisonous arsenic is a lot like the sins Satan uses to destroy us. Many times we don't realize we've been poisoned until it's too late. Wouldn't it be neat if we had a magic stone or a shiny goblet that could warn us whenever we were about to do something that would hurt us or cause us to sin? In a way, we do.

Just as the ancient kings tested their drink in a golden goblet before taking a sip, so we can test to find out what is good and what is evil by studying the flashing light found in God's Word and by listening to the hissing of our conscience.

Unfortunately for the royal bullies, the chemical powers of the golden goblet weakened with use, until all the gases were released. The monarchs didn't know until it was too late that the gold's magical powers were gone.

Aren't you glad that by properly using God's Word and our conscience, our power to detect Satan's poisons will grow stronger instead of weaker?

FEBRUARY 10

BRIDGES AND BARRIERS

Jesus answered, "I am the way and the truth and the life. No one comes to the Father except through me." John 14:6, NIV.

First-time drivers crossing the picturesque covered bridge to the Milo Adventist Academy campus in Oregon are often frightened by the clacking and clanking of the bridge's timbers beneath the weight of their automobiles.

Campus residents quickly assure visitors that the bridge has reinforced steel beams and columns of concrete supporting it underneath. In late summer, autumn, and early winter, the South Umpqua River flows lazily under the bridge and on to the valley floor at the little town of Canyonville, and then to the Pacific Ocean. While the depth of the water directly beneath the Milo bridge is in excess of 40 feet, most of the river is shallow. During much of the year you could hike upstream or downstream through brambles and berry bushes and ford the river.

In early spring, however, the snowpack from the Cascade Range melts, and the South Umpqua River surges through the rugged mountains of southern Oregon with a vengeance. The bridge becomes the only access to the campus.

Beneath the floor of the bridge, the level of the swirling, jade green water rises to within four or five feet of the supporting joists. The raging water slams gigantic redwood and Douglas fir logs against the underside of the bridge. Interestingly, from June through February, the longtime residents at the school vow that their bridge is safe. However, during spring's first runoff, their certainty becomes a bit shaky. The bridge didn't change; only the water did.

The only bridge from this world of death to eternal life is Jesus. He is the way, your only means of escape. When it comes to your faith in Jesus, are you like Milo's longtime residents? When the weather's fine and the water's calm, you trust God. But when troubles the size of redwoods beat against your faith, are you tempted to doubt the strength of your Bridge? If so, claim today's promise. Jesus says, "I am the way, the truth, and the life." He doesn't change, regardless of the size of your problems. He can be trusted to remain the same today, tomorrow, and forever.

HOOF 'N' MOUTH DISEASE

Let your conversation be always full of grace, seasoned with salt, so that you may know how to answer everyone. Colossians 4:6, NIV.

During the Seminole War in Florida, Colonel Zachary Taylor and his officers stopped at a village inn for the night. A young man fresh out of West Point entered the place and approached their table. As usual, Colonel Taylor wore a homespun sack coat and a broad-brimmed straw hat, whereas the young man wore a fresh linen coat to protect his uniform.

"Well, old man," the young man said as he sat down, "how are the Indians now?"

"I believe, sir," Taylor replied, "that they are giving considerable trouble."

"They are, are they?" The young man squared his shoulders a bit. "We'll have to see to that. I'm an Army officer and I'm on my way to take a hand. What are you drinking, old codger—you and your neighbors?" Taylor and his men declined the stranger's offer and left the inn.

A few days later the young West Pointer reported at Army headquarters for duty, only to come face-to-face with the "old codger," now wearing a colonel's uniform. Horrified, the young officer stumbled over himself in an effort to apologize.

Colonel Taylor listened patiently, then said, "My young friend, let me give you a little piece of advice. Never judge a stranger by his clothes."

If the stranger had listened instead of spouting his own opinions, he would have soon learned the identity of the "old codger." And he would have saved himself a lot of embarrassment.

While Colonel Zachary Taylor went on to become the twelfth president of the United States, no one remembers the name of the young officer who so misjudged his fellow traveler.

Do you judge people by the clothes they wear? by their age? their size? by their "coolness"? If you take the time to get acquainted, if you give the other person your respectful attention, you'll discover that friends come in all kinds of packaging. You'll learn that there is more to life than just being with the "right" people and wearing the "right" clothes.

GETTING YOUR FACTS STRAIGHT

Whatsoever things are . . . of good report . . . , think on these things. Philippians 4:8.

Since today is Abraham Lincoln's birthday, here are a few "facts" about our sixteenth president that three students reported to their history teachers. Do you know which are true? Circle the corrrect answer(s).

T or F 1. Abraham Lincoln's mother died in infancy, and the man was born in a log cabin that he built himself.

T or F 2. When Lincoln was president, he wore only a tall silk hat.

T or F 3. Lincoln wrote the Gettysburg Address while traveling from Washington, D.C., to Gettysburg, Pennsylvania, on the back of an envelope.

Answers:

1. Please, how could Lincoln's mother die in infancy and still manage to give birth to him?

2. I do hope that Abraham Lincoln's wardrobe consisted of more than just a tall silk hat, since the winters in Washington, D.C., can be mighty chilly.

3. No matter how much you can stretch your imagination, it is difficult to picture old Abe riding anywhere on the back of an envelope.

Silly mistakes? Yes, we chuckle at them because no damage was done, except perhaps to the three students' letter grades. However, misinformation is not always innocent or humorous. The results of human error are often irreparable.

Wars have been declared as a result of misinformation. The battleship *Maine* did not fall victim to an enemy mine, as was originally believed. The ship blew apart from an explosion within the hold. During the Spanish-American War, thousands died while shouting "Remember the *Maine*," when there was really nothing heroic to remember.

Once I heard a story about Sir Winston Churchill, the famous British statesman, and Sir Alexander Fleming, the discoverer of penicillin. After writing up the story, I sent it to *Guide* magazine.

A few months later the editor of *Guide* called and asked for the source of my great story. I told her that I'd research it and call her back. At the public library I found that my story had been a ridiculous rumor circulating during Sir Alexander Fleming's lifetime. Embarrassing? Yes. Tragic? No.

Like the story of the battleship *Maine*, all too often misinformation, better known as gossip, destroys people's lives just as thoroughly as those killed while charging up San Juan Hill. What misinformation are you passing on each day? Do you check your facts before you repeat a story? Are you careful to give only a good and accurate report?

FEBRUARY 13

TAR CREEK

The world and all that is in it belong to the Lord; the earth and all who live on it are his. Psalm 24:1, TEV.

If God tapped you on the shoulder, handed you a beautifully wrapped package, and told you to treasure His gift, to care for it and protect it, what would you do? Would you toss the package into your closet alongside your dirty gym socks? Or would you eagerly open the package and display the gift in a prominent place for all to see?

"Quiet on the set!" shouted the director. "Scene two, take one—roll 'em!" It was finally happening—the videotaping of Tar Creek. The story had begun the September before when a class of students from Joplin, Missouri, chose to do a scientific study on a local pollution problem—Tar Creek. The rusty-red and lifeless creek had been clear and clean when their parents were young.

After tramping out to the creek and taking numerous water samples, the students discovered that Tar Creek was being polluted by old lead and zinc mines in the area.

With the help of a local television station, the students made a video. They wrote the script, chose the filming site, and acted in it. They filmed two possible endings to their story—one portrayed an even more dangerous pollution problem if the community did nothing; the other showed the results of a successful cleanup of the creek.

The students showed their tape at the local shopping mall, on two TV channels, and at civic club meetings. The campaign mushroomed until the community petitioned the state and federal governments for help. It worked. The kids at Tar Creek learned that they could make a difference.

You and I are accountable to God for the way we use the gifts He gives us. Not only for the care of our bodies and minds, and the use of our money and time, but also for the care of our world. You and your friends can make a difference. Is there a vacant lot near your home that needs cleaning, or the lawn of an elderly person in your neighborhood that needs care? What can you do to ease the problems of pollution? Litter? Endangered animals? The ozone layer? Acid rain? The homeless?

Even by yourself you can choose to protect the treasure God has entrusted to you. You can decide whether or not to throw your candy bar wrapper onto the sidewalk, or to toss your soft drink container along the side of the road. It's your choice. This world, God's beautiful gift, is yours to protect or destroy.

FEBRUARY 14

WARM HEARTS AND LISZT KISSES

It is love, then, that you should strive for. 1 Corinthians 14:1, TEV.

Kisses and Valentine's Day seem to go together, don't they? So this morning let me tell you the story of one remarkable kiss.

At age 16, Andor Foldes, a gifted classical pianist who lived in Budapest, Hungary, was very discouraged. In the middle of his depression, he met a world-renowned pianist—Emil Sauer. Not only was Sauer famous for his keyboard skills, but he was the last surviving pupil of the great composer Franz Liszt.

Sauer arranged to have Andor play for him. Andor obliged with the most difficult pieces in his repertoire—works by Bach, Beethoven, and Schumann. When the boy finished, Sauer kissed him on the forehead.

"When I was your age, I became a student of Liszt," the celebrated musician explained. "He kissed me on the forehead after my first lesson and said, 'I have faith in you, son.'

"I have waited for years to pass on this sacred heritage," Sauer explained. "You are the first I've found to deserve it."

Andor Foldes left Sauer with more than a kiss on the forehead. The passed-on kiss from the master Liszt gave him a new confidence and sense of purpose.

Like the young pianist, kids today often need the encouragement of a "Liszt kiss." It isn't easy living with the stress of school, grades, peer pressures, and acne. Mothers need Liszt kisses too. Trying to juggle a career, the housework, and all the hundreds of tasks that go unnoticed is exhausting. Dads sometimes feel that they are loved only for the allowance that they dole out at the end of each week. Whether naturally gruff or tender, dads need Liszt kisses too.

With brothers and sisters, a Liszt kiss may be a gentle punch on the shoulder or the offer to take over a household chore, but the end result is the same. It says "You're OK, kid."

And believe it or not, even teachers blossom when students give them a Liszt kiss. A simple "Thank you" or "I enjoyed today's class" can make your teacher's day, possibly his or her entire week.

A Liszt kiss is one gift that manufacturers of candy hearts, greeting cards, flowers, and perfume cannot package. As with Emil Sauer, a Liszt kiss is uniquely yours to give. The catch is, it must be sincere. There's no room for phoniness.

The text that says "It is love, then, that you should strive for" doesn't mean you should search for love for yourself. Instead, it means you should hunt for ways to give love to others.

FEBRUARY 15

CHANGING THE WEATHER

Now this is eternal life: that they may know you, the only true God, and Jesus Christ, whom you have sent. John 17:3, NIV.

"You can't change the weather," they say. Weather—we all talk about it, but none of us can do much about it. I lived in two places where talking about the weather seemed rather silly. In Portland, Oregon, from November to April, it is pointless to comment on the weather since that's how long the rainy season usually lasts. And in Albuquerque, New Mexico, the sun shines 365 days a year. The sun is so certain to come up over the Sandia Crest on the east side of the city that the local newspaper publisher promises to give away free the day's edition of his paper if the sun fails to shine at least for a portion of the day. He's never been forced to keep his promise.

My husband, a trained scientist and mathematician, enjoys turning every facet of life into equations. Take the weather, for example. How would you create an equation for weather? His answer is air + water + sun = weather. Sounds simple, doesn't it? If it's so simple, why hasn't someone figured out a way to control or at least accurately predict the behavior of those three little ingredients? But even with all the recent breakthroughs in science, volcanoes continue to erupt, hurricanes continue to rip through the Southeast, blizzards paralyze the Midwest, earthquakes shake the earth at will, and showers rain on our picnics. This morning the street outside my office window is littered with tree branches and other debris left behind by an unpredicted 90-mile-an-hour wind that blew through the night.

Sin is simple too. When explained in an algebraic equation, it would read: human being + temptation + action = sin. So simple, but there's little that we can do about it—on our own, that is.

Each evening on the local and national news broadcasts, we hear of the violence and destruction sin creates. While governments outlaw sins such as murder, theft, and perjury, their laws fail to stop those sins. Instead, the laws seem only to produce outlaws. It's rather like the weather. Everyone talks about it, but we can do nothing about it.

That's why God came up with the winning formula—not a formula to control the weather, but to control sin. It's implied in today's text. Simplified to an algebraic equation, it is goes like this: Jesus + surrender + forgiveness = eternal life. Even if I knew absolutely nothing about math, I can understand God's solution to the sin problem. I like that, don't you?

FEBRUARY 16

JUST DO IT

Come, you who are blessed by my Father; take your inheritance, the kingdom prepared for you since the creation of the world. Matthew 25:34, NIV.

A famous gym shoe company recently used the slogan "Just Do It" in their advertising campaign. I'm sure they were not thinking of Agnes Bojaxhiu when they chose this slogan for their sneaker promotion. So who is Agnes Bojaxhiu, you ask?

In 1979 Agnes Bojaxhiu won the Nobel Peace Prize. What great deed did Miss Bojaxhiu do to deserve such an important honor? Did she negotiate a nuclear treaty between the United States and the Soviet Union? Did she rid her native country of Communism? Did she march in protest against some evil government?

Agnes Bojaxhiu went for the gold—the gold that lasts forever. Better known as Mother Teresa, she chose to live and work in the slums and ghettos of Calcutta, India, in order to help the people there. When reporters ask her why she does what she does, Mother Teresa, a tiny Catholic nun in white muslin, answers, "For the joy of loving and being loved."

"It takes a lot of money, doesn't it?" another inquires.

"No," she replies, "it takes a lot of sacrifice."

Politicians, presidents, and kings shake their heads in wonder. The world can't understand a woman like Mother Teresa.

Once a man informed her that his vocation was to work for lepers. "I want to spend myself for the lepers," he said proudly.

She stared at him for a moment and then said, "Your vocation is not to work for the lepers; your vocation is to belong to Jesus."

One day soon Jesus will return to earth to call His children to Him. The next two verses in Matthew 25 tell just who those people will be. Whether they be Roman Catholic or Baptist, or Jewish or Seventh-day Adventist, boys and girls and men and women, like Agnes Bojaxhiu, hold the keys to the kingdom of God.

"I love Jesus, but I'm just a kid," you say. "I can't go to India or Africa as a missionary. What can I do?" Think. Be creative. One young boy started distributing blankets to the homeless. A gang of "good buds" from school volunteered to help out one night a week at the soup kitchens downtown. Some "adopt" a grandma or grandpa at a local nursing home. Others help younger kids learn to read, and others act as a big brother or sister to kids who have no families. While their activities vary, they all have one thing in common: They don't sit around asking "What can I do?" Instead they find a place where they are needed, get busy, and "just do it."

FEBRUARY 17

COPS AND ROBBERS

By faith Moses, when he had grown up, refused to be known as the son of Pharaoh's daughter. He chose to be mistreated along with the people of God rather than to enjoy the pleasures of sin for a short time. Hebrews 11:24, 25, NIV.

Did you ever play cops and robbers? Or its tamer version hide-and-seek? You aren't alone. The popular game began in Egypt before Moses was born. The rulers of ancient Egypt believed that when they died, they would need all the comforts and wealth they'd enjoyed while alive. So they entombed in the pyramids treasures of gold, silver, and jewels—even horses and live servants for the dead king's enjoyment. Local thieves thought the treasures were a good idea too—for their pockets at least.

In a violent version of hide-and-seek, royal priests assigned to protect the pharaohs' wealth regularly chased thieves over the ghostly cliffs and through the narrow, winding passageways that led to the rooms of the dead. There is evidence on the cliffs and hollow chambers in the Valley of the Kings that fierce battles of "cops and robbers" were fought for the gold in the royal tombs. One tomb was so carefully camouflaged by the ancient priests that it remained untouched for more than a thousand years—the tomb of the boy ruler, Tutankhamen—King Tut. Mummified around 1340 B.C., the young ruler's face was covered with a golden mask; his body was decorated with a golden collar, belt, bracelets, and anklets; his fingers and toes bore golden shields. Hundreds of gold charms and amulets were wrapped around his mummified body, which was in turn encased in a solid gold coffin weighing more than 2,448 pounds. The coffin was protected by two gold-plated caskets placed within a stone sarcophagus surrounded by four golden-walled shrines, one as big as a bedroom. In the other rooms of the tomb, golden beds, thrones, chests, chariots, figures, idols, and even toys were stored for his use. All that gold—and the poor boy king never did get to enjoy it. For King Tut the season of fabulous wealth ended with his last breath.

From today's text we can surmise that Moses knew something that the pharaohs of Egypt didn't.

Do you know his secret?

(Story to be continued tomorrow.)

FEBRUARY 18

FORWARD THINKING

He [Moses] regarded disgrace for the sake of Christ as of greater value than the treasures of Egypt, because he was looking ahead to his reward. Hebrews 11:26, NIV.

Wow! Talk about fabulous wealth! Incredible! Let's review some of the contents in King Tut's tomb. The young ruler's face was covered with a golden mask; his body was decorated with a golden collar, belt, bracelets, and anklets; his fingers and toes bore golden shields. Hundreds of gold charms and amulets were wrapped around his mummified body, which was in turn encased in a solid gold coffin weighing more than 2,448 pounds. The coffin was protected by two gold-plated caskets placed within a stone sarcophagus surrounded by four golden-walled shrines, one as big as a bedroom. In the other rooms of the tomb, golden beds, thrones, chests, chariots, figures, idols, and even toys were stored for his use.

King Tut's grave remained hidden until 1922, when Lord Carnarvon and Howard Carter uncovered the fantastic tomb. While the two archaeologists became famous for their find, they were required by law to turn over their fabulous discovery to the Egyptian government. Just think—

wealth like that could have belonged to Moses. If Moses had stayed in Egypt and if he had become a pharaoh, he could have been mummified and surrounded by a hoard of gold when he died.

Instead, he chose to lead a bunch of rebellious, complaining people out into the desert. He led them right up to the border of the Promised Land, and then he died alone on a deserted mountain.

Aren't you glad that the story doesn't end there?

Soon after Moses' burial, his grave was robbed—not of a fabulous fortune in gold or jewels, but of Moses himself. Jesus, the Creator of all, not two archaeologists, raised His faithful servant, Moses, to life—life eternal. Moses made a wise choice, don't you agree? After all, a casket is still just a casket whether it's made of solid gold or cheap pinewood. And golden-lined burial shrines house only the bones of dead people, whereas a live Moses walks heaven's street of gold.

Jesus came to this earth to rob graves. He vowed, "I am come that you might have life, and have it more abundantly" (see John 10:10). Your decision whether to follow Him or the world might not be as dramatic as Moses', but the final outcome can be the same.

FEBRUARY 19

LITTLE ORPHAN ANNIE

I will not leave you as orphans; I will come to you. John 14:18, NIV.

Vanderhyden Hall—the massive red brick building loomed high above me as I scrunched down on the backseat of our car. I shuddered as the black wrought iron gate clanged shut behind my father. I wished my father would finish his business and return to the car—fast! My father, a painting contractor, did odd jobs at the orphanage during the winter months, when his outdoor jobs lessened. Occasionally he would take me along with him when he went to pick up his paycheck.

Even at 5 years old, I knew that an orphanage was a place where children who had no parents went. While I had two parents who loved me, I was still terrified of being trapped in the orphanage. What if I went into the building and somehow got separated from my dad? The orphanage people might keep me there and never let me go home again. What if my dad forgot and drove home without me? What if some naughty little girl who looked like me locked me in a closet and pretended to be me, then went home with my daddy? Crazy fears, huh? But in my fertile childish imagination, they were all too possible.

It wasn't until I grew older that I discovered the truth about the word *orphan*. I discovered that even if the worst possible thing happened that could happen—even if I did lose my parents—I could never, ever be a true orphan. Do you know why? It's easy. I love Jesus and He loves me. That makes me Jesus' sister—a daughter of the King of the universe. My baptism officially signed my adoption papers.

My dad died a few years ago. I miss him very much. I miss taking walks together, teasing him about his dislike of Ford cars, playing games together on Saturday nights around the mahogany dining room table, sitting in the pew beside him on Sabbath morning.

Even though my dad died, I'm not alone. The same guarantees God gave me, my earthly father claimed at his baptism and every day thereafter. My heavenly Father assures me that I will never, ever really be an orphan—unless I choose to be one.

When I chose to be baptized, the court of heaven processed my adoption papers. That day I became a full-fledged member of God's family, with all the rights and privileges that accompany the honor. I don't understand—some kids hesitate to be baptized, to become adopted children of God. I'm not sure I know why. Why would anyone choose to remain an orphan, trapped behind the iron gate of Vanderhyden Hall or Planet Earth?

FEBRUARY 20

A CHRISTIAN DIALECT

Surely you are one of them, for your accent gives you away. Matthew 26:73, NIV.

When Harry opens his mouth to speak, you know he's a New Yorker. Born and raised in Brooklyn, Harry travels to work each day in downtown Manhattan. Brooklyn to Manhattan, Manhattan to Brooklyn—that's the total of Harry's traveling experience, except for his honeymoon in Atlantic City, New Jersey.

Harry has never hiked in the Adirondack Mountains or smelled the cherry blossoms along the Potomac River. He has never picked fruit from a Florida orange tree or stretched his neck to see the top of a giant sequoia. To Harry, "Twees are for de boids." He has never stood at the rim of the Grand Canyon or camped along the lazy Rio Grande River. If asked, Harry would say, "Whoi would I wanna go dere? Dere's no people dere!"

Harry doesn't feel deprived. To him the city is his world. He works as a tour bus guide in Times Square. Harry loves the rush of the traffic and the vitality of people bustling about. It is Harry's job to convince the gawking tourists from faraway places like Tulsa, Oklahoma, and Tokyo to board his bus for a tour of the Statue of Liberty and lower Manhattan. He's good at it too.

Through the years, Harry has developed a unique talent. He can tell where a person's from by his accent. Whereas you and I might recognize an Australian, a Britisher, a Georgian, or a Bostonian, Harry can tell what county or province the visitor comes from. Often Harry can go one step further and identify everywhere the traveler has ever lived! Our speech gives us away.

In today's scripture, the people gathered about the fire in the courtyard could tell that Simon Peter was from Galilee, just like Jesus. Though Peter tried to hide it, each time he opened his mouth to speak, he revealed that he'd been around Jesus.

When you speak, can strangers tell that you have been with Jesus? Do you live so close to the Saviour that no matter where you travel in the world, people would be able to tell that you are a citizen of God's kingdom?

FEBRUARY 21

JUST A TINY WORM

You have set our iniquities before you, our secret sins in the light of your presence. Psalm 90:8, NIV.

The other day my doctor told me a story that I'd like to share with you. A male patient had been experiencing extreme pain in his abdomen. Emergency surgery was recommended.

In the operating room he was anesthetized, and a team of doctors and nurses watched as the head surgeon made his first incision. The specialist made a second incision—this time in the wall of the large intestine. After the area was cleaned and the arteries clamped, a most unusual event occurred. The entire operating team stared in amazement as a 12-foot-long pink worm slithered out of the open incision.

How could such a thing happen? How did the worm get into the man's intestine in the first place? Why hadn't the man's stomach acid killed it? Later the surgeon learned that his patient loved to eat Japanese sushi—raw fish. Apparently the man had eaten a piece of uncooked fish that contained a worm larva. And for some unexplained reason, the larva survived the journey through the man's digestive system and had set up housekeeping in the large intestine, where it attached itself to the lining. The larva matured and grew to be 12 feet long, which produced extreme pressure, or pain for its host. No wonder the man had a stomachache!

"Yech!" you say. "That's gross—eating raw fish in the first place, let alone having a 12-foot worm living in your insides!" Kind of reminds me of what the Bible calls "secret sins." You know the type—those committed behind closed doors or when no one is looking. Instead of growing in the intestine, they grow in a person's mind. At first they seem so insignificant, but they increase in size until they destroy the very life off which they feed.

Lies, impure thoughts, and hate are but a few larvae that can grow inside a person's fertile mind until they entirely destroy their host. Can you think of other secret sins you might commit, believing no one will ever find out? Yet, like the sushi-loving patient in today's story, sooner or later Satan's ugly worms will cause you pain. You can count on it.

FEBRUARY 22

WALKING TALL

I therefore, the prisoner of the Lord, beseech you that ye walk worthy of the vocation wherewith ye are called. Ephesians 4:1.

The gawky young man sat in the office of the president of a large Wall Street firm. The young man held a strange contraption on his lap. After explaining just how his invention worked, the 23-year-old, Thomas Edison, offered to sell it to the businessman.

"So, how much do you want for it?" the shrewd businessman asked.

Edison thought for several minutes, for he had no idea just what the contraption might be worth. Edison had invented an improved stock ticker machine, which would keep brokers updated on stock price changes. The young inventor scowled. Should he ask for $3,000, or take a daring chance and go for $5,000?

Losing his courage, Edison timidly said, "Make me an offer."

Thomas Edison stared in surprise when the stockbroker, after studying the invention, asked, "Would $40,000 be a fair price?"

Thomas A. Edison had been tempted to sell both his invention and himself far short of their true value.

Through false modesty or ignorance, Christian men and women, boys and girls, often sell themselves short. Instead of bringing glory to their heavenly Father for the talents He has given them, they belittle themselves or their successes. Christians can walk tall for God, not because of what they themselves have done, but because of what God has done for them and through them.

God gave the greatest Gift He could give for you. He gave His Son, Jesus. Just think how precious you must be to God? Doesn't that sacrifice give you the right to lift up your head, square back your shoulders, and walk tall for Him?

In a world where a lie is applauded, truth is mocked, and cheating rewarded, the honest man or woman, the trustworthy boy or girl, stands a body length above the crowd. One of my favorite authors, Ellen White, wrote, "The greatest want of the world is the want of men [people] . . . who will stand for the right though the heavens fall" (*Education*, p. 57). Now that's realizing one's true value! That's refusing to sell out cheap. That's walking worthy of one's vocation. That's walking tall for the Lord.

FEBRUARY 23

MORE THAN SPOT REMOVER

I will give you a new heart and put a new spirit in you. Ezekiel 36:26, NIV.

Jenny pawed through the freshly laundered clothes until she located her new blouse. The stain of catsup, mustard, and grease still ran straight down the front, from the neckline to the lower hem. At Kari's birthday barbecue, Jenny and Jeff had collided in the doorway, each dumping "shamburgers" on the other. She'd hurried home and washed the blouse immediately, yet the stain clung tenaciously to the fabric's delicate fibers. Determined, she sprayed the stain with an aerosol spot remover. No luck.

"One way or another," Jenny vowed, rubbing dry cleaning fluid into the stain, "I'll beat this stain!"

When she stopped to check her progress, the stain did appear to be lighter. *If I just scrub a little harder*, she thought. After a few minutes she realized she'd rubbed straight through the material. Her beautiful blouse was ruined, useless. She might be able to patch the hole and wear the blouse while cleaning the garage, but she'd have to buy a new blouse to wear for special occasions.

Jenny's blouse was stained with catsup and grease; but the Bible says that your heart and mine are stained with sin. When you first come to Jesus, He gives you a new heart. For a time, perhaps, you keep it spotlessly clean. Sooner or later, though, you collide with other people or perhaps yourself. Those collisions leave stains all over your beautiful new heart. Determined, you scrub those ugly spots. No matter how hard you try, the stains remain ingrained in the fabric of the heart itself. And worse yet, instead of having only one large spot, your once perfect heart becomes frayed and full of holes—not worth salvaging.

In desperation you cry to Jesus, "I'm so sorry for ruining the heart You gave me. Please, can You fix it?" The Creator of perfect hearts shakes His head no. Not even He can repair a ruined heart.

If the story ended here, all would be lost—hopeless. Instead, a smile spreads across the Saviour's face as He hands you a spanking clean, perfectly formed, brand-new heart—not a reject or an imperfect second. A gift—just for the asking.

FEBRUARY 24

BENNY'S BELIEFS

We must obey God rather than men! Acts 5:29, NIV.

When Benny, a tall, strapping farmboy, gave his heart to Jesus during the academy's Week of Prayer, he realized he'd need to make a lot of changes. First, he removed the magazines from his closet and from under the mattress. You know the magazines I mean—the ones you'd be embarrassed to have your mom accidentally discover. Then he sorted through his cassette tape collection. Somehow, he didn't enjoy listening to music performed by groups called Black Sabbath and the Grateful Dead any longer.

Benny's friend Rich noticed the changes and began teasing him. "Next thing you know," Rich joked, "you'll be trying to be friends with the geek!"

That night as Benny prepared for bed he remembered Rich's words, "You'll be trying to be friends with the geek!" Throughout his personal worship and when he knelt to pray, Benny saw Nick's face.

"No, Lord," Benny pleaded, "not Nick the geek."

Everyone on campus disliked Nick the geek. He had to be the most irritating human on Planet Earth. No one could be around the wiry little bantam rooster for more than five minutes before he was picking a fight, calling names, or starting an argument. The boys' dean was always rescuing Nick from senior boys whom the geek had angered beyond reason.

By morning Benny realized that he would at least have to make an effort to befriend the troublesome boy. From that day on, Benny became Nick's protector—or so it seemed—and all without a simple thank you from Nick. Instead Nick treated Benny even worse than he did the other students. When Rich asked Benny why he put up with the way Nick acted, Benny replied, "I believe it's the right thing to do. And beliefs aren't worth much if a guy's not ready to live by 'em."

The geek's days at the academy were numbered. Before long the faculty suggested he find another school where he might be happier. The night before Nick left campus, Benny helped him pack. As the two boys struggled to close one of the suitcases, Nick asked, "Why have you been nice to me? You don't really like me."

Benny laughed. "You're right. I don't like you—but God told me to love you. And by hook or by crook, I'm gonna' do it."

Nick stared at Benny for a moment, then cleared his throat. "I guess I don't understand."

"Someday you will, Nick." Benny punched him playfully in the arm. "Someday you will."

FEBRUARY 25

I DO WINDOWS

Why do you look at the speck of sawdust in your brother's eye and pay no attention to the plank in your own eye? Matthew 7:3., NIV.

Washing windows is not an enviable chore. Teaming up with a friend makes the job more bearable. On Friday afternoon my daughter Kelli and I each grab a rag and a bottle of window cleaner and attack the dirt on our sliding glass doors—she stands outside, and I stand inside. Within minutes sparkling clean glass replaces the muddy streaks our Border collie, Corky, left behind.

I step back to inspect our work. Oops! I notice a spot Kelli missed.

Tap, tap, tap. I smile and point to the spot.

She smiles and shouts, "It's on your side."

I shake my head. "No, it's on your side." I tap the glass a few times for emphasis.

Shaking her head, Kelli scrubs at the offending blemish. She steps back to take a look and then points at the glass. "It's still there."

"Look." I pull the door open and step out onto the deck. "I'll show you. You haven't worked at it enough." I wipe at the spot, then take a closer look, from her side.

Without another word I step back inside the house and run my cloth across the streak. The glass comes clean. Though I try, I fail to miss the self-satisfied smirk Kelli gives me from beyond our sparkling clean barrier.

Why is it always so easy to identify the faults of others and refuse to recognize our own problems? Jesus warns us of this very thing. He says, "Why do you see a speck in your neighbor's eye and miss the log in your own?"

Kelli and I saw the same spot of dirt through different sides of the same sheet of glass. Next time we clean the door together, I think I'll save myself a little embarrassment and teasing by first scrubbing at the spot before pointing my finger at her side. I wonder if I might apply this lesson to more than glass patio doors? Tell me, how clean are your patio doors?

FEBRUARY 26

ON HOLD

[The Lord] will listen to me and answer when I call to him. Psalm 4:3, TLB.

Last Sabbath I attended a church potluck dinner. While eating a bite of roast, I crunched down on a nutshell. I glanced about to be certain no one was watching, then spit out the shell into my paper napkin. To my surprise, a piece of my tooth came out with it.

The first thing Monday morning, I dialed the phone number of our family dentist. The telephone rang three times.

"Dr. Stafford's office," the voice on the other end of the line said. "May I put you on hold, please?" Then before I could answer, the strains of elevator music drifted over the phone line.

I felt like shouting, "No, I don't want to be put on hold! If I had wanted to listen to Lawrence Welk's bubble music, I would have turned on my radio, not my telephone."

After 60 seconds the receptionist returned to the line with a cheery "Thank you for waiting. May I help you?"

I arranged for an appointment in my sweetest, most patient voice. While I never told the receptionist how I felt, I still disliked being put on hold. To me my call was of utmost importance and shouldn't have been shunted aside for other, less important calls.

One summer my daughter Rhonda operated a telephone switchboard for a large downtown bank. It was not unusual for many calls to come in at the same time. She appreciated the on-hold button. Her stories of frustrated customers and harried phone operators make me more understanding of the poor receptionists' problems. Rhonda helped me look differently at being placed on hold.

Now instead of getting angry when I'm put on hold, I think about God and His incredible telecommunication system and say thank You. He never puts me on hold, no matter how many other calls He has coming in. He's always there for me. He's only a prayer away.

FEBRUARY 27

ICKY

Be always humble, gentle, and patient. Show your love by being tolerant with one another. Ephesians 4:2, TEV.

Rhonda and her friend Lori hopped into the family car and snapped their seat belts into place. Lori made herself comfortable, while Rhonda started the engine and eased the car into the afternoon traffic.

Lori noticed a tiny white fuzzy bear perched on the dashboard. Curious, she asked, "What's that?"

Rhonda replied, "Oh, that's Icky."

Disgusted, the tenderhearted Lori defended the plastic creature. "Oh, he's not icky. He's cute."

"No, Lori," Rhonda explained, "Icky is the bear's name. It stands for 'impatience can kill you.' It's my mom's little reminder to Kelli and me to drive carefully."

Lori bounced her head from side to side and giggled. "Hey, I like that—'impatience can kill you.'"

"The funny thing is," Rhonda chuckled, "I think Icky has helped Mother and Dad to be more patient when they drive too."

The lesson taught by Icky can go far beyond learning to drive safely. Impatience can kill you just as easily in the home as in the car. A grouch can kill everyone's good time at a party. Sarcastic remarks can kill friendships. Cutting comments can kill respect. Irritation displayed regularly can kill love.

Someone else's impatience killed Angie spiritually. She stopped attending the church's youth group and eventually church itself because the youth leader kept losing his cool with his wife at the Saturday night activities. Angie admired the pretty blonde woman. To have the youth pastor chew his wife out in front of the kids angered Angie so much that she chose never to return.

Isn't this where Christianity becomes more than a Sabbath day exercise? Isn't this Monday morning Christianity? Isn't it at these intersections of life when the rubber of Christianity meets the road of reality, when Christians need to "put their money where their mouths are"? For Angie, all the sermons in the world could not undo the youth pastor's hasty words to his wife.

FEBRUARY 28

THE FLIP SIDE OF ICKY

But the fruit of the Spirit is love, joy, peace, patience, kindness, goodness, faithfulness, gentleness and self-control. Galatians 5:22, 23, NIV.

One of my favorite Christian soloists is Sandi Patti. Recently my family and I attended her concert at the Portland Coliseum. To attend a sporting or cultural event at this coliseum is to subject yourself to a trial by fire. Parking is limited, and the exit gates are few. Fortunately we arrived at the Sandi Patti concert early enough to park within jogging distance of the auditorium. We enjoyed the concert right through to the final encore and made our way to the parking lot.

As we spied the crowds of concertgoers thronging the exits, my husband groaned, "It's going to take a good hour for us to reach the street."

We hurried to our car and eased into the lines of departing traffic. To our delightful surprise there were no long waits and no pushy drivers elbowing their way into the traffic. Instead the drivers took turns feeding into the exit lines. The only slowdowns occurred when two cars approached the lines simultaneously and paused to politely signal each other to please go first.

We found ourselves on the interstate heading home within 10 minutes of the end of the concert. Since then whenever anyone in our family talks about Christianity in action, someone brings up the Sandi Patti concert. Christianity in action—the gift of patience.

Icky may help you become a patient driver, but he can't help you become a patient Christian. Only the Holy Spirit can do that. And He will if you'll ask Him.

FEBRUARY 29

OVERTIME

This is the day of the Lord's victory; let us be happy, let us celebrate! Psalm 118:24, TEV.

Let's have a party! Today is a super special day—a day to celebrate! Today my friend Sam turns 16 years old. However, according to the calendar, this is Sam's fourth birthday. The other years, he celebrates his day on February 28 instead.

When his birthday actually comes around, Sam celebrates it by throwing an extra-large, slam-bang party. On that year Sam's mom makes and decorates 12 birthday cakes, one for each month of the year. Then Sam invites all his friends to come and celebrate their birthdays with him. Each friend makes a wish, and then blows out the candles and cuts the cake that represents his or her birthday. What a great mom, huh?

Today is special for Sam, but it is also special for you and me. We have one extra day to live this year. Let's celebrate today with Sam.

From what I read in the Bible, God enjoys celebrating too. What special events do you think we might celebrate in heaven? A new birthday—the day you first gave your heart to Jesus? The date of your baptism? Independence Day—the second coming of Jesus? Here's a mind bender for you:

1. List other possible new earth celebrations we might share.
2. Since our earthly holidays have customs associated with them (Christmas trees, valentine hearts, Fourth of July fireworks, etc.) come up with a list of the customs that might be attached to the celebrations you thought of in step 1 (in areas such as foods, decorations, games, songs).

Have each member of the family pray a one sentence prayer this morning vowing—through Jesus' strength—to celebrate Family Day together in God's kingdom.

MARCH 1

SAFARI FOR SON-SEEKERS

But if from there you seek the Lord your God, you will find him if you look for him with all your heart and with all your soul. Deuteronomy 4:29, NIV.

Treasures come in all shapes, sizes, colors, and values, as do the seekers of those treasures. I have a daughter who is a seeker, a sun-seeker. That's right—a sun-seeker. The hotter the sun, the better. She takes safaris, too. Like our cat Meow, Kelli searches for the perfect spot in which to sun. Her honey-beige complexion revels in the sun's rays. By the first rains of winter, Kelli is a toasty brown.

Kelli lives in Oregon, where from November through March sunshine is rationed. All winter long she pines for the sun. Sometimes, however, as early as mid-February the sun comes out in Oregon. That's when she dons her swimsuit, grabs a beach towel, tanning lotion, and portable radio, then heads for our deck to begin "working on her tan." For that matter, Kelli has been known to awaken before sunrise and drive a hundred miles east out into the Oregon desert to Keneeta to catch a few extra off-season rays.

Lately, with all the medical reports warning of skin cancer from too much sun, even Kelli chooses to limit her exposure by practicing safe sunbathing.

I attended a camp meeting a few years ago, and the theme for the week was "Son-Seeker's Safari." I thought of Kelli. For Kelli is a Son-seeker too—a Son-seeker as well as a sun-seeker. She chose to become a Son-seeker when she was only 8 years old. Kelli appreciates knowing that the more she seeks out God's Son, Jesus, the more color and richness He adds to her life. She doesn't need to limit her exposure. She can find Him on stormy days when her world is upside down, on gray cloudy days when nothing seems right. Even on her darkest days—He is there for her.

Since I burn and sizzle in the sun instead of tan, I will never be a sun-seeker. Yet like my daughter, I choose every day to spend time with the Son of God. Kelli and I are dedicated Son-seekers. Are you?

MARCH 2

NO WIMP IN SIGHT

Who knoweth whether thou art come to the kingdom for such a time as this? Esther 4:14.

"To enter into a war with the Northern states means certain bloodshed for the South. Your sons, your fathers, your husbands, will die if Texas secedes from the Union. Is this what you want?"

Governor Sam Houston's cries against the gathering storms of civil war were drowned out by a barrage of hate. The hero of the battle of San Jacinto and governor of the state of Texas fought and failed. On March 2, 1861, a special convention assembled at the state capitol in Austin to announce that Texas had seceded from the Union and joined the Southern Confederacy. When forced to take an oath of allegiance to the new government, Sam Houston said: "I refuse to take this oath. In the name of my own conscience and my own manhood . . . I refuse to take this oath. . . . I love Texas too well to bring civil strife and bloodshed upon her. . . . I am . . . stricken down because I will not yield those principles which I have fought for.'' Talk about peer pressure! Yet he chose to stand alone rather than go against his conscience.

In the book *Profiles in Courage*, author and future United States president John F. Kennedy wrote: "To be courageous, . . . requires no exceptional qualifications, no magic formula, no special combination of time, place and circumstance. It is an opportunity that sooner or later is presented to us all. . . . One may meet the challenge of courage, whatever may be the sacrifices he faces if he follows his conscience—the loss of his friends, his fortune, his contentment, even the esteem of his fellowmen—each man must decide for himself the course he will follow. The stories of past courage can define that ingredient—they can teach, they can offer hope, they can provide inspiration. But they cannot supply courage itself. For this each . . . must look into his own soul.''

Look into your soul this morning. Do you see a wimp or a hero?

1. When friends mistreat a less popular kid, do you speak out and say "This is wrong''?

2. Do your friends know that you will not cheat on your school assignments, quizzes, or tests, no matter what?

Mom and Dad, look into your soul also.

1. At work when your boss is blaming a coworker for something she or he didn't do, do you speak up?

2. When the clerk fails to charge you for the bag of dog food on the bottom shelf of your cart, do you make it right?

If you answered yes to all of the above questions, you are regularly exercising your muscles so when you are called to be courageous—there'll be no wimp in sight.

MARCH 3

GOD'S MEDICINE CHEST

But my God shall supply all your need according to his riches in glory by Christ Jesus. Philippians 4:19.

Many pioneer parents never said to their children "Eat your vegetables.'' Not even once! At that time many people called edible plants "herbs.'' They knew almost nothing about vitamins and minerals—that by eating green plants they could ward off some diseases. They did know about "spring tonics'' that could make loose teeth firm. Green plants that contain vitamin C helped heal scurvy, a disease that attacks teeth and bones. The American Indians also ate greens and berries as a cure.

My grandpa Ball was an herb doctor. He knew which herbs reduced a fever, soothed a queasy stomach, induced vomiting, or eased an infected lung. Today he'd be arrested for practicing medicine without a license. But in the late-1800s, when western Pennsylvania and other outposts of civilization experienced a shortage of licensed medical doctors, he saved hundreds of lives with his mysterious herbal concoctions. Yet as wise and knowledgeable as my grandfather was in herbs, he believed the fruit of the tomato plant was poisonous.

According to our text, God promises to supply all our needs. When it comes to vegetables, He could have limited our choices to rutabaga, horseradish, or squash. But He didn't. As usual He went way beyond the necessary. Some of His children prefer rice to potatoes, or corn to cabbage, or brussels sprouts to beans. To accommodate our individuality, He created an endless variety of vegetables, or herbs, that are not only good for us, but good tasting, too.

Then Jesus placed a touch of His own creative power in our minds. He supplied us with the gift of imagination. We use this gift to create delicious combinations of flavors. Who has never licked his lips in anticipation at the smell of spaghetti sauce bubbling in the pot or at the sight of a zesty bean enchilada?

If these two suggestions don't do it for you, picture a few of your own favorites. Take your imagination one step further. Try to picture the culinary surprises awaiting us in heaven—all from our Creator's hand.

Offer the following prayer. Fill in the blanks as you go.

"Thank You, Father, for the rich variety of herbs You have provided. Thank You for allowing for my individual tastes and preferences—for not limiting my eating choices to _______ or _______ , and for creating my favorites, _______ , _______ , _______ , _______ , and _______ . Thank You for promising to supply all my needs and so many of my wants too. Amen."

MARCH 4

SILVER SKATES

I waited patiently for the Lord; and he inclined unto me, and heard my cry. Psalm 40:1.

Indians regularly attacked the settlements around Concord, New Hampshire, where 12-year-old Daniel Abbott lived. During one such attack, Daniel was captured and forced to walk in a shackled line with other prisoners. The boy had heard all the horrid tales of Indian scalpings and massacres. Would they torture him? Would they kill him? Would they make him a slave? Daniel didn't know. But for the moment, just being alive was enough. During the long, cold trek north, Daniel determined, sooner or later, to escape and return home.

Once they arrived in Canada, the terrified prisoners were expected to help with the squaws' work as slave labor. Daniel refused. Instead, he competed with the young braves in their sports and repeatedly beat them at their own games. This astonished the Indians, who looked upon White men as a bunch of sissies. They grew to admire the boy and promised to adopt him eventually and possibly make him a chieftain of their tribe.

While pleased at his success, Daniel grew homesick for his family, especially his father. Daniel remembered the mealtime worship around the massive oak table when his father would read from the large family Bible. His father, a peaceable man, always cautioned Daniel against violence.

"Wait patiently on the Lord—He'll answer your prayer and provide a way of escape," he would tell his son. The words stuck. Daniel still determined in his mind that at the right moment he'd escape, but without using violence or endangering the lives of the other prisoners. All he had to do was wait for the right moment.

Week after week, month after month, Daniel bided his time. A raid on a settlement close to the Canadian border finally gave him his chance and brought to mind a second lesson Daniel's father had taught the young boy—how to ice-skate. When the braves returned from their foray with several pairs of ice skates, they didn't know what they were or what to do with them. Daniel patiently showed them how to put them on. On the ice the Indians wobbled and fell, much to their embarrassment. Although he was an expert skater, Daniel pretended to do the same. Before long the skates were tossed aside as worthless junk.

(Story to be continued.)

MARCH 5

THE ESCAPE

I can do everything through him who gives me strength. Philippians 4:13, NIV.

During those long months in captivity, Daniel remembered the Bible promise in Philippians 4:13. He knew that when the time came, God would give him the strength he needed to escape successfully and return to his family. The more he thought about the abandoned ice skates, the clearer his plan became. One day when he overheard the braves talking about the move north, "as soon as the ice on the river thaws," he realized that if he was ever going to escape, he'd have to do it soon.

Each day for a week he slipped out of camp unseen, then placed little caches of food in a deerskin pack hidden farther upriver. One morning, unobserved by his captors, Daniel fastened a pair of skates securely on his feet and disappeared around a point of the river. By the time the braves realized what he had done, Daniel was far out of the reach of their arrows. Angry and humiliated, they fastened on the skates and tried to catch him, only to slip and slide across the icy river.

Once free, Daniel collected his backpack of food, skated the entire length of Lake Champlain, then followed rivers and streams as far south as Albany, the capital of what is today New York state. Finally he reached his family and his home in Concord, New Hampshire.

In later years Daniel became a successful farmer and landowner. Over the years he retold the story of his long trip on the captured skates to his 18 children, who all learned to skate at an early age. He also taught them the good advice that his own father had taught him from the Bible—the words that helped him to decide what he should do—be as "wise as serpents and harmless as doves."

On a map trace Daniel's brave journey from the St. Lawrence River to Albany, then over to Concord, New Hampshire. How many miles did he travel?

Daniel Abbott is another profile in courage. He had the courage to wait for the right time and opportunity before trying to escape. I imagine it was difficult for Daniel to be patient—to bide his time. It was the Bible promise learned years earlier that helped him succeed. God holds the solutions to your problems also, if you'll but wait patiently.

MARCH 6

BILL NUNN IN BOONVILLE

The disciples came to him and asked, "Why do you speak to the people in parables?" He replied, "The knowledge of the secrets of the kingdom of heaven has been given to you, but not to them." Matthew 13:10, 11, NIV.

About 100 years ago the people of Boonville, California, invented an entire language called Boontling. No one knows why for sure. Some say the children of the community created it; others say the wives invented it so they could keep secrets from their husbands and children. The most popular belief, however, is that the men wanted to keep secrets from their wives and children. After a while the language spread throughout the community until all of the native people used it to prevent strangers from knowing what they were saying.

Most of the words came from association. For example, Bill Nunn, the term for syrup, came from the name of a man who loved pancake syrup. Even today children are taught Boontling along with English in school. A dictionary of 1,000 words has been published. Here are some of the terms used.

ab—crowd into a line
bahl—good
Bill Nunn—syrup
boo—potatoes
briney—ocean
briney glimmer—lighthouse

Did you know that Jesus spoke in code? When He told parables to the people, He was speaking in code. For He didn't want everyone in the crowd to understand. He knew that the Pharisees were scattered throughout the crowd, hoping to trick Him and to confuse the people who came to hear the gospel. Others were there to heckle and to criticize. His stories were hardly more than garble to these insincere troublemakers. But to the individuals whose hearts longed for the truths He had to share, He revealed the secrets of the kingdom of heaven.

If you and I come to Jesus with sincere hearts, we will be able to understand His clear, simple words. And like the citizens of Boonville understanding Boontling, we will know and understand the code of the kingdom of heaven.

MARCH 7

A TIMELY WORD

A man finds joy in giving an apt reply—and how good is a timely word! Proverbs 15:23, NIV.

My uncle Pete was a tall, skinny man with a very short fuse. Never admitting that he could possibly be wrong, he strode through life with a giant, double-fisted chip on his shoulder. I remember how his eyes would sparkle as he warmed up to his tales of how he really showed this person or told that person a thing or two. His sentences were always sprinkled liberally with "I's"—"I did this"; "I said that"; "I really told him off!"

"I wasn't about to let him push me around." Uncle Pete could always think of a nasty reply, a sarcastic comeback—the right word for every occasion.

As Uncle Pete grew older, he contracted a serious lung disease. That's when I discovered the results of my uncle's disposition. Though he'd lived in the same community his entire life, Uncle Pete died alone. His wife and five children had long since abandoned him. And any friends he might have once had he'd driven away with his caustic tongue and obvious delight in "setting people straight." Only my mother—his sister—cared enough to be with him at the end.

My poor miserable uncle never learned that joy comes from positive words *timely* spoken, not negative ones scattered about like broken glass at an accident site. I wonder how different his life would have been if he'd discovered the following secrets to happiness.

The six most important words—*I admit I made a mistake.*

The five most important words—*You did a good job.*

The four most important words—*What do you think?*

The three most important words—*I love you.*

The two most important words—*Thank you.*

The single most important word—*Please.*

The very least important word—*I.*

Author Frederick Buechner says, "It's fun to be angry—to lick your wounds; to smack your lips over what you should have said; to chew on the things you'll say next time, if next time ever comes; to savor both your pain and the pain you will inflict on your enemy. It's a feast fit for a king. The problem is, you are dining on yourself."

Uncle Pete dined on himself until all his human kindness and compassion were gobbled up. Only a crinkled, leather-like skin remained. What's on your menu today?

MARCH 8

A CHIP OFF THE OLD SPUD

But when he, the Spirit of truth, comes, he will guide you into all truth. John 16:13, NIV.

Earl Wise had a serious problem. His supplier had delivered too many potatoes to his restaurant. The spuds would spoil long before he could serve them to his customers. What could he do?

While contemplating his problem, Earl idly began peeling a potato out of the first gunny sack. One after another, he peeled the potatoes while thinking about his problem. The potatoes, as peeled potatoes do when exposed to the air, began to turn brown. Not knowing what else to do, Earl sliced the potatoes thinly and dumped them into a pot of hot grease bubbling on the stove. In a few minutes Earl's problem was solved and a new treat had been invented. You guessed it—Earl had made the first batch of potato chips! People came from miles around to try his "newfangled spud." And an entire industry sprang from one man's problem. Have you ever eaten potato chips from a bag with the picture of an owl on it? That's Mr. Wise's symbol.

Many inventions came by accident. Penicillin was such a product, as was the invention of safety glass and the discovery of radioactive rays from uranium testing—even Silly Putty. Such inventions come by what is called *serendipity*. That's the process of discovering one thing while looking for something entirely different. Usually the invention is better than what the scientist set out to invent in the first place.

A friend of mine learned of the true Sabbath while trying to prove that Sunday was the correct day to worship. Another friend studied the Bible to disprove that Jesus was really God in human form, only to come to believe in Him.

These last two stories are not really examples of the word "serendipity," though. There's a difference between discovering something by accident and the discoveries made by my two friends. Their discoveries resulted from the Holy Spirit working in their lives.

When the Holy Spirit works on your heart or mine, it is not an accident. He's just doing His job of leading us into all truth. Aren't you glad that your salvation and mine is not dependant on serendipity? Aren't you thankful that God has a definite plan for each of our lives—not the chance happening of a broken test tube leading to the discovery of safety glass or too many potatoes delivered becoming potato chips? Makes you love Him all the more, doesn't it?

MARCH 9

BALCONY PEOPLE

I always thank God for you because of his grace given you in Christ Jesus. . . . Because our testimony about Christ was confirmed in you. 1 Corinthians 1:4-6, NIV.

Katy was shocked when she entered the academy temperance speech contest and won. She clutched the second place ribbon and the check for $25. She still couldn't believe it. The shy, insecure girl's face glowed with happiness when Mrs. Gibbs, one of the judges, took the time to speak to her. "Katy," the woman said, "you have talent. Someday I expect to hear great things from you."

Whether or not Mrs. Gibbs thought much more about her encouraging remarks after that evening, Katy never knew. The woman's words became a precious treasure to the young girl. Years later, though Mrs. Gibbs was no longer alive to see it, Katy returned to the academy for her twenty-fifth alumni weekend celebration as a successful author. Would she have succeeded if Mrs. Gibbs hadn't taken the time to encourage her? Who knows? But I do know for a fact that Mrs. Gibbs did make a difference on the young girl's life, for I'm Katy.

The woman became one of Katy's favorite "balcony people." Balcony people are those who take the time to encourage you, to remind you of how special you are. I didn't invent the term *balcony people*. Another author, Joyce Landorf, did. She says there are two kinds of people in this world—balcony people and cellar people. A balcony person is the one cheering you on, the one who encourages you to get up and try again when you make a mistake, the individual who builds you up instead of pulling you down—the one shouting "Come on, you can do it!"

Jesus was that kind of person. He didn't scold people for their sins. He said, "Go and sin no more." That's the kind of person Mrs. Gibbs was, and that's the kind of person I want to be, don't you?

MARCH 10

CELLAR PEOPLE

Love your neighbor as you love yourself. But if you act like wild animals, hurting and harming each other, then watch out, or you will completely destroy one another. Galatians 5:14, 15, TEV.

Yesterday I mentioned a second kind of person—a cellar person. We've all met cellar people and been hurt by them. Cellar people evaluate everything you do, and let you know when your efforts aren't quite good enough. They haul your spirits down into the basement with theirs. When you try to do the impossible, they question, "Who do you think you are, trying to be someone you're not?"

They warn, "I don't know if you can make it. You're just not strong enough or good enough." When you fail, they taunt you with "See, I told you so." As in today's text, they enjoy destroying other people's enthusiasm. Their words cut so deeply into your spirit, it's hard to forget the pain.

If only I could remember the balcony people's remarks and forget the slurs of the cellar people! It's possible to do, you know. Try the following exercise.

Take three sheets of paper. On one sheet, make a list of all the cellar people and what they've said that hurt you. When you're finished, crumble it up into a tight little ball and throw it in the garbage. Forget it. You've given these people and their hurtful remarks enough attention already.

On the second piece of paper, list the names of your balcony people. Start with Mom and Dad or Grandma and Grandpa. Write a short thank-you note to each of them. Don't forget to include the people of the Bible on your list, such as Paul, Peter, Dorcas, and John, who encourage you with promises of love and forgiveness.

On the third sheet of paper, list the names of people for whom you are or could become a balcony person. Begin at home, then move out to your neighborhood—to your school, to your church, and perhaps even to the Pathfinders. Whom can you encourage? Pray for each name. And your last assignment is to ask God to show you how to stop being a cellar person and become a full-time balcony person.

MARCH 11

A RARE BREED

It is better not to vow than to make a vow and not fulfill it. Ecclesiastes 5:5, NIV.

Tears streamed down the faces of hundreds of war refugees on that bleak, desperate eleventh day of March 1942 as they watched the American troops, their last hope of escape from the advancing Japanese army, exit the Manila harbor. One island group after another had fallen to the advancing Japanese army until it was obvious that the U.S. forces would need to evacuate their stronghold. The enemy was marching into the Philippines as confidently as an honored high school band in Pasadena's famous annual Tournament of Roses Parade. And as he pulled out of the harbor, General Douglas MacArthur made a momentous promise to the people left behind: "I shall return."

Regardless of the odds of winning a difficult war in the Pacific, the 64-year-old general made good his promise two and a half years later. On October 20, 1944, he stood once again on Philippine soil. His radio speech went as follows:

"This is the voice of freedom, General MacArthur speaking. People of the Philippines, I have returned." MacArthur lived by the code that states: "A man is as good as his word." Such people were an endangered species, even in his day. And today, in a world where cheating is considered wrong only if you get caught, where returning lost money is considered stupid, where excuses such as "The dog ate my homework" or "The check is in the mail" are humorous clichés, such people still stand out as rare and exotic treasures.

Whether a business executive or a factory worker, a student or a teacher, a Christian or a pagan—we admire people whose promises we can trust. They stand out as heroes in a land of wimps. They do what they promise without being reminded, warned, or threatened.

Ask yourself: "Am I a hero or a wimp?"

1. When you say you'll be somewhere at such and such a time to do something, do you keep your word?

2. When you say "I'll pray for you," do you?

3. When you promise to pay back a debt at a certain time, do you?

4. When you say "I'll be glad to help," do you come through with that help or hope they forget you volunteered?

True, no one's perfect. Things do come up that prevent even the most sincere promises from being carried out. When this happens, are you quick to apologize without making a string of excuses? If you do, you are becoming a person of genuine integrity, a member of that rare breed of person who can truly be trusted.

MARCH 12

THE SUICIDE TREE

And I pray that you, being rooted and established in love, . . . may be filled to the measure of all the fullness of God. Ephesians 3:17-19, NIV.

When the leaves of C.B.'s favorite maple tree behind his Connecticut home fell to the ground in July rather than in early October, he wanted to know why. He inspected the leaves and the bark for insects or disease, but found nothing wrong.

Determined to save the tree, he talked with operators of a local landscaping firm. He contacted experts at the state university and at the U.S. Department of Forestry and followed their advice, but the tree continued to die. He'd have to cut it down.

First, he removed the branches, then he dug a trench around the tree so that he could get to the roots. As he dug around the tree's base, C.B. couldn't find any roots. Thinking there must be hidden roots, he tied a cable to the trunk of his car and wrapped the other end around the tree trunk. Backing slowly down the driveway, he expected to see the ground hump up over the roots below. Instead, the upright tree started to slide instead of tipping toward the car. The tree then became overbalanced and fell, missing the front bumper by only eight inches.

When C.B. climbed out of the car, he discovered something very strange. The tree had no roots to cut. One large root that encircled the base of the trunk had killed all but a few of the tree's tiniest roots. The large root had strangled the tree. One good windstorm would have toppled the maple. The tree had killed itself.

Perhaps the tree had been attacked by a disease or blight, or by a hoard of hungry insects, causing the tree to turn in on itself. While roots can differ in the direction they grow or in the size they reach, there must still be a root system of some kind to nurture and support a tree.

Christians need roots too—roots founded in love. It is as natural for God's children to love others as it is for a tree to send out roots beneath the soil. Without giving and receiving Christian love, we become like C.B.'s maple tree. When someone hurts us, when we feel rejected or are criticized by others, we are tempted to shut out the world. We hide away in our own little corner of the world so we won't be hurt again. But like C.B.'s tree, we end up destroying the very thing we tried to protect.

Jesus talked about roots and soil and growing in his parable of the sower. You can read the story in Matthew 13.

MARCH 13

DOLLARS AND SENSE

And he said unto them, Go ye into all the world, and preach the gospel to every creature. Mark 16:15.

The opposite bank of the river lay shrouded in the morning mist. I stared across the wide expanse of water. "There's no way he could have done what legend claims. No one could throw a silver dollar from here to the other side of this river—not even the great George Washington."

Every American student past the age of 10 has heard the story. According to legend, George Washington, our first president, threw a silver dollar across the Potomac River. However, anyone who has ever stood where the event was supposed to have occurred would find it difficult to believe the tale. Perhaps golf pro Arnold Palmer could slam a golf ball across, but even for the best Yankee pitcher it would be a stretch.

Likewise, if I were to tell you I could make a silver dollar go all the way around the world, your own good sense would cause you to doubt. But this claim I can back up with evidence. I can—and so can you. Instead of throwing the silver dollar, I put it in an envelope marked "mission offering" and place it in the offering plate at church.

After my local church treasurer counts the morning's offering, he deposits it in the bank, then writes a check to the local conference. From there the conference treasurer sends my dollar to the union conference, where the union conference treasurer mails a check to the General Conference treasurer, who disperses the accumulated money to the appropriate missions around the world.

So you see, I can make a silver dollar go all around the world, not by tossing it like George Washington is rumored to have done or by keeping it as Hetty Green tried to do, but by giving it.

I would prefer to go as a missionary teacher to South America or to India, but God has other plans for my life, which include supporting with my money and my prayers the people who do go as missionaries. That makes good sense to me—I am still fulfilling Jesus' command to "go into all the world and preach the gospel." Maybe God's plan for you includes mission service. If so, my dollars and cents along with those of other church members will help make your dream possible. However, until that dream becomes a reality, you can join me in sending your mission dollars to all parts of the world.

MARCH 14

MORE DANGEROUS THAN BIGFOOT

You have been a refuge for the poor, a refuge for the needy in his distress, a shelter from the storm and a shade from the heat. Isaiah 25:4, NIV.

On the last day of 1975, 16-year-old Gary Snyder and two of his friends from Walla Walla Valley Academy hiked up Oregon's Mount Hood in order to welcome the sunrise of the United States of America's bicentennial year—January 1, 1976. The three boys were familiar with the route. Since the age of 7, Gary had been mountain climbing with his father, a physical education teacher and professional mountaineer. Each of his climbing buddies had also done their share of mountaineering. The boys' packs contained the proper tools and adequate supplies for the short, easy climb to Mount Hood's Saddle Back area, above Illumination Rock.

The boys spent their first night at the 7,000-foot level. They were up before light the next morning. An icy crust had formed during the night, which made their climb more difficult. Triumphant, they reached their destination just as the sun broke over the horizon. The early-morning light sparkled on the ice crystals, creating a dazzling Disneyland-like light show. After a few minutes, the boys reluctantly turned from the magical carnival of lights and headed back down the mountain.

Partway down, they dug a gigantic snow cave, complete with ice shelves for their supplies and platforms for their sleeping bags. The three boys spent hours designing their creative cavern. The sun's disappearance into the west ended their efforts. Exhausted, the boys failed to take a compass bearing before turning in for the night.

While they slept, a storm howled outside their fortress. When the boys awoke, they found themselves in a total whiteout. They reminded themselves that mountain storms rarely last more than four days, so there was nothing to fear as long as they stayed put. To maintain a continuous supply of fresh air, they took turns clearing the new snow from the mouth of the tunnel.

They'd been in their cave for some time when they heard a strange, low growl. "It's probably Sasquatch," one of the boys joked.

"Yeah," one of the others added, "he wants out of the storm, right?" That Sasquatch, the mystical apelike beast of the Pacific Northwest, might have come calling at their snow cave struck all three boys as hilarious. Their laughter ceased as the strange, low growl grew into a giant, deafening roar.

(Story to be continued tomorrow.)

MARCH 15

SIXTEEN DAYS ON THE MOUNTAIN

For the Son of man is come to seek and to save that which was lost. Luke 19:10.

Gary and his friends stared in horror as a large portion of the roof collapsed, sending tons of wet snow to the floor of their cave. Startled, they scrambled out of the cave, barely escaping being buried alive. Should they head to the east or the west? Should they hike up or down? To choose the wrong direction could take them to their deaths. The right direction could bring them to the safety and warmth of Mount Hood Lodge. During the days that followed, the boys survived an avalanche, tumbled into a crevasse, dug six different snow tunnels, and once were buried under the snow.

Cramped, soggy, and suffering from the extreme cold, the boys huddled in their seventh snow cave, which was barely big enough to turn around in. They spent their days reading their Bibles, their nights singing hymns. When their fuel ran out, the small burner put out heat for five days beyond its fuel supply. After that they used a candle and their own body heat to melt snow for drinking water. The food ran out on the ninth day. Gary thought a lot about his father—the arguments and hassles they'd been going through recently. Yet he knew that his father was searching for him. Gary was right. Gary's father, along with experienced alpine rescue teams, was combing the mountain for the boys. Helicopters crisscrossed the sky above the mountain, their pilots hoping to spot the boys. Several times the boys heard the helicopters and rushed outside the cave, but the snow whipped up by the helicopter blades blocked out the boys and the orange tent they'd stretched out on the snow.

During their sixteenth night on the mountain, the boys emerged from their tunnel to view a clear, star-studded sky. Off in the distance they could see the lights of Portland. The boys debated whether or not to hike off the mountain before dawn. Finally they decided it would be smarter to remain where they were until they could see where they were hiking. They didn't want to step into any more crevasses.

The next morning as the three boys were scaling the bank of snow above their cave, a member of one of the rescue teams spotted them. Back at the lodge the boys learned they were heroes. Later experts agreed that it was the boys' faith in their eventual rescue that saved their lives. They just refused to give up their faith, no matter how bad their situation became.

Today, years later, Gary is passing on to his children that same faith that saw him through those 16 grueling days while lost on Mount Hood.

MARCH 16

REDHEADED GULLS

Professing themselves to be wise, they became fools. Romans 1:22.

John, a friend of mine, loves to go bird-watching. He keeps a list of the rare and interesting birds he has seen over the years. We eagerly await John's Christmas letter, which includes an up-to-date list of the birds he has sighted during the year. His travels around the world as a missionary have given him the opportunity to view some magnificent specimens. Since he and his family recently moved to sunny California, I dedicate this story to him and all his fellow birding enthusiasts—those with and without feathers.

In 1935 California ornithologists sighted an unusually marked bird—the first new species spotted in the San Francisco area in a number of years. The bird had all the identification marks of an ordinary sea gull except for its fiery red head. The scientists eagerly cataloged their unique find. This rare new species of gull was a major discovery. Bird-watchers from all over the world rushed to the city by the bay, hoping to locate one of these exotic gulls. Celebration soon turned to embarrassment. Quietly the bird-watchers slipped away into the night. No one ever admitted a mistake had been made, and no one ever revealed who discovered the error. The new species of bird proved to be nothing more than everyday, overly hungry sea gulls.

Workmen painting the new Golden Gate Bridge ate their lunch while perched on the bridge's steel girders, high above the ocean. The hungry gulls came begging for lunch scraps. To pass the time of day in their remote location, the workmen devised a game to see who could best daub the "international orange" paint on a swooping gull's head. The greedy gulls chose to risk the paint daubs for the food offered. Hence, redheaded sea gulls.

How foolish the internationally renowned ornithologists must have felt when they learned that the discovery of the century was no more than an innocent game between fowl and man. An innocent mistake, yet the experts were made to look like fools.

We laugh at the humorous goofs people make. And somehow they're even funnier when made by an expert. However, a mistake is not a laughing matter when it deals with spiritual issues. You and I cannot afford to make mistakes in the light of eternity. We must each take the time to study God's Word for ourselves. We must get to know Jesus so well that there is no room for stupid errors. Anything less would be foolish, don't you think?

MARCH 17

POWER PACKAGE

And so I am sure that God, who began this good work in you, will carry it on until it is finished on the Day of Christ Jesus. Philippians 1:6, TEV.

Long ago a large pink lotus plant bloomed next to a lake in northern Manchuria, China. The flowers dropped their petals, and the seeds fell into the thick, rich mud at the water's edge. In time the lake dried up. More time passed—a thousand years, in fact. During that time the Europeans went on crusades to the Holy Land, the Puritans sailed for America, the French dethroned their king, and the Industrial Revolution began.

In the early 1900s a team of American botanists explored the lake area in northern Manchuria. They dug up a handful of seeds—lotus flower seeds—from the hardened clay. The scientists tested and discovered that the seeds were extremely old. They placed the seeds in a display case in a museum. There the seeds remained until 1952, when a curious botanist decided to find out if by chance the seeds might bloom after such a long time. He placed a few of them in sulfuric acid in order to soften their shells. Then he planted the softened seeds in enriched soil. On June 29, 1952, the first pink Manchurian lotus blossom opened. If you were to visit the Kenilworth Aquatic Gardens in Washington, D.C., in July, you might be able to see these ancient flowers in bloom.

It's hard to imagine how a plant could possibly produce such a beautiful blossom after such a long time, how the tiny spark of life within those ugly, shriveled-up seeds could remain dormant for so long, then spring to life when the conditions were right.

Do you ever feel down on yourself? Do you think you're ugly? Lower than a slug? As talented as a pet rock or as useful as the common cold? Do you, after you've done something wrong, feel empty inside? Dead—like a dried-up lotus seed encrusted in mud?

Sometimes you may even wonder why Jesus even bothers with you. I imagine Simon Peter felt that way after Jesus' crucifixion, and what about how Mary Magdalene felt when she asked to be forgiven for her sins a seventh time? What about good, old, murderous David?

If you have ever felt like this, today's promise is for you. It says that God won't give up on you. When you first invited Jesus into your heart, the Holy Spirit planted a spark, much like the spark of life in the seeds. This spark prompts us to love and obey Him. From then on, God promises to keep working with you until He comes to take you home. The only one who can stop Him, who can choke out that spark of love, is you. Only you can force Him away.

So whenever you feel down on yourself like Simon Peter, whenever you feel as if you're a hopeless case like King David, whenever you've blown it again like Mary Magdalene, remember that if God doesn't give up on you, why should you?

NO CATCH

For it is by grace you have been saved, through faith—and this not from yourselves, it is the gift of God— not by works, so that no one can boast. Ephesians 2:8, 9, NIV.

Roger recently made his first visit to New York City. At Times Square, while he stood on the corner for a light to change, a street vendor tapped him on the shoulder.

"I've got genuine Rolex watches for sale here—$15 each." The man waved a forearm full of flashy gold watches in front of Roger's face. Roger watched the gold glimmer in the sunlight. Suddenly he just had to have one of those watches. Eagerly he bought one. When he returned to his friend's home in Brooklyn, he proudly modeled his purchase.

"See." He twisted his wrist first one direction, then the other. "Isn't it beautiful?"

His friend, a native New Yorker, shook his head. "Roger, think about it. What's the catch? Either the watch is stolen property or it's a cheap imitation."

"No," Roger argued, "it's not a fake—see?" He slipped it off his wrist and pointed to the words engraved on the back of the watch. Roger glanced down at his wrist and scowled. A greenish-gray ring encircled his wrist where the watchband had been. Carefully he tugged the sleeve of his jacket down to cover the evidence left by the watch's cheap plating. But his friend was too busy studying the watch to notice.

"Oh, no!" Roger's friend burst into laughter. "Did you know that your genuine Rolex watch runs backward?" Roger snatched the watch from his friend's hand. It was true; not only did the watchband turn his wrist green, but the hands ran counterclockwise.

"Well, at least you're safe with the law," his friend consoled. "There's no way this watch could be stolen property!"

Roger learned a valuable lesson from his watch—you don't get something for nothing. You get what you pay for or what you earn, nothing more. If something sounds too good to be true, it probably is. Now Roger takes the time to ask, "What's the catch?"

Roger knows that there is an exception to this rule. One freebie Roger knows he can trust is God's gift of eternal life. It is a gift of the highest quality, paid for by the life of God's Son. No amount of money can buy it; no amount of hard work can earn it. It really does seem almost too good to be true, except the gift comes with a written guarantee—direct from the throne of God.

MARCH 19

TH-I-I-I-S MUCH

This is love: not that we loved God, but that he loved us and sent his Son as an atoning sacrifice for our sins. 1 John 4:10, NIV.

Hiding in the pantry by the kitchen door, 5-year-old Rhonda danced impatiently first on one foot, then the other. Daddy's car would be pulling into the driveway at any moment. Every evening it was the same. Rhonda would hide in the pantry, then jump out when Daddy stepped into the house. Then even before Daddy had time to set down his briefcase, Rhonda would leap into his arms and plant a gigantic kiss on his cheek.

After exchanging the daily quota of kisses, Daddy would ask Rhonda, "How's my little girl?"

Rhonda would reply, "Just great. How's my big daddy?"

"Terrific," he would answer, squeezing her tightly again. "I love you so much!"

"M-m-m, I love you so much too."

"Just how much do you love me?"

Rhonda would stretch her chubby little arms out and giggle, "I love you th-i-i-s much!"

Daddy's lower lip would protrude into a pout. "Only that much?"

"Oh, no, I love you th-i-i-i-i-s much"—stretching her arms just as far as they could possibly stretch. Then she would wrap them as far around her father as possible, giving him a big hug.

Rhonda is a grown woman now. Today when she hugs her dad, her arms can stretch much farther and can hold him much tighter. Her love for him has grown too.

The other day when I visited a gift shop, I thought of Rhonda and her father. On the wall behind the counter I saw a plaque. It read "I asked Jesus, 'How much do you love me?' 'This much,' He answered, and He stretched out His arms—and died."

No one could stretch his arms farther or love us more than Christ did by dying on the cross at Calvary. So how much do you love Him?

WORD POWER

And whatever you do, whether in word or deed, do it all in the name of the Lord Jesus. Colossians 3:17, NIV.

Today I would love to have you conduct an experiment right there in your own house, but I'm not sure your parents would be too pleased with either you or me if you did. So instead, we'll go through the steps of the experiment in our imaginations.

Step 1. Remove—in your imagination, mind you—the cap from either a tube or a pump of toothpaste.

Step 2. Squeeze or pump—again in your imagination—the toothpaste onto a plate, circling it round and round until you have emptied it into a Dairy Queen swirl. Great!

Step 3. Return the toothpaste to its container.

Well, what's the matter? Is there some sort of problem? Of course, there's a problem, you say. Once toothpaste leaves the tube or the pump, you can't put it back inside.

Hmm, that's strange. Try again. Are you sure you tried hard enough? Come on; you can do it.

Words are much like toothpaste, you know. Just as toothpaste, once out of the tube, is impossible to stuff back inside, so words cannot be stuffed back into our mouths and brains once we have spoken.

Some words uttered in anger emerge from our mouths cruel and hateful like a basket of poisonous snakes, weaving and slithering around our victim's mind long after our tempers have cooled. Even when we ask for forgiveness, the offended person will have a hard time ridding himself or herself of the pain we caused.

Other words come out as lies, trapping and ensnaring the speaker in a tangled web while Satan dances in the middle, pulling the strings.

And at other times coarse, vulgar words are used in order to "sound cool"—these words buzz before our faces like gnats swarming on a hot summer night and can become nasty little habits, difficult to defeat.

Being able to communicate our thoughts and ideas through the use of words is a marvelous gift from God. By misusing that gift, speech becomes a vicious and destructive pestilence of Satan.

And now back to the toothpaste. When you look in the mirror and give yourself a just-brushed, toothy grin, remember the lesson of spoken words, of stuffing toothpaste back into the toothpaste tube, and today's memory text.

ALONE IN THE NIGHT

Listen to my prayer, O Lord, and hear my cry for help! Psalm 102:1, TEV.

The last thing Jeff remembered before his world went black was Grandpa's car careening off the muddy logging road and tumbling down the side of the mountain. He awoke some time later to the sound of night birds calling and crickets chirping. His head throbbed; his right leg felt numb and heavy. Struggling to sit up, Jeff peered into the gathering darkness to determine where he might be. When he tried to stand up, a cord tightened about his neck. He reached up and yanked. The black nylon strap from his camera broke free from the branch that had been holding it. Jeff glanced down at the cord.

"Where's my camera?" he mumbled. "Great! It's probably broken!" Then he remembered his grandfather.

"Oh, no," Jeff gasped. "Grandpa, where are you?"

Both being camera buffs, he and his grandfather often took drives into the back country for a day of picture taking. They'd snapped a number of animal photos when they decided to head home. Springtime rains had turned the usually stable gravel roads into a quagmire of mud, fallen rock, and broken tree boughs that had been left over from the winter ice storms.

Jeff strained to spot the car through the forest's old growth. A glint from the last rays of daylight caught on the Chevy's chrome bumper, farther down the mountain slope.

"Grandpa, Grandpa," he called. A lone owl answered his call. "I've got to get to Grandpa!" Painfully Jeff tried to stand, but his left leg wouldn't take his weight. He fell back onto the mattress of pine needles and dead leaves.

"Please, dear God, You've got to help me!"

(Story to be continued.)

MARCH 22

SONGS IN THE NIGHT

Where is God my maker, who giveth songs in the night? Job 35:10.

Jeff took a deep breath. *I can't just lie here*, he thought, half sliding and half rolling down the slope toward the car. After a long painful crawl over rough, fallen logs, through blackberry briars, and across patches of melting winter snow, Jeff spotted his grandfather's red plaid wool shirt.

He hurried to his grandfather's still form. Jeff reached out and touched his grandfather's neck, then sighed with relief when he felt a steady throb. "Grandpa, Grandpa, can you hear me?"

The shadows of night filled the narrow gorge where the boy and his grandfather lay. The woods had never seemed so frightening. He looked up the mountainside; he looked down. A river, wild with spring runoff, raged at the bottom of the mountain. And above, a 20-foot cliff of granite glowered over at him. Shadows became prowling bears; noises became stalking wildcats. A gentle rain began to fall, adding to both his discomfort and to the threat of hypothermia.

"Don't freak out," he repeated to himself. He must remain calm if either of them was to survive.

Suddenly his grandfather groaned and began to shiver uncontrollably. Jeff lay down and shared his body heat with the old man. To comfort him further, Jeff began to sing.

"'I love You, Lord, and I lift my voice to worship You. O my soul, rejoice . . .'" At first Jeff sang barely above a whisper, cracking on every note. But before long a strong clear tone filled the hollows and echoed off the bank on the opposite side of the ravine. He sang every chorus he'd ever learned in church, school, summer camp, and Pathfinders. Then he began singing his way through the *Singing Youth* songbook. It was during the last verse of "In My Heart There Rings a Melody" that Jeff heard someone calling his name. Within minutes Jeff and his grandfather were airlifted to the nearest trauma center, in time to save his grandfather's life.

"We were near the top of the mountain when we first heard you singing," one of the rescuers explained. "How we heard you above the roar of the river, I'll never know, but we did."

Jeff knew. He had no doubt. God had sent him songs in the night in order to save his and his grandfather's lives.

MARCH 23

WHERE, WHO, WHOSE?

For whether we live . . . and whether we die . . . we are the Lord's. Romans 14:8.

What makes people Christian? Is it because they go to church? Is it because they pay tithe? Do they become Christian by singing the right songs or saying the correct words? There's more to being a Christian than that, isn't there? Let me tell you about Tweeter and Candi.

A friend of mine named Candi loves animals—animals of any kind. Unfortunately, Candi has allergies. Once Candi had a German shepherd puppy named Romp. But the dog's hair made Candi sneeze. Her pet cat Sissy also made Candi sneeze. Even the talking mynah bird that her father brought home for her one day made Candi sneeze. No matter what animal her parents got her, Candi would get sick.

Being of a whimsical nature, the now-adult Candi has compensated by placing stuffed animals in unusual poses about her home. She has furry black spiders in a goldfish bowl, a tawny lion lounging in a doggy bed, and polyester-filled baby chicks climbing on a gerbil's jungle gym. My favorite animal in Candi's stuffed menagerie is Tweeter, the Siamese cat, who occupies a wicker bird cage by the front door.

Tweeter stays in the bird cage day in and day out. But residing in a bird cage hasn't changed Tweeter into a bird. He's still a stuffed beige-and-brown cat with plastic whiskers. Tweeter proves that it takes more than living in a bird cage to be a bird. Even if Candi stuffed bird seed down Tweeter's throat, the cat would never become a bird.

Could that be true of becoming a Christian also? Does it take more than regular church attendance or being born into a Christian family to become a genuine Christian?

It's true that living in a garage doesn't make you a car. Or sleeping in a barn won't turn you into a cow. And Tweeter didn't become a bird by living in a bird cage. So going to church faithfully will not automatically make a person a Christian.

Then what is a Christian? A Christian is someone who simply believes in Jesus and has asked Jesus to live in his or her mind. Inviting Jesus into your mind at home, at school—wherever you happen to be—makes the difference. The important thing about being a genuine Christian is not where you live or who you happen to be, but whose you are.

MARCH 24

GOOGOL AND GOOGOLPLEX

How precious also are thy thoughts unto me, O God! how great is the sum of them! If I should count them, they are more in number than the sand. Psalm 139:17, 18.

Sandy loved numbers from the time she was old enough to recite the rhyme "One, two, buckle my shoe. Three, four, shut the door." In 1989 when she watched a television special on the twentieth anniversary of the first moon landing, she became fascinated with the great distance between the moon and the earth. At school her seventh-grade teacher suggested that Sandy make a chart to help her classmates better visualize the distance the astronauts had traveled. Since all her friends read *Guide* magazine, Sandy decided to make an issue of *Guide* her "ruler."

Sandy measured the length of a *Guide* magazine—8 1/4 inches. By using her pocket calculator, she discovered she would need 7,680 *Guides* stretched end to end to cover just one mile. (At 52 *Guides* a year, that's 147.69 years' worth.) The moon's average distance from earth is 238,857 miles. So it would take 1,834,421,760 *Guides* laid end to end to reach the moon. A humongous number to measure.

The Bible is full of massive numbers that cannot be measured so easily. Abraham was challenged to count the grains of sand on the seashore and number the stars of the sky. He couldn't do it. Even today these numbers are so big that even Sandy's mathematical mind cannot grasp them.

Edward Kasner, a famous mathematician, wanted to create a name for such a number—a number that couldn't be counted. The number he chose is a 1 followed by 100 zeros. His 9-year-old nephew supplied him with a name for it—googol.

Then the nephew came up with an even larger number—a 1 followed by as many zeros as you can write before you get tired. The boy called this number a googolplex. Dr. Kasner refined his nephew's new number by saying a googolplex is a 1 followed by a googol of zeros.

Thanks to Dr. Kasner and his nephew, mathematics now has names for these numbers. Still, no one can count that high. The grains of sand remain uncounted; the stars of the heavens unnumbered. I have so many questions I want to ask Jesus when I get to heaven that the answer to the number of stars or grains of sand will be pretty low on my curiosity list. That doesn't bother me since I will have all eternity to look for the answers. Can you list some difficult questions you might want to find the answers to when you reach heaven?

MARCH 25

PRAISE IN EVERYTHING

In the name of our Lord Jesus Christ, always give thanks for everything to God the Father. Ephesians 5:20, TEV.

Marilyn heard the sound of metal crashing against metal, of glass shattering; she smelled the gasoline and the burning rubber, then nothing. When she awoke in the hospital two weeks later, Marilyn found herself paralyzed from the neck down. She couldn't talk, feed, or care for herself in any way. She prayed to be allowed to die.

Each day her family and friends would visit her. The local pastor visited as often as possible. *If only I could at least communicate with them,* she thought. First, she tried blinking—one blink for yes and two blinks for no. But what was happening inside Marilyn's mind still remained pretty much a mystery to the people who loved her.

One day the pastor arrived to find a personal computer set up beside Marilyn's bed. The screen was arranged so Marilyn and her visitors could view it. A private duty nurse sat at the keyboard, typing the morse code letters Marilyn tapped out by holding a pen between her lips and tapping on a bed table. The pastor watched letters turn into the names of people he knew. Then he noticed his own name being added to the list. When he asked her the reason for the names, she eagerly tapped out her reply, "This is my new mission. Before the accident, I was too busy to pray for those I love. Now God has given me all the time in the world to pray. Isn't He wonderful?"

The pastor cleared his throat and turned away. Just minutes before entering the hospital, he'd been complaining to God about his 10-year-old car, about the midnight telephone call that had turned out to be a wrong number, and about the long hours he'd worked during the past week.

He left Marilyn's hospital room with a new perspective on thankfulness. Marilyn was giving thanks to God for everything—both the good and the bad. Once the pastor reached his car, he asked forgiveness for his earlier griping and thanked God for Marilyn and the blessing she had given him that day.

MARCH 26

THE LETTER

But God commendeth his love toward us, in that, while we were yet sinners, Christ died for us. Romans 5:8.

Aunt Leta kept the letter in the bottom of her antique mahogany desk. Whenever she brought it out to show the children, we were not allowed to touch it. In later years she removed it from the desk, photocopied it, and placed the original in a safe-deposit box in the bank. On her death the letter went to a museum in Philadelphia. So what was so special about Aunt Leta's tattered old letter—the letter that hadn't even been written to her?

It was a letter a relative (I don't remember which one) wrote to my grandfather. Even that wasn't important. What made the letter special is that this uncle or cousin wrote the letter from the Confederate Army's Andersonville Prison two weeks before the end of the Civil War.

To be held prisoner of war at the Andersonville Prison had meant death for many. No prison in 1865, either Union or Confederate, would win a sanitation award from the Department of Health. The stench of disease, filth, and death permeated every cell block and prison yard. However, the infamous Andersonville Prison was the worst.

My relative's gruesome description of the conditions in the prison became a valuable piece of American history. If the war hadn't ended when it did, my relative would have been one of the death statistics listed in the history books. Fortunately, he lived to return to his farm in Pennsylvania.

When I first saw the letter, I was disappointed. Written on a plain, old, grimy piece of paper, the handwriting was almost illegible. *Big deal*, I thought. To my eyes it was just a letter from a common, ordinary soldier, long since dead.

"I have been offered more than $50,000 for it," Aunt Leta once confided. How could something that looks so worthless be of such value?

Dirty, ragged derelicts, drug users and drug pushers, bag ladies, prostitutes, deranged individuals shouting obscenities at their own reflections in store windows—the useless dregs of society. Like my first reaction to Aunt Leta's letter, we don't always see their value.

Aunt Leta's letter didn't change. I did. My eyes grew older and wiser. Likewise, the value of these homeless people changes when I view them through the wise, loving eyes of Jesus Christ. He died for the downtown drunk; He died for the nerd who bugs you in history class; He died for the foul-mouthed bully, for the wimpy coward, for the class tattletale, for me and for you. Valuable? Yes, beyond measure.

MARCH 27

SEE YOU LATER, ALLIGATOR

Dear children, let us not love with words or tongue but with actions and in truth. 1 John 3:18, NIV.

If you don't know what a hack, stormer, or draggin' wagon is, it's OK. It just means you were born later than 1950. Probably you also don't use such phrases as "har-de-har-har-har!" (response to a not-so-funny joke), "DDT" (drop dead twice), "ish" (yech), "moolah" (money), "sharp and nifty" (a snappy dresser), and "See you later, alligator" (goodbye).

And if you didn't grow up in the turbulent sixties, you probably don't often say "tough toenails" (too bad), "hairy" (difficult), "real blast" (fun), and "flake out" (relax). Some of you will remember that the seventies added such phrases as "let's rap!" (talk), "peace, man" (hello), "hang loose" and "stay cool" (take it easy), and "go for it" to the English language.

And the eighties added such slang as "give it your best shot," "nail it," "out of sight," "rad," "chill out," and "gnarley." What are some of the newest nineties terms and phrases?

In order to be distinctive, to be "with it" or "cool," each crop of teens develops its own sublanguage. The adults of each era find the latest teenage lingo bewildering and frustrating. To make it all the more frustrating, as soon as a phrase becomes part of everyday speech, it is discarded in favor of a new, more current phrase. Adults feel old, alienated, or out-of-touch when they can't understand what their children are saying.

Since the fall of the Tower of Babel, languages have divided people. However, from Bible times to the 1990s, there is one language that is understood around the world. After the earthquake in southern Russia and more recently the one in Iran, love poured in from all over the world in the form of food, clothing, and rescue teams. People around the world contributed to ease the food shortages in Ethiopia. Even here in America, after the San Francisco earthquake of 1989, people worked together to ease one another's suffering. Each year, every day, ordinary people fly to remote areas of the world to build churches, schools, and clinics. Whoever first said "Actions speak louder than words" was right. Wherever you may go, the language of love—not necessarily the words of love, but love in action—will be properly interpreted. This is God's language. When you show love to someone, you are speaking the language of heaven.

Just for today—keep a mental list of the times you "speak" the language of love.

MARCH 28

LANGUAGE OF LOVE

My little children, let us not love in word, neither in tongue, but in deed and in truth. 1 John 3:18.

"Hey," you say, "you must be slipping up. Isn't that the same text as yesterday?" Yes, it is. But the message is so important, it deserves a two-day coverage. Besides, in case you haven't figured it out yet, I love words, dialects, and languages of all kinds. To me, language is exciting and alive. It's always changing.

So turn back a page to yesterday's lesson and read your assignment for yesterday.

1. Keeping in mind that communicating love involves both giving and receiving, share your list with your family. Let each person at the table share his or her list. A good place to start might be with things that happen at home, then branch out to school and, for your parents, to work.

2. Once everyone has had a turn to share, appoint someone at the table to be the secretary to record everyone's answers to the following exercise. Beginning with today's reader, tell the family member seated next to you one thing that he or she does that you especially appreciate as an example of the language of love in action. Give everyone a chance to share.

Name of Speaker	Name of Person Spoken To	Compliment Given
1.		
2.		
3.		
4.		
5.		
6.		

Something to think about: What would happen if you made this little exercise a family custom?

MARCH 29

A WINDWAGON DARE

Go ye therefore, and teach all nations, baptizing them in the name of the Father, and of the Son, and of the Holy Ghost: Teaching them to observe all things whatsoever I have commanded you: and, lo, I am with you alway, even unto the end of the world. Amen. Matthew 28:19, 20.

"The Midwestern prairies are nothing more than dried-up oceans," the tall, lanky sailor explained. "Why, any smart seadog could sail across the country in record time. All he'd have to do is build a wagon four times—no, 10 times the size of the standard covered wagon and transport it across the plains at breakneck speed by using wind power."

Tom "Wind Wagon" Smith convinced the townspeople of Westport, Missouri, to give him money for his scheme. His vehicle looked like a cross between a Conestoga wagon and a crude oceangoing ship. Twenty-five feet long, seven feet across at its widest point, wheels 12 feet in diameter, with hubs as big as barrels, it drew crowds of curious onlookers. Its huge sail and mast rose 20 feet above the wagon. On the day of the launching, a few of the investors agreed to climb aboard. The craft seemed to almost soar across the plains, over small hills and gullies.

"Now I'll let her take the wind," Thomas announced to his passengers. The wind caught the ship, and despite all his efforts, the wagon went cockeyed in reverse. Then the steering gear locked, sending the wind wagon round and round in a mile-wide circle. When the craft slowed down, the "seasick" stockholders jumped overboard. Wind Wagon Smith held on until the wagon crashed into Turkey Creek. When he tried to talk the people into giving him a second chance, they threatened to sue him. Defeated and discouraged, he boarded his ship the next morning, cursed the cowardice of the "landlubbers," and sailed west.

Did he make it across the prairie as he planned, or did he die trying? An Arapaho Indian legend tells about a White man traveling in a strange, boatlike vehicle somewhere north of the Santa Fe Trail.

We chuckle at Tom "Wind Wagon" Smith and his impossible dream. While you and I will probably never cross Kansas in a wind wagon, throughout history courageous men and women have dared to risk the impossible. If such men as Tom Smith had not dared to pursue such wild dreams, you and I would be still living as people lived in the middle ages, using candle power instead of electricity, driving a horse and wagon instead of a Chevy, and eating food cooked over a spit instead of in microwave ovens.

Two thousand years ago a small group of men dared to risk everything to accomplish a seemingly impossible task. They would "go into all the world and share the good news of Jesus Christ." Their project succeeded better than they could have ever imagined. Like wild prairie fire, the entire then-known world learned of the Saviour and His sacrifice of love for them.

MARCH 30

PENNY'S KIND OF FREEDOM

Freedom is what we have—Christ has set us free! Stand, then, as free people, and do not allow yourselves to become slaves again. Galatians 5:1, TEV.

Penny, a brown-and-white Border collie, and her friend, a taffy-colored cat named Caesar, were traveling from Virginia to New Mexico by car. Before leaving home, their owners bought two collars, two leashes, and a double supply of animal tranquilizers. Both animals were isolated in the back of the family's overloaded station wagon. And at every stop the two animals were walked, watered, and loved.

Before many miles had passed, Penny grew accustomed to her leash and her confinement. She enjoyed the romps across the grass, dragging her owner behind. When it came time to return to the car, she willingly hopped aboard. Since Penny obeyed all commands, her owners soon decided to trust her to run occasionally without the leash.

Not so with Caesar. Throughout the entire trip, Caesar continued to pull, growl, and fuss whenever leashed. His owners could never lift his restrictions if he was ever going to make it to New Mexico with the rest of the family.

Both Penny and Caesar were very much loved—loved enough so that their owners would risk the animals' unhappiness and at times discomfort to take them on the long journey to their new home in the Southwest. They loved both animals enough to protect them. This meant that while Penny could be granted the freedom to run, Caesar had to be leashed for his own protection.

Caesar couldn't help it—he was a cat acting like a cat and doing what cats do. It was his nature to be independent. And Penny was behaving as dogs behave.

When it comes to God's leash—the Ten Commandments—some people, like Caesar, kick and scream and fuss against the very thing that will best protect them from themselves.

Sometimes your mom and dad attach "leashes" to your freedom—leashes such as curfews, assigned tasks at home, and homework before TV. You may feel that there are too many restrictions and, like Caesar, tug and strain against the leash. Could any of the leashes be removed if you, like Penny, could be trusted? Likewise, can you think of areas in which you, like Caesar, might still need a leash or two for your own good?

MARCH 31

OPERATION AIRLIFT

For the great day of his wrath is come; and who shall be able to stand? Revelation 6:17.

The U.S. Army was evacuating government personnel from Saigon just hours ahead of the advancing North Vietnamese Army. As soon as a helicopter landed in the American Embassy compound, diplomats, military personnel, and South Vietnamese officials who'd sided with the U.S. scrambled aboard to be airlifted to waiting ships. The helicopters were a dangerous means of transportation and might get shelled by the advancing army or crash into the South China Sea. But the refugees feared they'd be killed anyway if they didn't leave Vietnam when they had the chance. They willingly left all their belongings behind.

One South Vietnamese businessman who had become wealthy because of the war chose not to leave. He couldn't leave his Chinese jade art collection behind. When another woman tried to take her large jewelry box with her, she climbed out of the helicopter rather than sacrifice her jewels. Some chose to stay behind because of family members. A few stayed because they feared flying in the helicopter.

The Vietnam airlifts remind me of the scary tales of the time of the end. I've heard Christian adults and young people tell how frightened they are to live in the time just before Jesus returns. All that death and destruction! It can be a little frightening to think about. Sometimes people ask how a loving God would choose to allow such horrid things to happen to His creatures.

Could the problem of not understanding be because of our perspective? Is it possible that Satan has programmed the world to self-destruct and is blaming that destruction on God, just as he's done with every other terrible event he's caused over the years? Is the destruction an act of God's anger or just the logical end result of sin? Could Jesus' second coming be like the U.S. airlift out of Vietnam—an act of love performed by a loving God? Could His real purpose be to rescue those who love Him from the earth's certain destruction? Something to think about, huh?

APRIL 1

A ROYAL FOOL

"I have sinned. . . . Surely I have acted like a fool and have erred greatly." 1 Samuel 26:21, NIV.

Has anyone ever said to you "Don't be foolish"? Or "Stop acting like a fool"? Since it's April Fools' Day, it seems appropriate for me to tell you the stories of two fools.

On October 24, 1901, Anna Taylor climbed into a specially designed barrel, weighted on the bottom and cushioned on the inside, above

Horseshoe Falls on the Niagara River. Her friends sealed the barrel, pumped it full of air, then towed it out into the rushing current. At first the 43-year-old teacher and her barrel tumbled at an easy pace through the rock-filled rapids. Suddenly the current snatched the barrel and sent it hurtling toward the falls.

Her friends gasped as the barrel reached the rim of the falls and plummeted over the edge into the wild, churning water below. The boatmen waiting a safe distance below the falls rushed to rescue the bobbing barrel. Fifteen minutes later, when she climbed out of the barrel, she waved to the cheering crowd. After being treated for a number of cuts and bruises, she told reporters, "Don't ever try it! It was a very foolish thing I did."

The second fool was King Saul. He and his armies had been chasing David's ragtag band of soldiers for some time. Filled with an insane hatred, the king was determined to rid himself of the threat to his throne once and for all.

Late one night David and his aide Abishai sneaked into the royal camp and found King Saul sleeping on the ground. "Come on, let's kill him," Abishai suggested.

David refused. "I cannot take the life of God's appointed king." Instead, he wiped Saul's spear and water jug, which were lying by Saul's hand.

When Saul learned how David had spared his life, he repented. "I have sinned. Come back, David, my son. . . . I will not try to harm you again." The king added, "Surely, I have acted like a fool and have erred greatly" (1 Sam. 26:21, NIV).

Two very different fools—Anna and King Saul. While Anna Taylor never again attempted such a reckless stunt, King Saul repeated his same foolish mistake again. Maybe Anna wasn't such a fool after all. For it is one thing to make a foolish mistake once, but to not learn from that mistake takes a royal fool.

APRIL 2

LESSONS ON RUNNING

No man, having put his hand to the plough, and looking back, is fit for the kingdom of God. Luke 9:62.

Jim crawled out from beneath his downy comforter and shivered. *This is insane*, he thought, as he slid his feet blindly about the floor in search of his slippers. *I could sleep an extra hour and a half before getting dressed for school.* He yawned. Only the sound of water running in the bathroom sink kept Jim from climbing back into bed.

"Dad's already up," he groaned. Using all the self-control he could muster, Jim stood up, stretched, then opened the window drapery. The predawn darkness was broken only by the occasional streetlight on the avenue. A mantle of early-morning mist shrouded all but the closest details of the world beyond his window.

"If I had any sense at all, I'd get back in bed," Jim muttered, wondering if his dad was having the same misgivings. It was the thought of his father and the city's upcoming parent-kid 10-K race that finally forced Jim to shed his pajamas for his sweat suit and running shoes. Five minutes later he and his dad were stretching to prepare for their morning run.

A few weeks earlier Jim spotted the first poster advertising the upcoming 10-K race. He and his friends had badgered their fathers to enter.

During the first week Jim stood waiting by the door each morning, cheering his father on. But now, five weeks into their training and at 4:30 in the morning, Jim's bright idea was beginning to get dim. And the cooler the morning, the less bright Jim felt for even suggesting that they begin the project.

However, Jim knew that his gung-ho dad would allow nothing to stop him from seeing a project through once he decided to do it. As his father would say: "No man, having put his hand to the plough, and looking back, is fit for the kingdom of God." *And the man has definitely put his hand to the plow,* Jim thought ruefully as he retied one of his shoelaces. Short of unexpected disaster, Jim knew they were in it for the run.

(Story to be continued.)

APRIL 3

THE SECRET WEAPON

Even youths grow tired and weary, and young men stumble and fall; but those who hope in the Lord will renew their strength. They will soar on wings like eagles; they will run and not grow weary, they will walk and not be faint. Isaiah 40:30, 31, NIV.

A chilling breeze slapped Jim awake as he stepped out onto the front porch.

"Come on," his father called, "let's make tracks."

Jim groaned, then fell into pace beside his father. After running the first block, the two runners fell into a smooth rhythm. Only the sound of

Nikes slapping the pavement and an occasional passing vehicle broke the comfortable silence of their early-morning world. By the time they had completed their circle and finished their cooling-down routine, Jim was beginning to feel almost human again.

"Good run, son." Dad patted Jim on the shoulder and headed up the stairs to shower. "I think it's time for us to add another mile."

"Another mile?" Jim rolled his eyes and stumbled into the kitchen for a swig of orange juice. *Will I even survive until the race?* he wondered. Jim asked his dad how he managed to keep going.

"I must confess, son, that I have a secret weapon."

"You what?"

"I have a secret weapon. You'll find it in Isaiah 40:29-31. Look it up."

"Aw, Dad," Jim groaned, "I thought you had something there."

"Don't knock it until you try it."

Jim thought of his friends and their dads. While they'd all begun training for the race together, most had dropped out after the first few mornings. Jim straightened his shoulders and smiled to himself. *Maybe the old man does have something there after all.*

In the years to come, Jim discovered that Dad's secret had very little to do with running 10-K races and everything to do with running the Christian race. Some have said that dying for Jesus is often simpler than living for Him. To run the Christian race successfully for 70-plus years takes faith, prayer, and plain old determination.

(Story to be continued.)

APRIL 4

THE RACE

As for us, we have this large crowd of witnesses around us. So then, let us rid ourselves of everything that gets in the way, and of the sin which holds on to us so tightly, and let us run with determination the race that lies before us. Hebrews 12:1, TEV.

The morning of the race, Jim slipped his number harness over his red-and-white running jersey—207. Dad was runner 208. The two runners bent down to check the ties on their well-worn Nikes, then stood up, adjusted the waist bands on their running shorts, and took deep breaths.

"Ready, son?" Dad asked, waving to Mom and to Jim's two younger brothers standing by her side. Jim waved too. Farther down the row of well-wishers were his best friends, Tom and Bill. They exchanged a victorious "thumbs-up" with him.

I'm really going through with this, he thought. A surge of excitement caused the little hairs on Jim's neck to tingle. "Sure am," he hissed through tightened teeth.

The starting gun sounded, and the runners surged forward from behind the line. Within a short distance the runners had strung out, each team falling into their natural stride. A few teams of runners broke free of the pack.

This disturbed Jim. He was tempted to step up their pace. He didn't like having other teams ahead of him. But Dad had cautioned that this would happen—that some less-experienced runners would sprint ahead and use up their energies too early in the race, leaving nothing for the last hill.

"The object is to finish the race, son," he'd reminded.

At the beginning the morning sun felt good on Jim's back as he covered the first few miles of the course. But as time passed, it intensified. Sweat poured uncomfortably down his back and chest and dripped off his hair onto his nose. Jim swigged down a cup of ice water at each watering hole and ran on. Every so often he'd hear his friends' or his mom's and little brothers' voices cheering him on. When their shouts faded, Jim knew they had only hopped into the family car and driven farther ahead in order to cheer him and his dad on again at another point. Knowing that his family was there wishing him success kept him running. After all, he couldn't let them down.

(Story to be continued.)

APRIL 5

END OF THE RACE

I will be with you; I will never leave you or forsake you. Joshua 1:5, NIV.

Way station after way station passed. Jim and his dad continued to run side by side. It felt good to know his dad was there, matching him, pacing him, running with him every step of the way. As they climbed Cannery Hill, Jim remembered his dad's warning about picking up too much speed on the way down the other side.

Suddenly a 5-year-old boy in the crowd broke free of his mother and darted in front of Jim. Jim swerved to avoid the child, lost his own balance, and stumbled to one knee. Out of the corner of his eye, Jim watched other teams pass by. Angry tears sprang into his eyes. Blood streamed from his scraped knee and hand.

"You hurt bad, son?" Jim's dad asked.

"Naw, I don't think so. It looks worse than it is, I think."

Someone from the audience thrust a clean cotton handkerchief into Jim's hand. He tied it about his injured knee and stood up. "Ready to go on?" his father asked.

"Now? After this?"

"I am if you are," Dad replied.

The finish line came into view. The first team had broken the ribbon. Five more teams crossed the line before Jim and his dad. On the other side, Jim and his dad were engulfed by family and friends. Tom jammed a can of 7-Up into Jim's hand while Bill dumped a second can over Jim's head. Jim took a third can of soda and poured it on his father's head. Dad laughed and grabbed his son into a giant bear hug. Neither minded the sticky soda mingling with the sweat pouring from their bodies. They'd completed the race together.

It felt good to be a winner. It had been a difficult race. It had been great having family and friends to cheer him on. But the best part, Jim decided, was knowing that his father was not on the sidelines cheering him on, but beside him every step of the race.

Jim learned a little more about God that day. For like his father, Jim's God runs by his side, every step of the way. Aren't you thankful Jim's God is your God too?

APRIL 6

DARK GLASSES

For now we see through a glass, darkly; but then face to face. 1 Corinthians 13:12.

Stingray—the name sounds fearsome and frightening. And for good reason. The stingray can plant its serrated, razor-sharp, venomous tail in the foot or ankle of an unsuspecting wader. This causes tissue damage, swelling, and intense pain followed by vomiting, diarrhea, sweating, a drop in blood pressure, and occasionally death.

Diving in the shallows of the North Sound, off Grand Cayman of the Cayman Islands, Jay Ireland, photographer and deep-sea diver, watched in fascination as two stingrays cruised by his face mask. To his surprise, these creatures were gentle, even playful. "Usually you can't get close to stingrays, but here they were swimming into my camera," Jay explained.

The area off the Cayman Islands where Jay and his friends dive is the area where fishermen and tourists clean their catch of fish each day. The local population of stingrays has come to expect a daily buffet of fish scraps. Guides bring as many as 150 divers a day to view the graceful, birdlike fish. Because they have been treated with gentleness and respect, the creatures treat the human intruders accordingly. If the divers miss a day because of bad weather, the rays become aggressive and pushy the next day. It is almost as though they intend this as punishment for having been neglected.

Divers do not wear gloves since the fish's skin is easily irritated. One diver described touching the skin of a stingray like touching a mixture of velvet and silk. The rays enjoy being hugged and hugging divers. They will swim right up to a diver's mask and peer in curiously at the person behind the glass.

"In a world where the human being is a trespasser, coming face-to-face with a stingray is a moment even the most experienced diver never forgets," one vacationer admitted.

Deep-sea diving is a fascinating hobby that requires air tanks, fins, wet suit, and face mask. While it's a beautiful world of colorful fish and exotic fauna underwater, it takes training to dive safely into the alien world beneath the ocean surface.

The Bible speaks of "seeing through a glass darkly," separating the things of this earth from the heavenly treasures. When I think of heaven and all the exciting things I plan to learn, deep-sea diving is at the top of my list. And I won't need to be separated from the stingray by a face mask. I will not need to "look through a glass darkly."

What other adventures that, when done on this earth, require expensive equipment and/or personal risk will you be able to do safely and unencumbered in heaven?

APRIL 7

HOARDING TREASURE

Keep my words and store up my commands within you. Proverbs 7:1, NIV.

Remember Hetty Green, one of America's greatest misers? Hetty had two children—Ned and Sylvia. Upon inheriting half of his mother's $100 million in 1916, Ned—who had lost his leg due to his mother's penny-pinching—squandered the money during the next 20 years at the then-phenomenal rate of $3 million a year. When he died, he left the rest of it to the state of Massachusetts, a gesture that would have riled his dead mother, for she hated charity of any kind.

His sister, Sylvia, grew into a replica of her mother. She loved money and hated people. While she spent thousands on a new home, she filled it with her mother's old decrepit furniture and lived in isolation until she too died alone, with no known relatives. Her money was divided among 63 charities. All that the Greens' treasure ever brought them was loneliness and sorrow.

However, we can hoard one very real treasure that will bring happiness to the possessor—the treasure of God's Word. By memorizing Bible promises, they become ours. No matter how often we use them, they are still ours to use again and again.

If you have trouble hoarding Bible treasures, perhaps the following suggestions will help you:

1. Choose a time to memorize when your mind is free from distractions. Some people find early morning the best.
2. Learn the reference by repeating it every time you say the verse.
3. Read the verse several times, both silently and aloud. By hearing yourself say the words, you are actually cementing them into your mind.
4. Break the verse down into shorter phrases. Learn the phrases one by one, adding phrases as you learn.
5. Learn a little bit perfectly rather than a whole lot poorly.
6. Review the verse 10 to 20 times, then repeat it throughout the day.
7. Be creative. Sing the words to the verse. Or illustrate the verse in a picture or apply it to a story.
8. Share it with another person.
9. Apply it to a daily situation that occurs.
10. Recite the promise to God when you pray, thanking Him for the promise.

APRIL 8

STUDY WAR NO MORE

He makes wars cease to the ends of the earth; he breaks the bow and shatters the spear, he burns the shields with fire. "Be still, and know that I am God." Psalm 46:9, 10, NIV.

As the freckled-faced little girl dangled her feet over the back of the buckboard, she never imagined that one day her name would be added to the list of firsts in the history of the United States. Her thoughts were on the peppermint stick waiting for her at Wally's General Store.

In 1917 Jeannette Rankin, at the age of 36, became the first woman admitted as a member of Congress. Just being elected to Congress was remarkable since at the time women were not even allowed to vote in most states. Being a first could be a little intimidating. Everyone would be watching her performance in the all-male assembly. Surely she would move slowly and vote cautiously—to avoid standing out for unpopular issues. However, the wide-open plains of Montana had taught Jeannette to stand alone. Her beliefs were as solid as the granite mountains that gave her state its name.

Her first vote, two days after her arrival, almost ended her political career. She voted against going to war against Germany's kaiser. When her name was called, she replied, "I want to stand by my country, but I cannot vote for war." While she supported the cause for peace, the people of the country had been stirred to war. Defeated in 1918, she won again in 1940, just in time to vote against going to war after Pearl Harbor. Hers was the one dissenting vote in Congress.

People forgot about the gutsy lady who braved her countrymen's scorn to speak out for what she believed to be right—until 1968. The United States was facing a war in Vietnam. Jeannette, now in her late 80s, led a peace brigade of 5,000 women to Washington, D.C. She protested war until her death in 1973. Whether or not one agrees with Jeannette Rankin's views on war is unimportant. Her courage to stand for what she believed to be right—against seemingly impossible odds—should be honored.

Jesus is the only one who will completely eliminate wars and death, which He will do when He comes again. Without the courageous voices of men and women like Jeannette Rankin, the fragile bond of peace could never exist.

APRIL 9

JENKINS' EAR DAY

Do you have eyes but fail to see, and ears but fail to hear? Mark 8:18, NIV.

Today is Jenkins' Ear Day. Two hundred sixty-one years ago, Spanish pirates plundered a British ship of its treasure. During the battle a Spanish pirate sliced off the ear of an English captain named Robert Jenkins. When word reached England, Parliament declared war on Spain. The war was known throughout history as the War of Jenkins' Ear.

Sounds a little like the Bible story of Peter and the Roman soldier in the Garden of Gethsemane, doesn't it? Another man, an artist named Van Gogh, cut off his own ear in a fit of madness. Yech! But I must confess, there was a time when I hated my ears enough for that. In grade school my ears bothered me continually. I hated them. Where my friend Judy's tiny little ears lay flat against her pretty blonde head, mine resembled an elephant's—Walt Disney's Dumbo's, to be exact. At times, when I was called cabbage leaf ears, butterfly ears, and fly-away, I might have welcomed having a Spanish sailor cut off my ugly ears. Fortunately for me, no one cut off my ears. Instead, I grew into them.

I learned that when it comes to ears, the size and shape are not important. What they do is most important. When working properly, this marvelous pair of sound receivers perched on the sides of our heads can pick up a mosquito's whine or a massive thunder boom. This is terrific. This is remarkable.

My ears love the sound of wind whistling through the branches of tall Douglas firs, ocean waves crashing against the rocky New England shore, the words "I love you" whispered at times other than my birthday or Mother's Day, Handel's *Messiah* sung by a 300-voice choir, a kitten's purr.

The hearing Jesus speaks about in today's scripture is more than just receiving and recording the sounds around us. Remember when you were a little kid and someone wanted to tell you something you didn't want to hear? You'd shut your eyes, plug your ears, and shout, "I can't hear you! I'm not listening!" Some people do this with God when He tries to talk with them.

What kind of ears do you have? Huge or tiny? Round or pointed? Pretty or so-so? When it comes to hearing the sounds around you, do they do their job well, need help, or refuse to hear at all? But most important, do your ears listen and heed God's words?

APRIL 10

JOEY'S AWARD

Let brotherly love continue. Hebrews 13:1.

John Cappelletti, a senior at Penn State, won the treasured Heisman Trophy, an award for being the best college football player in the country. Big John and the rest of his family attended the awards banquet held in the grand ballroom of the Hilton Hotel in New York City. The huge ballroom was filled to capacity with more than 4,000 fans and friends—all toasting John's impressive achievement.

After accepting the 55-pound bronze trophy, John looked briefly toward his family for reassurance. Joey, the youngest in the family, was a surprise guest. He'd been very ill and was bedridden up until the morning of the banquet. When he heard that his big brother had won the award, he insisted on attending. His face beamed with pride as he watched John pose for photographs, then settled back to listen to John's acceptance speech.

John adjusted the microphone. He'd prepared a formal speech, but at the last minute changed his mind. "I'd like to dedicate this trophy to a lot of people I've been around, especially to the youngest member of my family, Joseph, who is very ill. He has leukemia," John quietly explained. "For me it's a battle only on the field and only in the fall. For Joseph it's all year round. I think this trophy is more his than mine because he's been such an inspiration to me."

John handed his brother the trophy, then sat down. The room was silent, almost eerie, then like a thunderclap, deafening applause broke out, followed by a standing ovation.

Joey was thrilled. He whispered to his father, "You mean he gave the trophy to me?" he asked. "But that's his trophy. He won it."

Mr. Cappelletti placed his rough hand on his son's shoulder. "Your brother wants you to have it."

Archbishop Fulton J. Sheen was to give the benediction. Instead he said, "For maybe the first time in your lives, you have heard a speech from the heart and not from the lips. . . . Part of John's triumph was made possible by Joseph's inspiration. You don't need a blessing. God has already blessed you in John and his brother, Joseph."

It was John's night, his moment of glory, the greatest triumph of his college career. In love, he generously gave the night and the trophy to his courageous little brother, Joey—a true act of brotherly love.

APRIL 11

SHOOTING THE SAINTS

If someone says he loves God, but hates his brother, he is a liar. For he cannot love God, whom he has not seen, if he does not love his brother, whom he has seen. 1 John 4:20, TEV.

British general Sir William Phips's orders were to load the ammunition in his fleet of boats at the mouth of the St. Lawrence River and to proceed inland to the city of Quebec, where he and his small force of soldiers were to wait until foot soldiers from the south could arrive in order to attack the French stronghold, thus claiming it for the Crown. That was the plan.

The fleet carrying the precious ammunition inched its way through the wilderness waterways to the walled city, where, under the cover of night, they strategically hid their ammunition-laden boats and waited.

All would have gone without incident except that General Phips, a strict Protestant, hated Catholics. As Phips viewed the walled city from his hiding place, the stone statues of saints mounted strategically along the crest of the city's walls irritated him so much that despite his orders, he commanded his men to shoot the statues off the walls.

The English sailors set up the cannons, loaded their muskets, and began firing on the stone saints. Round after round of ammunition was fired, toppling the statues to the ground. Poor General Phips got so caught up with his project that he failed to notice just how much ammunition he was using.

The shooting alerted the French Army to his position, and they began shelling the fleet. In his zeal to take pot shots at the saints, Phips exhausted the supply of ammunition. The first battalion of English foot soldiers arrived just in time to rescue General Phips and his crew.

General Phips had been commissioned to guard the treasured ammunition that would have given his country and his king a sure victory over the enemy. Instead he lost his opportunity. He'd been too busy blowing away defenseless stone saints.

You and I can do the same thing. Like General Phips, we use up valuable energy and ammunition taking potshots at our brothers and sisters in Jesus by gossiping, criticizing, and condemning God's defenseless saints. Then when it's time to do serious battle with our real enemy—Satan—we fail, not because God didn't send in His army of heavenly foot soldiers, but because we have used up our supply of moral strength and spiritual firepower.

APRIL 12

KENNY'S ULCERS

There shall no evil befall thee, neither shall any plague come nigh thy dwelling. Psalm 91:10.

Everywhere 12-year-old Kenny looked, he saw trouble. On the 6:00 evening news he watched as troops stormed the mansion of a Central American drug lord. He watched Middle Eastern terrorists hijack planes and blow up department stores. He listened to neo-Nazis spout their hateful venom and saw reports of the equally evil Bloods and Krips killing innocent children in their drive-by shootings. He shuddered at the gruesome murders committed by members of Satanist cults.

He found himself horrified yet fascinated with the violence. He read everything he could find on the subject. He watched every television special. He decorated the walls of his room with dark, garish posters that depicted the evil forces at work. He drew graphic pictures on his notebooks and folders of smoking pistols and gleaming knives dripping with blood.

His preoccupation with death touched every corner of his life, even his sleep—or lack of sleep. At night he would lie awake for hours, fighting his vivid imagination. When he did sleep he would have gory nightmares. He couldn't concentrate at school. His appetite lessened as his hunger for the excitement of danger grew.

When Kenny complained to his mother about the upset stomach he'd been having, she took him to see a friend, a Christian doctor. After extensive testing, the doctor told Kenny he had ulcers.

"Kenny," the doctor reminded, "I can treat your ulcers from the outside with medication. But if you really want to get well, you must treat your problem from the inside—from your mind. You need to cultivate the fine art of living in peace." The doctor picked up his prescription pad. "I'm going to give you a prescription to follow. If you take this medicine as prescribed, your stomachache will go away."

The doctor wrote: "Psalm 91—take daily, once in the morning and once at bedtime. Take Philippians 4:8 as needed for distress." Kenny followed his doctor's advice, and his ulcers healed.

The death, violence, and hate of the world didn't change—Kenny did. He became acquainted with the eternal God. While the world seems to be spinning out of control, he knows that in time the forces of evil will be totally destroyed. His God reigns today, yesterday, tomorrow, and forever. That's a truth Kenny can live with. How about you?

APRIL 13

BOSTON BLACKIE

The soul who sins is the one who will die. Ezekiel 18:4, NIV.

Boston Blackie, an alley cat, was an outlaw, a renegade. He was different from most cats who go astray, who either ignorantly or willfully wander from the proper path. Never a pitiful waif, Blackie hated other cats; he wanted to kill them—all of them.

Blackie would swoop down out of the woods on unsuspecting house cats, attacking them on their own premises, without regard to age or gender. He'd rip at their ears, gouge their eyes, and tear at their flesh. Cat after cat was carried to the vet to be stitched and given shots of penicillin.

Blackie fought without the usual rules and ceremonies established by generations of felines. Sometimes his mad, meaningless attacks began with the usual singsong dance of other cats; other times he'd forgo the formality and just pounce on his unsuspecting victim as he might on a mouse. This disarmed his foes; they didn't even have a chance to run.

Nothing distracted him from his urge to rid the world of other cats. If a human would try to thwart his attack, Blackie would continue undisturbed, regardless of the screaming and flailing.

One day Boston Blackie appeared at Liz's house, becoming cat number 24 for the cat fancier and her husband, Ralph. The renegade cat was in heaven. Not only did Blackie have regular meals each day, but also a built-in supply of cats to attack. "He's insane," Liz told her husband. "He's a psychotic killer."

"He can't be rabid," Ralph pointed out. "He would have long since died from the disease."

"If only the other cats would gang up on him," Liz suggested.

"Cats don't join armies," Ralph reminded. "Maybe we could grab him and take him to the vet. The vet could put him to sleep."

Liz's eyes grew wide with terror. "You're not suggesting we actually pick him up with our bare hands?"

"Not hardly. We'll use a trap."

Blackie avoided the trap, no matter what bait Ralph used. After Blackie injured the tiniest and cutest of Liz's cats, she suggested they poison Blackie. She discarded the idea when she realized that another cat might unsuspectingly eat the poisoned food. They considered shooting Blackie. That idea died also since neither could bring themselves to shoot a cat, no matter how evil that cat behaved.

Blackie's attacks on the neighborhood's feline population continued until late one Thursday evening the people of the community held court regarding the menacing cat. His sins were discussed at length. The cat was guilty; he deserved to die.

(Story to be continued.)

FROM BLACKIE TO BASIL

Come now, and let us reason together, saith the Lord: though your sins be as scarlet, they shall be as white as snow; though they be red like crimson, they shall be as wool. Isaiah 1:18.

At feeding time the next morning, the other cats took up their stations on the back steps and across the lawn. One by one, Liz fed her cats. She had gotten halfway across the lawn, when Boston Blackie came out of the bushes. Instantly, all the cats froze. Those closest to the woods began slipping away into the shadows. Three others broke and ran under the porch.

Liz stood frozen in place as Blackie walked toward her. He moved purposefully, without haste, ignoring the other cats as they melted away. He stopped in front of her and looked up. The cat's tail was high in the classic greeting gesture. Then he mewed. It was the first time he'd ever acknowledged a human's presence, let alone mewed. Liz wondered if it was a trick. Would he suddenly leap up into her face or dig his fierce claws into her ankles?

Now's my chance, she thought. *I can reach down, grab him, and throw him into the car for a fast trip to the vet*. Since she wasn't wearing protective gloves, she changed her mind. In a weak, quivering voice, Liz asked, "Are you hungry, Blackie?"

He lifted a front paw, curled it, and mewed again.

"Would you like a plate of your own?"

Apparently he did. Liz fetched him a plate from the house, filled it, and placed it by the bushes at the end of the lawn. The cat quietly ate his meal without a glance around. One by one the other cats sneaked back to their feeding stations. When he finished he washed his paws and whiskers, ambled over to a sunny spot near the back fence, stretched out on Liz's favorite day lilies, and napped. Liz and Ralph never saw the vicious Boston Blackie again.

For Boston Blackie is called Basil now. While Boston Blackie hated to be touched, Basil loves being rubbed under his chin. Whereas Boston Blackie would hiss and growl; Basil purrs like a Boeing 727 and has become one of Liz's most peaceful cats. What happened? Did the cat just one day make a decision to reform, to become a good cat? Who knows?

No one except the Creator knows what happened in Boston Blackie to change him forever into a purring sofa cushion cat. The same Creator knows what it takes to change boys and girls, men and women, from growling, snarling, spiteful children into happy, loving sons and daughters.

APRIL 15

FAMILY TREES

Thus there were fourteen generations in all from Abraham to David, fourteen from David to the exile to Babylon, and fourteen from the exile to the Christ. Matthew 1:17, NIV.

Heidi slinked further down in her chair as her classmates told about their families. Lee's parents had immigrated from Thailand. Gary's came from the Union of South Africa. Beverly proudly added, "I'm related to Daniel Boone."

"My grandfather fought for the South in the Civil War," Andy said as he grinned broadly.

"Very interesting, Andy," Miss Anders commented. "And what about the rest of you?"

Maria, Heidi's best friend, said, "My grandparents came from Puerto Rico."

On Tuesday Miss Anders had read the names of the people in Jesus' lineage from the book of Matthew. "Your ancestors make you distinctly you. That's how Joe got red hair and Kari got her freckles. Your height, the color of your hair and eyes, perhaps your favorite foods or special skills, even your temperament, may be influenced by people in your past." Then the teacher assigned each student to chart his or her own lineage by Thursday.

Heidi put off doing the assignment as long as possible. After all, how could she complete such an assignment? She was adopted! On Wednesday night at bedtime, she told her mother about her problem. Heidi's mom helped her devise a different way of looking at the project. Heidi made a timeline chart that began with Creation and the text "According as he hath chosen us in him before the foundation of the world" (Ephesians 1:4).

At the top of the chart she printed the following title, "Twice Chosen." Beneath the title Heidi listed every event she and her parents could remember since her adoption into the family. She charted her first birthday, the family's move from Chicago, her first day of school, and the day she began piano lessons. Beneath the date of her baptism Heidi printed "Adoption Into the Family of God."

When she showed Miss Anders her finished project, her teacher said, "Heidi, you've reminded us of a very important truth today. Perhaps that's why Jesus' lineage is the last recorded in the Bible. From that point on, our true inheritance became certain."

You and your family may enjoy doing Miss Anders' Bible assignment or, like Heidi, you may come up with your own creative alternative.

APRIL 16

EYE OF THE STORM

"Go out and stand before me on top of the mountain," the Lord said to him [Elijah]. Then the Lord passed by and sent a furious wind that split the hills and shattered the rocks—but the Lord was not in the wind. 1 Kings 19:11, TEV.

Will Keller tossed a forkful of hay over his shoulder and onto the growing stack. He glanced out across his vast Kansas farm. Suddenly his heart skipped a beat. To the west he saw a dark, funnel-shaped cloud. Having lived in the Midwestern tornado belt his entire life and knowing what such a storm could do, he ran for his storm shelter. He looked back and saw that the funnel was lifting off the ground. Fascinated, he stopped to watch. The open end of the funnel moved directly over him, placing him inside the "eye" of the storm. This is how Mr. Keller described the experience.

"Steadily the tornado came on, the end gradually rising above the ground. I stood there only a few seconds, but I was so impressed with what was going on that it seemed a long time. At last the great shaggy end of the funnel hung directly overhead.

"Everything was as still as death. There was a strong gassy odor. I couldn't breathe. There was a screaming, hissing sound coming directly from the end of the funnel," he explained. "I looked up and to my astonishment, I saw right into the heart of the tornado. There was a circular opening in the center of the funnel, about 50 to 100 feet in diameter and extending straight upward for a distance of at least one-half mile, as best I could judge under the circumstances. The walls of this opening were of rotating clouds made visible by constant flashes of lightning, which zigzagged from side to side. . . .

"Around the lower rim of the great vortex small tornados were constantly forming and breaking away. These looked like tails as they writhed their way around the end of the funnel. It was these tails that made the hissing noise. . . . The opening was entirely hollow except for a wind cloud in the center, moving up and down," the farmer reported.

The prophet Elijah learned of the tornado's power. Like Satan, tornados ripped across the land, leaving a trail of disaster while God spoke in a still small voice, bringing peace and the promise of protection.

APRIL 17

BOMBS AWAY

Happy are you poor; the Kingdom of God is yours! Happy are you who are hungry now; you will be filled! Happy are you who weep now; you will laugh! Luke 6:20, 21, TEV.

The Russian Army spent months training dogs to associate food with the underside of tanks. The plan was that when the German Panzer tanks rolled into Russia, they would tie bombs to the backs of these poor dogs, who would then crawl under the enemy tanks and boom!—the tank would be history.

The plan was initiated on the first day of the war—and abandoned the second. The dogs behaved exactly as trained: they searched for food under military tanks—*Russian* tanks! The bomb-laden dogs forced an entire Soviet division to retreat. Hooray! I can't help cheering for the poor pooches and booing the foolish military genius who devised such a hideous plan. It was a very bad day for everyone concerned, except for Hitler and his advancing army.

Do you ever have days like those Russian officers had when the dogs chased them off the battlefield? When the proverbial pits would be a step up from the misery you are wallowing in? Don't you just hate it when you share your agony with a concerned friend and all he says is "Don't worry; tomorrow will be better" or "Someday you'll look back on this and laugh"? Ugh! All you wanted was a little sympathetic listening, not advice or clichés, no matter how accurate the advice and or the cliché might be.

A friend once said, "Sometimes, it's hard to remember the sweet by and by while living in the nasty here and now." Thinking about a perfect heaven is great, but like it or not, as long as we live on this earth we will have good days and we will have bad days. And no matter how hard we try or how sincere we may be, some days are best forgotten. If we can't change a situation, then we should learn from it and move on. Some things that seem terribly important now will become humorous in time. It's wise to learn the difference between life's inconveniences and genuine disasters. When the real disaster hits, remember that God knew all about it in advance. And He is ready and waiting with the solution to your problem.

In today's text Jesus promises, "Happy are you who weep now; you will laugh!" Whatever troubles you might be facing, remember, one day you may laugh out loud over the very thing that gnawed away at your happiness. In other cases, while you may never be able to laugh over them, you will be able to say "Lord, You knew all along what was best for me."

APRIL 18

LAND RUSH

For, behold, I create new heavens and a new earth: and the former shall not be remembered, nor come into mind. But be ye glad and rejoice for ever in that which I create. Isaiah 65:17, 18.

Melinda's eyes filled with tears as she scanned the Oklahoma horizon. How she missed the gentle knolls and tiny villages that dotted the English countryside. This wild, untamed land threatened her even more than had the crowded New York City tenements before she and her husband headed west.

When Arnold learned of President Benjamin Harrison's declaration that opened up the Oklahoma Territory for homesteaders, she began to pack their meager belongings once more.

The young couple made their way from New York City to the Kansas border. Along with 50,000 other eager homesteaders, they camped all night on April 21. Grocery store clerks, bankers, real estate speculators, teachers, and cowboys waited for the high noon rifle shot that would start the stampede for land.

The first years on the plains were rough. Lack of rain, diseased crops, and renegade Indians made survival difficult. Letters from home told of the births, weddings, and deaths of loved ones. Yet in the arid Southwest, one day had a way of predictably following another. Clothes needed washing, bread needed baking, eggs needed gathering.

"Enough pining for what can never be," she scolded, picking up the loaded clothes basket and returning to the dark interior of her one-room sod house. "No time for wool gathering."

Melinda and Arnold were but two of the young people who chose to claim the promise of a new land where they could build and inhabit homes of their own.

Long ago the President of the universe set a date for opening up the heavenly territory—not an empty land covered with red, hard-packed earth, but one with dark, rich soil where young fruit trees won't wither in the hot July sun, but will produce in abundance. Best of all, the Melindas and Arnolds will not be lonely, but will be surrounded eternally by loving family members and friends.

While the date has yet to be announced, I want to be waiting on the edge of that new land, ready and eager to enter, don't you?

APRIL 19

UNCLE SAM'S GRAVE

I am the resurrection and the life. Whoever believes in me will live. John 11:25, TEV.

Samuel Wilson owned a large meat-packing business outside Troy, New York, during the War of 1812. Before long an opportunity to serve his country knocked at his door in the form of a government official from Washington, D.C.

"Armies are made up of men, hungry men," the official reminded. "It is my task to set up a food supply line for the troops. Will you sell your beef to the Army?"

Wilson agreed to supply the Army with beef. One day a group of visitors was touring Wilson's meat-packing plant and noticed the letters EA-US stamped on the barrels of salted beef. "What do those letters stand for?" one of the visitors asked. The reply was that the EA stood for Elbert Anderson, Jr., the contractor the company worked for, and the US stood for the owner of the meat-packing plant "Uncle Sam" Wilson. The expression "Uncle Sam" had already been used, but in derision. After this experience it took on a more positive meaning.

Before long, everyone from upstate New York to the battlefields of Pennsylvania called him uncle and his U.S. stamped meat "Uncle Sam's Beef." Later a newspaper cartoonist picked up on the tale and drew a picture of a tall, angular man dressed in red, white, and blue—the Uncle Sam we know today. In 1961 Congress passed a resolution honoring "Uncle Sam" Wilson of Troy, New York, "the progenitor of America's national symbol."

While every schoolchild now recognizes the legendary Uncle Sam, few have heard of the real Uncle Sam—Samuel Wilson. And although his legend lives on, the man sleeps forgotten in a large cemetery overlooking the city of Troy, New York.

Today is Easter, a day when people in all parts of the world celebrate the resurrection of Jesus Christ. Some will listen to His stories, marvel at His teachings, and celebrate His life and death, but refuse to let Him make a difference in their lives. To these people He is only a legend, much like Uncle Sam. While they might travel thousands of miles to visit His grave site, all they'll find is an empty tomb. Because the story of Jesus Christ is more than a legend. He's not a pile of dust and bones in the side of a Palestinian hill. He's more than a caricature of a friendly old man with a white beard or a white bunny rabbit carrying a basket of eggs. He's a living Saviour, not a dead uncle. And He won the war with sin and death for us.

APRIL 20

NOBODY OF NOTE

Let another praise you, and not your own mouth; someone else, and not your own lips. Proverbs 27:2, NIV.

Ready for a pop quiz? You have probably heard of Paul Revere and his famous midnight ride to warn the American colonists that the British were coming. Did you also know that two other men helped carry out the same assignment that night? Their names were William ''Billy'' Dawes, Jr., and Dr. Samuel Prescott. So why do we speak of Paul Revere's ride and not of Dawes' and Prescott's?

When the poet Henry Wadsworth Longfellow wrote the poem ''Paul Revere's Ride,'' the name Revere rhymed better.

''Listen my children and you shall hear
of the midnight ride of Paul Revere.''

I wonder if Dawes and Prescott felt like nobodies, or did the people of Massachusetts give all three men credit for their bravery? Don't you just hate it when you're in a group and you come up with a clever remark that only the person next to you hears, he repeats it, and everyone laughs at ''his'' terrific joke? Or how do you feel when you and your best friend work hard on a school science project that you thought up, then your friend acts as if the entire idea was his?

We all like to be appreciated. It's never easy to sit back and let another take the credit for what we do. It's never fun feeling like a nobody, but it's worse being left a nobody when you really deserve recognition.

Can you name the ''nobodies'' in the list below?

1. Who inspired Martin Luther to translate the New Testament from Latin to German?

2. Who visited the famous preacher Dwight L. Moody in a shoe store and talked to him about Christ?

3. Who cared for the apostle Paul in the dungeon as he wrote his last letter to Timothy?

4. What were the names of the parents who trained the prophet Daniel?

5. What are the names of the women who, along with Clement, helped Paul spread the gospel?

The answers to the above questions are in tomorrow's reading.

APRIL 21

NOBODIES WHO COUNT

Help these women; for they have worked hard with me to spread the gospel, together with Clement and all my other fellow workers, whose names are in God's book of the living. Philippians 4:3, TEV.

Yesterday I asked you five questions. Allow me to refresh your memory.

1. Who inspired Martin Luther to translate the New Testament from Latin to German?

2. Who visited the famous preacher Dwight L. Moody in a shoe store and talked to him about Christ?

3. Who cared for the apostle Paul in the dungeon as he wrote his last letter to Timothy?

4. What were the names of the parents who trained the prophet Daniel?

5. What are the names of the women who, along with Clement, helped Paul spread the gospel?

The answers are:

1. Philipp Melanchthon

2. Edward Kimball

3. Onesiphorus

4. and 5. Anonymous—no names available.

Where would the Reformation have been without Luther? Or the modern Protestant movement without Moody? Where would we be without Daniel's witness and Paul's writings—all made possible by a bunch of nobodies, nobodies who exalted Somebody: the Son of God.

Without the "nobodies" on Sabbath morning, we'd shiver in cold, unheated churches and last week's bulletins would litter the pews. Without the "nobodies," the grass on the ball field would trip you up when you were running the bases, your wastebaskets would overflow with spoiled banana peels and rotten apple cores, your restroom sinks would be corroded with dirt, fingerprints, and water stains. And think about the "nobodies" who work in obscure, out-of-the-way missions around the world—all nobodies exalting Somebody.

That Somebody knows the names of Daniel's parents and will reward their faithfulness. He knows your school janitor's name. He knows the names of the missionaries in the Andes Mountains. He knows your name and my name too. For in God's eyes there are no "nobodies."

APRIL 22

NOBODY DID IT

Do not merely listen to the word, and so deceive yourselves. Do what it says. James 1:22, NIV.

Once upon a time there were four Christians whose names were Everybody, Somebody, Anybody, and Nobody. One day Somebody asked for volunteers to help out at the local shelter for the homeless. Everybody knew that Somebody should do something. Anybody could help, but Nobody did. Well, Somebody got angry because it was Everybody's job. Everybody thought Anybody could help out, but Nobody realized that Everybody didn't. Everybody ended up blaming Somebody when Nobody did what Anybody could have done.

Once upon a time there were four young Christians. One day, Everybody noticed that Somebody was throwing trash on the school lawn. Everybody knew that Somebody should pick up the litter . . .

Once upon a time there were four Christians. One day Somebody noticed that a new kid in school was being picked on. Everybody knew that Somebody should befriend him . . .

Once upon a time . . .

Think about it. What is your once upon a time? What needs do you see that Everybody knows Somebody should do and that Anybody could do, yet Nobody does them? You can change your world by refusing to become just another Everybody, Somebody, or Anybody. Love is more than words or talk or good intentions. Genuine love demands action.

APRIL 23

AN ANCIENT PUZZLE

I do not want you to be ignorant of this mystery, brothers. . . . "The deliverer will come from Zion; he will turn godlessness away from Jacob. And this is my covenant with them when I take away their sins." Romans 11:25-27, NIV.

"Sir," the young archaeological student asked the old Andean chief, "what is the reason all these paths and trails converge on the plain, then veer off into the forest as they do?"

The chief shrugged his shoulders. "Who's to know?" he answered. "They were here before I was born, before my father and before his father. They are the trails of the ancient ones."

This ancient puzzle lies half buried in the blowing dust bowl of a windswept plain in Peru. Crisscrossing like a giant spider's web, strange lines and markings stretch more than 37 miles in the valley of the Andes. When archaeologists first discovered the tracks, they concluded that the lines were an ancient network of roads emerging from the ancient city of Nazca. However, the more the scientists analyzed the roads, the more choppy and confusing they seemed.

When the researchers flew over the valley in an airplane, it became evident that the interlaced markings were part of a great design, a desert mural of staggering proportions. While scholars propose theory after theory, no one really knows the secret to the ancient puzzle. It is one of God's little mysteries to be solved in heaven.

Sometimes the Bible has seemed a great mystery of crisscrossing patterns of history, doctrine, and poetry. Viewed close up—when taken one at a time—some Bible texts can be as confusing as the interlaced markings of the Peruvian puzzle. However, while God may choose to keep the origin of the mysterious road patterns in Peru a secret until the kingdom, His plan to save us from this world of sin and death is no secret. Throughout the 66 books of the Bible, He shows us in every way possible just how He loves us. And like the flight over the Peruvian valley revealed the sense and beauty of a bigger picture, so an overview of the Bible will show us a bigger picture of God's love for us—God's grand design for eternity.

APRIL 24

HOW EMBARRASSING

Look to the rock from which you were cut and to the quarry from which you were hewn. Isaiah 51:1, NIV.

A news reporter once asked Marian Anderson, the Black American soloist who won worldwide acclaim for her superb contralto voice, what the greatest moment of her life had been.

Her choices included: (1) the compliment by the great conductor Arturo Toscanini ("A voice like hers comes once in a century"); (2) being the first Black to sing with the Metropolitan Opera Company in New York; (3) publishing her best-selling autobiography *My Lord, What a Morning*; (4) being appointed delegate to the United Nations; (5) receiving medals from governments around the world; (6) giving private concerts at the White House for the Roosevelts and the king and queen of England; (7) winning the president's Medal of Freedom; and (8) singing beneath the Lincoln statue on Easter Sunday for a crowd of 75,000, which included cabinet members, Supreme Court justices, and members of Congress.

Which of these did she choose? None. Miss Anderson told the reporter that her greatest moment was the day she went home and told her mother that she wouldn't need to take in washing anymore.

Some famous people go to great lengths to hide their origins for fear others will think less of them. They buy cars they can't afford and clothes they can't pay for in order to look good in someone else's eyes. A truly great individual knows that his or her success is partly the result of the struggles he or she has been through. How can someone who has never hurt understand someone else's pain?

Your or your family's past need never stop you from doing great things for God. Whether you come from a good Christian home or no home at all, whether your parents work as missionaries or are serving time in prison, you need never be embarrassed. Your only embarrassment should be if you're too proud or too stupid to recognize God as your Father and Lord.

APRIL 25

LYDIA'S SCARY GOD

This is how we know what love is: Jesus Christ laid down his life for us. 1 John 3:16, NIV.

Switching schools in the middle of the year was normal for Lydia. She'd lived in nine foster homes since she was 7. Her latest foster parents, Mom and Pop Werner, were the best of all, she decided, especially since they enrolled her in fifth grade at the local church school.

For a while Lydia had found the new school difficult, and at times a little scary. Everything was so different—morning worship at home, prayer at mealtimes, worship in the classroom. After a few weeks, though, she liked the changes.

One Monday Lydia's teacher introduced a visitor, Pastor Mike, to the students. "He will be here each morning to speak with you."

Lydia loved Pastor Mike and the stories he told about Jesus. She knew absolutely nothing about Him or His "scary" Father, who lived somewhere up in the sky. At the end of the week Pastor Mike invited her and her friends to join a baptismal class he was starting. She agreed eagerly. Weeks went by. When Pastor Mike asked Lydia if she would like to be baptized also, she frowned and shook her head. She couldn't do such a thing—not knowing her horrible secret.

"That's fine, Lydia," he soothed. "I know you love Jesus. I can see it in your face. When the time is right, you'll give your heart to Him."

"Oh, Pastor Mike, I've already given my heart to Jesus . . ." her voice trailed off.

"Yes," the pastor encouraged.

Unable to contain her guilty secret any longer, she burst out, "I hate God. He's mean and cruel and . . . and I hate Him!"

The pastor blinked at the young girl's anger, then smiled. "At one time or another, I've felt like that."

"You?" She couldn't believe it of Pastor Mike.

"Yep, even me. When I was growing up, I had a dad who drank and beat my mom and me. Whenever I heard the words 'father' or 'dad,' I felt only anger and hate."

Lydia looked down at her scruffy tennies. "I never knew my dad."

"You think you hate God because you don't know Him yet. When you get to know Him, you'll see that He loves you just as much as does His Son, Jesus, and you won't be able to keep from loving Him in return. I know, because it happened to me."

(Story to be continued.)

APRIL 26

LYDIA'S GOD BOOK

God is love. 1 John 4:8, NIV.

Lydia scowled. Could Pastor Mike be right about God? She liked the idea of a Jesus who lived in heaven, watching over her and caring for her. But Jesus' Father?

Pastor Mike interrupted her thoughts. "Do you want to know what I did about my feelings?" The minister leaned forward and whispered, "I started my God book. I still have mine at home in my files."

"Your God book? You mean the Bible?"

"No. My God book is a notebook in which I record all the discoveries I make about God the Father. It helped me to get to know Him better," the pastor explained. "And whenever I was tempted to doubt His love, I reread the precious lessons I'd learned."

"Can you help me get started?" she asked.

Lydia's God book grew from one notepad into volumes of notepads. The more she searched for God, the more excited she became. It was like acquiring a brand-new family all her own. She was baptized one Sabbath that summer.

You might like to create a God book of your own. It helps to locate Bible texts to support your answers. But most important, this book is yours. In your God book you can write whatever you like. Here are a few suggestions to get you started.

1. Describe what God looks like.
2. Does God laugh? Can you think of times when He might have laughed? Does He cry?
3. What do you think God's voice sounds like?
4. List five things you believe about God the Father.
5. Does God have a favorite season? A favorite color? A favorite song?
6. Why did God rest after Creation? Was He tired?
7. What do you wish God would change in the world? Why do you think He hasn't?
8. Write about a time when you were frightened of God.
9. Write about a time when you were angry at God.
10. Tell about a time He answered one of your prayers.

APRIL 27

GHOST IN THE GRAVEYARD

So man lies down and does not rise; till the heavens are no more, men will not awake or be roused from their sleep. Job 14:12, NIV.

"Now, let me get this straight, Johnny," Eb teased. "You were walking past the cemetery and you saw a ghost hovering over one of the graves? And I suppose the rattling noises you heard were the sound of the devil's chains on the poor old spirit's wrists?"

"It's true," Johnny argued. "It's all true! I know what I saw and heard."

"You and your cheap whiskey," Sam, the owner of the general store, chuckled.

"I wasn't drinking," Johnny insisted.

The men nodded to each other, then resumed playing checkers beside the store's potbellied stove.

Johnny's ghost story would have died there if the local shoemaker hadn't passed the cemetery in time to see a moonlit object bobbing up and down by a headstone. When a third citizen of the community sighted the same ghostly being in the cemetery, the men of the community decided to take action. Shotguns and lanterns in hand, Johnny and his "ghost brigade" made their way to the cemetery.

One night, two nights, three nights passed—no ghost. On the fourth night the men had just settled down for their long vigil when they heard a low, muffled moan followed by the rattle of chains. In the bushes beside a tall slender headstone, a white object bobbed up and down.

One of the terrified ghost hunters lifted his lantern while the others leveled their shotguns at the creature—a white-faced black cow scratching herself on the branches of an old lilac bush. The rattling metal was the sound of the cowbell around her neck. How silly the men must have felt sneaking back into town that night. How unnecessary their nightly vigils had been. If they'd taken the time to read the Bible, they would have known that their mysterious creature could not possibly have been a ghost.

If you have taken the time to read this morning's text, you will not be fooled when people like Johnny come to you with fantastic tales of ghosts and goblins and mysterious beings. You will know the truth, and the truth will keep you from being deceived.

APRIL 28

"MATT THE MAGNIFICENT"

Dead flies can make a whole bottle of perfume stink, and a little stupidity can cancel out the greatest wisdom. Ecclesiastes 10:1, TEV.

Matt and pianos! At the academy he attended, when you saw one, you saw the other. They were inseparable. Everyone loved to hear him play. Matt could run his fingers over the keys so fast that they blurred before your eyes. One of the favorite activities at the boys' club was the "Stump Matt" night. The fellows would try to suggest a song that Matt didn't know and couldn't play. The club actually offered a cash prize to the student who succeeded in stumping Matt, but no one ever collected it.

Besides being a popular person on campus with students and faculty, Matt also pulled A's. The girls drooled over his wavy black hair and Close-up toothpaste smile. On the basketball court Matt—even as a freshman—could out-dunk the tallest senior, and he could always be counted on to hit a home run when he played softball.

During his four years at the academy, Matt the Magnificent (as the other students called him) soared beyond popularity to become one of the school's superstars—the kind of person that the student body and faculty members rave about for years after graduation. As a senior he had received scholarship grants from the federal government, the state government, and the colleges to which he applied. On graduation weekend he received the annual Chopin award and the All-around Sportsman award. And the class night program, with the traditional slides of baby pictures and a live class performance, ended with Matt stealing the show by a stunning rendition of *Revolutionary Étude*.

Before returning to the dorm after class night, Matt and his friends drove to the local pizza parlor to celebrate. No one planned to drink too much. They'd only intended to take a few sips of beer as they leaped into adulthood. But those few sips turned into many, until no one could remember just how much alcohol anyone had guzzled.

I'm sure that you can guess what happened next. On the way home they were driving at too high a speed when they encountered a sharp curve. The driver's reactions had been impaired by the alcohol, and Matt the Magnificent spent the rest of the night and 17 months in and out of the hospital. The prognosis wasn't very good. He'd probably never walk again. The young mother of three kids—the driver of the other car—wasn't so fortunate. She died before the ambulance reached the emergency room.

Whenever Matt's academy friends think of him today they invariably say, "If only . . ." Matt's sweet perfume of success changed to a noxious odor of tragedy, all because of one foolish choice. Matt himself will tell you that "a little stupidity" can cancel out a thousand fabulous dreams and change life to an unending nightmare of pain and regret.

APRIL 29

A SLIGHT MISCALCULATION

He that doeth wrong shall receive for the wrong which he hath done: and there is no respect of persons. Colossians 3:25.

Even in the 1990s, with all our sophisticated radar and satellite communication conveniences, pilots can still get completely turned around in fog. One wouldn't think such a thing could happen, but it does. Without radio contact, a pilot can still lose his or her sense of direction when fog sets in.

A few years ago a commercial pilot landed his jet at a small airport a few miles from Portland International Airport. The control tower was guiding him in when he saw a break in the clouds and runway lights. Before the tower controller could warn him, he landed on the small plane runway. Fortunately, he managed to stop right at the end of the runway.

Once landed, the pilot's problem was only half solved. How would the jet manage a takeoff on such a short runway? Furious airline officials, along with flight engineers and aeronautical experts from the plane's manufacturer in Seattle, flew in to determine the damage. It was decided that the plane must be emptied of all excess weight.

The passengers were bused to the regular airport. They transported all the cargo by trucks. The jet's tanks were emptied of all fuel except for the amount it would take to takeoff and make the two- to three-minute flight to Portland International Airport. The experts still feared the plane would be too heavy to manage the lift-off, so they removed every excess piece of equipment, including the passengers' and crew's seats, except for the pilot's. And last, the airline officials brought in another pilot to fly the expensive aircraft out.

I feel sorry for the original pilot. While he didn't goof on purpose, he was never allowed to fly a commercial airliner again. It would be nice to be able to tell you that the results of our mistakes are erased once we ask forgiveness, but it's not true. The law of cause and effect is not as forgiving as our loving God.

APRIL 30

HANDKERCHIEF MOODY

I said, "I will confess my transgressions to the Lord"—and you forgave the guilt of my sin. Psalm 32:5, NIV.

The congregation at the Second Church of York, Maine, sang the opening hymn. When the young pastor walked out onto the platform, the people gasped in surprise. His face was draped with a black crepe handkerchief. Whispers and titters traveled throughout the audience as Pastor Joseph Moody began preaching his sermon with his back to the audience. Worse yet, he refused to tell anyone the reason for his bizarre behavior.

From that day on the 32-year-old preacher's once-cheerful personality changed. Joseph Moody's fame spread throughout the New England area, and eventually he acquired the nickname "Handkerchief Moody." His draped face dampened the joy of weddings and other church celebrations. After more than 20 years, Joseph finally resigned his post and moved into a small cabin near the edge of town, coming and going from the cabin only at night, when he would prowl the local graveyard.

People speculated as to his reason. Some said his proposal had been rejected by a local girl. Others said he was just plain crazy. It wasn't until he was on his deathbed, at the age of 53, that he revealed his secret to a fellow minister.

It seems that on a hunting trip Joseph accidentally shot and killed a close friend. Rather than tell anyone what had happened, he ran away. When the body was found, the townspeople believed the man had been shot by a marauding Indian. They never suspected their pastor, and he never admitted his guilt.

The longer he waited to admit his guilt, the more difficult it became for him to reveal the truth. Joseph became so obsessed with guilt that he finally vowed never to show his face again.

What a shame! He had the assurance of forgiveness right in his hand—in the Word of God. I can see him on his knees in that small New England cemetery begging for the peace God promises. Unfortunately, Joseph Moody never found that peace because he could not believe in God's forgiveness. How could God forgive, since Joseph Moody could never forgive himself?

MAY 1

PLAY MONEY

Be careful not to do your "acts of righteousness" before men, to be seen by them. Matthew 6:1, NIV.

Newspapers, scissors, construction paper, and glue bottles covered the mahogany dining room table. Patti and Helen whispered between themselves as their fingers wove the brightly colored paper strips into miniature baskets. It was fun making and giving out May Day baskets filled with flowers, but the most fun was delivering them in secret. Each year, the girls constructed the baskets, filled them with violets from the abandoned field behind the Presbyterian church, and then gave the baskets to people in the neighborhood. They would ring the doorbells and hide in the shrubbery so they could see their neighbors' happy faces.

"We can make one for Mrs. Fairfield," Patti said. "She makes the best chocolate-chip cookies."

"Yeah!" Helen agreed. "And one for Mrs. Tague and one for Mr. Brown and . . ."

"And we can't leave out Mr. Bryant," Patti reminded. "Let's see. With my mom and your parents added, we'll need to make at least eight baskets."

Over the years, Patti and Helen added more people to their May Day list until the girls needed to begin making the baskets two weeks before May 1. They also included the people in the nursing home down the street.

The custom of making and giving out May baskets became a habit for Patti. Today she no longer restricts her generosity to one day or even one week a year. Her secret May baskets have become what she now calls play money. This is money she sets aside from every paycheck to "play" with by secretly helping someone else. She started calling it play money because it was so much fun to give to others without their knowing who was responsible for it—like playing a game. Patti has secretly paid school bills for academy students, and doctor and hospital bills for the elderly in her church, and given parents a free night on the town—all expenses paid.

Now, I have to admit, Patti is a very rich woman—not in dollars and cents, but in joy and happiness. Try Patti's game. You can be wealthy too.

MAY 2

RESCUE FROM THE SKY

I will lift up mine eyes unto the hills, from whence cometh my help. Psalm 121:1.

Less than four months after his high school graduation, 18-year-old Marty found himself aboard a troop plane heading for South Vietnam. All those episodes of *Combat* and *The Gallant Men* that he'd watched during his teenage years, as well as the three months of intensive medic training that the Army had supplied, failed to prepare him for the gruesome horrors of war.

Days after his arrival, his unit tramped into the jungle for the first time to face the Vietcong. Suddenly the 18-year-old boy was forced to make decisions and supply medical treatment usually reserved for licensed physicians to dispense.

Marty hadn't been in Southeast Asia long when his unit walked into an ambush. Immediately the troops sought shelter. The American soldiers hadn't fired too many rounds of ammunition before they realized that the enemy was firing at them from all sides.

Time passed. Though the men continued to fire on the enemy, they knew that unless reinforcements arrived soon, it was only a matter of time before their position would be overrun and they'd either be killed or be taken as prisoners of war. Marty and his buddies also knew that their rescue would need to come from the sky.

Between dodging bullets and bandaging the men's wounds, Marty prayed, "Please, God, send in the helicopters in time to save us." The enemy kept them pinned down for hours. It began to rain; then the shelling stopped. The soldiers huddled together in the eerie silence as raindrops splattered where minutes before bullets fell. A familiar sound sent Marty's heart soaring. Over the hilltop, U.S. helicopters appeared! They would airlift the troops to safety.

Marty had never been so happy to see anyone in his entire life. In the middle of the muck and mud, he fell to his knees in thanksgiving as he remembered a text his grandmother taught him: "I will lift up mine eyes unto the hills . . ."

MAY 3

BALANCING ACT

Set your minds on things above, not on earthly things. Colossians 3:2, NIV.

Today Marty shares the story of his rescue with young people in his church. At the end of his exciting tale, he reminds his audience that they too are being ambushed on every side by a formidable enemy. Television, videos, radio, music, magazines, and even billboards along the state highways bombard our senses with temptations of every kind. There's no earthly escape.

Sometimes Marty uses the following experiment to illustrate a point. You can try the experiment at home. Take an ordinary kitchen-variety broom to an open area, preferably outside. He doesn't recommend that you accidentally turn your mom's crystal vase into irregular crystal prisms! Once you are certain you have room to maneuver, turn the broom upside down and place the end of the handle in the palm of your right hand, keeping your palm as flat as possible. Stabilize the broom vertically with your left hand on the broom handle, and then remove your left hand and balance the broom. Can you do it?

If you concentrate your attention on the spot where the broom and your right hand meet, you'll fail. The broom will crash to the ground. Watching the point of contact between your hand and the broom handle is like the times you look at your worries and fears, at your sins and weaknesses, and try to handle them on your own.

The only way to balance the broom in the palm of your hand is to look up, to watch the broom's bristles instead of the broom's handle. With a little practice you'll be able to balance the broom just fine. The same principle is true when you try to maintain a balance in your life. If you look up, if you lift your eyes to Jesus, you can handle the troubles, even in this topsy-turvy world.

Better yet, why not just place your life full of troubles totally in God's hands and let Him balance everything? The results are worth it.

MAY 4

STRONG MAN

Wisdom is better than strength. Ecclesiastes 9:16.

So you want to be strong? Let me tell you about a few strong individuals. Imagine a 3-year-old who lifted weights. In 1934 Charles Louis Fuchs, age 3, of New York City, could lift a 45-pound barbell. His father began training him in weight lifting at the age of 6 months. Once when Charles became angry, he threw a full-size china closet at his sister.

His parents called him the cyclone. Whenever he'd break furniture or dig holes in the wall with coat hangers, they'd laugh and tell him how cute he was. He might have had incredible strength, but wisdom? Hardly. I'm not too impressed with his parents' wisdom, for that matter.

As the fad for body building continues, some athletes foolishly take steroids in order to build up their muscles. Do the drugs make them stronger? Yes, for a very short time. Is it wise for them to do so? No! They discover that the steroids destroy the very body they'd hoped to build up. Strength without wisdom is a curse, not a treasure.

Strength comes in all kinds of packaging. There's physical strength, like our 3-year-old mighty kid had. There's strength in power, fame, money, good looks, even knowledge. I can think of a number of strong people in the Bible—strong but not wise.

Which kind of strength did each the following people demonstrate?

1. Absalom
2. Judas
3. Samson

4. David
5. Miriam
6. King Saul
7. Matthew
8. Delilah
9. Solomon
10. Moses

Which of them possessed both strength and wisdom?

MAY 5

GARBAGE DISPOSAL

There will be no more death or mourning or crying or pain, for the old order of things has passed away. Revelation 21:4, NIV.

"Don't forget to take out the garbage." If you're between the ages of 8 and 16, you probably hear that sentence almost every day. Carrying out the garbage is truly an unenviable task. Bags rip, handles break, trash spills out all over the sidewalk. Imagine. When Jesus takes us to heaven, garbage will be part of the old order of things as described in today's text—not part of the new.

There was no such thing as garbage in the Garden of Eden. When Adam and Eve sinned, God had to initiate a garbage disposal system. Actually, His system could be better described as a trash recycling system. Without it the world would quickly be overpopulated with rotting, smelly trash.

In your imagination, take a walk with me in a wooded area. Carefully scoop up one pound of forest soil. In it are 30 billion soil bacteria. This is the stuff that breaks down the leaves, twigs, flowers, fruits, seeds, and dead animals that fall on the forest floor. If you look at the soil sample under a high-powered microscope, you'll find more than 1,000 animals living in it—mostly insects and mites.

The forest's soil is like a history book. The top layer is last year's twigs and leaves. The next layer contains alder twigs and leaves partly decayed by bacteria and fungi. The third layer is called humus—the top layer of actual soil. Here's where tiny animals such as mites, springtails (so named because they turn backflips when they are exposed to the open air), millipedes, earthworms, rove beetles, sow bugs, and many more creepy-crawlies live. Digging deeper, you will discover that the ground is punched full of holes, tunnels, and burrows, making the forest floor feel like a soft, spongy carpet.

In the new earth there will be no death, hence no garbage. Plants, flowers, trees, animals, and people will live forever. Have you ever wondered what will happen to the bouquet of flowers you pick if nothing ever dies? Or the pinecones? Or the leaves if and when they fall? Some people worry about this. These doubters limit God to earth's garbage recycling system—as if it's God's only option. How silly! If God can conquer death, if He can reconstruct a person's molecules from the grave, then you and I and our doubting friends can safely leave this little cleanup problem to Him.

MAY 6

THREE SACKS OF SPUDS

If we confess our sins, he is faithful and just to forgive us our sins, and to cleanse us from all unrighteousness. 1 John 1:9.

The news traveled fast through the small Irish community. Before O'Ryan managed to open his barbershop for business, the entire town had heard the news. Housewives hanging out their weekly washing clicked their tongues in disgust. Old men playing checkers at the dry-goods store pounded their fists and decried the theft. How could such a thing happen in their town? they wondered.

Just before dawn it was discovered that a thief had broken into Squire Tucker's cold cellar and had stolen two gunnysackfuls of potatoes.

The people of the community discussed the unusual occurrence all morning long. Poaching rabbits off the squire's estate they could understand—that was a national tradition—but stealing spuds from a man's cold cellar? "Why, that's like taking food right off his children's plates!" they decided.

The village priest in the little Catholic community was passing the post office when one of the town gossips told him the tale of the missing potatoes. The old man just patted the irate woman's hand gently and shook his head. Weeks passed. The sheriff failed to catch the thief, and new gossip soon replaced the excitement caused by the robbery.

One morning a man named Paddy showed up at the church. Paddy confessed to the priest, "I stole the three sacks of spuds." The priest listened and pointed to repentance and forgiveness.

It wasn't until Paddy was ready to leave that the priest said, "I heard about the theft, but weren't there only two sacks taken? You mentioned three."

"Yes," the man answered, "but tonight I am going to steal the third one."

Somewhere along the way, poor Paddy missed the point of God's forgiveness. When Jesus said, "Thy sins be forgiven thee," He could very well have added, "Go, and sin no more."

MAY 7

CLAY PEBBLES

If you look for it [wisdom] as for silver and search for it as for hidden treasure, then you will . . . find the knowledge of God. Proverbs 2:4, 5, NIV.

Gary, a young businessman from Detroit, Michigan, flew to Key West, Florida, for a vacation. Tired of the rush of his everyday life, he chose to spend his two-week vacation beachcombing along the southern Florida coast. Each day as he ambled along the water's edge, Gary collected interesting shells, unusually shaped driftwood, and bits of wreckage from discarded boats.

On one of his beachcombing forays, he noticed a small hole partway up a sandstone cliff. Curious, he scaled the cliff and peered into the dark hole. Hoping he'd located an abandoned bird's nest, he stuck his hand deep inside. Gary felt around until his hand rested on what he thought were bird's eggs.

He scooped up the pebble-sized eggs and withdrew his hand from the hole. When he looked at the round, smooth eggs in his hand, they turned out to be hard gray clay balls varying in size from that of a large pea to that of golf balls. Disappointed that what he'd found turned out to be of no value, Gary dumped the clay balls into a pocket of his sweater and climbed back down to the beach.

As the afternoon sun melted into the golden haze of sunset, Gary walked back toward his hotel, occasionally practicing his aim by tossing a clay ball at a piece of floating driftwood. Once he tried to skip a few of the pebbles out over the surface of the ocean. By the time he reached his hotel, the strange clay balls were gone.

At the end of the two weeks, Gary returned to his home in Detroit. While sorting through his dirty clothes, he checked the pockets of his favorite sweater and discovered one of the smallest of the clay balls, one he had missed. He rolled the pebble about a few times in the palm of his hand. Recalling the pleasant day he'd spent on the beach, Gary decided that the clay ball would make a good memento of his vacation.

(To be continued tomorrow.)

MORE THAN CLAY

Through these he has given us his very great and precious promises, so that through them you may participate in the divine nature and escape the corruption in the world caused by evil desires. 2 Peter 1:4, NIV.

Months passed. Gary's busy schedule forced the memory of the Florida vacation from his mind until the day he met Bert. Bert's hobby was reading tales about pirate ships and buried treasure. Bert fascinated Gary with stories about the pirates of Florida and the Caribbean islands. Having visited the area, Gary could easily picture sailors with wooden peg legs and sea captains with eye patches burying treasure chests of gold and emeralds in the smooth white sandy beaches of southern Florida.

One afternoon while at work, Bert told Gary the story of how pirates would hide precious jewels from their enemies by molding wet clay around gems and then hiding the clay balls in holes high on the sandstone cliffs.

No, Gary thought. *That's impossible*. His curiosity piqued, Gary left work early. Hurrying home, he rushed into his bedroom and removed his box of souvenirs from the closet shelf. He pawed through the scraps of driftwood and broken shells for the small pebble. Finally he found the tiny clay ball. He took out a penknife and began scraping away at the clay. At first there was nothing but clay. Then the ball cracked—and out rolled a small but perfect blue-white diamond. Speechless, Gary stared at the gem sparkling in the lamplight.

Then his heart leaped to his throat and his stomach turned sick, for suddenly he remembered the other 23 marbles of clay that he'd tossed away—lost forever in the ocean's changing tides.

God gave you and me hundreds of precious promises in His Word. Some of these gems, at first glance, are wrapped in common clay. Others catch our attention the minute we read them. Too often we, like Gary, toss the mud-wrapped jewels away before we take the time to discover their true value.

Take time to discover and think about God's promises to you. You will be surprised just how much treasure you will uncover if you do.

OCEAN OF LOVE

You must forgive one another just as the Lord has forgiven you. Colossians 3:13, TEV.

This morning I would like to introduce you to a remarkable Christian lady. If you've already met her, you will agree with my opinion. Her name is Corrie Ten Boom.

Corrie lived with her father and sister, Betsie, in Haarlem, Holland, where they operated a watch repair shop. When Hitler's army invaded Holland and proceeded to persecute and then deport the Ten Booms' Jewish neighbors, the Ten Booms began hiding these desperate people in their attic. This Christian family helped many Jewish refugees escape death at the hands of the Nazi gestapo before getting caught themselves.

As prisoners of the Third Reich, Corrie and Betsie were transported to a prison camp called Ravensbruck—a cruel, inhumane place designed to torture and destroy the prisoners within. Betsie was one of its victims, but Corrie survived.

After the war Corrie wrote a book about her experiences, *The Hiding Place*. A movie was made from the book. Corrie traveled all over the world, telling Christians everywhere about the love of God and how He demonstrated His love even behind prison doors.

One evening she spoke to a large congregation in Munich, Germany. After the meeting a stranger walked up to her and extended his hand. Immediately she recognized him as one of the guards at the Ravensbruck concentration camp. Hate seethed within her as she remembered all the brutal things he had done to both her and her sister. Then, as suddenly as the hate appeared, it was replaced by a wave of love. Corrie reached out and took his hand. The man had become a Christian.

"If we forgive our enemies," Corrie said, "we experience the ocean of God's love as never before."

I like that—an ocean of God's love. It's a miracle—the miracle of forgiveness. Only the love of Jesus is strong enough to erase the kind of hate Corrie and the former Nazi guard felt for each other. Only the love of Jesus can allow you to forgive those who hurt you. The miracle of forgiveness is well worth the effort.

MOTHER'S VOICE

As one whom his mother comforteth, so will I comfort you. Isaiah 66:13.

There are a lot of frightening firsts for a kid growing up. I remember them all too well. My first day of school, my first visit to the dentist, my first trip to junior camp, my first vocal solo in church, my first piano recital, my first day at boarding academy—those are just a few frightening firsts that I remember.

As I encountered each new experience, I felt alone and scared. I didn't know then that I was far from alone. My mom was right there should I need her help. When I really blew it, like the time I forgot my music at the piano recital, she was there to tell me everything was OK. When I had my first tooth pulled, she bought me a bowl of hot pea soup (my favorite at the time).

I also remember my first crush. I was devastated when my seventh-grade heartthrob preferred a perky little sixth grader named Judy. While my pride wouldn't let me admit to my mother that I'd been rejected for another, she recognized my need to be comforted.

Now that I'm an adult, I know—and Mom knows—that she was not perfect. She made plenty of mistakes. In fact, she often wishes that she could do some things over again in a different way. During my teenage years I held those mistakes against her. Yet, in spite of all the hassles, I knew she loved me. And I learned to comfort others by the way she comforted me.

God says, "As one whom his mother comforteth, so I will comfort you." He promises to comfort us like a mother comforts. However, I read something more into this promise. I read that the man Jesus, who was also God, followed His mother's example of comforting in order to comfort you and me. That's neat—to know that the Son of God learned compassion at His mother's side.

Today is Mother's Day. Whether or not you choose to give a card to the woman who gave you life or who makes your life more enjoyable, at least take time to say thank you. Give her a big kiss and an extra hug. Take a few minutes to share memories from your past or hers—talk about a few firsts you experienced together. Show her that you're learning the art of compassion.

If by chance for one reason or another you have no mother with whom to share this day, then claim today's promise. The promise says that God, through Jesus, is ready to share with you the experience of a mother's comfort.

MAY 11

THE GOLDEN SPIKE

God forgave us all our sins; he canceled the unfavorable record of our debts . . . by nailing it to the cross. Colossians 2:13, 14, TEV.

Harriet tingled with fear and excitement. Her family were leaving their home in Roanoke, Virginia, for San Francisco, California. She had heard frightening stories of families who died attempting to cross the continent by covered wagon, as well as tales of ships sinking, killing all on board. She shuddered. She knew that once she kissed her grandmother and grandfather goodbye, she would never see them again. The distance was too great, the dangers too deadly. Grandpa and Grandma could never make such a difficult trip either by covered wagon or by sailing ship around the tip of South America.

But Harriet was wrong. Less than 10 years later, her grandparents also moved to California, where they lived well into old age. They didn't travel by either ship or covered wagon. They traveled by train, thanks to the dream of a number of wealthy businessmen who decided to link the eastern and western United States with a railroad.

Working from east and from west, workmen laid miles and miles of track over mountain passes, across raging rivers, and through sweltering deserts until the rails met in Promontory, Utah. There on May 10, 1869, the final spike—a gold one to commemorate the occasion—was pounded into place. The spike was later removed and placed in a museum.

When Eve and her husband, Adam, sinned and fled the Garden of Eden, they were afraid they'd never see their heavenly Father again. But they were wrong. God loved them so much that He and His Son, Jesus, reassured the grieving couple by sharing Their plan that would forever link the earth with heaven. Adam's and Eve's sins would be forgiven, their debts paid. All this became possible through the death of Jesus on the cross of Calvary. There was no national celebration held, and no golden spike was used to bridge the gulf, just plain iron spikes pounded through the flesh of our Saviour. The cross and the spikes have long since disappeared, but the connection made that day will last for eternity.

THE WEATHER AT NOON

But where shall wisdom be found? and where is the place of understanding? Job 28:12.

You have seen road signs for deer crossing, elk crossing, cattle crossing, and children crossing. In England local lawmakers erected a sign giving toads the right-of-way. The most unusual crossing I have ever seen was a "dragon" crossing outside a school in Springdale, Oregon. Since the students, not the state, placed the sign alongside the road, state officials forced the kids to take it down.

Another one-of-a-kind animal crossing sign can be seen along Interstate 5, near the city of Roseburg, Oregon—a sign for a mountain goat crossing.

The human citizens of this small Oregon city protect these "city dwelling" goats for two reasons. First, since the city of Roseburg grew up around the goats' natural mountain home, the people of Roseburg believe the shaggy creatures have squatters' rights. The animals were there first. The second reason, and a more important reason to the people of Roseburg, is that the town's mountain goats can and do accurately predict the weather. That's right—predict the weather. The goats know when the day will be fair or foul.

The people of Roseburg trust the goats' predictions more than they trust those made by the scientifically sophisticated U.S. Weather Bureau. When the official forecast conflicts with the goats', the local TV weatherman broadcasts the goats' prediction first.

The local television station is located at the foot of the in-town mountain. And before each of the daily broadcasts, a station employee looks out the window to learn the goats' whereabouts. If the goats are grazing at the base of the mountain or descending the mountain, a storm is on its way. If the goats are nowhere in sight or climbing the mountain, the weather will stay fair.

Why does this happen? Your guess is as good as the experts, since no one, except the goats, knows the real reason for their strange behavior.

People get so caught up in their own wisdom that they forget there is more in nature that we don't understand than we do. Where can we go to find wisdom? Where can we acquire the knowledge of the universe? We look to the mountain goat, the playful dolphin, or perhaps the desert roadrunner. Each of God's creatures can share new and unusual insights about God's wisdom and love.

THE LAST WAR WHOOP

Do not deceive yourselves; no one makes a fool of God. A person will reap exactly what he plants. If he plants in the field of his natural desires, from it he will gather the harvest of death. Galatians 6:7, 8, TEV.

"The British are on the march north," spies for the American Army reported, "with new recruits straight from Europe." The spies also reported that the new British soldiers who had arrived from Europe were terrified of the wild, uncivilized country with its strange, ferocious animals.

Legend has it that Americans stationed at Saratoga, New York, decided to take advantage of these new recruits' fears. The rebel colonists waited until the advancing army made camp for the night, and then spies slipped into the British camp, not to gather information, but to regale the enemy with hair-raising tales of wild bears, of scalpings and torture during Indian raids.

After dark, American sympathizers too young to be in the army sneaked into the woods surrounding the British camp, where they serenaded the terrified soldiers throughout the night with screams, war cries, and frightening animal sounds. By morning the exhausted British soldiers were too terrified and too tired from lack of sleep to fight well. Great strategy, huh?

Years earlier, the war between England and France had spread to the New World. It was during this French and Indian War that the British Army supplied the native tribesmen with steel knives and promised to pay a bounty for each French scalp they brought in. The custom spread. The British never imagined that one day the lesson would haunt their own people. As the text says, a man reaps what he sows. Unfortunately, those around him often suffer too. Can you name a person in the Bible whose bad choices caused others pain?

How would making the following bad choices affect those around you?

1. Refusing to wear your seat belt.
2. Drinking and driving.
3. Partying with drugs.
4. Having sex before marriage.
5. Dropping out of high school before graduating.
6. Shoplifting at K Mart.
7. Gorging on sweets.

8. Watching late-night TV regularly.
9. Making fun of the class dummy.
10. Cheating on your math quiz.

The next time you are tempted to say "I'm not hurting anyone but myself," remember today's text and reconsider.

MAY 14

A TASTE OF HONEY

The law of the Lord is perfect, reviving the soul. The statutes of the Lord are trustworthy, making wise the simple. . . . They are more precious than gold, than much pure gold; they are sweeter than honey, than honey from the comb. Psalm 19:7-10, NIV.

I have two assignments for you today.

Assignment 1: Spread a layer of peanut butter on a slice of whole-wheat bread. On top of the peanut butter, add a thick coating of honey. Yum! It makes your mouth water just looking at it, doesn't it? Even without the peanut butter, you will have a meal "fit for the gods." (If you don't have all three of these ingredients, use your imagination.)

Actually, the people of ancient times did consider honey to be "food for the gods." Egyptians believed it to be "the sustainer of life" and placed a generous supply of honey in the pyramids for their deceased pharaohs' enjoyment, along with a number of horses and slaves, as well as an abundant supply of gold, jewels, and toys. British archaeologists of the twentieth century unearthing these tombs have found these treasure caches still intact. They have discovered that the honey buried centuries ago has remained unspoiled—edible, in fact.

Isn't it interesting that the psalmist would use honey to describe the law of God? He declared the law to be "sweeter . . . than honey from the comb." While the sweetness of honey is pleasant, its longevity is profound. Much like God's law, honey neither spoils nor changes its consistency throughout the passage of time.

Assignment 2: Read the rest of Psalm 19 to discover more comparisons you can make between God's perfect law and honey.

MAY 15

THE PROMISED LAND

And they [Abel, Enoch, Noah, and Abraham] admitted that they were aliens and strangers on earth. People who say such things show that they are looking for a country of their own. If they

had been thinking of the country they had left, they would have had opportunity to return. Instead, they were longing for a better country—a heavenly one. Hebrews 11:13-16, NIV.

Can you imagine what it would be like to leave home knowing you can probably never ever return? To 16-year-old Frank, it seemed that the entire hometown population of Amantea, Italy, had come to the train station to say goodbye. He made his way through the crowd of well-wishers, stopping for violent hugs from the men and sloppy kisses from the women who had, until today, been his whole life. His body and mind felt heavy with the sadness of leaving all he loved behind, yet alive with excitement at the adventure before him. He was leaving his homeland of Italy for America, the promised land.

Frank had no dreams of finding wealth in his new home. He'd heard the silly stories of gold in the streets and money growing on trees. But he knew better. His brother Pasquale's letters told tales of hard work, unfair prejudice, and greed. Yet the country was a land where hard work and determination could change dreams into reality. And that was more than the Old Country could give him.

He climbed aboard the train that would take him northwest to the bustling port of Naples. Sticking his head out an open window, he waved and blew kisses to his family and friends as the train whistle filled the air. The giant black steam engine's blinding smoke wafted back into his face, giving him a good excuse to wipe the tears from his eyes.

The next few days passed in a swirl of bright colors, strange odors, and loneliness as he made the arrangements for his voyage. Over and over he read his brother's letters from America. Without Pasquale's encouraging words, Frank was certain he'd turn around and head back home to the familiar dusty little coastal town.

You and I are travelers looking forward to our heavenly home. Sometimes it seems more like a dream than a real place. It's like trying to imagine Disneyland without having been there. That's why our heavenly Father has sent us Letters (the Bible) to encourage us, to remind us that the new land is worth the sacrifice.

(To be continued tomorrow.)

MAY 16

THE NEW LAND

For he [Abraham] was looking forward to the city with foundations, whose architect and builder is God. Hebrews 11:10, NIV.

Frank bought his ticket aboard a ship heading for New York City. He watched, forlorn, as the ship eased out of the harbor and as Italy disappeared over the horizon. Except for the occasional storm, one day at sea was much like the next. West along the Mediterranean, through the Strait of Gibraltar, and across the vast Atlantic Ocean they traveled.

One morning the passengers and crew members were repeating the expectation "Today's the day! Today we will reach America!" Eager to catch their first glimpse of the New York City skyline, Frank and his traveling companions scanned the misty horizon.

Frank's breath caught in his chest when he first spotted the giant green statue in New York Harbor—the Statue of Liberty. After a week on Ellis Island, where all the immigrants stayed until they were permitted to enter the country, Frank boarded the ferryboat that would take him on his last lap to his new home.

Tears brimmed in his eyes as he passed the island that held the Statue of Liberty. He studied the folds of her metal garments, her facial features, the torch above her head. His tears went unnoticed because his companions were experiencing the same emotions. Their long journey had ended and they were home at last.

Frank eagerly adopted his new land. Through good times and bad, through wealth and despair, he never wavered. He never looked back.

A few years after his arrival in America, Frank became a pilgrim again. This time he began a journey that would take him the rest of his life to complete. He learned of a new Promised Land, a better land, of the city whose "builder and maker is God." Frank claimed God's promise that one day the new land, and the shining city of God, would be his. And you know what? Frank was right. He will not be disappointed.

MAY 17

WINNING THE SUPER BOWL

See, the Sovereign Lord comes with power. . . . See, his reward is with him. Isaiah 40:10, NIV.

The Super Bowl? In May? That's right. Each year, toward the end of May, a national Super Bowl is held in Angels Camp, California. And do you know what the winners get as their reward? Not a million-dollar bonus or an Olympic gold medal or a trip to Disneyland, but an extra serving of dead flies at suppertime. Yum!—if you're a prize-winning jumper of a frog. More than 3,000 frogs compete each year for the blue ribbon and the dead flies.

The first actual Frog Jumping Jubilee was held on May 19 and 20 in 1928 to honor Samuel Clemens, alias Mark Twain, for making their town famous in his short story "The Celebrated Jumping Frog of Calavaras County." Fifty-one frogs entered the contest that year. The winning frog, The Pride of San Joaquin, was owned by Louis R. Fischer of Stockton, California. Since then frogs from all over the United States and Canada have come to compete in their very own Olympic events—the Frog Jumping Jubilee.

I wonder how the owner coaches his frog to jump farther. Does he put his star frog through a rigorous training program? Probably not. Most likely there are very few similarities between the frog's jumping event and the world Olympic jumping events.

When I told this story to a young friend of mine named Casey, she asked me what color the frog's track uniform was and who designed it. Regardless of the silly comparisons we could make between the athletic frogs and the Olympic stars, there is one very definite thing that both types of performers share—they will both receive a reward for winning.

I never plan to train for the Olympics, and I know I'll never qualify for the Frog Jumping Jubilee, but I have been promised that I will receive a prize for completing the longest, most difficult race ever run. When Jesus returns to this earth to take me home, my reward will be in His hands. And that prize will be better than all the dead flies, the gold medals, and the trips to Disneyland possible.

MAY 18

IQ OR $$$$

OK, what's going on? Where's today's Scripture text? Be patient. The text will appear near the end of the reading instead of at the beginning.

Today I want you to do more than just read a story. I have two questions for you and each member of your family to answer.

If you had to choose to be born either a poor genius or a not-so-bright billionaire, which would make you happier? Why?

A real, live genius answered these two questions for me. Decide if you agree with her answers.

She said, "If I had to choose whether to be intelligent and poor or rich and stupid, I would choose to be intelligent and poor. Being smart, I could come up with a way to become wealthy if I really wanted to. But the person who is rich but not-so-bright would lose his wealth to the first clever con man that came along. And he'd lack the intelligence to rebuild his fortune.''

Well, do you agree? Before you answer that, you should know that my genius friend's answer corresponds with the advice given by another genius, King Solomon—the wisest man who ever lived and the richest.

Consider your answers to the questions posed. Did you agree with the experts in today's story? If you didn't agree earlier, do you now agree?

It is better—much better—to have wisdom and knowledge than gold and silver. Proverbs 16:16, TEV.

But let's take today's lesson one step further. Both my genius friend and King Solomon agree that true happiness never comes from possessing gold and silver. Nor does true happiness necessarily accompany wisdom and great learning. However, true happiness always comes when we choose to obey God and love other people.

MAY 19

DAY OF JUDGMENT

Well done, thou good and faithful servant: thou hast been faithful over a few things, I will make thee ruler over many things: enter thou into the joy of thy lord. Matthew 25:21.

May 19, 1780, dawned clear and bright except for a haze in the southwestern sky. As the morning progressed, the haze grew darker until the entire sky was covered with a rapidly moving thick cloud that swept through eastern New York, Maine, New Hampshire, Rhode Island, Massachusetts, and Connecticut, and reached the Canadian border by midmorning. By 1:00 in the afternoon, some areas of the country were so dark that a piece of white paper held only a few inches from one's eyes could not be seen.

Teachers sent the children home from school. The lamplighters of Boston lit the streetlamps early. The light from the lamps cast a strange green hue over the city. Farmers watched their chickens go to roost at midday. Even the wild birds flew to their nests to sleep. The people, afraid that the end of the world had come, rushed to their churches to pray and await the judgment day.

By noon the state legislature of Hartford, Connecticut, threatened to break up in panic until one member of the house of representatives rose to speak. ''Mr. Speaker,'' he began, ''my colleagues of the house fear for their lives due to this strange darkness that has befallen us. They are calling it the wrath of God's judgment. Well, the way I see it, either this is the judgment day or it is not. If it is not, then there's no need to adjourn," the man reasoned. "And if it is the judgment day, I desire to have my God find me doing my duty to the best of my ability. I move that we bring in candles and proceed with business." The session continued, with only a few terrified legislators leaving for home.

The darkness continued into the night. The full moon didn't appear until 1:00 a.m., and then it was blood-red. Nearly a day after the darkness arrived, a new morning dawned. The sun was as bright as ever.

Even today some people become anxious and fearful at the thought of Jesus' coming. The true child of God would be wise to adopt the Connecticut representative's attitude when he sees signs of the end of time. What better way to have Jesus find us when He returns than faithfully carrying out the tasks He's given us to do?

If you wish to learn more about May 19, 1780, read pages 306-308 in *The Great Controversy*, written by Ellen White.

MAY 20

FILL 'ER UP

And God's peace, which is far beyond human understanding, will keep your hearts and minds safe in union with Christ Jesus. In conclusion, my brothers [and sisters], fill your minds with those things that are good and that deserve praise: things that are true, noble, right, pure, lovely, and honorable. Philippians 4:7, 8, TEV.

Picture yourself sitting in school. It's 11:15 a.m. You have 45 minutes to go before lunch. Right in the middle of your math teacher's explanation of the factoring of polynomials, your stomach growls. Your hear the class clown chortle. Your face reddens when you realize the entire class heard the growl. You cover your stomach with your arms in an effort to silence all future growls, only to feel a slight headache coming on. You're certain you will shrivel into starvation before noon if you don't get something to eat—now!

Suddenly you hear your mother's voice. "I told you to eat your oatmeal this morning. Breakfast is the most important meal of the day."

Your mother's voice fades into a TV jingle. "Snickers satisfies you . . ." M-m-m! Your mouth waters. Oh, for a Snickers bar right now to tide you over until lunch. Your appetite tells you that unless you get at least one bite of the gooey caramel and crunchy peanuts in the creamy chocolate bar, you'll simply die before 12:00 noon. Ah, but your brain knows better.

You know that your stomach is never completely empty and that hunger pangs come when the stomach squeezes itself into a little ball around a pocket of air and digestive juice. You also know that while filling your stomach with sugar will ease the pangs, the candy bar's nearly empty calories will leave no room for the nutritious sandwich and big juicy apple in your lunch box—true body builders.

Your mind, like your stomach, is never empty. And like with your stomach, you can fill your mind with junk food such as frothy love stories, trashy TV programs, anger, jealousy, and self-pity. Just as the body needs nutritious food in order to build strong muscles, the mind needs nutritious thoughts in order to remain strong and healthy.

Just as your stomach gets so full of food that you can't eat another bite, so your mind can be stuffed with the good food listed in today's promise, leaving no room for hate, self-pity, and regret. So what are you waiting for? Fill 'er up!

MAY 21

THE HEADLESS INSECT

Keep your temper under control; it is foolish to harbor a grudge. Ecclesiastes 7:9, TEV.

"Chill out!" "Keep cool!" "Don't get your back up!" "Don't get hot under the collar." "Don't work yourself into a lather." "Don't get your dander up." "Don't blow your top." "Don't lose your head." You've heard them all—warnings to keep your temper under control. Unfortunately, by the time someone is telling you not to lose your temper, you've probably already lost it, right?

I know this will sound crazy, but did you know that an insect can lose its head and still survive? That's right! Each of its two body parts can carry out its own reflex actions without first having to go through the switchboard of the brain. For instance, if an insect is decapitated, it could live until it starves to death. If I hadn't read it in a book called *Amazing Facts*, I wouldn't have believed it either.

Lucky bug! He can lose his head or blow his top without dying instantly. However, it is important to note that even if the insect doesn't die instantly, he will not recover, but will surely die from the experience.

Unlike insects, our bodies can't function without our heads. We would die instantly—just consider "Madame Guillotine." This instrument of capital punishment was named after a Dr. Guillotin. He hated the practice of hanging criminals, so he suggested using what he believed would be a more humane method of execution. Whether or not the hundreds of people during the French Revolution who lost their heads and didn't live to tell about it agreed with the good doctor, we'll never know.

Humane or inhumane, losing one's head is sure death. Medical teams have learned how to replace fingers, arms, and legs accidentally severed. They can replace worn-out hearts with healthier hearts, and blind eyes with eye transplants that can enable people to see. But no one has figured out a way to reconnect a severed head to one's neck or to exchange one head for another.

Have you ever lost your head (figuratively, of course) and later wished you could just die? I have. Maybe that's what the wise man is saying in today's scripture. Only a fool will lose his head over every little real or imagined slight. Physically, losing your head is instant death; figuratively, watch out! You may survive, but, like the insect, you'll probably live to regret it.

MAY 22

THE ULTIMATE ZOOKEEPER

Then you will know the truth, and the truth will set you free. John 8:32, NIV.

The Psychology of the Giraffe. Isn't that a great book title? I doubt there is such a book, since who knows what a giraffe is thinking? There is, however, such a course of study for zookeepers at the San Diego Zoo. After observing that giraffes are afraid to walk down stairs, the caretakers at the zoo have used psychology to control them. When you think about the weird balance that giraffes must maintain to keep from tipping over, it's easy to understand the animals' fear of stairs.

So when a new giraffe area of the zoo was being constructed, this discovery was put to good use. To prevent the giraffes from wandering about the zoo, the keepers placed the animals on a platform. The animals' natural fear of stairsteps became their prison.

Another such discovery involved bears. The scientists learned that the bears could not scale even a low fence if the fence is at the bottom of an incline or ramp. Again they used the information to cage in the animals better.

Funny, huh? But don't laugh too loudly. You could be living in a zoo too. Your zookeeper, Satan, has been studying humans for 6,000 years. He observes your daily habits, as well. He knows what cereal you eat in the morning. He knows your favorite flavor of gum. He learns everything he can about your likes and your dislikes, your pleasures and your fears, and then uses the information to control you—to keep you sinning. He takes advantage of your every weakness to keep you trapped in his zoo.

The last thing your zookeeper wants is for you to learn the truth—that you can be free. He doesn't want you to know that Jesus is your escape. The best part is, unlike the giraffe and the bear, which cannot change their natures, it's your own choice to allow the Creator to re-create in you the nature He originally planned for you to have, the truth that will set you free. Aren't you glad you know the truth? Aren't you thankful Jesus has set you free?

MAY 23

CHICKEN SURPRISE

Stop judging by mere appearances, and make a right judgment. John 7:24, NIV.

"Buy a chicken I can roast," Anna's mother admonished. Fourteen-year-old Anna and her family had just arrived in Los Angeles from Cambodia. Since Anna was the only member of the family who could speak a little English and knew the value of the strange-looking American money, she was the one chosen to do the family grocery shopping. At the market Anna searched up one aisle and down the next for the rack where the plucked chickens were hanging. Distressed that she could find none, Anna asked the grocer, but he waved her away. He couldn't understand her broken English.

She walked down the aisle where he had pointed. Suddenly she spotted something she recognized, a can with a picture of peas on the label. Next to the canned peas, she found a can with a picture of carrots on it. *H'mm, this is easier than I thought,* she mused as she picked up one large blue metal container. On the label was a picture of a golden-brown fried chicken. *Mama will be so happy*, she thought. *Imagine, in America they put a dead chicken in a can instead of hanging it by its feet.* Anna excitedly removed the can from the shelf and hurried to pay for her purchases.

When she arrived back at the apartment, she bubbled over with excitement. Her entire family eagerly listened to the details of Anna's adventure in the grocery store. However, when Anna's mother opened the large aluminum can with the chicken on the label, instead of a golden-brown chicken, the woman found a thick, greasy mass of white. Anna had purchased a can of Crisco shortening.

Some people shop for friends in the same way Anna shopped for a chicken—by "reading" labels. You know the labels I mean: fat, skinny, black, yellow, stupid, nerd, ugly, klutz—the list goes on. Perhaps you've read a few such labels yourself. Perhaps you, like Anna, jump to conclusions by judging from the outside the contents on the inside. People labels are no more accurate than the picture on that Crisco label.

If you are going for the gold when choosing friends, you will not judge people by their outside layer alone. You will take time to discover the specialness of the class nerd, the beauty beneath the uncool student's pimpled face, and the unique treasure buried even within yourself. Golden friendships like these can make you rich beyond imagination.

MAY 24

MIRRORS AND PRISMS

The Lord is my light and my salvation. . . . One thing I ask of the Lord is that I may gaze upon the Lord . . . and to seek his face. Psalm 27:1, 4, 8.

Rhondi loved to eat spaghetti swimming in rich, red marinara sauce. To help make eating the spaghetti easier for the 4-year-old, Mother always cut the strands into short, manageable lengths. One night Rhondi decided that she was too grown up to have her spaghetti cut. She wanted to wind it around her fork like her daddy did. Mother reluctantly agreed to let her try.

Rhondi stabbed her fork tines into the pile of stringlike pasta on her plate and began to turn the fork around and around. When she felt certain that she'd wound it enough she lifted the fork to her mouth, but only four or five long strands dangled from it in midair. She tried again and had the same results. Finally in desperation she stuffed the spaghetti into her mouth the best she could.

By the end of the meal Rhondi's face, dress, hands, forearms, and lap held more cold, sauce-covered pasta than did her tummy. Rhondi was so busy enjoying the spaghetti that did make it into her mouth that she didn't notice when her dad slipped away from the table so he could grab his camera. The resulting photo shows two bright blue eyes staring out of a mass of red. Rhondi didn't need the picture to show her how messy she was. She could see and feel it. After changing clothes and washing her face, Rhondi glanced in the bathroom mirror and discovered that she'd forgotten to wash her eyebrows, which were still streaked with red.

While Rhondi's experiment with long strands of spaghetti was not sinful, some experiments that you and I make are. When we sin we usually know we've done something wrong—that we made a mess of things. And like Rhondi we try to clean up the mess we have made. Just as the mirror revealed the spots Rhondi had missed when she tried to clean herself up, so God's laws do the same thing. They show us the dirt still on our face.

This is where the mirror illustration fails. Whereas Rhondi could clean up her own face, hands, and arms pretty well without her mother's help, you and I can never clean up our sins by ourselves. Only Jesus can do that for us. And that's where the prism comes in.

While I am mixing my metaphors here, remain with me while I explain why you and I will be happiest if we possess both the mirror of God's law and the prism of His love. You know how a prism works, don't you? When a specially cut crystal prism is placed in direct sunlight, the light shines through the facets of the glass and breaks the white light into all the colors of the rainbow. When we turn our messy lives toward Jesus and ask Him to make us clean again, we will be able to take in His beauty, and His love will shine through us in living, breath-taking color.

MAY 25

SLIGHTED BY GOLD

Then Peter said, "Silver or gold I do not have, but what I have I give you. In the name of Jesus Christ of Nazareth, walk." Acts 3:6, NIV.

Henri straightened his jewel-studded jacket, twirled the ends of his waxed mustache, and strutted into the royal dining hall. The light from a hundred candles glistening off the mirror-lined walls dazzled his sight. Priding himself over his good fortune in being invited to dine at the table of the most powerful man in France, Henri allowed the maître d' to lead him to his place at the table.

Henri smiled graciously at the guests seated on each side of him and across the table from him. But when he glanced down at his setting of a knife, forks, and spoons, his smile froze in horror. He cast a sly glance to his right and to his left, checking out the other guests' dinnerware. What might he have said or done to deserve such disgrace? Henri reddened at the thought of his shame and embarrassment once his friends learned of his fall from grace.

"Once I was an honored guest. Now this?" What was Henri's problem? What had he seen that threw him into such a state of mind?

Henri's knife and a fork were made of gold! Everyone knew that Louis Napoleon's favored guests were honored by being allowed to dine with rare aluminum dinnerware. Everyone else had to make do with plain old gold knives, forks, and spoons.

Throughout time, the value of a metal has always been determined by its scarcity. Aluminum was rarer and much more difficult to process than gold or silver in Henri's day. For instance, today even gold is not the most precious metal available. Platinum is. And Louis's aluminum? Today aluminum is used for wrapping leftovers.

When the apostle Peter told the beggar in our text today that he had no gold or silver, I imagine that the man sighed in despair. Most likely passersby had been using the same excuse all day long. However, the rest of Peter's words made the lack of gold or silver unimportant: "In the name of Jesus Christ of Nazareth, walk."

As the man leaped to his feet and jumped about, do you think he felt slighted because Peter failed to give him money? As he tested out his new strength, do you think he cared that he lacked pocket change? Peter's gift was of far greater value to him than a few metal coins.

Think for a moment. Do you ever fret like Henri over real or imagined slights? Do you ever forget just how blessed you really are? What gifts do you enjoy that are more valuable than gold or silver?

List 10 blessings from God that are worth more to you than any amount of wealth.

MAY 26

BOUNCING SMILES

Smiling faces make you happy, and good news makes you feel better. Proverbs 15:30, TEV.

Eager young faces stared up at the former Miss America. "One of the most important lessons a beauty contestant must learn is to smile," the stunning brunette explained. "That isn't as easy as it sounds. She must smile when her feet hurt; smile when her head aches; smile when she's just snagged her best pair of panty hose." The woman paused to allow her message to sink in. "Miss America not only represents her home state but is also an ambassador for the greatest country in the world. Therefore she must, at all times, appear confident and happy."

An interesting thought—Miss America needs to maintain her smile because she is an ambassador for her country. Her smile is important to America's image.

I wonder. God's children are often called to be ambassadors for the King of the universe. Could smiles be important for them to maintain also? Do other people really judge Christians by their cheerfulness?

Joe, a friend of mine, invented a game to play while waiting for his mother to finish her shopping in the local mall. He calls the game "bouncing smiles." Joe doesn't know much about Miss America and her reasons for smiling, but he has noticed how sad or grouchy most shoppers look as they trudge up and down the mall corridors. The object of Joe's game is to bounce a smile to a passerby. He scores a point each time the shopper smiles back. He loses a point when the shopper fails to smile back.

Joe's scores are astounding. Only 1 out of 20 refuses to bounce his smile back to him. He's learned that people find it difficult to frown when someone takes the time to smile at them.

I am going to give you an assignment. Just for today, play Joe's game of bouncing smiles. As an ambassador for your heavenly Father, take the former Miss America's advice—and smile. Make your world a happier place—today.

Tonight during family worship, share with one another the results of the assignment.

MAY 27

SAUERKRAUT AND OTHER DELIGHTS

O taste and see that the Lord is good: blessed is the man that trusteth in him. Psalm 34:8.

The last notes of Taps had barely drifted across the moonlit lake when Angie's shadow appeared over the edge of the bunk bed. "You guys got anything to eat?"

"No," Mary Jo wailed, "we ate all the goodies I brought to camp last night."

"And mine the night before," Leigh reminded. "How about you, Sue? Sue?" Leigh shined her penlight in the unconscious girl's face. "She's asleep already?"

"Hey," a voice from the far end of the cabin whispered, "I've got three slices of pizza I smuggled out of the cafeteria at suppertime."

"Pizza?" Angie's voice climbed an octave. "Kim, my buddy, my pal!"

"Shine that light over this way. I'll divide them between us, OK?" The girls scrambled out of their sleeping bags and across the cabin to Kim's bed. One by one, Kim handed each of the girls a share of the hoard.

''Wait; before you take a bite, imagine yourself back in civilization at your neighborhood pizza parlor,'' Angie suggested. ''Imagine the aroma of hot melted cheese assaulting your senses.''

''Ah . . . ,'' Mary Jo sighed, ''double cheese, green olives, and hundreds of mushrooms.''

''Oh, no,'' Angie corrected. ''The best pizza imaginable is covered with green olives, onion rings, and—''

''E-e-e-u!'' Mary Jo grimaced. ''Not slimy onion rings.''

''Mary Jo, you have to have onion rings,'' Kim interrupted, ''and tomato slices and pineapple and—''

''Pineapple on pizza?'' Angie shuddered in disgust. ''Take it from a genuine Italiano, you do not put pineapple—''

''We do in California. It's called Hawaiian-style pizza,'' Kim informed her. ''And then there's Mexican-style pizza with refried beans and hot sauce—''

''Can we eat our pizza yet?'' Mary Jo interrupted.

''Wait! How about your favorite pizza, Leigh?'' Angie asked.

''Oh, that's easy—Pennsylvania Dutch pizza. It's topped with sauerkraut.''

''Sauerkraut pizza?'' Mary Jo gasped. ''You're kidding!''

''No, it's true. The first time you try it, you might not like it, but after a while, it kinda grows on you.''

''It wouldn't grow on me!'' Angie groaned. ''My 9,000 or so taste buds would never allow the likes of a sauerkraut-topped pizza to enter their domain!''

''Don't be so closed-minded,'' Leigh insisted. ''It's not so bad.''

''Never in a million years, sweetie,'' Angie mumbled as she crunched into her slice of cold pizza. ''Sauerkraut!''

Food likes and dislikes vary from home to home, state to state, and country to country. Whereas Kim enjoys Hawaiian pizza after living on the West Coast, so Leigh enjoys a totally different style.

When it comes to the Bible promise ''Taste and see that the Lord is good,'' the delightful results are the same for each sincere child of God—whether born in Calcutta or Cairo, Sausalito or Savannah.

God is so good. Taste and see for yourself.

A ROUND TUIT

Be very careful, then, how you live—not as unwise but as wise, making the most of every opportunity, because the days are evil. Ephesians 5:15, 16, NIV.

"Procrastination" is an interesting word. What does it mean? I think I'll look it up in the dictionary—tomorrow. When I think of procrastination, I remember a circular piece of cardboard my friend Debbie gave me. In the middle of the circle she'd written, with a bold black marker, the letters TUIT.

On the back of the circle it said "This is your very own TUIT, a round TUIT, to be exact. Now you will never need to put off until tomorrow what you should do today. You will never need to say 'I'll do it when I get a round TUIT,' because you will always have a round TUIT." I laughed. How appropriate coming from Debbie!

My friend Debbie is one of the most able young women I've ever met. God gave her so many unbelievable talents. She sings beautifully; she paints gorgeous pictures. She can act; she tells great children's stories. You name it, Debbie can do it. She even whips up the best blackberry pie you've ever tasted. On top of all these talents, she is sweet, kind, and always willing to volunteer when something needs to be done.

This is where Debbie's troubles start. Her flaw to perfection is—you guessed it—procrastination. She puts off until tomorrow the tasks she should do today. The results of her belated efforts, if she manages to fulfill her promises at all, are far less than her best.

When scheduled to sing for church, she says, "I'll practice when I get around to it." When learning her lines for a school play, she thinks, *Oh, I'll get around to memorizing them tomorrow*. Debbie's talents would be phenomenal if only she had a round TUIT.What about your round TUIT? Are your science projects as good as they can possibly be? Are your stories for English as clever as possible? Your math papers neat and correct? Your social studies posters carefully designed? A task worth doing is worth doing well. The habits you are developing today will be the ones you will live with tomorrow. Jesus wants you to be the very best you can be. He can give you the strength to find your very own round TUIT.

TOUGH-LOOKING HOMBRES

Be alert and always keep on praying for all the saints. Ephesians 6:18, NIV.

I like stories about answered prayer. One of my favorite stories comes from Brazil. A missionary and his wife had set up a small medical clinic in a remote jungle region of the country. When a priest from another church learned of the couple's success in reaching the Indian population, he became jealous and threatened to hurt the couple.

In her letter back to friends at home, the missionary wife told about the priest's threats. She asked her friends to pray for them. It wasn't long after she wrote the letter that she took sick with appendicitis. Her husband rushed her to the nearest hospital for emergency surgery. Since she would have to remain in the hospital for a few days, the missionary was forced to return to the mission compound without her.

For an entire week the missionary worked alone in the clinic. On Sabbath morning as the people from the area began arriving for church, a man known for his drinking and his violence approached the missionary.

"Last night," the man said, "the priest and a few of my drinking buddies intended to kill you, but we couldn't."

"Why not?" the missionary asked.

"Hey we're not stupid. There were only four of us against 18 of you tough-looking hombres."

The missionary frowned. Eighteen? He'd been home alone all evening.

Later his wife received a letter from her friend in the United States. In the letter the friend told the missionary how she and 16 friends spend 10 minutes at a specific time every Friday evening praying especially for the missionaries' safety. When the missionary woman and her husband calculated the time zone difference, they discovered that their friends had been praying for them at the same time the priest and his hooligans had come to kill the missionary. How many men did they see? Seventeen strangers + the missionary = 18. And how many people were praying at precisely the same time? Sixteen friends + the letter writer + the missionary = 18.

One famous woman of prayer said, "Satan laughs when we exert ourselves. He sneers at our wisdom, but he trembles when we pray."

PULLING MY LEG

Blessed is the man who makes the Lord his trust. . . . Many, O Lord my God, are the wonders you have done. Psalm 40:4, 5, NIV.

Today I have some objects sitting in front of me that no human has ever seen. The man who "made" them never once saw them. The man who sold them to me never saw them. In fact, I've never seen them. And yet the objects are sitting right in front of me.

"Aw, come on, Mrs. R," you're probably saying, "you're pulling my leg. Such a tale is impossible!" To you my claim sounds too incredible—too unbelievable. If you're smart, you would doubt my word. After all, you don't really know me. We've probably never met face-to-face.

If you attended my church, if you and I took walks together, spent lots of time getting to know each other, then maybe you could trust what I say, right? For trust has very little to do with the story I tell, but much to do with the storyteller. By knowing me and knowing that I would not intentionally lie to you, you would be more likely to believe what I have to say, right?

Well, in the case of the objects I described, however incredible it may sound, what I said is true. No one has ever seen the peanuts inside the unopened peanut shell lying on my desk. Not the farmer who grew them, not the grocer who sold them, and not I. I bought the peanuts sight unseen.

When I break the shell, I will see for the first time exactly what I purchased. I am hoping there will be two kernels inside. I am hoping they will be a smooth golden color, crunchy, and good to eat. I will be disappointed to find two shriveled-up nuts, blackened by some disease or eaten by a harmful insect.

Mmm! I can't wait any longer—here goes. *Crack!* I break the peanut shell open and find exactly what I'd hoped I'd find—two ready-to-eat peanuts. Imagine how surprised I would have been if when I opened the peanut shell, I found a tiny daffodil curled up inside or perhaps a miniature tomato.

"Aw, that's pretty silly," you say. "That can't happen."

You're right, it can't happen—naturally, anyway—unless someone was trying to play a practical joke on me.

Just as I trusted the farmer and the grocer when I bought their unshelled peanuts, so I trusted the Creator of the peanut to put peanuts and not popcorn inside the shell.

I DOUBT IT

In all he does he is faithful and just; all his commands are dependable. They last for all time. Psalm 111:7, 8, TEV.

When I was a kid, my friends and I used to play a game called "I doubt it." The object of the game was to convince the other players you didn't have the card asked for. Usually the best liar won. Not too great a game, huh?

In a world full of fakes and rip-off artists, there is always someone playing games with the truth. Sooner or later you'll meet one—if you haven't already. Perhaps my friend Mitch ran into too many of these crooked characters. Whatever his reason, Mitch refused to believe in beings or things he could not see. For example, when someone spoke of such beings as angels or demons, Mitch would ask, "How do you know they exist? How can you be sure?" He had doubts about other truths of the Bible, as well.

When he expressed his doubts, my answer was "I believe what the Bible teaches because I have taken the time to know the Author—not only by what He says in His Word, but by what He has done for me."

Knowing Jesus makes all the difference. I can believe the stories about the talking donkey and the sun standing still. I have no trouble accepting the fact that Peter walked on the water and miraculously escaped from prison. I believe because of the miraculous changes God has made in my life. I can know God will keep His promises because I've taken the time to get to know Him.

The older you get, the more likely it is that you'll meet doubters like Mitch who try to destroy your faith. However, the more you get to know God, the more you can trust Him to keep His promises. You can obey His commands without hesitation. When you are tempted to doubt, remember the promise hidden inside an unshelled peanut and believe. How can you know? How can you be sure you're not being deceived? By getting to know God better each day.

JUNE 1

AT THE CONTROLS

For this God is our God for ever and ever: he will be our guide even unto death. Psalm 48:14.

Five-year-old Amy giggled as Daddy scooped her into his arms and carried her onto the Boeing 747. The man handed the girl over to Sue, the head flight attendant. "Now, Sue, you take care of my best girl, you hear?"

The pretty woman smiled. "I will, Captain." Then she took Amy to her assigned seat and fastened the seat belt for the little girl. "Now," the flight attendant instructed, "you keep your seat belt on until the little red light goes off, OK?"

Within minutes into the flight, the child grew sleepy. After checking to be certain the red light was out, Amy removed her seat belt, snuggled into a little ball, and fell asleep.

Midway across the Atlantic a violent storm hit. The jumbo jet bounced around like a kite in a March wind. Lightning flashed around the plane. Sue and the other flight attendants hastened to assure the nervous passengers that all would be well. When the captain announced further turbulence ahead and asked the flight attendants to take their seats, Sue remembered the captain's daughter. She'd been sleeping the last time the flight attendant had passed her seat. Perhaps Amy had loosened or removed her seat belt. When Sue reached the little girl, Amy was still asleep. The belt strap dangled beside the seat. Sue awakened Amy in order to reclamp the belt. At that moment an extra-large lightning bolt flashed directly outside Amy's window. The child jumped.

"Are you all right?" the attendant asked. "Are you afraid?"

Amy looked up at the concerned woman. "Is my daddy flying the plane?" The attendant nodded yes.

"Good!" The child sighed, smiled, closed her eyes, and fell back to sleep.

Amy trusted her father completely. When you and I trust our heavenly Father just as completely, we never need to be afraid either.

JUNE 2

STINK WEED

Better a meal of vegetables where there is love than a fattened calf with hatred. Proverbs 15:17, NIV.

The first winter had been hard on the Jamestown settlers. Many had not survived. When spring arrived and the first green shoots broke through the snow, the women left their stuffy cabins to search for herbs (vegetables) to supplement their dwindling food supply.

Unfortunately, the plant many of the women chose to prepare was an unfamiliar weed whose leaves and green, spiny fruit when crushed give off a very pungent odor. It is also very poisonous. Several settlers and some of the Indians died from eating it. Because of this tragedy, the plant became known as the "Jamestown weed" or as we call it today, the jimsonweed. Other names for the plant include the mad apple, devil's trumpet, and stinkweed.

The stinkweed plant can be found in abandoned fields and back lots. It grows almost anywhere. You can recognize it by its wide-spreading branches, large oval leaves, and spiny fruit. The plant is so poisonous that some people break out in a rash if they accidentally touch it. One bite can kill you.

It is understandable for the Jamestown settlers to have unwittingly eaten the poisonous plant. They didn't know any better. Today no one would purposely cook up a stew of jimsonweed for family or friends, right? If only that were true. Both you and I have seen people's minds poisoned when fed meals of steamed gossip, stewed gripes, and boiled backbiting. And we've seen—and felt—the pain of such actions ourselves. Let's vow today that you and I will never be guilty of serving up such poisonous meals to our friends and families.

JUNE 3

MILLION DOLLAR PRICE TAG

The kingdom of heaven is like a merchant seeking beautiful pearls, who, when he had found one pearl of great price, went and sold all that he had and bought it. Matthew 13:45, 46, NKJV.

A friend of mine has made millions of dollars, lost millions, and made millions again during his lifetime. He drives Porsches and Mercedes; lives in a modest mansion, if a mansion can ever be modest; and jets about the world at will.

When I asked him about his success at making money, he laughed. "It's easy to make a million dollars—ya just gotta want it bad enough. It takes total commitment."

"Ya gotta want it bad enough"? *What kind of advice is that?* I thought to myself. *If that were true, everyone would be a millionaire*. I glanced about my three-bedroom bungalow and at my 12-year-old Chevy, which would find it difficult to make a trip to Omaha, let alone to an exotic and exciting locale. I fought to sweep away a thin, green streak of jealousy wrapping itself around my thoughts. Yet the more I mulled over my friend's remark, the more profound it became.

The next morning at the breakfast table as I filled my bowl with Total cereal, suddenly my friend's words made sense. That's when I discovered that I will probably never put myself out to earn the "big bucks." I can't imagine giving myself totally to that particular goal. I am, however, totally committed to another goal—heaven.

Jesus says, "You want to inherit the kingdom of heaven? Give Me your heart." That means total commitment. Today's text pictures Jesus as the pearl of great price, so valuable that the merchant sold everything he had in order to possess it.

If I can focus my total attention, my total energy, my total commitment, on Jesus and the kingdom of heaven and still be blessed with a million dollars or more, that's OK with Him. But if in order to get that million I must give my Jesus anything less than my total being, then the million-dollar price tag is just too expensive.

JUNE 4

HOT-TEMPERED FRIENDS

Do not make friends with a hot-tempered man, do not associate with one easily angered. Proverbs 22:24, NIV.

I read about a stray dog that wandered into the New York City Aquarium. No one knows quite how he managed to sneak undetected by the guards, but sneak he did. The story became even more incredible when, in the dog's wanderings, he tried to make friends with an electric eel by licking it. How the dog climbed up to the rim of the aquarium is another mystery. And why the eel paid any attention to his canine visitor, I don't know. However, the author of the book reported that the eel wasn't impressed with the dog's overtures of friendship and zapped him with a bolt of electricity. The resulting shock sent the dog flying up in the air. After spinning around in midflight, the dog hit the ground running, putting as much distance as possible between himself and the ill-tempered creature. While the author stated that the dog survived the jolting encounter, he didn't say what happened next in its life. I know that if I had been the dog, I would be more careful when choosing friends in the future.

While the canine in the story learned his lesson the hard way about choosing friends, you and I can learn from the advice of the wisest man who ever lived. King Solomon had a lot to say about friends and friendship. In the texts below, find the traits of character that should serve as red warning lights to us when choosing friends. For your personal worship, read the rest of the book of Proverbs to discover more advice on choosing friends wisely.

1. Proverbs 4:14
2. Proverbs 4:24
3. Proverbs 6:12-15
4. Proverbs 6:16-19
5. Proverbs 11:9
6. Proverbs 12:13
7. Proverbs 12:15
8. Proverbs 12:20
9. Proverbs 13:1
10. Proverbs 13:10

JUNE 5

LIVING WATER

Whoever drinks this water will get thirsty again, but whoever drinks the water that I will give him will never be thirsty again. John 4:13, TEV.

Here's a quiz to start your day. Imagine that you are walking across the Mojave Desert of California. You've had nothing to eat or drink for three days when on the horizon you see a mirage. But it isn't a mirage at all. It's a gas station and convenience store combination. Dehydrated, you stumble into the store and gasp, "Grape Nehi, please!" or perhaps "Caffeine-free Diet Pepsi, please!" Maybe you ask for a can of Orange Crush.

Not likely. Anyone who has ever been truly thirsty knows that nothing quenches thirst like a glass of fresh, plain, old H_2O—water. Actually, there's nothing plain about the substance called water. And a glass of fresh water? There is no such thing on this earth. *Fresh* water does not exist. The water coming from your tap has been around since Creation. Every droplet of water on the earth today was here when Jesus used some of it to make mud to place on the blind man's eyes. The same molecules of water pelted the roof of Noah's ark and threatened to drown Jonah. Think about it—you and Jesus drank from the same supply of water. You and He were baptized in the same molecules of water.

Next to soda pop or hot chocolate, water can seem plain and common, but to a chemist or physicist, biologist or engineer, it is one of the most marvelous and versatile substances on earth. Its lopsided molecular structure, H_2O (schematically, the one oxygen atom resembles the head of Mickey Mouse and the two hydrogen atoms are his ears), allows the molecules to behave like little magnets. Water literally yanks matter out of other substances. Picture what happens when you drop a sugar cube in a glass of water. The sugar crystals are wedged apart, or dissolved, by the water molecules.

We use water for almost everything. It is truly a life-giving compound that all life forms on earth need. Perhaps that is why Jesus used the miracle of water to describe the changes He makes when we let Him into our lives. He fills us with life-giving water so that we will never thirst again. This is the water He offered the woman at the well, and it is the water He offers you and me today.

JUNE 6

STREETS OF GOLD

And the main street was pure, transparent gold, like glass. Revelation 21:21, TLB.

Imagine walking on a road paved with gold ore. There is such a road—and on this earth. I walked on it. It's the "Million-Dollar Highway," between Silverton and Durango, in western Colorado. When I walked on this road, I was disappointed. It didn't look any different than any other I'd ever seen. The gold ore had been covered with tar.

Back in the 1800s the veins of gold in the mountains of western Colorado were so rich with pure gold ore that the miners didn't want to waste time on the lower grades of gold ore that they dug from the earth. This lesser-quality ore would cost too much to process, so they tossed it aside.

When the road builders came through, they used the discarded ore as a foundation for the roadway. Thus the highway is called The Million-Dollar Highway. The first time I heard of this fabulous road, I was eager to see it and walk on it. I drove a very long distance from Albuquerque, New Mexico, in order to satisfy my curiosity. But once I saw the road and had myself photographed while standing on it, I lost interest.

There are some people who would have you believe that heaven will be like that—an interesting place to visit where one can float on clouds all day, strumming away on a harp. Boring!

The Bible gives us a very different view of heaven. It talks about streets of gold, gates of pearl, and of a city built on layers of sparkling jewels. All these phenomena will be exciting to see. But tell me, does it really matter to you if the streets you walk on every day for the next billion years and beyond are covered with gold or concrete? Or that the city's gates are made of one giant pearl? (Imagine the size of the oyster that grew the giant pearl!) So why did the Bible writers describe these wonders for us?

Maybe God wanted us to see how upside down our thinking is. After all, if gold is so abundant in heaven that it's used for paving the streets, or if one pearl is large enough to use as a city gate, perhaps God's children should spend less time worrying over gold and other riches and more time preparing to inherit the real treasure of heaven—Jesus. I am glad that heaven's treasure is a whole lot more than just glittery streets and the pearly gates. Aren't you?

JUNE 7

NO FACTORY GUARANTEE

Be merciful, just as your Father is merciful. Luke 6:36, NIV.

The television reruns continue about the perfect family—an easygoing obstetrician, his glamorous and successful lawyer wife, and their children. No matter how serious the problems are that they face each week, they solve them in about 20 minutes of air time, and with good humor to boot! Wouldn't it be great if real life were like that? Sometimes it's easy to forget that it's not, though.

The *Bill Cosby Show* isn't new. It's just one more in a long line of family-based situation comedies that portray ideal people dealing with difficult problems in a much too simple fashion. Does that make it bad? Probably not, if television viewers don't mistakenly expect their life and their problems to fall into such a predictable pattern.

Ken did, however. After watching reruns of such programs as *Little House on the Prairie* and the *Bill Cosby Show*, he would complain about having a father who was always too tired from working two jobs in order to keep food on the table and who had so little time to spend with him; he would gripe when his clothes weren't ready for him to wear, conveniently forgetting that his mother worked eight hours a day as a janitor in order to keep the kids in church school. He jawed about teachers who didn't seem to care and about the Pathfinder leader who just didn't try to understand him. Ken filled his life with a series of miseries until he really believed everyone was out to get him. He wasn't even certain about his best friend, Pete.

One day as usual, Ken was griping to Pete about the people in his life. "How can I be expected to be a good Christian? I could be if I had a dad like Dr. Huxtable or a mom like Caroline Ingalls."

His friend laughed. "Those aren't real people; you know that."

"Well, they could be."

"Yeah, and you could be a medical genius like the kid on *Doogie Howser* too," Pete replied. "People don't come with factory guarantees. You're not perfect, so why do you expect them to be?"

Pete's advice to Ken was right on. As the text says, be merciful—let people be people. Forgive their mistakes. And in doing so, they'll be more likely to forgive you yours.

JUNE 8

BLUE SKIES

And I saw a new heaven and a new earth: for the first heaven and the first earth were passed away; and there was no more sea. Revelation 21:1.

Remember in kindergarten when the other kids would laugh at the child who dared to paint his sky red or green instead of blue? Well, surprise of surprises, skies aren't always blue everywhere. When you look at a picture of outer space, the area between the stars is black. It's only on earth that the heavens appear to be blue. That's because our planet has something that doesn't exist on the moon or in outer space—an atmosphere. It's the sunlight interacting with the atmosphere that makes the sky blue. Sunlight is composed of a rainbow of colors. Somehow the air filters the blue light from the white sunlight, making the color of blue visible to us. It does this by the nature of the particles that make up the air: various gasses, water, and dust. These particles scatter the sunlight. The veil of blue you see in the Blue Ridge Mountains of Virginia or the Blue Mountains of Washington is a result of this artistic effect of nature.

OK, enough of the science lesson this morning. Let's do some "blue-skying" (that's what people in the business world call dreaming). What is heaven's atmosphere like? If God is creating a "new heaven and a new earth," do you think this might include the atmosphere? If so, wouldn't it be exciting if He made the sky some color other than blue? What about plum purple? Or lemon yellow? Or strawberry red? Or maybe God has an entirely new rainbow of colors to add to our vision. Maybe we'll get to help name the new shades and variations. There are some new ideas to add to your God book.

Right now we can only imagine and dream. Yet the reality of God's new heaven and new earth will be so much better than our wildest dreams or most far-out imaginings that there's no danger of our ruining the surprise. I don't know about you, but I can hardly wait to see, hear, taste, smell, and touch the exciting new adventure God is preparing for us. What about you?

JUNE 9

THE FUNERAL

Glory in his holy name; let the hearts of those who seek the Lord rejoice. 1 Chronicles 16:10, NIV.

Martin ignored the singing birds outside his bedroom window. He paid no attention to the blossoming petunias in the window box. Dragging himself from bed, he washed, dressed, and made his way to breakfast. For a long time he had been discouraged. It seemed as if nothing could make him smile. His family and friends couldn't figure out just what was depressing him so. His wife, Kate, had tried to break through his constantly rotten mood. Nothing had worked. Instead, Martin spread gloom and doom wherever he went.

He entered the empty kitchen and glanced about. Just where was Kate, he wondered. He inhaled the aroma of freshly made bread. Even this didn't make him smile. Suddenly he heard a noise and turned around. Standing in the doorway was Kate. Dressed up as if she were going out, she wore black from her head to her toe. Martin scowled.

"Are you going somewhere this morning?"

"No," she replied and went about preparing breakfast.

"Well, then, who died?" he asked, referring to her totally black outfit.

"Martin," Kate answered with a wide-eyed innocence, "the way you've been acting lately, I thought God must have died, so I came prepared for His funeral."

Martin Luther, the great Reformer, winced at his wife's pointed rebuke. Kate was right. Only the death of his heavenly Father warranted the misery he had been spreading among family and friends. As a result, Martin vowed never to allow the troubles of the world—or even his own troubles—to destroy his happiness and praise to God. If you seek God, rejoice, laugh, and sing, for God is eternal. Therefore, there is always something about which to be thankful.

When was the last time you praised God when you didn't feel like it? If you wait until you feel like it, the time may never come. Today is the day to praise Him. Today is the day to shout "Thank You, Jesus!" And your thank You list will be endless.

JUNE 10

SINGING SANDS OF SCOTLAND

Let heaven and earth praise him, the seas and all that move in them. Psalm 69:34, NIV.

Eric imagined the fine Scottish sand castle he'd build. His castle would sport turrets, a moat, and a perfect drawbridge. He had traveled with his uncle Charley to the isle of Eigg, off the coast of Scotland. While Eric's uncle had come to hear the legendary "singing sands," Eric had but one thought in mind—building the best sand castle in the whole world.

At first the white sandy beach on the rocky and isolated island seemed like any other beach until it was walked on or touched. This is when the sand produces a musical sound—not just one sound or one note, but musical tones ranging from high soprano to low bass.

Eric couldn't believe his ears. All thoughts of sand castles dissolved with the first note he heard. "This is incredible! How does it work?"

"Well, Eric, from what I understand, the singing sounds are believed by some scientists to be the result of the structure of the sand itself." Uncle Charley bent down and ran a handful of grains through his fingers. They tinkled like wind chimes. "Look, the grains of sand are made up of tiny pieces of the mineral quartz, which the sea has ground into a rounded shape. Each grain is surrounded by a minute pocket of air; the friction between the grains sets off a vibration that creates a musical note." Uncle Charley rolled a few grains around in his hand.

"The musical note varies according to the amount of moisture in the atmosphere and the amount of pressure being applied. Any amount of dust or foreign matter present in the air will alter the sound—even a pinch of wheat flour can change the tone."

Eric experimented with the sand by tossing it in the air, dribbling it through his fingers, treading on it and letting it run through his bare toes. The resulting music fascinated him for hours. Before he realized it, he had to leave in order to catch the evening ferry back to the mainland. So many questions ran through his mind. Why had the sand been produced only in this one remote place? And why the music?

On the ferry ride back, whenever he thought of the singing sands of Scotland, Eric couldn't help humming the music to the old Christian hymn "I Sing the Mighty Power of God." Whether the birds of the air or the sands of the earth—all give praise to their Creator.

JUNE 11

THE CAT CAME BACK

When he came to his senses, he said, "How many of my father's hired men have food to spare! . . . I will set out and go back to my father." Luke 15:17, 18, NIV.

Jenny Woods cried into her pillow. At suppertime her parents announced that the family was moving from their home in Anderson, California, to a farm in Gage, Oklahoma. Jenny didn't mind moving to the farm. She even thought she'd like it. She was crying because her father had also announced that Sugar, Jenny's cream-colored Persian cat, wouldn't be able to make the trip. Sugar hated to travel to the point of becoming wild and uncontrollable, even during the shortest trip to the veterinarian for shots.

As the plans progressed, Jenny reluctantly accepted the fact that Sugar would have to stay behind. When the moving day arrived, Jenny handed Sugar to her next-door neighbor. The neighbor lady assured the child that she'd love Sugar for the rest of her life. Jenny pressed her face against the car window and sobbed.

"Don't worry, honey," her father reassured her as their former neighbor and Sugar disappeared from sight. "We'll get you another cat once we get settled in Oklahoma."

"But that cat won't be Sugar," Jenny wailed.

As the miles rolled by, Jenny pushed her pain aside to make room for her building excitement about their new home. The new farm was everything Jenny had dreamed of. She loved her new room, her school, and her new friends. She was totally happy until a month later when her mother received a letter from their former neighbor, saying that Sugar had vanished one night and had not come back home. Thirteen weeks later Jenny's mother was sweeping the front porch when a familiar golden ball leaped into her arms. It was Sugar. He had come home and had walked 1,500 miles to do it. How he'd done it, no one knew, but there was no doubt but that the cat was Sugar—even to his deformed right hipbone. Sugar knew where his home was, where his family was, where love was.

The young man in today's text knew where home was and where he'd find love—back with his father. You and I sometimes feel like we're a long way from home too. Unlike Sugar, it is we who have strayed away. But like the prodigal son and Sugar the cat, we too know how to find our way home to God and His love.

JUNE 12

HAPPY BIRTHDAY, GEORGE

Give everyone what you owe him: If you owe taxes, pay taxes; if revenue, then revenue; if respect, then respect; if honor, then honor. Romans 13:7, NIV.

Today is President George Bush's sixty-eighth birthday. Instead of celebrating Presidents' Day in February as most people do, I decided to be different and celebrate Presidents' Day on President Bush's special day—June 12. "Happy Birthday, George." George Bush is the second George in the history of the United States presidency. The first president with that name and the first president period, of course, was George Washington—or was he? Are you sure? Believe it or not, political experts argue about that fact. In 1781 a lesser-known American named John Hanson, from the colony of Maryland, became the first "president of the United States in Congress Assembled." In 1774 the colonies established a Continental Congress with delegates from each colony. This group of men voted into existence the Continental Army, under the leadership of George Washington. And on July 4, 1776, the Continental Congress issued the Declaration of Independence. They also issued the Articles of Confederation, which represented the laws of the new country. One of the articles stated that a delegate could be appointed "to preside" over the Congress, and in 1781 John Hanson was appointed.

George Washington himself congratulated Hanson, stating that he held "the most important seat in the United States." And between 1781 and 1789, seven other men followed him in that office. Washington didn't become president until Congress replaced the Articles of Confederation with the United States Constitution. In the years since the first George served as president, a succession of scoundrels and saints have run our country. Their popularity with the people never determined their greatness. Often even character had little to do with their success. Time has sorted out the good from the bad. Is President Bush a good president or a bad one? Will the man elected this fall be a great leader or a terrible one? Only time can really tell.

Perhaps that's why Paul gave the advice he did. Considering that the man who ruled Rome at that time was the hated Nero, Paul's advice was probably unpopular with his audience. Yet throughout time that same advice has served those well who love God. You and I serve God by honoring our nation's leaders, whether they deserve the honor or not.

JUNE 13

ANGELS GO CAMPING

The angel of the Lord encamps around those who fear him, and delivers them. Psalm 34:7, RSV.

Rhonda and Kelli leaned their elbows atop the picnic table and rested their chins in their hands as Daddy read from the Bible, "The angel of the Lord encamps around those who fear him, and delivers them."

"That is certainly an appropriate text for tonight," Mother said. "What with us camping out, it's nice to know that our angels are camped here with us."

Rhonda's gaze skimmed across the small man-made lake and up the jagged mountain that rose high above the valley floor. A cool breeze whipped across her bare arms as the hot June sun disappeared behind the mountain range. She rubbed her arms briskly and started at the sound of her name.

"Rhonda," Daddy repeated, "are you with us?"

"Huh? Oh, sure."

Daddy and Mother glanced toward one another and laughed. "I asked you what you saw when you thought about angels camping around—"

"I know, I know!" Kelli interrupted. "I see a circle of little white tents surrounding our camping trailer—kind of like the circle of covered wagons that would form when the pioneers stopped for the night."

"Very good, Kelli," Mother replied.

Rhonda scowled as another chill tingled up and down her spine. *It sure is getting cold*, she thought. "Well, I see a circle of little campfires around us. And two or three angels are sitting at each campfire—like the cowboys used to."

"That's very colorful too, Rhon," Daddy added. "However they're managing to guard us, we can be certain they are here because God promised. And He never breaks His word."

"OK, kids," Mother announced, "off to bed now."

(Story to be continued tomorrow.)

JUNE 14

CAMP UNDER SIEGE

Call upon me in the day of trouble; I will deliver you, and you will honor me. Psalm 50:15, NIV.

After thanking God for their protecting angels, Rhonda and Kelli kissed their parents good night and disappeared into the camping trailer. The girls could hear Daddy and Mother outside. They were discussing the disturbing news that Daddy had heard from the only other camper in the park. Bikers had terrorized the campers the night before, turning over trailers and tearing down tents. Most of the campers chose to leave rather than risk injury or danger.

"Perhaps we should pack and leave too," Mother said.

"The state police have been patrolling all evening," Daddy reminded. "Besides, where would we go? There isn't another campground for at least 150 miles. Come on, let's take a short walk down by the lake."

Rhonda and Kelli cheered silently when Daddy told them that he and Mother would be gone for a few minutes. As soon as their parents had walked a short distance from the trailer, the girls took out their penlights and Uno cards, and settled down for some serious play.

Their parents had been gone for less than 10 minutes when the girls heard the sound of revving engines. Before Rhonda and Kelli could think of what to do, a gang of tough-looking bikers roared up the hill—their boom boxes turned up as loud as possible. When one of the meanest-looking men hopped off his Harley-Davidson and strode up to the trailer, Rhonda leaped across the trailer to a side window. She scanned the shoreline, hoping to see her parents, but no one was in sight.

The invaders parked their bikes. "Let's trash it," one biker shouted.

"Let's ransack it first," another replied.

Inside the trailer Rhonda and Kelli huddled together, shaking with fear. Although the girls forgot the promise Daddy read during worship, they remembered to do the right thing. They prayed.

(Story to be continued.)

JUNE 15

THE RESCUE

For it is written, He shall give his angels charge over thee, to keep thee. Luke 4:10.

Suddenly the girls' eyes grew round with fear. Someone started shaking the trailer as if to overturn it. "Mama! Where's Mama?" Kelli wailed.

Rhonda peered out between the venetian blinds in the direction her parents had disappeared. "Look," she gasped, "Daddy's coming up the hill toward us."

Her relief turned to terror when the blaring radios suddenly died. Rhonda peeked out of the back window at the six massive men wearing grubby jeans, black leather jackets, and red bandannas, their arms firmly planted on their hips and glaring at the small man climbing the hill.

Then the girls heard their father's voice. "Excuse me, gentlemen, may I help you?"

May I help you? Rhonda thought. Just what could their 5-foot-11-inch teacher-father do to control these gigantic, evil-looking creatures? She could see her mother inching up the hill behind her father, but what could she possibly do to help? Maybe God would send the state police to stop them. Yet she had to admit that she could hear no approaching sirens.

An eerie silence descended over the deserted campsite as her father continued walking toward the trailer. For an exaggerated moment the men stood frozen in place. Their mouths and eyes flew open in terror. Suddenly, without a word, the six men leaped on their motorcycles and roared away in a cloud of dust and spitting gravel.

Rhonda and Kelli ran from the trailer into their parents' waiting arms.

"What happened, Daddy?" Kelli asked. "What made the men run like that?"

Daddy shook his head in bewilderment. "I honestly don't know."

"I think they saw our camping angels and got scared," Kelli announced.

Mother chuckled and tousled her daughter's long brown curls. "Maybe so, little one, maybe so."

"Do you think," Rhonda asked as she snuggled into the crook of her father's arm, "someday when we get to heaven we'll know?"

"You can be sure of that, princess," Daddy replied, giving her an extra big squeeze. "You can be sure of that."

JUNE 16

THE ULTIMATE DELICACY

There is a way that seems right to a man, but in the end it leads to death. Proverbs 14:12, NIV.

Imagine being invited out to dinner by a wealthy friend. He has arranged with an exclusive Japanese chef to treat you to the delights of fugu, especially for your pleasure. You discover that fugu, a type of fish, will cost your host $150 a person. Your friend describes for you the delicate, delicious flavor of this rare and exotic cuisine. "There's nothing better tasting in the entire world," he assures you. "And the fish's liver is the best part." He licks his lips in anticipation.

When you inquire about this fish dish called fugu, you learn that your friend is speaking of eating the raw flesh of the deadly puffer fish—one of the most poisonous creatures in the sea. Its poison is far more deadly than the chemical cyanide.

While the flesh may taste delightful, the poison's action on the victim is grim. First, the toxin acts on the nervous system. Your lips and mouth tingle, then the fingers go numb, and paralysis spreads throughout the body. Death may follow within minutes or may take as long as six hours. There is absolutely no antidote for the poison and no way to tell if the fish contains the toxin until it has been eaten. Not such a terrific delicacy after all, huh?

Puffer fish can be found around the world, and most are equally as deadly. Yet only the Japanese puffer fish seems to attract such fanatical devotion from its enthusiasts. They pray to it, build statues to it, and eat it. Yet Japanese fugu enthusiasts consume as much as $50 million worth of the ugly, vicious, and deadly fish every year.

"Friend or no friend! One hundred fifty dollars a plate or not! I'd be out of my mind to risk eating that stuff, right?" I agree. No way would I even consider trying even the tiniest morsel.

Your friend may never tempt you with $150 plates of fugu, but sooner or later a friend will try to lure you into trying other more common, yet deadly, poisons—such as crack, marijuana, cocaine, speed, and alcohol. I'd rather learn my lessons from other people's mistakes than suffer while learning from my own. What about you?

Today's advice works for more than just fugu and cocaine, you know. Think about it.

JUNE 17

OOPS! DID I SAY THAT?

There were also false prophets among the people, just as there will be false teachers among you. 2 Peter 2:1, NIV.

"Everything that can be invented has been invented!" This is the message that the director of the U.S. Patent Office sent to President William McKinley in 1889. He also recommended that the president abolish the office.

Thomas J. Watson, Jr., of IBM predicted in 1958: "There is a world market for about five computers." Professor A. W. Bickerton called the proposed flight to the moon "basically impossible." In 1896 one magazine author wrote: "The vast majority of people would prefer a smooth-running, reliable steam engine . . . to the evil-smelling, dangerous, wasteful, and at best uncertain and unreliable [gasoline] engine." A spokesman for the Daimler-Benz Company (granddaddy of the Mercedes-Benz Company) announced in 1900: "There will probably be a mass market for no more than 1,000 motorcars in Europe. There is, after all, a limited number of chauffeurs who could be found to drive them." During the next seven years Henry Ford sold 15 million Model T's.

In 1903 a preacher predicted, regarding air travel, "It is only for God and the angels to fly." The prophet's name was Bishop Milton Wright, father of Orville and Wilber.

"He will never amount to anything," one Munich teacher predicted about a high school student of his. The student? Albert Einstein. Thomas Edison was labeled a "dunce" by his father and "addle brained" by his first teacher. He himself described his invention the phonograph as "not of any commercial value."

In 1948 radio pioneer Mary Somerville predicted: "Television won't last. It's a flash in the pan." Newspaper editor C. P. Scott agreed. He wrote: "Television? No good will come of this device. For one thing, the word itself is half Greek and half Latin."

In December 1989 West German politicians confided to pop singer and actor David Hasselhoff that the Berlin Wall would still be in place long after their children and grandchildren had died. Two weeks later it came down.

Predictions come and go. The wise child of God heeds only those that speak according to God's law and the Bible testimony. The others, like poor Bishop Wright's, disappear like dust in the wind.

JUNE 18

A THIEF IN THE NIGHT

You will not fear the terror of night, nor the arrow that flies by day, nor the pestilence that stalks in the darkness. Psalm 91:5, 6, NIV.

A sound startled me awake. I lifted my head from my pillow and glanced toward the clock on the night table beside my bed—4:37 a.m. I listened. There it was again—someone was outside our window, walking on our graveled driveway. I elbowed my snoring husband. ''Honey, someone's outside.''

''Huh, umph, rumma, rumma grauble, grunt,'' he mumbled.

''Honey,'' I insisted, ''someone's outside.'' Again he replied in a nonintelligible form. Before I could poke him again, I heard the kitchen doorknob rattle and the back door open.

Did we even lock the doors last night? I wondered. Living on a rural academy campus, I hadn't worried much about home security—not until that moment, anyway.

I shook my sleeping husband's arm. ''Richard! Wake up!'' His reply was a variation on his last.

''Call 911,'' I told myself. The phone was on my husband's side of the bed.

I could hear someone moving about our kitchen. I heard him open the refrigerator, close it, then walk across the dining room and descend the three steps into our living room. He was less than 15 steps away from me. By now I saw a soft glow of a light flashing on the wall outside our bedroom door.

I knew I couldn't just lie there and be mugged in my bed. I tried to sit up, but my terror-frozen brain refused to send the proper signals to my muscles. *Maybe I am trapped in a nightmare*, I thought. After shaking my husband's arm once more and receiving no intelligent response, I decided any defense of home and hearth was up to me.

''Oh, dear Jesus,'' I prayed, ''I'm so scared. Help me know what I should do.''

(To be continued.)

JUNE 19

STOP! THIEF!

For you yourselves know very well that the Day of the Lord will come as a thief comes at night. 1 Thessalonians 5:2, TEV.

I forced myself to slip my feet out from under the covers and onto the plush carpet. As quietly as possible, I stood up and glanced about the darkened room. A glint of light from the window fell on one of my ornate brass candlesticks. Without thought for the consequence, I wrapped my fingers around the cool metal surface of one candlestick, removed the candle, and laid it on the dresser. Step by step, I inched toward the bedroom door, listening as my assailant tiptoed toward the same door from the opposite direction. By now I could see his shadow on the wall and the muted penlight glowing on the hall carpet. Once in position, I raised the candlestick high above my head and held my breath.

When the man's form filled the doorway, I screamed my loudest high C and swung. Chaos erupted from all over the house. First, my unsuspecting assailant shouted in terror. His hand gripped my wrists to prevent the candlestick from reaching its mark. Locked in combat and nose to nose, we shrieked in each other's faces.

I never heard the thud when my husband leaped from the bed and slammed his shins into the nightstand. His shout of pain along with the startled cries from our children, who had, moments before, been asleep in their rooms, joined the trespasser's and my yell to form a chilling choral concert in terror. Outside the back door our dog howled in response.

"It's me, Gary." A familiar voice broke through my sustained high C.

Gary, a former student, explained his presence. "I got an unexpected military leave and decided to take you up on your offer to visit any time. Since it was so late, I thought I'd slip in and stretch out on your sofa until morning, but I decided to let you know I was here so I wouldn't scare you." Gary wasn't a thief in the night—an enemy bent on destruction. He hadn't broken into our home; we'd invited him.

The Bible says that Jesus will return as a thief in the night for some people. Others will welcome Him with open arms. Since my husband and I invite our Friend, Jesus, into our home and into our hearts every day of our lives, I can be sure that He will return, not as a thief, but as a friend.

JUNE 20

LEAST ATHLETIC SON

Forgetting what is behind and straining toward what is ahead, I press on toward the goal to win the prize for which God has called me heavenward in Christ Jesus. Philippians 3:13, 14, NIV.

Carl's family loved sports—of any kind. Both his mother and his father coached track in the city of Willingboro, New Jersey. In addition, Carl's two older brothers excelled at track. Small for his age and shy, Carl seemed to have been the only member of the family not talented in sports of any kind.

At 15 Carl began to grow. He grew so fast that he had to walk on crutches for three weeks to give his body time to adjust to his new height. His coordination and skills on the track seemed the only thing capable of keeping pace with his phenomenal growth spurt. By 1981 he ranked number one in the world for the 100-meter dash and in the long jump. In 1983 he won the 100- and 200-meter dash and the long jump at the U.S. National Championships and qualified for four events at the 1984 Los Angeles Olympics, at which he matched Jesse Owens' 1936 record of winning four gold medals.

In the first two rounds of the 100-meter event, Carl scored far better than his two leading opponents, Sam Graddy of the United States, and Ben Johnson of Canada. In the final round Graddy and Johnson were out faster. Graddy stayed in the lead until the 80-meter mark. Graddy thought to himself, *Hey, I'm going to win the gold medal.*

Then suddenly Graddy saw Carl Lewis out of the corner of his eye. Lewis passed and pulled away so strongly from his nearest opponents that his winning margin was a remarkable eight feet—the widest in Olympic history. Later Lewis learned that he'd been clocked doing 28 miles an hour during that race.

Carl could have excused himself for not excelling in sports by saying: "I'm a shrimp and a klutz. Everyone says I'm nonathletic" or "I'm way behind the other guys running the race." And he would have been right—if he'd stopped trying at that point in his life. But he didn't. Instead, he left the past behind and looked forward toward the prize—the Olympic gold—and won.

Have you ever heard people make excuses as to why they didn't do something as well as they had hoped? Or excuse away their bad behavior with "I can't be a good Christian—look at my father" or "My mother's an alcoholic" or "I'm too poor"? Any excuse will do. But none will work with today's text. Leave the past behind and go for the gold!

JUNE 21

TUESDAY NIGHT FIREWORKS

And Enoch walked with God. Genesis 5:22.

"There he is!" Richard squealed and shouted. "Daddy's coming!" he continued as he dashed out the front door and down the porch steps to meet his father. Throughout supper Mother needed to remind 7-year-old Richard again and again to slow down, to not eat so fast, and to chew his food thoroughly.

After supper and family worship, Richard grabbed his sweater while his father grabbed his hat. Together, hand in hand, they walked out of the house and down the street toward the elevated subway station. Their topics of conversation were predictable. First, Father would ask Richard about his day. Then Father would tell all about his. Then they'd walk along silently, with Father waving occasionally to neighbors they passed.

Richard straightened his shoulders and walked a little taller beside his father. He knew that the people in the community respected the man. Father was a colporteur. He had sold books to and prayed with almost everyone they met. While he greeted each person he met with a big smile, Richard secretly hoped they wouldn't meet anyone who would keep his father talking long enough to make them late for the beginning of the fireworks display.

They reached the subway station in time to catch the train headed for the island. Usually there were no seats left by the time the train reached their station, so Richard held on to his father's hand extra tightly so as not to get separated by the standing crowd of people. Once they arrived at their exit, they got off the train and weaved their way through the people milling about the fun park.

Richard didn't beg for a carnival ride. That would come later—one merry-go-round ride after the fireworks, then home. It was always the same, and that's the way Richard liked it—he and his father spending special time together.

When Richard reads the biblical account of how Enoch walked with God, he remembers his Tuesday night journeys to see the fireworks at Coney Island—walking with his father, holding his hand, talking together. And he thanks God for the gift of a Christian father.

Today is Father's Day. What activities do you and your father share that help the two of you to become better acquainted? What do you do that helps you become better acquainted with your heavenly Father?

JUNE 22

PERFUME OF FAITHFULNESS

He shall grow as the lily, and cast forth his roots as Lebanon. . . . They that dwell under his shadow shall return; they shall revive as the corn, and grow as the vine: the scent thereof shall be as the wine of Lebanon. Hosea 14:5-7.

"Noble Alexander," the Cuban officer snarled, "you will admit to being a spy for the American CIA, or we will see just how long your God will save you." With that the soldiers threw Noble Alexander into the prison's sewage pond. The filthy water reached his chin. The young Seventh-day Adventist pastor prayed for strength to endure yet another torture in Castro's prison.

I must keep my chin up high enough, he thought, his nostrils pinching together from the terrible odor, *or this contaminated water will get into my eyes or my mouth. The resulting infection will kill me. No! I will not die in prison. I will die free!* Noble had heard about others who had experienced the same torture and had died from disease and infection because the filth had entered their mouths. He discovered that he could almost touch the bottom of the sewer if he stood on tiptoes. Time passed by slowly. He had no idea how long he would be kept in this horrid environment. Could he survive? he wondered. Did he really want to survive? Was it worth surviving just to spend another day in the dreaded Communist prison?

Perhaps he was tempted to pray the prayer Jesus prayed while on the cross: "My God, my God, why have you forsaken me?" Whether or not he prayed those exact words is unimportant. For that's how he felt—forsaken, alone, and defeated. Noble doesn't know how long he was there before something other than the floating sewage caught his attention. He saw a plant—a pure, white lily—growing up out of the filth. He studied it, captivated by the miracle of the stubborn little plant. In spite of its dreadful surroundings, the flowering lily blossomed clean and pure. He could smell the sweet perfume of the flower above the odor of the sludge surrounding him.

The lily's fragrance became a precious promise to the tortured servant of God. God had not deserted him. Noble knew without a doubt that his God still reigned, even amid the filth of the Cuban prison. When the officials finally removed him from the pond, Noble's faith was stronger than ever. Through a lily God reminded Noble that he was still safely in His care.

JUNE 23

GOD'S CURE-ALL

Praise the Lord, O my soul, and forget not all his benefits. He forgives all my sins and heals all my diseases. Psalm 103:2, 3, NIV.

When was the last time you had the flu? Remember how miserable you felt—chills, high fever, your head throbbed and your entire body ached with pain? Perhaps your mother called the doctor and he advised you to stay in bed, drink lots of liquids, and take some children's pain medicine. Normally staying in bed would be a most horrible punishment, but when you feel so sick, you'll do anything in order to feel better, right? Perhaps your Aunt Frieda suggested that you drink some of her hot herb tea. Or maybe Grandma Frazer advised your mother to rub your back and chest with a smelly lotion. If you felt miserable enough, you probably begged your mother to at least try each suggestion. After a few days your flu ran its course, and your discomfort lessened. Within a week you were back at school, a little paler and perhaps a little thinner, but not too much worse for wear.

Well, if you were living in London in 1665 instead of 1992, your bout with sickness would probably have had a different ending. Instead of feeling better after a few days, your condition would worsen. You'd break out with a rash that would develop into open sores. Swellings under your armpits would develop, and your lower abdomen would ache. In time the disease would reach your lungs, making it hard for you to breathe. The symptoms I've described are not flu symptoms, but those of the Bubonic Plague. And we think we have it bad!

Yet even today new diseases appear that send scientists scurrying to their microscopes and test tubes. Just as soon as medical experts congratulate themselves for finding a cure for one form of illness, a new strain develops. The psalmist says, "Praise God—He's the one who can heal all of your diseases." He offers to give us the only sure cure for the ugly disease of sin. The cure is eternal life.

JUNE 24

GOTCHA!

We cannot understand the great things he [God] does. Job 5:9, TEV.

Let's play a mind-reading trick this morning. Got a piece of paper and pencil handy? Here goes. Write down any three-figure number in which each succeeding figure is smaller than its predecessor (example: 752). Reverse that number (257). Now subtract the smaller from the larger (752 − 257 = 495). Reverse that number (594). Add the last two numbers together (495 + 594). And your answer is 1,089. I read your mind, right? No, not really. No matter what three-figure number you chose to begin with, if you did the problem correctly, your answer would be 1,089.

Here's another game you can play on your friends that involves an optical illusion. On a rectangular card print carefully the following letter-number sequence: S6I5NC5. Now take a second card and place it over the bottom half of the letter-number sequence. When your friends look at just the top half of the sequence, they will think they are seeing the top of the word *SCIENCE*. Their brains will automatically fill in the familiar word. They will be imagining things that aren't there or jumping to a conclusion, a very dangerous sport indeed.

If you've ever seen a magician "float" a pretty lady in midair, you might have wondered how he could possibly be breaking the laws of gravity to do such a thing. Well, wonder no longer. The magician has a special piece of equipment similar to the hydraulic lift used for repairing cars. The majority of the machine is behind the curtain. The part out front is a flat board, upon which the woman lies. However, extending back from the board and behind the curtain is an S-shaped arm that is attached to the machine. So when the magician waves his magic wand, the lift raises the woman's body to the level of the magician's waist. Notice, the woman is probably wearing a full-skirted dress to drape over the edge of the board so as to hide the connections beneath the board. The flat S-shaped arm allows the magician to pass the hoop first over one end of the floating woman, then over the other, thus making you think she is truly floating. Sneaky, huh?

Tricksters fool their stunned audiences by using a handful of knowledge, a piece of rigged equipment, and optical illusions. You and I can uncover their secrets in no time.

God's wonders don't work that way. The more we study His wonders, the more mysteries we uncover. That's one reason heaven will never be boring. You and I will have an eternity of exciting "magic" to study and appreciate.

JUNE 25

THE HUMAN CALCULATOR

I remind you to keep alive the gift that God gave you when I laid my hands on you. 2 Timothy 1:6, TEV.

How many years, days, and hours have you lived? If you're like me, you just shrug your shoulders and grunt, "I dunno." When Thomas Fuller was asked that question, he answered in a minute and a half. He said 70 years, 17 days, and 12 hours. His questioners challenged his answer until he reminded them that they hadn't taken into account leap years. Thomas Fuller, born in West Africa in 1710, was shipped to Virginia as a slave and remained illiterate his entire life.

Another gifted mathematician was Carl Friedrich Gauss. On his first day of school Carl's teacher became upset with the young boy because the child answered each of the arithmetic problems before the teacher could finish dictating them.

Vito Mangiamele, the son of an Italian shepherd, could figure out the cube root of 3,796,416 in less than a minute. The answer is 156, if you're interested. He did this before the French Academy of Sciences at the age of 10.

Wow! Talk about feeling stupid! I use my hand calculator to tabulate my groceries each week. Maybe my problem lies in the fact that I'm more right-handed than left-handed. Scientists have discovered that these human calculators are often left-handed. So all you lefties out there, maybe you can develop your brain in such a way too.

If you're not a mathematical genius, don't despair. You have a lifetime to uncover the other talents God has given. Yet there is one gift that we all share once we give ourselves to God. That is the gift of the Holy Spirit. And while our talents in mathematics, art, music, and sports have limits, there is no limit to what you can accomplish through the gift of the Holy Spirit.

JUNE 26

THE CANOE TRIP

A good name is better than fine perfume. Ecclesiastes 7:1, NIV.

Kathy's ebony curls and dimpled smile set 12-year-old Joel's heart a-flutter as he anticipated the Pathfinder outing on the North Umpqua River. On the day of the outing Kathy and Joel were assigned to a four-person canoe with Kathy's best friend, Pam, and her boyfriend, Billy. During the first part of the trip down the river, the nine canoes stayed together. There was the usual amount of splashing and horseplay associated with water sports. As the newness of the adventure wore off, the canoeists settled down to enjoy the ride.

Just before noon, dark clouds formed, shrouding the sun. A wind arose, churning the river into a challenge for the amateur canoeists. Within minutes a drenching rainstorm hit. Mr. Hicks, the Pathfinder leader, waved the young people toward shore. Unfortunately, Joel and Kathy's canoe hit a snag. The current whipped the boat about, hitting the main rush of water and hurtling them downstream—backward. One big wave snatched the paddles from the boys' hands and sent them into the swirling water. They didn't know how long the river bashed them about until the canoe slammed into a sandbar. The sudden stop tossed all four of them from the canoe into the shallow water.

Already soaked by the continuing rainstorm, the two couples waded out of the river and onto the rocky shore, dragging their crippled canoe behind them. Cold and wet, they searched for a shelter from the wind and rain. Joel noticed that halfway up the craggy cliff that loomed over the river, there were a number of dark holes that looked like they might be caves. Billy gave Joel a sly look as he announced, "Pam and I will take the cave on the left; you two take the one on the right. Know what I mean, man?"

Joel knew what Billy meant—all too well. He glanced toward Kathy in time to see her blush. Everyone knew of Billy's and Pam's reputation for "making out." He'd heard Billy bragging in the locker room. He'd heard rumors about Kathy, too. It made Joel feel uncomfortable when the guys snickered about Kathy and Pam. And while he might not mind taking a canoe trip with Kathy, she probably wouldn't be the girl he'd choose as a special friend—reputation or not. Yet he knew that when he got back, the other guys would demand a full report.

How did I get myself into such a mess? he wondered as he led the way to their assigned cave.

(Story to be continued.)

JUNE 27

IN THE CAVE

He knows the secrets of the heart. Psalm 44:21, NIV.

Kathy scrambled into the cave after Joel. After exploring their temporary refuge thoroughly, the two of them settled down on the ground near the mouth of the cave. From there they could see the river below should Mr. Hicks come searching for them before the rain stopped.

Kathy wrung the water out of the hem of her sweatshirt and pushed her bedraggled curls from her forehead. Her teeth chattered as she huddled against one wall. "Boy, it sure is chilly."

"Here." Joel whipped his nylon windbreaker off and wrapped it around Kathy's shoulders. "This should help keep you a little warmer."

"Oh, no, you need it."

"Hey, it's an oversized one. It's my dad's. We'll share it."

Joel put his arm around Kathy's shoulders and wrapped the leftover portion of the jacket around his own shoulders. "You can't risk developing hypothermia, you know."

Joel liked having Kathy so close. The fragrant odor of Kathy's shampoo accosted his senses. He thought about Billy and Pam in the other cave. An unexpected breeze brushed across Kathy's arm. She snuggled closer. He glanced at her out of the corner of his eye. She was looking at him and biting her lower lip expectantly. *Big deal*, he reasoned. *Here I am sitting with a pretty girl in a cave in the middle of the forest. She expects me to kiss her. I'd have to be deaf, dumb, and blind not to know what's on her mind. It's not like I'd be the first guy to kiss her. And I certainly won't be the last.*

A persistent thought nagged at his mind. *Admit it, Joel. It's the setting, not the girl. In a normal situation you wouldn't choose to be with Kathy. She's just convenient, that's all*, the voice reminded. *That's not fair to Kathy or to you, in fact.*

"So who would know?" Joel snapped.

"Did you say something?" Kathy inquired.

Joel shook his head vigorously. "Huh? Oh, oh, no . . . nothing."

(Story to be continued.)

JUNE 28

BUILDING ARKS

Noah did everything just as God commanded him. Genesis 6:22, NIV.

Long before he climbed the cliff to the cave, long before he made the canoe trip down the river with Kathy, Joel had made some important decisions. Months earlier the church pastor had given a Week of Prayer talk at school about ways to plan now for a happy home. Pastor Roberts related the story of Noah.

God told Noah to build an ark, a place of safety, for the members of his family—his wife and children. "But did you know," the pastor asked, "that God's command came 20 years before Noah's first son was born? Talk about planning for one's family! You too are making choices today that affect the happiness of your future home. Like Noah, you are building an 'ark of safety' for your own children, for the person you will one day marry."

He continued: "The best way to 'build' your ark of safety is to develop respect for yourself and for members of the opposite sex—for other people, no matter who they may be. Misuse of drugs, premarital sex, cheating in school, laziness, quitting too easily, reading magazines or watching stories that cheapen marriage and make fun of purity, are all dangers directly designed to strip away your self-respect and your respect for other people."

Inside the mouth of the cave Joel thought about Pastor Roberts and about Noah's 20-year plan as he stared out into the pouring rain. Suddenly he started as if burned by a hot poker. Kathy had kissed his cheek and was gently turning his face toward hers. His face reddened.

"No, Kathy. I'd rather not."

"What's the matter? Don't you like me?"

"Believe it or not," Joel said as he removed her hand from his cheek and clasped it between his two larger hands, "it's because I like you that I won't make out with you. You're a nice girl—too nice to mess around with just any guy."

"Well!" Her eyes filled with tears as she leaped to her feet. "Of all the arrogant . . ."

Joel looked up into Kathy's eyes. "Come on. Sit back down and let me tell you about the ark I'm building."

JUNE 29

THE HEALING PLANT

There is a way that seems right to a man but in the end it leads to death. Proverbs 16:25, NIV.

Terror followed the hated plague as it rampaged its way through Europe. The first scourge hit Europe a few hundred years after the apostle Paul died. In the city of Rome alone, an estimated 5,000 people a day died from the disease. In 1334 the plague swept across Europe, India, and China; one out of every three people in England and Europe died from the disease. In the 1660s it again ravaged Europe. As late as 1894 the plague broke out in the port of Hong Kong. Ships with contaminated crews spread the disease. Ten million people died in India alone during this epidemic. One popular treatment for the dread disease was the "healing plant."

Medical experts around the world touted the "healing plant" not only for its properties for treating the plague but also as a cure for such unrelated diseases as cancer and for healing open sores, scabs, and battle wounds. Doctors recommended it for shrinking goiters and repairing broken limbs. The plant was proclaimed to be a miracle of modern science.

You and I know the "healing plant" today as tobacco. Can you imagine your family doctor today recommending you take up smoking to cure yourself of the flu or to heal your broken leg? Suppose he recommended that you begin chewing tobacco? You'd probably look for a different family doctor, huh? Instead, the people of America are constantly warned on television, in magazine articles, even by the U.S. surgeon general, that the use of tobacco is dangerous to one's health. And they're right. Tobacco is a poison. It kills—and often causes great suffering in the process.

While our doctors have the benefit of extended testing and studies, the scientists and physicians of the Dark Ages weren't trying to kill off their patients. These dedicated men truly believed they were right about tobacco, yet they were wrong—dead wrong.

Have you ever believed you were right about something and later learned you were mistaken? I have—all too often, in fact. That's why when it comes to the important issues in life, such as faith in God, Christian behavior, forgiveness of sins, death, the second coming of Jesus, eternal life, and such—you and I can't afford to be wrong. God's way is the only way.

JUNE 30

HONEY IN THE DESERT

Every one of you knows in his heart and soul that the Lord your God has given you all the good things that he promised. Every promise he made has been kept; not one has failed. Joshua 23:14, TEV.

Ruthie fretted a lot. Besides worrying, Ruthie grumbled, complained, and made dire predictions of disaster. To make matters worse, she was often accurate. At school she predicted that no one would want her on their softball team. She was right. At Pathfinders she just knew that when the kids buddied up for swimming, she'd be lone person out. She was right. Before Ruthie attended summer camp, she predicted that the other kids in her cabin wouldn't like her. You know what? She was right again.

At home, from the moment she entered the kitchen for breakfast in the morning until she kissed her mother and father good night, Ruthie whined and complained about first one terrible problem, then another. Ruthie's parents thought they'd go crazy with their daughter's constant complaining. Mother and Father had tried everything to break Ruthie of her habit of grumbling.

If her mother said, "Isn't it a pretty day?" Ruthie would reply, "I don't know; it's a little too warm for me." If her father suggested a family outing at the coast, Ruthie would sigh, "It'll probably rain." On days when everything was going well, Ruthie just knew something terrible was about to happen. If trouble brewed, Ruthie was certain things would soon get much worse. And if her predictions failed to materialize, the girl seemed to sulk even worse.

One day when Ruthie was complaining about how awful everything was, her mother interrupted. "Ruthie, let me tell you about two birds—the vulture and the hummingbird. Both birds fly over the California desert. One looks down and searches for rotting carcasses; the other searches for the fragrant flower half hidden in a cactus. And each bird finds exactly what it is looking for." Mother paused to let the idea sink in. "There's something good and something bad in every person, in every plan, in every dream. Remember, what you see is what you get. So look for the good."

It is important to look for the good, to look optimistically to the future, and to look at how the Lord has blessed you in the past.

JULY 1

RECORD-BREAKING PRAISE

What is man, that you think of him; mere man, that you care for him? Psalm 8:4, TEV.

The beginning of the 1992 Summer Olympics is only days away. Swimmers are swimming their last practice laps; runners are running their last practice meters; and gymnasts are reviewing their floor routines for the last time before leaving for Barcelona, Spain, where they'll compete for the gold, silver, and bronze medals and for the honor of being the best in the world.

Today, however, we'll put aside mankind's impressive Olympic records and learn a little about a few lesser-known record holders. In 1963 U.S. athlete Robert Hayes set the record for 100-yard sprinting at 27 mph. Yet an everyday cheetah can run an average of 56 mph and can sprint at more than 60 mph. Even greyhounds and red foxes sprint along at more than 40 mph. Zhu Jianhua of China set the world's high jump record at 7 feet 10 inches in 1984. However, a native Australian, the Australian red kangaroo, jumped over a 10-foot-high stack of lumber in 1965. Impressive!

In 1984 the world's weight-lifting record was set by the U.S.S.R.'s Alexsander Gunyashev, at 1,025 pounds, but gorillas have been known to lift as much as 1,800 pounds. And whereas humans can barely swim faster than five mph, sailfish can average 68 mph on a bad day. Even a penguin can move through the water at more than 10 mph.

And what Olympic athlete would want to compete against the common everyday flea in a long jump—weight for weight? While the long-jump record hovers around 29 feet, a flea can hop six inches into the air and cover as much as two feet in a single leap. Pound for pound, this jump would be the equivalent of a man leaping a quarter of a mile in one bound. Kind of puts human athletes in their places, huh? And we consider ourselves kings of the beasts, overseers of creation!

So why is God mindful of human beings if His other animals can run faster, leap farther, outswim, outsprint, outlift, even the fittest of humans? Because of their special gift—they are made in the likeness of their Creator. Monkeys look like other monkeys; giraffes, other giraffes; and zebras, other zebras. But people were made in the image of God.

JULY 2

THE BLUE FLASH

What is the way to the place where the lightning is dispersed, or the place where the east winds are scattered over the earth? Job 38:24, NIV.

Hester—a cat with long, yellow hair—lounged on the back of his master's sofa and stared out of the picture window one summer afternoon at a crew of workmen restoring phone service to the neighborhood after an electrical storm. The rains had stopped; sunlight filled the sky. Suddenly a softball-size ball of lightning appeared from nowhere, swirled across the street, and zapped the picture window. The ball hit Hester, broadside, producing a startling blue flash. The cat flew into the air and landed running.

The workmen rushed to the house and reported what they had seen to Hester's owner. The strange incident of the "blue flash" made international news. The reporters were quick to add that the cat was found a few minutes later, cowering under his owner's bed. He was apparently unharmed except for a few spots of singed fur. After that, Hester refused to go anywhere near the sofa and the picture window. Smart cat! When scientists were asked to explain the blue flash, they had many theories, but no proof. The phenomenon of lightning balls is still a mystery.

I've never seen a lightning ball, have you? But they do exist. One housewife from Smethwick, England, noticed a ball of violet hovering over her kitchen stove. Before she could decide what to do, the light floated across the room and touched her. She brushed it away. An explosion shook the room, and the ball vanished, burning a small hole in her dress and underwear.

In 1897 in the Midwest during a storm a farmer spotted pea-sized electric sparks at the ends of every twig on a tree. When he touched one, the spark transferred to his thumb; when he let go, the spark reappeared on the twig, yet he felt no shock. In Cordoba, Spain, in 1892, immediately following a flash of lightning, large drops of rain fell and each one, on hitting the ground, emitted a spark and a faint crack. Curious, huh?

God reminded Job that we don't know everything, even about the simplest of nature's elements. I'm glad I don't have to worry about the mysteries of the universe, that my God is big enough to handle them all, including Hester's blue flash.

JULY 3

DIRTY FARMER

You call him Father, when you pray to God, who judges all people by the same standard, according to what each one has done. 1 Peter 1:17, TEV.

The travel-weary man entered the main lobby of an elegant Baltimore hotel. The hotel manager eyed the traveler critically as he approached the reservation desk. *A dirty farmer*, the manager thought in disgust.

"Excuse me, sir," the traveler said, "I need a room for the night." The manager stared down his nose at the man and sniffed. "We have no room for you, sir."

The farmer, appearing not to have heard the stuffy manager's remarks, repeated his request and got the same answer. The man then turned around, ordered that his horse be resaddled and brought to the front door of the hotel, then departed. Watching the entire exchange, a second traveler, dressed in expensive clothes and carrying himself with style, strode up to the counter.

"Sir," the second traveler said to the hotel manager, "do you know who that man was—the one who just left your establishment?"

"No," the manager lifted his nose a tad higher and added, "and do I care?"

"Perhaps," the wealthy traveler said. "That man was Thomas Jefferson, the vice president of the United States."

"The vice president of the United States?" the manager wailed. "I didn't know!"

The manager sent his servants after Mr. Jefferson to tell him that the best of everything at the hotel was his. The servants reported back to the manager that they'd located Jefferson in another hotel in town.

"He said to tell you, sir," the servant explained, "that while he values good intentions highly, if you have no room in your hotel for a dirty farmer, you have no room for the vice president of the United States."

Thomas Jefferson, later to become the third president of the United States, taught the hotel manager a valuable lesson. Don't judge people by the clothes they wear. Perhaps it's a lesson you and I need to learn also.

JULY 4

LET FREEDOM RING

Everyone who sins is a slave to sin. Now a slave has no permanent place in the family, but a son belongs to it forever. So if the Son sets you free, you will be free indeed. John 8:34-36, NIV.

"This is the Fourth?" The 83-year-old man struggled to lift his head off the down-filled pillow. It was 11:00 p.m. on July 3, 1826, and Thomas Jefferson, the author and signer of the Declaration of Independence, had traveled to Washington, D.C., to participate in the fiftieth anniversary of the great Declaration. Knowing how important the Fourth of July was to the old man, Nicholas P. Trist, a trusted, young lawyer friend, couldn't bring himself to say "Not yet," so he remained silent.

At the gong of midnight, Jefferson again asked, "This is the Fourth?" This time Trist nodded his assent.

"Ah," the old man breathed, a look of satisfaction crossing his face. He then fell into a coma. The next day, a little after noon, the third president of the United States died.

Unknown to Jefferson, the second president of the United States and the man who worked on the Declaration of Independence with him so many years previous, John Adams, died on the very same day at Adams' home in New England. Two men loved freedom so much that they were willing to risk their very lives for the cause of their newly formed country. Had these two favorite sons of America been caught by the British before the end of the Revolution, they would have been hanged. As a result of their love of freedom, they kindled the desire for freedom in the hearts of people around the world.

Jesus, the Son of God, risked more than everything. He risked all eternity; He gave all He had so that you and I could be free. Freedom—is it expensive? No, it's priceless.

SIMPLE DIRECTIONS

Thomas said to him, "Lord, we do not know where you are going; so how can we know the way to get there?" John 14:5, TEV.

Sara's excitement bubbled over the minute she entered the front door of her house. Pastor and Mrs. Niel had invited the church youth group to their horse ranch the next day for a Sunday of games, swimming, and horseback riding. All her friends were going.

After Sara explained her problem, her dad, who did not attend church with the rest of the family, asked, "So where does this Pastor Niel live?"

"Oh, don't worry. His daughter, Ana, told me how to get there."

Sara's father frowned. "Told you how to get there? Before I get up at some unearthly hour on Sunday morning and go traipsing about the countryside, I want to know where I'm heading."

Mother, who had been listening to the exchange, tried to interrupt. "Excuse me . . . ," she interjected repeatedly, but no one heard her.

"Aw, Dad," Sara groaned. "First, you take Powell Valley Road to Gresham, then take a right on the Mount Hood Highway. Go to Barnes Road and turn left," she paused. "Or was it right? No, no, turn left. Then go five miles until you come to a large school on the corner—turn right and . . . Wait, wait, wait—it was a firehouse. The school comes later," Sara explained. "Then go . . ."

"Hold it," Dad said. "Right now, if your directions are correct, we should be smack dab in the middle of the Columbia River. We need a map!"

"Would you two listen to me for a moment?" Mother dangled the church bulletin in front of her daughter's face. "I have a map that Mrs. Niel drew for me after church."

"Good!" Dad exclaimed. "Now we're getting somewhere."

That afternoon Sara thought about her dad and his insistence on having a map before making the trip to the pastor's house. *Hmm*, she thought, *if only Daddy would use the simple map God gave for living a happy, successful life—the Bible—maybe he wouldn't be so mixed up so often about where he is headed.*

Dad didn't know just how wise a daughter Sara really was. In time he learned and because of her faithful witness, Sara's dad began following God's map too.

JULY 6

NASTY ZACH

You may think that everything you do is right, but remember that the Lord judges your motives. Do what is right and fair. Proverbs 21:2, 3, TEV.

Big Zach wasn't always big. In fact, when Big Zach was a child, the other kids on the block teased him about being so little. They heckled the little boy so much that he vowed that one day he would get even, one day everyone would be sorry for being so mean. Luck and hard work paid off for Zach. When the grown-up Zach walked or drove down the streets of his town, the people no longer called out ugly names at him; instead, in fear, they glared at him from behind window shutters and spread nasty rumors. But he no longer cared, for Zach had become wealthy. He became rich by stealing from his neighbors. Best of all, as far as Zach was concerned, the neighbors knew Zach was stealing their money but could do nothing about it. This in turn made them hate him all the more.

Zach knew what the Bible says about stealing and lying and all those other sins he prided himself on doing. Yet while he knew he shouldn't do those things, inside he argued that by robbing his neighbors he was exacting little enough payment for the pain and discomfort he'd experienced when his snooty neighbors had looked down on him over the years. So instead of worrying over his guilt, every time he was shunned in his community, he just chuckled to himself, patted his wallet, and hurried on his way.

Zach would probably have lived his entire life as the hated, evil man he'd become if it hadn't been for one man's sudden appearance in Zach's life.

One day as Zach hurried from his office, he noticed that the villagers barely noticed his presence. They weren't taking the time to glare or to growl at him. They weren't even avoiding him. Instead, they were pushing and shoving right past him. Eavesdropping, he discovered that a Celebrity was coming into town.

(Story to be continued.)

JULY 7

BIG ZACH

If he [the evil man] stops sinning . . ., if he returns the security he took for a loan or gives back what he stole . . ., he will not die. . . . I will forgive the sins . . . , and he will live. Ezekiel 33:14-16, TEV.

The minute he learned of the Preacher's arrival, Zach knew he had to see the Man. For months Zach had been keeping track of the Man's rise to fame. Zach felt almost a kinship to the Man, considering the way the government and church officials were treating Him. Yet Zach knew that that's where the similarities between the two men stopped. For the Preacher had something Zach wanted, and Zach was determined to get it.

"Get out of my way." Zach tried to elbow first one person then the other out of his way, but no one would budge. Instead, the townspeople formed a barrier, making it even more difficult for Zach to break through. *Just like 'em*, Zach grumbled to himself. *But I won't let them stop me, not this time*. Suddenly Zach stopped right in the middle of the road.

"I know what I'll do," he said. "Get out of my way," he growled.

Zach remembered a tree—a sycamore tree he'd climbed as a child whenever he felt alone and mistreated.

You remember the rest of the story. Zach climbed the tree. Jesus, the preacher, passed beneath the tree and called for Zacchaeus to come down out of the tree. Zacchaeus gave his heart to Jesus that day. Good story, huh?

Ah, but the rest of the story should not be overlooked. After being forgiven for his sins, Zacchaeus not only paid back all those he'd robbed, but gave them four times what he'd stolen. And that's how Nasty Zach became Big Zach. Can you imagine how shocked the townspeople were when Zacchaeus went door to door giving away bags of gold? Do you think they treated him the same afterward? Probably not. Remember Zach's lesson. It took a change in Zach to bring about a change in others. If you want someone in your life to change for the better, ask God to show you what changes you need to make first. You might be surprised at the results.

JULY 8

CATHY'S COOTIES

Jesus said, "Forgive them, Father! They don't know what they are doing." Luke 23:34, TEV.

"Cooties! Cooties! Cathy has cooties," Ben and his fourth-grade buddies chanted during the Vacation Bible School's morning play period. Even later when the junior-age group were busy making macrame pot holders, the whispered chant "Cathy the cootie" drifted from table to table.

Cathy was the outsider. You know about outsiders. Sometimes they are the newest kids in the class. Other times, they're the ones whose hair isn't styled just right, or they wear polyester pants instead of jeans, or they wear cotton sport shirts rather than the trendier sweatshirts. It doesn't take much to become an outsider, but it takes true courage to brave being an outsider.

All the other juniors had attended the same church since they were in cradle roll, and the same school since first grade. Cathy had walked in off the street, dragging her little sister beside her.

Now while they never discussed it, Ben and his friends knew they should be kind to Cathy. After all, wasn't the purpose of Vacation Bible School to witness to nonchurch members? But it was so much fun to show off by teasing girls, especially one they'd probably never see again once the week passed.

Lynn, one of the girls of the group, knew she should tell Ben to "bug off," to "get off Cathy's case." She should try to make friends with the outsider, but if she did, maybe the guys would begin harassing her, saying she had cooties. No, it was too dangerous to stick up for Cathy, who would be around only a few days. After all, Lynn would be attending school with Ben and his friends for years to come. Lynn's friends had similar thoughts. So day after day, the guys poked fun at Cathy and her cooties. And the girls stood by, pretending not to care.

(Story to be continued.)

JULY 9

LYNN LEARNS A LESSON

Lord, do not hold this sin against them. Acts 7:60, NIV.

Friday night Cathy and her little sister brought their father to the closing program. When the juniors lined up front to sing their theme song for the parents and other departments, Ben made a big show of moving as far from Cathy as possible. The other boys imitated him. Lynn noted the sudden flush on Cathy's face. Swallowing her fear, Lynn stepped in beside the embarrassed girl.

Throughout the program, Lynn's conscience needled her. She didn't feel very good about herself. She realized that she'd done too little too late to help Cathy. After the program, Lynn was standing at one of the craft tables when she overheard Cathy's father talking to the craft director.

"I have really appreciated being able to send Cathy and her sister to the Vacation Bible School programs this week. You see, I've spent the entire week with my wife. She's in the hospital—cancer. She probably won't make it.'' The man choked up, then continued speaking. ''Cathy volunteered to bring her little sister Zoe each day because Zoe loved the meetings so much. I think they got her mind off her mama's illness.''

Tears sprang into Lynn's eyes as she flew to the restroom. *Poor Cathy,* she thought, *we didn't know. I've got to find Cathy before she leaves*. Before Lynn could find Cathy and apologize, Cathy and her family were gone. Lynn never saw them again.

That night, in her room, Lynn prayed, ''Dear Jesus, forgive me. I didn't know what I''—Lynn stopped midsentence—''was doing. Oh,'' she gasped. She recognized the prayer Jesus prayed while on the cross and realized with a new certainty that He had prayed that prayer for more than just the Roman soldiers and the angry crowd. He had prayed that prayer for her.

Lynn never saw Cathy again. When Lynn went with the Vacation Bible School teacher to invite Cathy to church the next week, the house was empty. The family had moved.

Big Zach made amends for his sins. Lynn couldn't. All she could do was accept the forgiveness Jesus requested for her at the cross and pledge never to stand back and just let her friends or anyone else hurt a Cathy, a Jody, a Harold, or a Francis without trying to prevent it.

JULY 10

FOLLOW THE LEADER

"Come, follow me," Jesus said, "and I will make you fishers of men." Matthew 4:19, NIV.

The academy band members filed into the band room. Only an occasional whisper could be heard as the players removed their instruments from their cases and took their places. They'd blown it—not just their trumpets and saxophones, but the entire band had messed up badly at the last concert. And Mr. Clarke, the band director, was bound to be angry and would lecture them throughout the entire class period.

When Mr. Clarke came through the doorway, even the customary warm-up racket ceased. All eyes watched as he strode to the front of the room. There was no need for him to tap the music stand with his baton in order to gain everyone's attention. He already had it.

''Trumpet section, turn around and face the saxes. Woodwinds, face the wall on your left. Slide trombones and bass horns, face the wall on your right.'' He paused to give the band members time to follow out his instructions. "We'll begin rehearsal today with your favorite, 'Stars and Stripes Forever.' Oh, yes, percussion, I almost forgot; play whatever you like. Ready? A one, a two, a three . . ."

The band members played with all their might. Trumpets deafened the saxophonists. The bass horns oompah-pah-pahed from side to side to avoid being hit by a slide trombone. The flutes and the piccolo ended the chorus four measures behind everyone else. And the five members of the percussion section went wild doing their own thing. After the director shouted everyone to order, he said, "You are good musicians. You've put hours and hours into individual practice. Each one of you is a soloist in his or her own right, with the exception of you, Kandi. I've never been partial to cymbal solos myself." Everyone, including Kandi, laughed. "But to be a good band takes more. It takes working together. That's where the director comes in. Me—you've got to watch me. You messed up last night because no one was following the leader."

The band members learned a valuable lesson that day—one that you and I must remember also. Jesus is our leader. When we turn our eyes from Him, when we look at one another, when we do our own thing, we mess up badly. It is only by keeping our attention on Him that He can produce beautiful music through us.

JULY 11

5 BILLION MADE

For those God foreknew he also predestined to be conformed to the likeness of his Son, that he might be the firstborn among many brothers. Romans 8:29, NIV.

Today is Matej Gaspar's birthday or the "Day of the 5 Billion"—not the 5 billionth customer served at McDonalds, nor the 5 billionth car produced at the Ford Motors plant, nor the 5 billionth visitor to Disneyland. Five years ago today Matej was born in Zagreb, Yugoslavia—the 5 billionth person born on Planet Earth. Happy birthday, Matej.

That's a lot of people—5 billion—more than I can count. And each person of that humongous number is different from every other person. Some people look a lot alike—twins, triplets, and such. But even in the case of identical twins, there are probably as many differences as there are similarities between them. Isn't it neat how God never seems to run out of variations on the same theme of arms, legs, eyes, noses, and ears?

After God makes us each uniquely individual, He invites us to "be conformed to the image of His Son," Jesus. That seems a little confusing at first. What does it mean to "be conformed" to an image? Does it mean we are to be little Xerox copy machines turning out exact copies of Jesus—His hair, His eyes, His chin? A copy machine's job is to make an "image" of a typewritten page—to make an exact copy. If you place in the machine a piece of paper that says "I lyke choklite candee," the machine will reproduce the words "I lyke choklite candee." It must conform to the image received.

Perhaps the "image" of Jesus that God wants in us is the image of Jesus' character—being loving, caring, honest, trustworthy, pure—not just how we look. Perhaps when it comes to reproducing these traits of His character, we need to become His human copy machines—activated, not by a dime, nor by pushing a button or turning a dial, but by plain and simple love for Him.

So have a happy fifth birthday, Matej—number 5 billion on Planet Earth. Enjoy occupying your very own special place in the human race. Enjoy being different. Enjoy being you. Enjoy meeting Jesus and discovering how to become His uniquely individual copy machine.

JULY 12

THE STONE COLLECTION

And he said to the people of Israel, "In the future, when your children ask you what these stones mean, you will tell them about the time when Israel crossed the Jordan on dry ground. . . . Because of this everyone on earth will know how great the Lord's power is, and you will honor the Lord your God forever." Joshua 4:21-24, TEV.

"Here's a picture of our house at Milo. Remember the fun we used to have scaring the night watchmen as they passed the old shed behind the house?" Rhonda asked.

"Yeah," I interrupted, "and the time you got caught by the assistant dean, too."

"Oh, look," Kelli sighed, "a picture of Rhonda and me in the Baltimore airport. I really loved those red shorts."

"That was the day our jet almost collided with a private plane, remember?" Rhonda reminded.

"I'll never forget the surprised look on the face of the pilot of the small plane as our jet passed just a few feet over his head," Dad added. "I'll bet he didn't sleep well that night."

Friday evening at the Rizzo house often begins by gathering around the family photo albums and family vacation slides. Memories of good times—and bad—soon tumble out for all to share. Inevitably the conversation develops into a time to remember and thank God for how He has protected us throughout the years. We have discovered that remembering how God has led us in the past builds faith with which to face our problems. It's a great way to start the Sabbath, and it's a great way to keep from forgetting just how often God has protected us and how He continues to bless us.

Just as in Joshua's time a pile of stones helped the Israelites remember God's care, so the family photos are the Rizzos' stone collection. Remember the story? After God parted the waters of the Jordan River and the people of Israel crossed on dry ground, Joshua had one man from each tribe carry a large rock from the bottom of the river to build an altar to God. The altar, built of 12 rocks from the riverbed, would forever remind the people of Israel of how God had led them in the past.

How has God led you and your family? Take out your rock collection, whether it's a photo collection like ours or a box of trinkets or a carton of shells—whatever it is, spend a few minutes sharing family memories together. Talk about God and His place in your family treasures.

JULY 13

MY VERY OWN RAINBOW

I am putting my bow in the clouds. It will be the sign of my covenant with the world. Whenever I cover the sky with clouds and the rainbow appears, I will remember my promise to you. Genesis 9:13-15, TEV.

I love rainbows—rainbows and daffodils—daffodils because, regardless of the icy winds and rains of springtime, these vibrant, yellow flowers bloom defiantly happy, and rainbows because they contain one of God's most specific promises to us. He called the rainbow "His covenant with the world." I like that. To send a rainbow after bolts of lightning slash across the sky and thunder booms out over the hills reveals the gentle side of our heavenly Father. His rainbow says, "Whatever the trouble may be, I'm with you. I'm there for you."

By first grade every child knows the colors of the rainbow—violet, indigo, blue, green, yellow, orange, and red. But few have been lucky enough to see some of the rarer rainbows. For instance, did you know that some rainbows are all purple or all red? Red rainbows can be seen at sunset, whereas purple rainbows can be seen only at sunrise. Since white light is made up of all colors, white rainbows can appear either in daylight or moonlight.

While you may have seen a double rainbow, have you ever seen a straight, vertical rainbow? Scientists say this unusual type of rainbow only appears over large bodies of water, like oceans or seas. My favorite rainbows were the bits and pieces of rainbows, called sun dogs, that we used to see in the New Mexican desert after an electric storm. It's hard to imagine that all these miracles are caused by nothing more than light reflecting off tiny droplets of water.

However, my favorite piece of rainbow trivia is this: every rainbow I see is my very own personal rainbow. No one else in the entire world can view it exactly as I view it because no one else can stand in the exact same spot as I. The rounded shape of the water droplets causes the light hitting each droplet to reflect the colors slightly differently to each person. So while God put His rainbow in the clouds as a promise to the world, He also customized that promise just for me and just for you. It takes a very special God to care enough to create rainbows after storms and rainbow promises. So look to the sky for God's special promise designed just for you.

JULY 14

BAT MAN

For you were once darkness, but now you are light in the Lord. Ephesians 5:8, NIV.

Other students on campus called Jonathan, "Bat Man." You see, Jonathan and his friends earned their way through academy by collecting bats for the local college biology department. Professor Engels had a research grant from the government to do experiments on bats and their natural ability to maneuver in the dark, and he paid the boys, who enjoyed spelunking (exploring caves) to catch them for him.

One Sunday morning each of Jonathan's spelunking friends backed out of the scheduled trip up to the caves. Jonathan knew he should just cancel the trip, since it is never safe to explore a cave alone. Yet he needed the money badly. After leaving a note on his desk, Jonathan headed for the caves. As a precaution, he packed two additional flashlights along with his helmet light and his customary two battery-operated lights attached to his utility belt.

Jonathan's collection of bats grew as he moved deeper into his favorite cave. As he'd fill one container with bats, he'd set it against the wall for his return trip. The more bats Jonathan caught, the less cautious he became, until, while reaching for a bat on a stalactite high above his head, he lost his balance and fell. In the fall, he crashed his helmet against a rock—the light blinked and went out before he stopped tumbling into a large underground avalanche of rocks. His body landed in a cold puddle of water a foot deep.

Darkness surrounded him, clawed at him, and almost seemed to smother him before he could slip one of his belt flashlights from its holder. When he tried to operate the light, he discovered the bulb had broken in the fall. The second flashlight didn't work either. Suddenly he felt very much alone and more than a little frightened. He took out the first of his spare flashlights. Relief flooded through him as the small penlight pierced the darkness of the cave. Thankful for that light and his last spare in his pack, Jonathan made his way back through the labyrinth of tunnels, singing a song he'd sung years earlier in Sabbath school, "This little light of mine . . . ," and praying that his penlight would continue to shine.

(Story to be continued.)

JULY 15

BAT MAN SEES THE LIGHT

I am the light of the world. . . . Whoever follows me will have the light of life and will never walk in darkness. John 8:12, TEV.

Jonathan picked up the containers of bats that he'd left along the way and continued walking. When he checked his watch, he discovered he'd been underground for more than three hours. He made great progress until he came to a place where three tunnels branched off in different directions. For some reason, he couldn't remember which path he'd taken, and he could find no identifying landmarks.

His head and his right leg had been hurting since his fall. When he swung around to check out one of the tunnels, his right knee buckled, sending him to the ground with a crunching thud. Instantly he knew he'd broken a bone. The penlight slipped from his hand and rolled out of his reach. He removed his last light from his pack and discovered that it too had been smashed in one of his falls. While frantically scrambling about with his hands, searching for the light he dropped, Jonathan prayed, "Oh, dear Father, please, please help me. No one knows where I am. And I can't walk out of here without some kind of light. I can't even crawl out now."

As if in answer to his prayer, Jonathan noticed the soft green glow from the hands on his watch. In the intense darkness of the cave, the light was comforting. It was as if God reminded him, "I am the light of the world." Jonathan knew without a doubt that he was not alone, that he was resting safely in God's care.

Jonathan fell asleep. How long he slept, he didn't know, but he awoke to the sound of his name. His friends had come for him. They'd found his note, surmised which cave he'd likely go to, found his abandoned car, and started searching for him. After administering first aid to his injured leg, his friends carried him out of the cave into the sunlight—the beautiful sunlight. Tears glistened in his eyes—not because of the light, but because of his overwhelming gratefulness to his heavenly Father—the Father of light.

JULY 16

BLINDING LIGHT

Every good and perfect gift is from above, coming down from the Father of the heavenly lights, who does not change like shifting shadows. James 1:17, NIV.

Today is the anniversary of the first atomic bomb explosion nearly 50 years ago at the testing grounds of Holloman Air Force Base in Alamogordo, New Mexico. Spectators said that the explosion produced a blinding light. Less than a month later, thousands more would see the blinding light of the explosion and die from its effects. Not exactly a happy event to celebrate, is it? Definitely an event no one on Planet Earth wishes to see repeated.

While God invented the atom that the scientists exploded that day on the New Mexican desert, man used it to destroy. While light comes from God, the Father of lights, people can still use it to hurt, kill, and destroy. The blinding lights of a speeding car in the night can cause an oncoming automobile to crash into a concrete embankment—is God to blame because that which He created was responsible for the death of the second driver? If one believed such a thing, God could be considered responsible for sin, for didn't He create Adam and Eve? When a beam from a laser light is used to kill instead of heal, when someone dies from electrical shock—is it God's fault because He created the tool that did the killing? Some people would have you think so. When troubles come, these people search for the cause of their troubles and unfairly put the blame on God. I confess that I've done it sometimes. What about you?

I love the words of today's text—"Every good gift and every perfect gift" comes "from the Father of heavenly lights." Every good and perfect gift! With God there is no changing like shifting shadows. I like that, too. We can depend on Him for all that is good and perfect in our lives.

And we can put the blame for the bad, the unfair, the cruel "atomic bombs" that regularly explode in our lives right where it belongs—on Satan, the father of darkness. Best of all, we can know that old Satan's days are numbered. Jesus will soon come in a blaze of glorious light, and we will go to live with Him in a place where there is no darkness, no sin, no pain, and no misuse of God's good and perfect gifts.

JULY 17

PERSIMMON PINK AND STRAWBERRY RED

Consider the lilies of the field, how they grow; they toil not, neither do they spin. Matthew 6:28.

Persimmon pink, strawberry red, lemon yellow, lime green, and plum purple—don't these colors just sound delicious? I love colors—colors of every kind. If anyone asks me what my favorite color is, I just can't decide. I like 'em all.

When I was in grade school, my mom and dad couldn't afford to buy more than the standard Crayola crayon box containing the eight basic colors. I remember looking at Billy's brand-new box of 64 colors—you know, the one with the built-in pencil sharpener on the side—and wishing I had a box with so many colors to choose from. One day I borrowed his crayons. The next day his mother came to the school and told me to use my own crayons in the future.

At home I learned that there was a time and a place to color, that coloring the white flowers on the living room wallpaper was a no-no, and that unwinding the toilet paper to create red and yellow tulips on each sheet was none too popular with my family either. You can only imagine what happened when I discovered Magic Marker liquid pens. I went absolutely banana yellow! The bold, vibrant colors made my pictures look like a real artist had painted them, or so I thought. My sketch pad full of "designer original" paper doll dresses blossomed to life.

Even today, one of my Sabbath pastimes is to grab my paints, brushes, and a canvas and head for my favorite Columbia Gorge overlook for an afternoon of painting. While I'm strictly an amateur artist, I can appreciate the wild array of colors God mixes and blends in order to create His masterpiece—nature.

There's a game I play when I spend a few minutes studying one of God's canvases. I imagine myself as the owner of the company that makes

Crayola crayons, and I devise yummy names for each shade of color He used. Besides being fun, the game provides me with a way to stop and give a little praise. So today, if you're so inclined, stop and give a little praise to our vibrantly creative, our wildly wonderful Creator—the Creator of such colors as peachy yellow and pomegranate red.

JULY 18

COLOR GONE WILD

The wall was made of jasper, and the city itself was made of pure gold, as clear as glass. The foundation stones of the city wall were adorned with all kinds of precious stones. The first foundation stone was jasper, the second sapphire, the third agate, the fourth emerald, the fifth onyx, the sixth carnelian, the seventh yellow quartz, the eighth beryl, the ninth topaz, the tenth chalcedony, the eleventh turquoise, the twelfth amethyst. The twelve gates were twelve pearls. Revelation 21:18-21, TEV.

Can you even imagine such a city? What a riot of color! Blue, green, red, yellow, orange, purple, and every other in-between color there is, all glittering and shining in the sunlight of God's love. Wow! Think about it. Even if I owned a set of 64 Magic Markers, their colors would appear dull in comparison. That's a sight I certainly do not want to miss! Do you?

OK. We agree that the colors in the walls of God's eternal city are worth seeing, but here's another thought you might consider. Since light contains all the colors we see, have you ever wondered about our robes of light—the clothes we will wear in heaven? Are these garments white like artists usually portray? Or could they—like light—possess all the colors of the rainbow, which I could, according to my creative mood, rearrange and redesign at will? Yesterday I mentioned my sketch pad full of designer original clothing. Well, listen to this heavenly dream.

One morning after I return from the planet Sophatha (or any other name you might choose), I design a shimmery scarlet dress to wear to my music lesson (Gabriel is teaching me how to sing a trio by myself); a coral pink scuba suit to wear to my deep-sea diving class (Jonah, my diving instructor, is introducing me to a great white shark today. I can hardly wait!); and a little paisley number I'll wear later in the day to a picnic in the park with Jesus (He's going to bring His special recipe for potato salad made out of a completely new variety of potato Adam has been working on). And I'll create all these new and fantastic outfits out of the very same robe of light.

Now, I don't know if my robe of light will match my crazy dreams, but I do know that whatever the robe can or cannot do, I will not be disappointed with it—nor with any other possibility heaven has to offer. And I know that the more I talk about heaven, the more real it becomes and the more I want to go there. So, what's your most wild, outrageous, imaginative idea regarding living in heaven?

JULY 19

BEST PALS

He will give his angels charge of you to guard you in all your ways. Psalm 91:11, RSV.

Armed with his secret new weapon, Alex peeked around the corner of the big stone wall. He looked first one way, then the other. Relieved that Ralph was not in sight, he scooted out of his hiding place and down the alley toward school as fast as his skinny little legs could carry him. All the bravery he'd felt at the breakfast table had vanished during the short walk to the Anderson estate.

Alex loved school. He felt quite grown-up to be able to walk the three blocks to the eight-grade church school. He loved first grade. He loved his teacher, Mr. Carlton. But one thing Alex didn't love—Ralph. Ralph lived in the Andersons' gray stone mansion behind the big stone wall. And most mornings Ralph sat waiting for Alex in order to terrorize the young boy. Worst of all, Ralph enjoyed scaring Alex.

Alex had almost made it to the end of the Andersons' property when he saw Ralph coming around the corner of the garage. Ralph spied Alex at the very same moment. And the chase was on—Alex running scared and Ralph bounding after him. When Alex reached the crosswalk, he had to stop. The light and the traffic were against him. In fear, Alex braced himself. He could hear his assailant getting closer and closer. The little boy cringed at the thought of what Ralph might do when he reached him.

Dear Jesus, Alex prayed to himself, *You said that You would give Your angels charge over us—to keep us and to protect us. Well, I need those angels—bad!* Suddenly Alex whirled about and faced his bloodthirsty opponent.

Startled, Ralph screeched to a halt inches from Alex's face. They eyed each other speculatively. Ralph growled his fiercest growl and took a few steps backward, all the while staring angrily into Alex's eyes.

In his loudest, most threatening voice, Alex shouted, "Go home, Ralph. Go home!"

How God's angels changed Ralph's mind about Alex, I don't know. But change it, they did. For Ralph, the oversized pit bull, dropped his head and walked slowly back toward his master's house. Ralph never bothered Alex again. In fact, the two became best pals.

JULY 20

HERMAN'S MOON DAY

The moon marks off the seasons, and the sun knows when to go down. Psalm 104:19, NIV.

"Mark my words," Herman shouted, his face suffused with anger, "God will never allow man to place his sinful foot on the surface of the moon." Within two months of his prediction, the *Eagle* had landed, and at 10:56 p.m. E.D.S.T. astronaut Neil Armstrong climbed down the *Eagle's* ladder and set foot on the lunar surface. A quarter of a million miles away on Planet Earth, I was sitting in a farmhouse living room near Columbus, Wisconsin, watching and listening as he said, "That's one small step for a man, one giant leap for mankind." The United States had landed on the moon before 1970, just as President John F. Kennedy promised the U.S. Congress they would.

Twenty minutes later Edwin "Buzz" Aldrin came out of the *Eagle* and joined Armstrong. The two men took photographs, collected soil samples, bounced about on the moon's low-gravity surface for two hours before returning to their spaceship.

And where was my friend Herman? Sound asleep in his bed. He refused to watch what he called the "farce" on television or listen to the reports of it on the radio. To him, the government was playing a gigantic hoax on the American people to justify the misuse of tax money and to convince Russia that we were ahead in the space race. No one could change his mind. Finally everyone realized his mind was made up, so the subject was avoided in his presence. Herman went to his death still believing that man never landed on the moon, that God would not allow it to happen, and that the United States government was guilty of deceiving its people.

Twenty-three years have passed since Herman's fateful prediction proved to be inaccurate. It's no big news now, right? For that matter, I hardly ever think about the moon landing. Yet God did reveal the important things in His Word—the things on which we can depend, like how the moon marks off the seasons, how it affects the tides, how it becomes visible only after the sun goes down. Our text tells us that God is in control of the situation on earth, that He reveals what we need to know through His Word, and that the rest is in His hands.

JULY 21

THE DESERTER

Happy are those whose sins are forgiven, whose wrongs are pardoned. Psalm 32:1, TEV.

William, a quiet sensitive English boy, joined the British Army to fight against the German kaiser in World War I. When the bullets began to fly and the cannons boomed, William ran—he deserted. The punishment for desertion at that time was death. Somehow the military police couldn't find the young man in order to punish him.

In time William Herschel became the great astronomer who discovered the planet Uranus. The king of England, King George III, sent for the talented astronomer in order to award him for his discovery. Did the king know of William's desertion during battle? If he did William knew that the king could order him shot. Yet King George was the king, and William's presence had been commanded.

After talking with family and friends and praying about his situation, William decided he'd hidden his terrible sin long enough. He'd lived with his guilt too many years. He'd go to see the king, and whatever happened would happen.

William arrived at the king's residence on time and was escorted to the waiting room outside the room where the kings of England receive their important guests. Within a few moments of his arrival, William was handed an envelope. The king's aide instructed William to read the contents of the envelope before the king arrived. William opened the envelope and read the official-looking document inside. It was a royal pardon. William had been forgiven.

When the king summoned William into the reception room, he said, "Now we can talk." With William's guilty conscience cleared, he no longer needed to fear the king. William was later knighted. He became known as Sir William Herschel and was invited to live permanently in Windsor Castle, King George's winter home.

William Herschel knew he was guilty. He didn't try to deny it. But King George had mercy on him, even making him a member of the royal household. That's what God promises to do for us—pardon our guilt and take us to live in the royal palaces of heaven.

TERROR ON TENTH

I call on the Lord in my distress, and he answers me. Psalm 120:1, NIV.

Richard dusted the sand from his bathing suit, stuffed his belongings into his sports bag, slipped into his jeans, and gingerly pulled his T-shirt down over his sunburned shoulders. One glance at his wristwatch and he realized he'd have to hurry to catch the next train home. The elevated train was just pulling into the station as he stumbled up the stairs and through the gate.

A short time later, the 13-year-old boy exited the train and bounded down the stairs to the bustling street. The taste of his mom's spaghetti sauce lured him into a run toward home. He stopped at the busy Tenth Avenue intersection to wait for the traffic light when two police cars roared to a stop in front of him, successfully blocking his pathway. Before Richard could decide what to do, two burly policemen leaped from the automobiles, drew their guns, and ordered him to put his hands up. Instantly he obeyed.

After frisking Richard and learning his name, address, and where he'd spent the day, the two men asked to see inside Richard's sports bag. "Sure," the young boy replied, "but what are you looking for?"

"We know that you and a 29-year-old felon have been breaking into several houses in the neighborhood during the afternoons while the owners are at work. We know your MO," one of the policemen explained while the other tore into Richard's bag.

"My MO?" Richard scowled.

"Your method of operation, OK?" The first officer explained. "We're on to you, kid."

"But sir, there must be some mistake," Richard said, gesturing with his hands.

"Keep 'em up, kid!" The first policeman shouted, aiming his handgun at the side of the boy's head. "The only mistake around here is yours—yours and your no-good friend's."

Frightened, Richard watched as his belongings were spread across the sidewalk. Richard watched and prayed.

(Story to be continued.)

MISTAKEN IDENTITY

Even a child is known by his actions, by whether his conduct is pure and right. Proverbs 20:11, NIV.

The first police officer rose to his feet. "There's nothing here, Sergeant," he said to his partner.

"Are you sure? No bracelets buried in the side pockets, no rings stuffed into the lining?"

"No, sir," the man replied. "Nothing."

Not finding the goods he'd been looking for seemed to make the policeman angrier. "Look, kid, we don't know where you dropped the goods, so we can't take you downtown. But we know how and where to find you. And we'll be investigating you."

Richard nodded his head vigorously.

"Pick up your stuff and get out of here!" The sergeant ordered.

"Yes sir, yes sir." Richard scooped his wet clothes into the bag, hardly daring to watch the two policemen walk back to their cars. He rose to his feet in time to see and hear the police cars squeal away from the curb and down the street.

A week passed, then two weeks. One after another, people in the neighborhood confided to Richard's mom that the police had been around asking questions about her son.

"What did you tell them?" His mother asked.

"What could I say? Richard has always been a good boy. He's never in trouble."

After a time, the police caught the real team of burglars. Yet through the experience, Richard learned the value of having a good reputation. He also learned another valuable lesson. He learned that whoever you are, wherever you go, and no matter your age, people watch. "Even a child is known by his actions."

JULY 24

THE MYSTERY OF THE STONE

But these are written that you may believe that Jesus is the Christ, the Son of God, and that by believing you may have life in his name. John 20:31, NIV.

In 1799 in Rosetta, Egypt, a troop of French soldiers accidentally found an ancient stone. This stone had three kinds of writing on it: Greek, and the other two were ancient Egyptian—hieroglyphics, and Demotic characters. All three writings appeared to say the same thing. They brought the stone to the linguists to decipher. The translators had no trouble with the Greek inscription, but they couldn't seem to break the code of the two Egyptian messages.

In 1818, 28-year-old Jean François Champollion discovered that in Egyptian hieroglyphics some of the pictures stood for sounds. It took Jean four more years before he completely solved the mystery of the stone that had baffled the experts for so many years. He had broken the code of the Rosetta stone. This discovery was the key that allowed scholars to read other ancient manuscripts and discover how Old Testament history related to other events of its time.

Another great discovery that revealed God's Word to us occurred not through a man's hard work but by accident, or so one might think. A young shepherd boy was watching his father's sheep one day on the scrub-covered hills that rise above the Dead Sea. One of the new spring lambs wandered into a cave. When the boy discovered that the lamb was missing, he went looking for it. He found the lamb near the mouth of a cave he'd never noticed before.

Curious as to how deep the cave might be, the boy threw a few stones back into the darkness. Suddenly he heard a loud crack. His stone had hit some object and it had broken. Upon searching further, he found some old clay vessels. Inside the vessels were ancient scrolls—early copies of Holy Scripture. These scrolls became known as the Dead Sea scrolls. They helped prove the authenticity of the text that makes up our modern Bible.

I am certain that neither one of these great discoveries was accidental, because I believe God, in His own wisdom and His own time, supplies what His people need in order to believe in Him and to make it to His kingdom.

JULY 25

A BATHYSCAPHE ADVENTURE

You will again have compassion on us; you will tread our sins underfoot and hurl all our iniquities into the depths of the sea. Micah 7:19, NIV.

Jacques Piccard swelled with pride as he eyed the latest invention of his father, Auguste Piccard—the world's first bathyscaphe. The submersible ship, designed for underwater exploration, challenged the young boy's imagination. He listened as his father explained how the vessel worked. He climbed into the spherical watertight cabin attached to the ship's underbelly and imagined himself navigating the coral reefs of the South Pacific.

On January 23, 1960, Jacques' dream came true. He and U.S. Navy Lieutenant Donald Walsh would put Auguste Piccard's invention to its greatest test. At 8:23 a.m. Jacques and his companion climbed into the bathyscaphe *Trieste* and sealed it shut. The *Trieste* was then lowered into the water, and slowly began its descent to the bottom of the Mariana Trench, the deepest spot in the Pacific Ocean. Before noon the *Trieste* reached a depth greater than the height of Mount Everest. At this point the two men heard a loud crack. The tremendous water pressure—nearly eight tons per square inch—had cracked a small outside window. The window held, so the men continued downward. At 1:06 p.m. they touched bottom: 35,000 feet below sea level, nearly seven miles.

For 20 minutes they watched fish, seldom if ever seen before, swim back and forth in front of the bathyscaphe's lights. Reluctantly they began their long voyage back. At 4:56 p.m. the *Trieste* broke through the ocean's surface, and the men learned that they had indeed conquered the ocean's greatest depths.

While God promises to cast our sins into the deepest part of the ocean, I doubt that Jacques and Donald spotted lies floating by the ship's beams of light or temper tantrums bursting up from the ocean floor. They probably didn't see any murders or thefts bobbing around the area, either. But that doesn't belittle God's promise. What our loving heavenly Father wanted us to understand was that our sins were cast as far away from Him as possible. They were gone—forgiven and forgotten, forever. Aren't you glad that all Jacques Piccard and the *Trieste* found were fish, coral, and seaweed? That they couldn't uncover the naughty things I have done or the bad mistakes you have made and that God has buried them forever?

JULY 26

GOLD, GOLD, AND MORE GOLD

To him who by means of his power working in us is able to do so much more than we can ever ask for, or even think of; to God be the glory in the church and in Christ Jesus for all time, forever and ever! Amen. Ephesians 3:20, 21, TEV.

When Mark Spitz flew to Munich, Germany, in 1972, he dreamed of bringing home a gold medal for his country, never realizing at that time that he would make Olympic history. On August 28 he swam to a new world record for the 200-meter butterfly stroke. A half hour later he earned his second gold medal by swimming the final leg of the 400-meter freestyle relay.

The next day Spitz broke the world's record for the 200-meter freestyle and earned a third gold medal. His fourth gold medal was in the 100-meter butterfly, and his fifth was won as anchorman for the 800-meter freestyle relay. On September 3 he splashed ahead to capture the 100-meter freestyle gold. The next day he swam the butterfly in the 400-meter medley relay and put his team ahead with a 4-yard lead and another world record. He had won an unbelievable seventh gold medal—the most won by any athlete at one time in the history of the Olympic Games. He had accomplished more than even he had ever dreamed possible.

So what is your dream? Would you like to fly jet planes? Would you like to be the first to ski Mount Everest? Find the cure for cystic fibrosis, AIDS, or the common cold? Would you like to conduct the National Symphony Orchestra or sing the soprano or bass solos in the *Messiah* at Carnegie Hall? Or __________ (you fill in the blank)? And are you sometimes afraid to tell anyone, afraid of being laughed at? Tell Jesus. He won't laugh. No matter how big and seemingly impossible your dream might be, God's plans for you are bigger. So go ahead, "blue sky" to your heart's content, think as big as you dare. Just don't ever, for one minute, forget that the secret to reaching your success and going beyond even your wildest dreams is in the rest of today's text. It is only when we remember to give God the credit for our "wins" that He can multiply them and make them grow.

JULY 27

OFF THE BEATEN PATH

Man's hand assaults the flinty rock and lays bare the roots of the mountains. He tunnels through the rock; his eyes see all its treasures. He searches the sources of the rivers and brings hidden things to light. But where can wisdom be found? Where does understanding dwell? Job 28:9-12, NIV.

Morris Baetzold and two of his friends on an outing from the Methodist Children's Home of Berea, Ohio, explored the famous Wild Cat Cave at the Hinkley Reservation south of Cleveland in northeastern Ohio. The three boys had already hiked back into the "room" where popular legend said local people hid runaway slaves before and during the Civil War. Two of the boys tired of the caves and crawled out. Morris lingered behind near a fallen stone slab that blocked the crossing of the main passage, allowing two dark triangular openings into a side passage of the cave. On a sudden impulse, Morris slithered into the narrowest of the two openings. He wanted to go farther even though the tunnel was dark and cold and his friends had the only flashlight. Convinced there was a hidden room farther into the mountain, he inched along in the dark. If he found a never-before-discovered room, he'd be famous.

Outside, the teachers discovered that they were one child short as they loaded the children onto the school buses for home. When his hiking companions were asked when Morris had last been seen, one of them indicated that they'd left him in Wild Cat Cave. They hurried to the cave.

"Morris," Mr. Powell, one of the teachers, shouted. From deep inside the cavern came a feeble reply.

"Help!" the trapped boy called. Morris had fallen into a crack—10 feet down. His chest and hips were wedged into a V of stone. He had toppled on his side, trapping his right arm beneath him. Though he'd scratched his fingers raw with his left hand, he could not reach a handhold. He was as good as paralyzed. While his search brought him all sorts of new wisdom, Morris no longer wished to explore or discover a secret room. He just wanted out.

"You'll never get me out," Morris wailed. "I'm gonna' die here."

(Story to be continued.)

JULY 28

HELP ON THE WAY

Do not be afraid; do not be discouraged. Deuteronomy 1:21, NIV.

Fire fighters and state policemen arrived within minutes of being called. Television and newspaper reporters followed. And as soon as the accident was reported on local TV and radio, volunteers came from all over to help rescue the boy. The boy's father, whom he hadn't seen in years, was rushed to the scene by additional state policemen.

Everyone had ideas on how to rescue the boy. They threw him a rope, a steel hook, a long pole. All attempts failed. The Cleveland Mining Company was called in to assess the situation. At first the mining engineers suggested drilling their way to the boy, but upon studying the rock formation, they discovered that the heavy equipment would most likely cause a cave-in, crushing Morris to death before they could reach him.

A trained rescue team from the National Speleological Society in Washington, D.C., was flown to the site. However, none of the team was skinny enough to reach Morris and hook the equipment to the boy. A five-foot-two-inch volunteer nurse made it within two feet of the boy, then dissolved into uncontrolled panic and had to be hauled out.

As the experts studied the situation, they were frustrated. The boy was within 60 feet of the mouth of the cave. If only Morris had fallen head toward instead of away from the rescuers, or if he had more than one hand free, or a belt on his pants, or even had worn clothing sturdy enough to hold a hook.

A few miles away in Cleveland, the Ulrich family watched the drama at the cave unfold on their television.

"I'll bet one of our boys could help this kid," Andy Ulrich commented to his wife. The couple had eight sons, all strong, agile athletes.

"I don't know," his wife replied. "With so many people there, we'd only get in the way."

In the morning when Andy Ulrich turned on his car radio on the way to work and learned that Morris was still stuck in the cave, he decided to act. His second and fourth eldest sons, Michael, 15, and Gerald, 12, were small, sturdy fellows. If anyone could reach Morris, these boys could. An hour later he and his boys were clambering up to the cave to volunteer their skills.

After explaining his idea to the men in charge of the rescue, an argument ensued. The experts were reluctant to send the young boys down into the hole. They might get stuck too, creating an even worse emergency.

(Story to be continued.)

JULY 29

NO GREATER LOVE

Greater love hath no man than this, that a man lay down his life for his friends. John 15:13.

First Gerry Ulrich tried. They tied a rope to his waist and he started into the hole. Since Morris had been trapped more than 12 hours, body odors permeated the closed in area. Gerry got to within six inches of the trapped boy's foot and suddenly became nauseated at the strong, foul-smelling air in the cave. Gerry gasped for air and cried to be pulled out.

Disgusted, the firemen pulled Gerry out, muttering, "That's what you get for using a kid." But Andy didn't mind. He just grabbed his son in his arms and held him tight.

"Why don't you try the other guy?" Andy said above the sobs of his younger son.

Michael, the other guy, stood silently by, watching the proceedings. When the men stopped muttering to themselves about the failed attempt, they agreed. Michael removed his coat to lessen his bulk. A rope was tied to his leather belt, and a nylon strap was placed around his waist. He also took with him an extra rope, strap, and clamp to attach to Morris should he reach his goal.

Michael talked to Morris as he edged closer. "It's only a matter of time and you'll be out of here," he promised. Michael attached the hook to Morris and ordered the men above to pull. They did—two inches and no more. Morris could not be dragged from the jaws of the cave, but must somehow be lifted. Michael worked for some time, trying to figure out a way to dislodge the boy. Finally, with the help of his father and the other men hovering above the hole, they rigged up a pulley system. It worked. Twenty-six and a half hours after Morris's accident, he was freed because of Michael's quiet, persistent courage.

Michael Ulrich later received a bronze medal from the Andrew Carnegie Hero Foundation. Inscribed on the back of the bronze coin are the words, "Greater love has no man than this . . ."

Through the medium of love, God prepares His people to help and serve others.

JULY 30

BEATING THE ODDS

We call them happy because they endured. James 5:11, TEV.

One morning Ray ached all over. His head felt hot; his stomach felt queasy. His worried mother called the doctor. The doctor examined the young boy, then called the mother aside.

"Mrs. Ewry," the doctor said, "I hate to tell you this, but I suspect that Ray has polio."

After months of illness Ray was allowed to go home. "There is little we can do now. Most likely he will never be able to walk properly again."

The woman dabbed her eyes, though she wasn't surprised to hear the doctor's prediction. "Must he keep doing the exercises? They are so painful for him."

“I would.” The doctor removed his spectacles, cleaning the lenses on his white handkerchief. “If he keeps exercising those injured muscles, he’ll be able to hobble around somewhat. Though walk again? Don’t hope for too much, Mrs. Ewry.”

But the doctor was wrong. He couldn’t measure Ray’s persistence. By the time he reached adulthood, Ray was the number one jumper in the world. In 1900 and 1904 he won gold medals in three jumping events—the high jump; the long jump; and the standing hop, step, and jump. In 1906 and 1908 he won only two medals each year, since the Olympic committee had eliminated the standing hop, step, and jump competition. Ray Ewry’s once-crippled legs won him 10 wins in 10 tries, more medals than any other Olympic competitor.

My heroine, Jackie Joyner-Kersee, the gold medal winner of the 1988 Summer Olympic long jump, grew up as an asthmatic. Asthma and track seldom go together. Attacks of coughing leave the victim gasping for breath, and overexertion brings on attacks. In spite of her coughing, in spite of her wheezing, in spite of fighting for each breath, Jackie persisted and won not only a gold medal but also the 1988 women’s heptathlon—a seven-event competition that includes running, jumping, and hurdles. Her broad smile of success flashed across TV screens around the world. Why was she happy? Like Ray Ewry, Jackie had endured years of pain and discomfort while training and had won.

Paul describes the everyday life of a Christian as a race and heaven as the gold medal. I don’t know about you, but the smile on my face when Jesus comes back for me will be broader than that of any Olympic winner. I will be so happy I endured the pain and the discomfort necessary to my training.

JULY 31

THE PECKING ORDER

There are six things the Lord hates, seven that are detestable to him: haughty eyes, a lying tongue, hands that shed innocent blood, a heart that devises wicked schemes, feet that are quick to rush into evil, a false witness who pours out lies and a man who stirs up dissension among brothers. Proverbs 6:16-19, NIV.

Andy tramped back to the farmhouse with an injured chicken in his arms. He couldn’t believe it. His hens had been at it again—trying to peck out each other’s eyes. The birds would strut about the hen yard looking for trouble—daring each other to challenge their authority. Pride was destroying his flock. They definitely had a severe “I” problem. Somehow he’d have to put a stop to it. But how do you force chickens to get along with one another? *There must be an answer,* he thought. *But then, some folk seem to have the same "I" trouble.*

That's how the first spectacles for chickens were invented—a simple but extraordinary invention designed to correct the chickens' "I" trouble. The spectacles were not designed to improve the chicken's eyesight, but as a protector that blurred the chicken's vision so that the bird couldn't see the other chickens and, likewise, they couldn't see it. Hence, they wouldn't feel threatened by another hen's presence and want to fight. In 1903 Andrew Jackson, Jr., was granted a patent for his invention. While his invention worked well, it never became popular.

In the next 15 years, in Munich, Germany, instead of Munich, Tennessee, people prepared for war, a war inspired by pride—"I" trouble—just like in the case of Jackson's chickens. Many people died. Too bad Mr. Jackson didn't design spectacles that would cure humans' "I" trouble.

Troublemakers—prideful, hateful troublemakers. That's what God despises. That's pretty strong language. Can you understand why? Have you ever been hurt by someone trying to get even or get ahead? Have you ever met people who need a pair of Jackson's spectacles? Have you ever needed a pair yourself? I have.

Two hundred two years ago today, the first U.S. patent was issued. Yet God had the cure for pride long before. And His miracle process still works. God will cure your "I" problem if you ask Him to.

AUGUST 1

BURNING OFF THE CLOUDS

Your love, O Lord, reaches to the heavens, your faithfulness to the skies. Psalm 36:5, NIV.

"Oh," my houseguest groaned as she peered out of our living room window, "it's cloudy. I was hoping to see Mount Hood before I left Oregon."

"Don't worry," my husband assured her, "the clouds will burn off by noon."

From October to April, Richard wouldn't have dared make such a prediction. During the Northwest's rainy season, clear skies are rare. But in midsummer it is almost a guarantee that the clouds will be burned off by the sun's rays.

While visitors to the area often fret over the clouds or occasional rain shower, true Oregonians don't mind at all. They even joke about the rainy weather. "We don't tan; we rust," they say. Or "At the beach you can always tell an Oregonian from a tourist; the Oregonian is the one with webbed feet."

One of Oregon's college basketball teams is called the Ducks—for obvious reasons. I've even heard Oregonians exaggerate to tourists about the amount of Oregon rainfall each year in order to discourage them from moving here permanently.

Not only do those clouds overhead maintain the incredible forests of giant trees and wild fern undergrowth but they also contribute to the snow pack gracing our mountain peaks and to the ample spring runoff that cascades down the caverns and over dramatic waterfalls into our reservoirs.

But you know, more than just Oregonians live with clouds hanging over their heads. I'm not talking about clouds predicted by the TV weatherperson, but the ones that bring discouragement and sorrow. Death, sickness, losing one's job, are all heavy clouds that block out personal happiness. Just as Oregonians appreciate the winter rains for the blessings they enjoy come springtime, so Christians know that God and His richest blessing can be found in the midst of the darkest of personal storm clouds. In Exodus 19:9, He says, "I come to you in a thick cloud." And like the Oregon sunshine, God can burn off the clouds of discouragement and bring us clear, blue skies once again if we will only trust Him.

AUGUST 2

TOO HEAVY TO CARRY

I am drowning in the flood of my sins; they are a burden too heavy to bear. Psalm 38:4, TEV.

Stephen grew up on the streets of New Delhi. He couldn't remember ever living in a house. Long before he reached school-age, he learned the skills of street survival. He mastered theft and violence instead of mathematics and reading. Each day he pawed through people's garbage cans for food. When night fell, Stephen and the other street people of the city clawed, bit, and struggled for a place to sleep under bridges or in the doorways of closed businesses. Whatever memories he once had of his parents faded from his mind before he reached the age of 10.

Yet the tough little street kid didn't remain a street kid. A Christian orphanage worker found him and took him in. At the orphanage Stephen learned to read and work with numbers. He also learned that if he wanted anything more out of his life than he already had, he would have to leave India. He worked at odd jobs, saving every cent in order to leave India. Acquiring a student visa, he traveled to Ontario, and there he finished high school and college. Once graduated, he found a job in Vancouver, Canada, teaching school. There he met and married a young woman. And by making a few good investments in real estate, Stephen Sanders became rich—very rich.

He traveled around the world for both business and pleasure. Wherever he traveled, Stephen was forced to remember his roots. Because everywhere he went he found poor people—living in dirty little shacks or on the street as he once had. The more misery and suffering he saw, the guiltier he felt about the billions of dollars he possessed. After more than 20 years of living in utter luxury, Stephen decided to do something about his past. He would give his money to help the poor.

"I can drive only one car, live in only one house, and wear only one suit at a time. I can eat only so much food in one sitting," he reminded his wife. "I cannot tolerate the suffering all over the world and do nothing about it. I feel so guilty for having so much while others go without."

The two agreed—they would save out adequate funds for themselves and their children to live on, then they would use the rest to help other people. Though not a Christian, Stephen discovered a new kind of happiness by giving to others. In 1990 he told a TV reporter, "It felt so good to unload the burden of self-importance. I am happier today than I've ever been."

AUGUST 3

A LITTLE GIFT

[Your gifts] are a fragrant offering, an acceptable sacrifice, pleasing to God. Philippians 4:18, NIV.

When I told a friend about Stephen Sanders' remarkable gift, my friend replied, "Well, it's easy for a man like Mr. Sanders to give away millions to the poor and keep a measly $10 million for his own use. That's not much of a sacrifice."

If you agree with my friend, let me tell you about another man I know. R.B. (I'm using his initials so greedy people won't try to con him out of his fortune) lives in eastern Pennsylvania. He too started out poor, though not as poor as Stephen Sanders. From a little boy, R.B. has been a Seventh-day Adventist Christian. He learned early that the secret of happiness is in helping others.

R.B. started a small business selling mobile homes. He married and began a family. As his business grew, R.B. recognized that everything he had was God's—the company profits, the inventory—to use however it was needed, no matter how small or how large the business grew. When the local congregation needed to build a new church, he gave freely of his time and money. When the academy needed a new bus, he gave all that he could. When a family needed food and shelter, he opened up his own home. No matter what the need might be, if R.B. had money for it, he gave.

"The more I give, the more God gives," R.B. once explained to a friend. "He gives me $2 for every $1 I give away. Trying to outgive each other has almost become a game between us." No television reporter interviewed R.B. regarding his gifts of love. Even as they grew in size, most of his donations he made in secret.

Mr. Sanders said his happiness came as the result of shedding his burden. R.B. described his joy as a game—playing a game with God. While both men possess a sense of peace and happiness from sharing their wealth, R.B. has enjoyed a whole lifetime of giving compared to Mr. Sanders' newly acquired joy. Which man, do you think, has received the greater reward? Is today too soon to begin giving to others? Or will you wait until you've made your first thousand, your first million, or your first billion?

AUGUST 4

GOING TO AFRICA

But you will receive power when the Holy Spirit comes on you; and you will be my witnesses in Jerusalem, and in all Judea and Samaria, and to the ends of the earth. Acts 1:8, NIV.

"Lord," the young singer prayed, "I don't want to go to Africa—anywhere else, but not Africa." Scott Wesley Brown had just heard the news. His singing group had scheduled concerts all across the continent of Africa, and he was expected to go.

Scott couldn't think of a worse fate than being sent to Africa—Africa with its rogue elephants, raging lions, and poisonous snakes; Africa with its violent revolutions, devastating famines, and terrible diseases. When the other musicians learned of his fears, they teased and harassed him during the entire flight across the ocean. But as the singing group toured from one city to the next, Scott decided his fears were unfounded. Africa wasn't so bad after all. The modern cities had paved streets, skyscrapers, and luxury hotels. He met loving and friendly people.

After one particular concert, a man from the audience introduced himself. "I am chief of a rural tribe. Please, could you come and sing for the people of my village?" The chief went on to explain that his heart had been touched by the words to their songs, and that his people had never heard of Jesus and His love. "I would especially like my people to hear the song sung by that young man, Scott Wesley Brown."

Reluctantly, Scott agreed to go along with four other singers of the group to the chief's remote village. As they packed their belongings in the Land Rover, the chief reminded them that there was no electricity, so their music would need to be performed a capella.

It took 12 hours to reach the village. They didn't see another motorized vehicle for the last six hours of the journey. During that time Scott became silent. They reached a small village of mud huts at dusk. While the village drummers hammered out a message to the other villages in the area, telling them of the guests who had come to sing for them, Scott and his friends immediately dined on a stew of undetermined origin.

Hot, dusty, and tired, Scott glanced about the village and realized that his worse fears were coming true. Somehow the words of Jesus about going into all the world to preach the gospel weren't much of a comfort to the wary young man.

(Story to be continued.)

AUGUST 5

CONQUERING LION-SIZED FEARS

Lo, I am with you alway, even unto the end of the world. Matthew 28:20.

Well, thought Scott Wesley Brown as he hurried back to his sleeping quarters to prepare for the evening concert, *this place certainly qualifies as the end of the world*. After a cool bath and a change of clothes, he felt better. *I might make it yet*, he thought.

The tropical heat didn't drop much after the sun went down. By the time Scott and his fellow musicians had returned to the clearing, the area was packed with hundreds of people eager to hear the message of Jesus Christ in word and song. Scott looked out over the field of upturned faces, some marred with disease and others scarred from injuries. He'd never performed before a more eager crowd. At the end of the concert, the people didn't want the musicians to stop. They begged for more. The musicians sang into the wee hours of the night. Finally, exhausted and hoarse, the singers had to stop singing.

The chief's top aide took the men back to their quarters and instructed them to call for help should any of them need to leave their huts during the night. "There are poisonous snakes in the surrounding jungle."

"Why do you maintain the ring of campfires around the village," Scot asked. "Certainly not for warmth."

The aide laughed. "No, the fires are not for heat. They keep the lions out of the village at night."

That did it. Scott knew he'd not get one wink of sleep. Long after his hutmate had fallen asleep, Scott sat by the door and stared into the jungle night as he recited memory texts he'd learned as a child. *So this is what it is like to go as a missionary for God—to preach to the uttermost parts of the earth?* As he sat alone in the night, Scott realized that for the first time in his life, he was in a place where God had no other voice but his voice; where God had no other tongue but Scott's tongue to proclaim the wondrous love Christ had for His people. God had chosen to use Scott's reluctant tongue to tell the story. In the middle of an East African jungle, Scott decided that there is no greater honor than to be used for God's service, whether in Hartford, Connecticut, or there in the jungles of East Africa. Tears blurred his vision as he lifted his eyes toward the indigo sky and told God thank You for letting him use his talents, for helping him conquer his fears, and for sending him to Africa.

AUGUST 6

TOO GOOD TO GET BETTER

There is one thing worse than a fool, and that is a man who is conceited. Proverbs 26:12, TLB.

Maria, as we will call her, had no doubt but that she possessed great musical talent. Her parents told her so. Her voice teachers told her so. The crowds that flocked to the town's small concert hall told her so. The newspapers proclaimed her talent throughout her region of Italy. Talented and exquisitely beautiful, the young woman soared to fame in record time. When an invitation came for Maria to travel to Rome to be lead soprano in an opera conducted by the famous Italian conductor Arturo Toscanini, she decided that all these people must be right. She truly was great. Her family and her agent noticed a change in her almost immediately. Acting the role of a prima donna, Maria demanded her way in everything, threw tantrums, corrected everyone, and spewed hateful words whenever someone crossed her. Rather than endure her wrath, her family and friends gave in to her demands and spoiled her more.

The great day finally came when Maria began rehearsing with Toscanini and the orchestra. Her nerves were strung out as the great conductor put the musicians through their paces. During the dress rehearsal for opening night, Toscanini stopped the orchestra and corrected a mistake Maria had made.

Embarrassed, angry, and shocked that anyone would dare humiliate her in front of the entire orchestra, Maria's eyes flashed with fire. "Mr. Toscanini, I would remind you that I am the star of this evening's performance!"

Toscanini turned toward the young woman, lifted his arrogant head, and stared down his nose at the furious prima donna. "Madam," he explained, "the only stars that be are up in heaven. On this earth there are only good musicians and bad musicians, and so help me, you are a bad one!"

Maria rushed to her dressing room, packed her belongings, returned home, and refused to sing again. Poor Maria—destroyed by her pride. I have seen professional athletes, movie stars, writers, and presidents—even people like you and me—destroy themselves by being too proud to learn from other people. How foolish! What a waste of talent—to lose so much because of one's feeling of self-importance.

AUGUST 7

START AT THE VERY BEGINNING

In the beginning God created the heaven and the earth. Genesis 1:1.

Let's have a quiz this morning. You've read through the Creation story many times. So you know all the correct answers, right?

1. On what day did God make fish?

2. On what day did He decide that cod would have scales and that clams would have shells? That crabs would run sideways instead of straight? That daddy sea horses would carry the sea horse eggs in their pouches instead of the mother sea horses carrying them?

3. On what day did He put the dots on the ladybug's back or the shell on the snail?

4. On what day did He design Orion or the Big Dipper or the moon's pull on the oceans to produce tides?

5. On what day did He make Arabian horses? Palominos? Morgans?

Boy, the Creator sure had a lot to think about when He made the world, didn't He? Think of the hundreds of thousands of other decisions God needed to make! Talk about planning ahead! Nothing was left to chance, as a few of the world's scientists would like you to believe. Each day's task was carried out in an orderly fashion.

A woodcarver I know says that when he looks at a piece of wood, he sees an owl or an eagle or a dolphin trapped inside, waiting for him to release it with his carving blades. An artist friend of mine plans exactly how her finished canvas will look by first sketching her idea out on a piece of paper. Nothing is left to chance. An architect draws thousands of tiny lines on a sheet of paper before even one brick is stacked on top of another. When I write a story I close my eyes and picture just how the story should go, then I turn on my computer and begin typing.

When I think of the time before Creation, I like to imagine God and Jesus relaxing on the green lawn beside the sea of glass and talking about creating a long-necked creature with spots or a shiny black creature with eight legs. Or perhaps sketching the basic structure of the little dipper in the sand beside the water. Of course, I have only the Genesis story to go by. But that's more than enough for us to see God's love, His power, and His carefully organized plan for His children. The rest of the story we'll learn straight from the Creator Himself someday.

AUGUST 8

LITTLE THINGS MEAN A LOT

Do not add to what I command you and do not subtract from it, but keep the commands of the Lord your God that I give you. Deuteronomy 4:2, NIV.

Imagine getting on an airplane and thinking you're heading for Florida, but you land in Alaska instead. That's what happened in 1981 when Mr. and Mrs. Lewenetz left Moscow, Russia, to visit Mr. Lewenetz's father in sunny St. Petersburg, Florida. When they emerged from their long flight, the couple, who spoke no English, went through customs without learning of the mistake. Mr. and Mrs. Lewenetz didn't discover the error until they hailed a cab and handed the driver their father's address. The cab driver located a friend who spoke Russian and helped straighten out the couple's problem.

"The Lewenetzes wound up in Petersburg, Alaska, instead of St. Petersburg, Florida, because a loyal Communist airport official in Moscow took offense at the Saint in St. Petersburg. So he removed the two letters from the couple's tickets," an Alaska Airline official explained. That tiny error stranded the couple in Petersburg, Alaska, a fishing village 100 miles from Juneau. "The airline will, of course, fly the Lewenetzes safely to their son's home in Florida at no additional charge." Two little letters, an S and a T, caused a 3,000-mile error.

Have you ever heard people claim, when they've done something wrong, "It's no big deal"? I have. Students cheat on exams—no big deal. Would you want a brain surgeon who cheated on his medical exams operating on you? People drink a little too much—no big deal. How many people die each year because the other driver drank a little too much? Just a little lie—no big deal. Super transport jets have crashed, killing everyone on board, because the safety inspector lied on his report. Little things—the spacecraft *Challenger* tragedy occurred because a drop of a few degrees in temperature caused the O rings to fail.

To God there are no little things. The tiniest creature is important to Him. The tiniest bad habit can destroy the greatest Christian. God didn't give Moses 10 suggestions, 10 little pieces of advice, but 10 commandments to live by. When someone says "It's no big deal," listen to the warning signals going off in your head. If you don't, the least that might happen is for you to end up in Petersburg, Alaska. The worst? Well, I'm sure you can guess.

AUGUST 9

IN FULL RETREAT

Flee the evil desires of youth, and pursue righteousness, faith, love and peace, along with those who call on the Lord out of a pure heart. 2 Timothy 2:22, NIV.

Have you ever heard anyone say "You can't run away from your troubles" or "You can't win the battle by running away"? That's not entirely true. I can think of at least two times in history when running away was the only way to truly win. And I'm sure there are thousands more that I do not know about.

In August 1588 the English defeated the Spanish Armada. Actually, the inferior English fleet defeated King Philip's mighty fighting force by running—that's right, by running away. Sir Frances Drake lured the

Armada into the English Channel, then on in to the storm-swept North Sea by fighting minor skirmishes, then running.

The heavier, more powerful Spanish fleet was carrying foot soldiers along with artillery and food supplies necessary to sustain the large fighting force, while the lighter English ships could play the role of the pesky mosquito—zapping the Spanish, then flitting out of reach. By the time the Spanish realized just what was happening, they were running short of supplies and had no friendly ports to go to so they could restock. The pride of Spain was forced to limp home, defeated by an enemy they barely saw.

The second example of running to win took place thousands of years before England and Spain became great naval powers. It happened in Egypt. You remember the story about the young, handsome slave being pursued by the "lady" of the house until one day she cornered him. Joseph tried to reason with Potiphar's wife, but the self-indulgent woman was determined to have her own way. What did Joseph do? He ran from her. He ran from the temptation.

Both Joseph and Sir Frances Drake must have fought the temptation to stand and fight, but both men were wise enough to realize that to do so would mean defeat. What about you? Are you wise enough to know when the best move you can make is a quick reverse? Make a list of situations that you might face when running is the only sensible way to fight. An example might be when a friend is pushing drugs.

AUGUST 10

A MISSED OPPORTUNITY

Let us fix our eyes on Jesus, the author and perfecter of our faith. Hebrews 12:2, NIV.

The year: 1931. The event: the opening of the World Series between the St. Louis Cardinals and the Philadelphia Athletics. The man of the moment: President Herbert Hoover.

With thousands of men out of work, farmers going bankrupt, and factories closing as a result of the Great Depression, President Hoover felt that his appearance at the first game of the World Series would boost the nation's morale. Besides, the president loved baseball. On the day of the game he traveled by special train from Washington, D.C., to St. Louis in order to throw out the first ball, a tradition begun in 1910 by President William Howard Taft.

When the president arrived at the stadium, news reporters besieged him with questions. Photographers insisted he stage a few practice throws for their cameras. He obliged the many requests, throwing the practice baseball again and again. The baseball officials, seeing him busy with the news media, started the game without him.

After posing for so many pictures, Mr. Hoover noticed the game had already started and simply dropped the practice ball into his pocket and sat down to watch the game. In spite of all the effort he'd made for the privilege of throwing out the first ball in the World Series game, he missed his opportunity. He allowed himself to get sidetracked from his objective. How funny; how sad.

When it comes to preparing for heaven, you and I can make the same mistake. If we lose sight of our reason for going, if we allow other people to come between us and Jesus, we can become sidetracked and lose out on the gift of a lifetime—eternity.

AUGUST 11

GOOD JOB

In the beginning God created the heavens and the earth. . . . And God saw that it was good. Genesis 1:1-10, NIV.

Eleven-year-old Crissy looked forward to painting the kitchen with her dad. For the first hour she happily splashed the paint on the low cupboards while her father worked on the higher shelves. When she finished the last cupboard, she stood up to stretch. Her arm ached. For that matter, her entire body ached. Yellow paint dotted her nose, hair, and arms. She glanced down at her fingernails, coated with paint, and groaned. *I'll never get them clean again*, she thought.

Dad glanced toward his daughter and smiled. "Crissy, you've done a good job today. I appreciate your good work. We just have one more area to finish, then we'll be done."

One more area, Crissy thought. *Ugh!*

"Could you paint the back wall beneath the sink for me, please?" he asked.

"Sure, Daddy." Crissy grabbed her paint can and brush, then climbed under the sink. Minutes went by as she changed the green wall to yellow—all except the area behind the water pipes. *Aw, who cares*, she thought as she climbed out of the cupboard.

"All done?" Daddy asked.

"Yeah, all except for behind the pipes. And who's ever gonna know that part wasn't painted?"

After a pause, Daddy said, "You'll know, and I'll know. And that's what's important."

Like Crissy, you and I enjoy knowing we did a good job. Even if we feel a little embarrassed or uncomfortable when complimented, we glow with happiness inside when someone notices that we've done a good job. But do we do a good job just for the compliments we might receive? What happens when no one is around to give us a pat on the back after we do a good job? It's easy to sluff off if we think no one will see or know. That's when the Creation story takes on a new dimension.

God showed us the correct way to approach our tasks. He looked at what He had made and said, "That's good!" It didn't take a compliment for Him to know He'd created a perfect world. He knew within Himself. You and I should know too. Whatever task we undertake, we should be certain we've done our best. Then it won't matter whether other people compliment us or criticize us or totally ignore what we've done. "A job worth doing at all is a job worth doing well."

AUGUST 12

THE ANT MAN

Go to the ant, thou sluggard; consider her ways, and be wise: which having no guide, overseer, or ruler, provideth her meat in the summer, and gathereth her food in the harvest. Proverbs 6:6-9.

Can you imagine spending your days watching a colony of ants crawl about? That's what Dr. Jim McIver of Oregon State University does. Some people call Jim the ant man; others say he's just plain "buggy." For, you see, he takes today's text seriously. He spends his time looking for and studying ants. He doesn't study how their bodies are constructed. Science has known that for some time now. Instead, he studies how ants behave, how they respond to one another, how they make their society work.

It's trickier than you might think to study ants. For one thing, how do you tell one ant from another? To humans, including Jim, the creatures all look alike. To follow the individual ant's progress, he glues a tiny disk about a millimeter across to its abdomen with glue. He tried enamel paints, but the ants don't like the paint. They will clean it off themselves or off each other as quickly as possible. Jim has traveled to such faraway places as Australia to tag ants for his study.

Jim has learned that ants can construct massive structures without any kind of crew boss or supervisor telling them what to do and how to do it—just like the Bible says. Like people, ants know to do the right thing as a result of a combination of inherited tendencies and learned behavior. There are no lazy ants in an ant colony. Each ant has his own small area in which he operates and is needed—without being told to.

Jim has discovered that, like many humans, young ants are more impressionable than older ants. The "kiddie" ants can be easily trained to adjust their behavior; whereas the older, more mature ants resist making any changes—even to save their own lives.

I know both adults and young people like that, don't you? They smoke, drink alcohol, or take dangerous drugs—even when they know the habit will kill them! Sad, huh? It's another lesson you and I can learn from the ants.

Have some fun today. Take Solomon's advice and go a little buggy. Go to the ant! See what lessons you can learn from these tiny creatures.

AUGUST 13

THE HUNTING EXPEDITION

Come over into Macedonia, and help us. Acts 16:9.

Captain William Clark, superintendent of Indian Affairs, sat at his desk one morning in 1831 when four Indians, strangers to St. Louis, strode in. Clark, of the famous Lewis and Clark team to the Pacific Northwest, sized up his visitors and determined that three of his guests were from the Nez Perce tribe and the fourth was a Flathead Indian. "Gentleman," Clark greeted the men in the language of the Nez Perce, "what can I do for you?"

"We are on a hunting expedition," the leader explained.

Clark studied the Indian's impassive face. "Aren't you quite a distance from your village?"

"Yes, our hunt has brought us across mountains, across desert, across rivers, and across the grasslands to you."

"To me?" Clark asked. "What creature could you be seeking that would bring you to me?"

The Indian paused a moment, then continued. "We have come for the White man's Book of Heaven. You can help us?"

Clark stared in surprise. *The heathen are coming for the Bible? Unbelievable!* he thought. Although knowledge of Christianity had been leaking into the mountain regions for some time, and although there were a few Christian Iroquois in the Rockies because of the witness of French fur traders, he'd never imagined that word of the Bible would reach the remote tribes of the Northwest.

"Tell me," Clark questioned, "how did you learn of the White man's Book of Heaven?"

"Once, a long time ago, some traders came upon Indians worshiping their own way and explained the only true way to worship the Great Spirit," the Indian explained. "These men had a book that contained all the directions. We wish to have such a book also."

Like the man from Macedonia whom the apostle Paul saw in vision, these Indians had traveled hundreds of miles to learn more about the God of heaven—not just for themselves, but to share with their family and friends back home. I wonder if I am as eager to share the good news of God's love with my family, with my friends? How about you?

AUGUST 14

ONE LETTER

It is like a lamp shining in a dark place until the Day dawns and the light of the morning star shines in your hearts. 2 Peter 1:19, TEV.

William Walker, a simple businessman of little importance, strode down the street toward the office of the superintendent of Indian Affairs. In addition to conducting a piece of business, he also hoped to spend a relaxing afternoon trading tales with the genial Captain Clark. One thing he didn't expect was to start a missionary movement to the West.

The tale Clark told about the four Indians' search for the Book of Heaven stunned Mr. Walker. "And so they're here? Now?"

"That's right," Clark replied. "Even though I'm not a preacher, I feel I should help them all I can. I told them the stories of Adam, of the Flood, and of Jesus. I took them over to the church. I don't know what else to do since they can't read English, especially the King James' Bible."

"What do you think they'll tell their people when they get back?" Walker asked.

"I doubt they'll ever get back. Man-of-the-Morning and Black Eagle have already died. There are only two left to tell the story."

All the way back home to Sandusky, Ohio, Walker couldn't forget what he'd heard and seen. On January 19, 1833, Walker wrote a letter to a friend, G. P. Disosway, detailing the Indians' story. Disosway had it published in a newspaper called the *Christian Advocate and Journal.* Christians carried the story from city to city, from state to state, and even across the ocean to Europe.

Although Black Eagle and Man-of-the-Morning died in St. Louis and No-Horns-on-His-Head died on the trip home, Rabbit-Skin-Leggings reached his village across the mountains and told of what he had learned. Walker's letter lit a missionary torch for Christians—a light in a dark place. By the time the missionaries arrived in the West, a group of Indian believers were there to greet them. One conversation, one letter, and the light of God's love flooded into a remote corner of the continent—changing it forever.

William Walker never imagined that his one letter would ignite the fire it did. He just shared what he knew and let the Spirit of God do the rest. That's all you and I are asked to do, isn't it?

AUGUST 15

A REAL CHAMPION

Do not be overcome by evil, but overcome evil with good. Romans 12:21, NIV.

"What will become of him?" the teachers at the El Cajon, California, elementary school wondered. Given up for adoption at birth by his 15-year-old parents, the half-Samoan and half-Swedish boy felt alone and unwanted. Because of his dyslexia, the kids at school called him "retarded." Because of his darker skin, the kids in the neighborhood called him "Nigger."

He began smoking by age 8. When he was 13, his adoptive parents turned him over to the authorities after finding illegal drugs in his room. Throughout his early teens, he drank so much that he considered himself an alcoholic. No one, not even his adoptive parents, believed Greg stood much of a chance of making it big in life. For that matter, most people who knew him believed the boy would be lucky just to make it to adulthood. But Greg proved them wrong when he discovered his talent for diving.

A few months ago I told you about Greg Louganis' courage—how he climbed back onto the diving board after his accident and went on to win the Olympic Gold Medal. The worthless kid from the streets of El Cajon, California, didn't become a hero by winning at the Olympics. He developed into hero material by practicing his dives hour after hour, day after day, year after year. Persistence and hard work, sacrifice and determination, turned him into hero material.

Whether Greg turned to God for his strength, I don't know. But I do know that Greg didn't allow hateful words, destructive habits, and evil people to overcome him. Instead, he overcame their evil with good.

You and I can do the same—no matter what habit we may have, no matter what other people call us or think of us.

And we have an added benefit when we depend on God's strength—guaranteed success! Your gold medal in the Heavenly Olympics already has your name engraved on it. So don't hold back—go for the gold!

AUGUST 16

TAKE A CHANCE

He who has the Son has life; he who has not the Son of God has not life. 1 John 5:12, RSV.

Greg, a young friend of mine, loves to play *Monopoly*. He and his friends would play it for hours on end if his mom would consent. The object of the game (in case you have never played *Monopoly*) is to make lots of money from the bank and from other players. The winner is whoever winds up with the most money while the losers go broke. Once Greg and his buddies played the game so long that the bank ran out of money and the boys had to make a new supply.

Greg finds it exciting to roll the dice and move his piece around the board without landing on someone else's property, where he'd have to pay high rent. But what Greg dreads most is landing on Chance, which generally happens sooner or later. Greg must then take a Chance card. Some cards bring him bad luck: "Go to jail! Do not pass Go and do not collect $200." or "Go to the nearest Utility, roll dice and pay owner ten times the value." No fun! When Greg lands on Chance, he has a secret wish. He wishes he could remove all the bad cards from the stack so that he could pick only a good Chance such as "Every player must pay you $100."

Whether Greg realizes it or not, *Monopoly* is a lot like real life. You and I like being able to make choices (kind of like visiting a chocolate factory and choosing either light or dark chocolate or a piece with or without nuts)—just not choices without risks.

It wouldn't be fair for Greg to remove all the cards with "bad" chances, and in life it wouldn't be very realistic to think that nothing bad will ever happen to us—especially once sin entered the world.

Greg can't avoid having bad things happen—either when he plays *Monopoly* or in life. Last winter he got tonsillitis. His best friend moved to Georgia. His pet cat, Chauncey, got hit by a car. That's life!

But thank God that real life is more than a *Monopoly* board of aimless chances. In the most important choice of all—that of eternity—you have a choice between heaven and hell, life and death.

Jesus, the Son of God, died on the cross so that all the Gregs of the world, all the Kays of the world, and all the "yous" of the world could live forever. Sooner or later each person must choose for the "chance" of a lifetime. There is no risk, however, in choosing Jesus. His promises are sure—not uncertain like the Chance cards in *Monopoly*. "He [Greg] who has the Son has life; he [Greg] who has not the Son of God has not life." Read the text again. This time insert your name where Greg's is, then pray the following:

Dear Father, help me never to forget that Your promise of eternal life is not the result of a throw of the dice, a turn of a Chance card, but rather results from my choice. Today I want to make that choice and accept Your Son Jesus into my heart and my life. Amen.

AUGUST 17

TASTE AND SEE

Like newborn babies, crave pure spiritual milk, so that by it you may grow up in your salvation, now that you have tasted that the Lord is good. 1 Peter 2:2, 3, NIV.

The fluffy little ball of fur stretched out four very large paws and opened her mouth into a giant yawn. "Me-o-o-o-w," she wailed.

"Oh, you poor little baby," the zoo attendant cooed as he tried to insert the nipple end of a large baby's bottle into the tiger kitten's mouth. "You must be terribly hungry. Won't you try a little of this milk? I know it's not your mommy's, but you'll get to like it, I promise." The kitten clamped her mouth shut and turned away just as the nipple touched the edge of her lips. "It's just not her mama's. She's gonna die if she continues to refuse to eat. If she'd only taste it, I know she'd like it."

The zoo director shook his head sadly. "It's too bad her mother died giving birth. There must be a way to make her nurse."

"Sir," the attendant suggested, "I have a house cat at home that just gave birth to a litter of kittens. I wonder . . ."

The director snapped to attention. "It would certainly be worth a try."

The plan worked. Frisky, the attendant's house cat, adopted the little tiger cub immediately. One taste of the mother cat's milk, and the cub made herself right at home—so much so that when it came time to housebreak the kittens, the tiger cub learned right along with the rest of Frisky's family. The zoo director and the attendant have no idea what will happen when the tiger cub grows to full size. Will they have to supply the housecat-trained tiger with her very own restroom facility?

While the tiger cub's story made national news, it would have had a much different ending if the tiger cub had refused Frisky's milk. The zoo attendant and the director could have coaxed, badgered, and scolded the tiger kitten until they grew hoarse trying to convince her to nurse, but until the kitten tasted the milk for herself, the milk couldn't save her life.

You and I are like the tiger cub. Our moms and dads can tell us how great God is. Our teachers can explain to us how trustworthy He can be. Brothers, sisters, pastors, and Pathfinder directors can all remind us of how loving He can be. But until we get to know Him for ourselves, He can't really save us.

AUGUST 18

TWO ALTARS

You are good to us and forgiving, full of constant love for all who pray to you. Psalm 86:5, TEV.

When Chi Ho became a Christian, his neighbors treated him cruelly. When he tried to speak to them of Jesus, they laughed and made fun of him. One morning Chi Ho got an idea. He would build an altar to his new God.

The town's basketmaker watched Chi Ho make trip after trip through town as he lugged massive river rocks in his wheelbarrow. Finally he called to him, "Chi Ho, what are you going to do with all those rocks?"

Chi Ho turned and grinned. "I'm building a monument to happiness."

Later when the rice vendor asked Chi Ho about the rocks, the smiling young man replied, "I am building a monument to happiness."

For weeks Chi Ho carried massive rocks from the riverbed to his home. Each time a villager asked Chi Ho what he planned to do with the rocks, Chi Ho's answer was the same: "I am building a monument to happiness." One day when Chi Ho failed to make any more trips through town for river rock, the rice vendor and the basket weaver wandered out to Chi Ho's home at the edge of the forest. "Chi Ho," the rice vendor called as he knocked on Chi Ho's door, "we missed you today. Chi Ho?"

Chi Ho didn't answer.

"Maybe he's out back," the basket weaver suggested. Together the men walked to the back of the house, and there they found Chi Ho. Before him stood two chest-high pillars of massive river rock. Atop each pillar was a bonfire of incense.

"What are you doing?" the basket weaver asked.

Chi Ho turned to his friend and said, "I have built two altars to my God. This altar over here is where I burn incense to say thank You for all the good things that happen to me and for all the good thoughts He gives me."

"That's fine," the rice vendor admitted. "It is good to give praise. But what is the other altar for?"

"That is where I thank God for all of my troubles, all of my hurts, and all of my bad thoughts."

"Thank God for your troubles and your bad thoughts?" the rice vendor exclaimed. "I do not understand."

"You see, God's Son died for every thought I have—good or evil. He died for each of my troubles, too. So on this altar I burn incense to praise Him for all of my troubles, all of my hurts, and all of my evil thoughts." Chi Ho smiled. "I give them all to my Father so I don't need to carry them anymore. That's why it's my monument to happiness."

Chi Ho had stumbled onto a good way of dealing with anger against a brother, even if his method might have been a little clumsy.

Give your bad feelings and your hateful thoughts to Jesus. Then every time one of those thoughts tries to return to disturb your peace of mind, give it back to Him with a large "Thank You, Jesus." And you will have built a monument to happiness too.

AUGUST 19

TEST YOUR WINGS

If I rise on the wings of the dawn, . . . even there your hand will guide me, your right hand will hold me fast. Psalm 139:9, 10, NIV.

Today is National Aviation Day. It is also Orville Wright's birthday. And I have a secret I want to share with you. Of course, after today it will never be a secret again. Perhaps you are hiding the same secret. My secret is, I can fly. I soar; I dip; I climb high above the morning clouds. I've done this since I was a little child. I don't need an airplane or a parachute. I don't need a sailplane or a kite. I just extend my arms and fly.

Before the editors of this book wipe this lesson off their computer screens, before your parents dash off an angry letter to the publisher, or before my husband declares me insane, let me explain. I fly in my dreams. These dreams are so real that when I awake and discover my latest journey was just a dream, I feel a little depressed.

When I was 5 years old, I had a dream so real that when I awoke, I flew down a flight of stairs into our living room, where my father sat reading the newspaper. My father stared in horror as I bounced face first down the stairs, coming to a sudden stop at his feet. There I lay gasping for air and unable to explain just what I'd tried to do without feeling totally foolish. Later, after seeing *Superman* on television, I decided that what I needed in order to fly was a cape. But the sheet tied around my neck didn't help. And my leap off the kitchen roof proved as disastrous as my previous flight. I didn't break any bones, but I learned an important lesson. Since then I've confined my flying either to commercial jets or to my dreams.

It makes me wonder if God once intended human beings to fly, but sin grounded us. That He built the desire to fly within us cannot be denied. Long before Orville and Wilber succeeded at Kitty Hawk, North Carolina, men dreamed of flying. In the late 1400s one of the greatest artists of all time, Leonardo da Vinci, sketched out complex diagrams of parachutes and helicopters. King David, the author of today's text, dreamed of flying too. I guess I'm in good company. The text also reminds us that wherever we go, no matter how high we fly, God is there.

The best part is that one day my dream to fly will no longer be just a dream. In heaven it will be an actuality. And best of all, even then God's hand will still be there to guide me. What about you? Are you eager to test your wings? I sure am.

AUGUST 20

THE HARE DRYER

Speak the truth to each other. Zechariah 8:16, NIV.

Have you heard this one? One morning a woman came out of her house to find her pet German shepherd, Gonzo, shaking a dead animal in his jaws—a rabbit. The woman took the dirty, mangled animal from the dog and immediately recognized it to be the pet Easter bunny kept caged on her neighbor's back porch. Horrified at the thought of having to tell her neighbor that Gonzo had killed the neighbor's beloved pet, she took the dead carcass inside her home, shampooed it, blow-dried its fur as best she could, sneaked into her neighbor's yard, and slipped the restored rabbit in its cage in a lifelike position. Then the woman left for work.

When she arrived home from work that evening, she saw a police car parked in front of her neighbor's house. Curious, she went over to a policeman standing beside the patrol car.

"What happened?" she asked. "Anything wrong?"

The policeman shook his head. "Nah—just a nuisance call. Their pet rabbit died yesterday, and some sicko in the neighborhood dug it up and put it back in its cage."

The Hare Dryer story or one of its variations, traveled across the United States and back again a number of times in 1988. Jan Harold Brunband, author of *Curses, Broiled Again*, calls the story an urban myth. An urban myth is a fanciful tale that an unknown person told as a joke and which later became accepted as gospel truth by being told and retold a couple million times.

Have you ever fallen for a tale such as this one? I have—many times. No matter how many people hear the story or retell it, the Hare Dryer remains a myth—untrue. Truth is not determined by the number of people who believe it.

What you and I believe regarding the Hare Dryer story is not important. However, what we believe regarding Jesus and His soon return is! Jesus is coming back again—regardless of the number of people waiting for Him. What happens when a person dies remains a fact, no matter how many entertaining little movies, storybooks, or TV programs claim otherwise. God didn't keep the truth about things that are really important from us. He reveals them in the Bible. Zechariah urges that we speak the truth to each other, and Jesus says: "Ye shall know the truth, and the truth shall make you free." Study for yourself to be sure you have your facts straight. Be certain that you are free from religious urban myths that can destroy your right to eternity.

AUGUST 21

DESERT MESSIAH

If anyone says to you, "Look, here is the Christ!" or, "There he is!" do not believe it. For false Christs and false prophets will appear and perform great signs and miracles to deceive even the elect—if that were possible. Matthew 24:23, 24, NIV.

Many people believe in false christs and false prophets. A few years ago (like it or not—and most Oregonians didn't like it) we had one of our very own—the Bhagwan Shree Rajneesh. Proclaiming himself to be the messiah, the Bhagwan and his followers bought land in the eastern Oregon desert. There they built a complete city, with streets, curbs, sewers, a school, a mall, and an airport. Adopting the color red as their symbol, believers came from around the world to live in the city of Rajneesh Purim in order to be near their messiah. When one of the Bhagwan's Rolls Royces passed by (he had 49), the mob of people lining the roadway fell on their faces to worship him.

At first Oregonians shrugged their shoulders and went on with the business of living. Let him and his followers do whatever they want out there in the desert, more than 70 miles from the nearest city and 20 miles from the nearest small town. As phony as he was, the Bhagwan wasn't hurting anyone, was he? They were wrong.

Daily in Portland scores of followers arrived—on buses, planes, and Amtrak trains—until the town of Rajneesh Purim organized a bus service to transport them all to the Bhagwan's city of promise. Tourists and news reporters swarmed out to the city for a closer look. Even the local ranchers in the region "drove over for a glance" at this self-proclaimed christ.

My family and I didn't go. Do you know why? Jesus Himself warned me not to go. Read about what He said in Matthew 24:23-27.

(Story to be continued.)

AUGUST 22

RED SKIRTS AND POISONED WATER

Notwithstanding the land shall be desolate because of them that dwell therein, for the fruit of their doings. Micah 7:13.

All went well in the city of Rajneesh Purim until the Bhagwan and his officials got greedy for more power and more land. Besides cheating hundreds of their followers out of their money and investors out of their investments, the Bhagwan and his leaders schemed to overthrow the local government, to change the laws to their favor, and finally to poison the water supply of The Dalles, the county seat, and assassinate one of Oregon's senators. All doubts about the Bhagwan's messiahship were erased when the U.S. government deported him for his crimes. The Bhagwan and his spokesperson, Anand Sheila, became known by their fruits.

The 49 Rolls Royces were sold at auction to a wealthy man in Texas, the Bhagwan's expensive jewelry and Rolex watches were held to help pay back the money to city investors, and the entire city was put up for sale. Hundreds of discouraged and disillusioned men, women, and children, carrying what was left of their belongings on their backs, streamed through Portland, Oregon. Their leader had been revealed as a false messiah. Their dream for the perfect city, their heaven on earth, faded. And ultimately their messiah died.

A year or so after the Bhagwan left the country, my husband and I visited the deserted city. Prairie grass had reclaimed the lots where tents had been. The abandoned buildings stood in stark silhouette against the barren hillside. The guard tower and the sign that greeted the guru's enthusiastic followers were pockmarked and gutted by souvenir hounds and angry ranchers determined to wipe the last memory of Rajneesh Purim from the land. "The land shall be desolate . . . for the fruit of their doings." No matter how long it takes, even the most clever dishonesty will be uncovered. Sooner or later, the craftiest, most deceitful individual will be revealed for his true self.

It is easy to shake my finger at the Bhagwan and say "Naughty! Naughty! You got just what you deserved" and forget that other people can know me by my fruit, whether it is sweet and pure or whether it be sour and bitter to swallow. Let's pray together this morning that the fruit of our actions will always be good to the taste as God, the Creator, intended.

AUGUST 23

WHO'S CHEATING WHOM?

Whatever is covered up will be uncovered, and every secret will be made known. So then, whatever you have said in the dark will be heard in broad daylight, and whatever you have whispered in private in a closed room will be shouted from the housetops. Luke 12:2-4, TEV.

Recently on the late-night television news show *Nightline*, the commentator reported the results of a nationwide survey (taken anonymously, of course). He said that 38 percent of sixth graders across the United States admitted to cheating off either other students' papers or cheat sheets at one time or another.

So what's new? Cheating has been around since before Jacob cheated his brother, Esau, out of his inheritance, and we all know what happened there. But think about it—would you want a surgeon who had cheated his way through medical school working on your brain, or an airline pilot who'd fudged on his exams flying the commercial jet on which you had scheduled a flight? OK, taking a peek at how the class math whiz solved the geometric equation might not result in a plane crash someday, but it could result in your downfall, even your death.

Cheaters are self-made, not born. They begin by telling little fibs, creating little cover-ups, getting away with little dishonesties until they have formed a steel web of deceit.

Just ask the millionairess who washes dirty laundry in a federal penitentiary because she tried to skim a little off her income tax report—less than 1 percent of her earnings—or ask the political candidate who lost his bid for his party's nomination for president in 1988 because of a secret rendezvous he had with a woman other than his wife, or ask the dictator and his wife who lived in exile because they had stolen millions of their country's money while their people lived in poverty.

But of course, you and I wouldn't cheat on our taxes, especially if we had billions of dollars already; we wouldn't pretend to be a messiah in order to get rich; we wouldn't steal from the poor; and none of us would be so stupid as to cheat on our marriage partners. Yet I wonder. I wonder if Leona ever sneaked a peek at someone else's answers on a geography test. I wonder if the Bhagwan ever cheated at math. I wonder if Ferdinand Marcos ever stole money from his dad's wallet. I don't know, but I wonder. And in the long run, who's cheating whom?

AUGUST 24

JUST ME

Repent, then, and turn to God, so that he will forgive your sins. If you do, times of spiritual strength will come from the Lord, and he will send Jesus, who is the Messiah he has already chosen for you. Acts 3:19, 20, TEV.

All week long I've told you stories about people whose sins ruined their lives. The same sins you and I see every day. That's discouraging and a little frightening, isn't it? It doesn't have to be.

Let me share an embarrassing story with you. When I was 10 years old, new Sabbath shoes and pretty dresses were a rare treat. That didn't bother me since I knew that my parents didn't have much money. What did bother me was feeling rejected. I had friends in my neighborhood, but no one at school liked me, or so I thought. One day a classmate's mother brought cupcakes to school for his birthday. Suddenly usually picked-on Roger was the center of attention. The attention spilled over into noon recess and on into the afternoon.

At home that night I thought about all the attention Roger got. Since my birthday wasn't until August, I came up with an alternate plan. I would take all the money from my piggy bank to school and buy each of my classmates a Fudgesicle for lunch. Then they'd like me, maybe even choose me sooner for the softball team.

It worked. The rest of the day was the best day I'd ever experienced at school. However, the next day everything was back to normal. A week later I considered doing it again, but I had used up all my money. That's when I stumbled into Leona's (or the Bhagwan's trap)—I stole a dollar bill from my mom's pocketbook. Guilt flooded through me. I discovered that I didn't even enjoy being the center of attention at school that day. Thanks to the baptismal class I was taking at the time, I also discovered the secret to relieving that guilt and putting the sin behind me forever. Not only would the Lord forgive me, but He would also give me the strength to apologize to my mother and to do what was right in the future. Mom did forgive me. And in time I forgave myself. (Maybe that's the hardest part—forgiving yourself.)

Take it from one who knows. You don't have to wait until your life falls completely apart before you break a bad habit. You don't have to wait until your crime makes national news. Whether it's your first lie or lie number 18,975, your first theft or theft number 1,139, God forgives—that's His line of work. And He can give you the strength to resist next time if you'll just ask Him.

AUGUST 25

THE BLACK HOLE

Woe unto them! for they have gone in the way of Cain. . . . These are . . . wandering stars, to whom is reserved the blackness of darkness for ever. Jude 11-13.

For years a sign on the closet door of Kelli's room read "The Black Hole—Open at Your Own Risk!" When she couldn't find her favorite skirt, someone would say, "Have you checked in the black hole?" If her car keys were missing, they were probably swallowed up in the black hole. Family and friends alike teased her with dire warnings of falling into the hole and disappearing forever. No one ever did—at least that we know of. During her "black hole" era, Kelli often replied to attacks with "Even God allowed for black holes in the universe." In time, she matured into a very neat and efficient homemaker—with no black holes allowed.

However, black holes are believed to exist, and no one is sure why. Noted astronomer Sir Arthur Eddington wrote: "I think that there should be a law of nature to prevent a star from behaving this way." But, not counting Kelli's messy closet, just what is a black hole?

A black hole is a star that has collapsed and condensed until it becomes invisible. It seems to have destroyed itself through its own gravity. All of the star's mass is still there. It's just packed into a smaller space. An example of this would be if you could remove nearly all the empty space in the atoms of the Empire State Building, you could then shrink the 102-story building to less than the size of a toothpick—a very heavy toothpick, of course, since it would still weigh the same. This makes the gravity around black holes very strong. So if an object, whether a rocket ship or a beam of light, falls into the gravitational pull of one of these collapsed stars, it cannot escape. Astronomers call it "black" because light cannot escape from it, and a "hole" because it would suck in matter like a swirling gravitational drain. You can see for yourself how this works in your own kitchen sink. Run some water into the sink and watch the water's gravitational swirl as it is sucked down the drain.

So what does all of this black hole stuff have to do with today's text? Kelli's black hole closet might be funny, but the black hole of sin isn't. Remember Cain? After he killed his brother, God cursed him and sent him away to wander in darkness for the rest of his life. Those who go "the way of Cain"—who sin against God by harming other people—become like black holes or "wandering stars" and will be cast into darkness forever.

AUGUST 26

THE BIG BLUE MARBLE

The Lord made the earth by his power; by his wisdom he created the world and stretched out the heavens. Jeremiah 51:15, TEV.

The other day I watched NASA launch the space shuttle carrying a giant telescope into outer space. With the Hubble telescope, named after famed astronomer Edwin Hubble, astronomers hope to study the universe from outside earth's atmosphere. I remember the first time I saw pictures of our planet from outer space. It looked like a big blue marble.

Scientists tell us that the earth's atmosphere distorts and even obliterates what we peer at through our telescopes. By sending the Hubble telescope into orbit outside our distorting atmosphere, we might be able to locate other star systems. Even as I write this piece, the telescope is being activated.

Since publishing a book takes a long time, I am writing this piece in April of 1990. By the time you read this in August of 1992, you will know just how successful the project has been. You will know whether or not it stayed on track or burned itself out in the earth's atmosphere. If it is successful, you will probably have seen incredible photos splashed across your TV screen and newspaper.

In the meantime, until they learn otherwise, scientists believe that there are "cold" stars or mini-black holes clumped around galaxies. Some scientists speculate that these may have played a part in the creation of our planet and in the structure of the cosmos.

Astronomers estimate that there are possibly 10,000,000,000, 000,000,000,000 stars out there somewhere—many of which are suns much like ours. With so many possible suns, they reason, there must be planets. And some of these planets must be situated the same distance from the sun, hence with enough light and heat to support life. Figuring distance, light, and heat, and giving these planets a one-in-a-million chance, then the numbers would indicate that there might be at least 10,000 inhabited planets. How do you like those odds? No matter how you look at it, that's a lot of marbles.

As Christians we can agree with these men of science. A God as generous as ours, who loves giving good gifts to His children, must thoroughly enjoy creating other planets and other children in His image. And one day soon, He has promised to rocket us to planets still unseen and unknown—not with the help of NASA, but through His wonderful creative power.

AUGUST 27

TAKE IT FROM JOEY

Ever since you were a child, you have known the Holy Scriptures, which are able to give you the wisdom that leads to salvation through faith in Christ Jesus. 2 Timothy 3:15, TEV.

As Joey climbed out of the school bus, he told himself that the new school year would be different. But there to harass him were the same old troublemakers.

"Here comes dummy Joey," Brock, a burley fifth grader, yelled.

"Yeah, dumb-dumb himself!" Sam, Brock's best buddy, joined in.

The boys waited for Joey to lose his temper and start fighting. Instead, he smiled, waved, and hurried toward Miss Edison's fifth-grade classroom.

Joey and school had never gotten along. Whether it was reading, spelling, math, or Bible, he always messed up. *Maybe Brock's right*, he thought. *Maybe I am too stupid to learn. No,* he decided, *this year will be different. I just know it!*

As the school term progressed, Joey began to notice changes in his learning ability. His problems weren't solved instantly, but somehow his schoolwork did seem easier than before. After a bit, even Brock stopped calling him dumb-dumb.

During that summer Joey had discovered a secret to learning. He formed the habit of reading his Bible every day—really reading, not just a quick-Bible-text-then-hurry-to-breakfast kind of reading. It wasn't always easy. Sometimes he couldn't understand what he had read, yet he continued studying. By the time Joey reached academy, he had read his Bible through 17 times and had read many of Ellen White's books almost as many times. He especially liked reading *Steps to Christ* and *The Desire of Ages*.

That was years ago. Today Joey is a heart surgeon. Pretty good for a dumb-dumb, huh? Perhaps his techniques will improve your learning skills too.

This is how Joey changed from being the class dummy to a straight-A student. You will need a Bible, preferably one written in everyday language—one like Today's English Version or the New International Version. Also, have a pencil and a notepad or diary handy.

1. Get up 15 minutes earlier in the morning to study. The quietness helps.
2. Sit at a desk or table to keep you from getting too sleepy.
3. Pray. Ask God to open your mind so you will understand what you read.
4. Start with one of the Gospels—Matthew, Mark, Luke, or John. Read only one story at a time and take turns becoming each person in the story. Imagine how they felt when they encountered Jesus. Imagine how Jesus would have felt. Then read the same story from *The Desire of Ages* to see how Mrs. White describes the event. From there, move on through the book of Acts and the rest of the New Testament.
5. Write today's date in your notebook, the texts you read, and what you learned about Jesus from the story you read.

AUGUST 28

RICKSHAW JIM

The Lord has anointed me to preach good news to the poor. He has sent me to bind up the brokenhearted, to proclaim freedom for the captives and release for the prisoners. Isaiah 61:1, NIV.

Remember when as a little kid in the kindergarten Sabbath school you waved goodbye to the missionary doctor, teacher, preacher, and nurse as you sang a song about leaving for the mission field? Or perhaps you were one of the lucky ones to be chosen to carry the Bible or wear the nurse's cap. When did you discover that God needs more than just doctors, nurses, teachers, and preachers—that He needs pilots, lab technicians, secretaries, mechanics, gardeners, computer programmers—all kinds of people with all sorts of skills? God uses college students to teach English to Korean students and thereby share the knowledge of God's love. He uses retired carpenters and plumbers to build churches and repair run-down schools. Being willing to let Him use you is what's important, not your age.

Recently, I read about Rickshaw Jim. Fifty-six-year-old Jim Tice went as a self-supporting missionary to Sri Lanka, India, Malaysia, and Singapore. When he and his wife returned home in 1984, he discovered that many Christians seemed uninterested in missions. Frustrated, Jim decided to do something about it.

First, he built an adult-sized tricycle rickshaw. Then Jim began a bicycle trip in Washington, at the Canadian border, traveled south to the Mexican border and across the American continent. By the time he completes his journey, he will have ridden more than 5,000 miles. Rickshaw Jim believes in missions and has found a unique and creative way of spreading the good news of Jesus Christ to at least one major part of the world.

Think about the words to the song you used to sing in the kindergarten department—the one about missionaries going to the mission field. What are your plans for the future? Is God grooming you for His special service abroad? Will you answer the commission in today's text and one day pick up the work where men such as Rickshaw Jim leave off?

AUGUST 29

TO USE, NOT TO KEEP

Teach us to number our days aright, that we may gain a heart of wisdom. Psalm 90:12, NIV.

What would you do if a stranger were to knock on your front door this morning and hand you a checkbook for an account in which he has placed $86,400? When you try to hand it back to him, he shakes his head and says, "It's yours—keep it. And tomorrow I'll place another $86,400 in it for you to use—every day for the rest of your life."

The first thing you'd probably say is, "What's the catch?"

"The only catch," he explains, "is that you must spend the entire $86,400 in one 24-hour period. Every cent must be used up each day."

"I can spend it any way I please?"

"Yes—any way you please."

"Wow! What fun!"

The good news is, you already possess such a bank account—not in dollars, but in time. Every day you live, you are given 86,400 seconds to use however you see fit. And the only catch is that you can't save them; you must use them all every day.

Busy, busy, busy! We all feel too busy every now and then. Have you ever said "I'd help out at church if I had the time" or "I'd help my little brother study for his math test if I could find the time" or "I'd clean out the garage for Dad and surprise mom by fixing supper tonight . . . if I had the time"? Kind of a weak excuse, huh? You have the time—the same amount of time your grandparents had each day they lived, the same amount of time Jesus had every day of His life, the same amount of time Adam had, or Ruth, or Daniel.

God's gift of time is free to all. While a person might be smarter or richer or more talented than someone else, time is the great equalizer. We all have the same amount to use or to waste. And you and I are responsible for how we use it. Tell me, how will you spend your 86,400 seconds today? You could learn a new hobby, read a book, hike, gaze at the stars, make a new friend, take out the garbage without being told—the list is endless.

AUGUST 30

MORE THAN SOW BUGS

The Word became flesh and made his dwelling among us. We have seen his glory, the glory of the One and Only, who came from the Father, full of grace and truth. John 1:14, NIV.

Five-year-old Kristy turned over a rock at the edge of her grandmother's garden and squealed, "O-o-h! Bugs!"

Grandma looked up from her weeding and grinned. "Sow bugs—they're called sow bugs."

Kristy wrinkled her nose in disgust as the little black creatures scurried for cover. "I wonder why God ever made such ugly things."

Grandma laughed. "Why, child, they're not ugly, at least not to another sow bug. And did you know that you and I can learn about God from even the tiniest creature?"

She reached out and picked up one of the slower moving sow bugs. Instantly the bug rolled itself into a ball. "See, he's afraid. He thinks I might hurt him." Kristy peered at the small, black ball in her grandmother's hand.

"How can I show him that I don't intend to hurt him?" Grandma asked. "Got any ideas?"

Kristy thought for a moment. "I suppose you could give him some food."

"What else?"

"Uh, you could put him back under his rock," Kristy suggested, "or build him a little house."

Grandma laughed. "Maybe I can tell him so. Hey, little bug, I won't hurt you. I love you."

"Oh, Grandma," Kristy giggled, "he can't understand you."

"Do you think he would understand me if I could shrink down to his size, even make myself look like another sow bug?"

"Grandma, that's silly!"

"Is it? Jesus did that and a whole lot more to show His love for us. He left all of heaven to come down here to this earth and become a piddly-little human being so we could understand Him better. That's one lesson the sow bug can teach us," Grandma reminded.

AUGUST 31

THE MEASURE OF A MAN'S WORTH

A good man's words are like pure silver; a wicked man's ideas are worthless. Proverbs 10:20, TEV.

In 1862 President Lincoln received a letter from the king of Siam (now Thailand). The king had learned of the Civil War from an Englishwoman named Anna Leonowens. When the king discovered that Lincoln had no elephants with which to fight the war, he wrote, offering to ship pairs of elephants that could be bred in the United States for military purposes. The king then instructed Lincoln on the care and keeping of the beasts.

With his war troubles and the other political pressures Lincoln faced, it would have made sense for him to chuckle over the king's suggestion and then just toss the letter into the garbage or tell his secretary to mail off a brief thank-you note to the king. But that wouldn't have been Abraham Lincoln's style. Instead, President Lincoln sat down and personally wrote a thank-you letter in which he carefully explained the reasons that elephants could not thrive in the United States. He also expressed his appreciation for the king's generous offer and kind concern. He signed the letter, "Your good friend, Abraham Lincoln."

The king of Siam was no political threat to Lincoln, nor was he the ruler of a powerful nation. He wasn't even a voter. The man's kingdom was thousands of miles away from Washington, D.C. Yet Lincoln treated the naive king with as much respect as he would have the king of England or the czar of Russia. A wise man indeed.

Perhaps the true measure of a human being's greatness is not money, power, or fame, but how he treats the unimportant people he meets, those who can do absolutely nothing for him. The man who stops to help a child untangle a kite string, the woman who takes time to help an old lady with her groceries, the boy or girl who sees the school bully picking on a younger child and tells him to "pick on someone your own size"—these are the greatest people, the wisest people, the wealthiest people in the whole world. Their words and their actions are pure silver through and through.

SEPTEMBER 1

FIX A FEW TEETH

Again Jesus said, . . . "As the Father has sent me, I am sending you." John 20:21, NIV.

Friends and neighbors of Shirley and her dentist-husband, Bob, could understand flying to Brazil for a holiday. But to travel into the backcountry aboard a mission launch and repair teeth? That made no sense at all.

"How will you communicate? Do you speak Portuguese?" their friends asked.

"I don't know how we'll communicate because we don't know Portuguese," Shirley admitted. "I imagine we won't get to do much real missionary work while we're there except for filling and extracting teeth."

The desire to go to a foreign country as a missionary began years earlier for Shirley. When she was a little girl, her father, also a dentist, had died in a plane crash in the Pacific Ocean while on his way to begin a term of mission service. So when the opportunity came to go to Brazil and work on a mission launch as an assistant to her husband, the dentist, she urged him to accept. Even Bob wondered just how much real mission work they could do in such a short time, not knowing the language. For Shirley just watching real missionaries in action would be enough.

Working on the mission launch proved to be all Shirley had imagined. While she found it frustrating not to be able to communicate directly with the people, every day she witnessed new adventures and incredible miracles. The medical team from the United States had been forced to travel without adequate supplies of food and fresh water. The Brazilian government would exchange only a small portion of their U.S. dollars—so the cash supply was also scarce. Yet during their time in the backcountry the medical/dental team never went hungry or thirsty. They always found adequate quantities of fuel for the launch. And each day ended long before the long line of hurting patients stopped coming.

I know that God only requires me to do my best in His name, Shirley reasoned to herself, *but I'd so much like to do some real missionary work—work different than I'd do back home in Portland.*

(Story to be continued.)

SEPTEMBER 2

LADY SHIRLEY

In all thy ways acknowledge him, and he shall direct thy paths. Proverbs 3:6.

The mission launch traveled farther and farther up the Amazon River. The tangle of jungle undergrowth grew thicker and thicker as they traveled. The only contact the villagers had with the outside world came by river. So the arrival of the mission launch gave the people cause for celebration. When the launch arrived in one particular village, the local school let out for the day in order to allow the children time for a trip to the dentist. While Bob and the other doctors dealt with the usual line of patients, Shirley and one of the other doctors' wives decided to visit the schoolhouse. Shirley took along her Bible and a copy of the book *Steps to Christ*—both in English.

At the school, the women tried to communicate with the teachers, but the teachers didn't speak English, and the two women didn't speak Portuguese. When it was time to leave, the women waved goodbye and started back to the launch. Suddenly a man came running after them.

"I speak English," he shouted. "I am school's English teacher."

But when the women began talking, it was evident that the man couldn't understand what they were saying, nor did they understand him. All they accomplished was to exchange their first names. Since the teacher knew a smattering of English, Shirley gave her Bible and the book to him. *Perhaps,* she thought, *he reads English better than he speaks it.*

When Shirley arrived back at the launch, she asked the pastor about the man and learned that the teacher belonged to the local Catholic church and was the only person in the entire village who knew any English whatsoever. If on her own she'd gone looking for the only English-speaking person in the village, she'd probably never have found him. Instead, God directed the teacher to her.

Thrilled, Shirley tried to tell some of the other launch people about the encounter, but they didn't seem to catch her excitement. To them Shirley's miracle was such a little thing compared with the challenge of saving lives and easing pain; yet to Shirley the miracle was everything. Her mission to Brazil had become more than just cleaning teeth, as important as that may be.

God wants to direct in your life, too. You may not be old enough to go to Brazil in South America or to Uganda in Africa, yet God promises to direct your path if only you, like Shirley, will let Him. And someday, who knows? Maybe you'll board a mission launch, travel up the Amazon River, and meet a man who came to know and love Jesus Christ through a Bible and a book called *Steps to Christ* that a certain "Lady Shirley" gave him years ago. Maybe, who knows?

SEPTEMBER 3

HOW DOES GOD SPEAK?

"Speak, Lord, your servant is listening." 1 Samuel 3:9, TEV.

What does God's voice sound like? Does He have a deep bass voice? Or does He speak with a rich tenor tone? Every time I read the story of young Samuel and God's midnight visit, I wonder again, for I've never heard God's voice speaking out loud to me. Yet He speaks to me regularly. That sounds like a contradiction, but it isn't—not at all. For, you see, God speaks to me in several different ways. Sometimes He speaks through impressions.

Late one night my parents and I were traveling home from visiting my sister at Atlantic Union College. Route 2, the most direct route from the college to our home in Troy, New York, winds and twists through the mountains of eastern Massachusetts. For some reason there were a lot of cars on the road, forcing us to ride for miles in bumper-to-bumper traffic. I had been asleep in the back seat when suddenly I woke up feeling incredibly thirsty.

"Daddy," I whined, "can we stop at a gas station or something? I'm so thirsty I could just die."

My father, who never liked to stop for anything while traveling, answered, "I doubt we'll find anything open at this hour, but if you see any place we can stop, let me know."

Suddenly a light caught my attention—a light in the window of a cafe up ahead on our side of the road. "There, Daddy!" I shouted, "there! See, that place is open. See the light?"

My mother glanced toward my father and grinned a she-got-ya-there type of grin as he eased us out of the long line of traffic toward the tiny coffee shop. I could hear him mumbling under his breath about all the cars that would be getting ahead of us on the road.

"I'll go check to see if they're still open," my father said. After walking entirely around the building once, he returned to the car and scratched his head. "That's funny; I could have sworn that I saw lights on when we drove in, but this place hasn't been in operation for months."

I groaned. "But the light," I argued. "That's strange—there is no light. Must have been a reflection of some kind." He climbed back into the car and drove back onto the highway.

I had just curled up to go back to sleep when we saw red lights flashing. There'd been a seven-car accident. A patrolman waved us around the wreckage. As we passed the third car—the most seriously damaged vehicle and the one that had the most injuries—Mother, Daddy, and I gasped. Minutes earlier the third car had been behind us in the long line of traffic. We would have been that third car, except for the mysterious light. God used my thirst to remove us from danger.

SEPTEMBER 4

GOD SPEAKS THROUGH THE BIBLE

Obey me, and I will be your God and you will be my people. Walk in all the ways I command you, that it may go well with you. Jeremiah 7:23, NIV.

Meet three friends of mine—Kendra, Rick, and Merideth. Each came to me with a problem. Each asked me for advice. Each wanted to know how to discover God's will.

A handsome young man named Hank had stolen Kendra's heart. They'd dated for quite some time when he proposed to her. The problem: Hank didn't believe in God; Kendra did. She wanted me to tell her it was OK to marry him anyway.

Rick had been best buddies with Tim and Andy since first grade. In third grade the three made a blood pact of loyalty. Their friendship continued throughout grade school and into academy.

The problem: One night Tim and Andy broke into the academy administration building and stole all the audiovisual and computer equipment, then hocked it for cash with which they bought a supply of crack. When the principal brought in the police to investigate the break-in, Tim and Andy confessed to Rick what they'd done and made him vow not to tell anyone. Should Rick rat on his friends?

Merideth entered and won her state beauty pageant. She would compete for the Miss America title in Atlantic City, New Jersey. The problem: Merideth would be required to participate in all the activities—Friday night and Sabbath as well. Wouldn't Merideth's witness to the other pageant contestants make up for breaking the Sabbath just a little?

What advice would you give my three friends? Each of my young friends claimed not to know God's will. Each said he or she wished God would speak to them face-to-face. Each wanted to hear God's voice. And do you know, God did speak to each of them, not in a clap of thunder or a desert whirlwind, or even a still small voice, but through His Word, the Bible. God answered their questions directly several thousand years ago. And those answers haven't changed, no matter how much my friends wished they had. Kendra, Merideth, and Rick knew what God required of them before they asked. Can you find the answers in the Bible that helped my friends choose the right solution to their problems? What texts would you give them to read? A place to begin might be 2 Corinthians 6:15 and Exodus 20:8-11.

SEPTEMBER 5

WARNING BELLS

The Spirit of the Lord will rest on him—the Spirit of wisdom and of understanding, the Spirit of counsel and of power, the Spirit of knowledge and of the fear of the Lord. Isaiah 11:2, NIV.

Kurt tossed the sponge basketball to Will. "So are you comin' with us tonight or not? Mandi's expecting you."

Will caught the ball and bounced it twice before answering. *Why not go to Kurt's moonlight swimming party?* he thought. I've hung out with some of these guys since fourth grade. It was only after Kurt let it slip that there would be no parents or chaperons at the party that warning bells had gone off in Will's head. Those warning bells! He'd been excited when he'd first been invited to Kurt's parents' palatial estate overlooking the city of Portland. He could feel Kurt and the other guys watching him intently. "I don't think so."

"Aw come on. You chicken or something? It's no big deal," Kurt pushed.

"I'm sorry." Will shook his head. "I'll have to pass this time."

As his best buddies left him standing beneath the hoop in the schoolyard, he heard Kurt whisper, "What's with him?" The others shrugged their shoulders and continued walking. Will punched the basketball with his fist. What *was* wrong with him? He didn't understand himself. Normally he would have leaped at the chance—he loved swimming and good food, and Mindi wasn't too bad either, he admitted.

It was those pesky warning bells again! *Gram and her old wives' tales,* he thought. Gram lived with Will and his parents. Normally he loved talking with the spirited old lady. She could be so funny, yet so wise—until the day she told him about the warning bells.

"Those are the loud, clanging bells that go off in your head, warning you that something isn't quite right. Always heed those bells," she said. "They ring straight to you from God's throne."

Those bells! What could possibly be wrong with a bunch of kids goofing off at a friend's pool?

(Story to be continued.)

SEPTEMBER 6

BELLS, BELLS, AND MORE BELLS

The Lord knoweth how to deliver the godly out of temptations. 2 Peter 2:9.

As Will rode his bike the short distance to school the next morning, Gram's words rang in his head. "The bells are more often right than wrong. If something seems not quite right, it probably isn't."

Will's friends wasted no time telling him how much he'd missed at Kurt's pool party the night before. The more his friends raved about the party, the worse Will felt. *Gram and her warning bells*, he grumbled to himself.

"Yeah, the fun really started when Kurt swam up behind Lynn and untied her swim top," Jim, the youngest in their group, added. The rest of the guys smirked as Jim continued the story. "Then he grabbed her top and swam to the other side of the pool."

Kurt and the other guys doubled over with laughter as they remembered the girl's embarrassment.

"What did the other girls do?"

"That's just it. Kurt tied the top into a ball, and we started a game of keep away."

Will winced. Poor Lynn. She must have been mortified.

His concern for Lynn must have shown on his face, because Kurt added, "Aw, come on. Don't be such a wimp. We didn't hurt her or anything."

"Yeah, later we let her win the chug-a-lug contest," Jim added. "She sure got mighty silly after drinking so much wine cooler."

Jangle! Jangle! Clang! Clang! Gong! Gong! Will smiled to himself. Gram and her pesky warning bells. *Booze at the pool party?* Will thought. "What did your folks say when they got home, Kurt?"

"Uh, well, uh, we didn't tell 'em. We're not that stupid, you know."

"Sounds pretty dumb to me," Will mumbled and glanced down at his watch. "Hey, guys, I gotta go make a phone call. I just thought of something I forgot to tell my grandma this morning."

Will's friends stared as he turned and ran up the stairs toward the registrar's office and the telephone. As he dialed his home number, Will admitted to himself, *I'm not ready for those kinds of parties—and I don't think I ever will be. Thanks, Gram.*

SEPTEMBER 7

TINY BURRS

To every thing there is a season, and a time to every purpose under the heaven. . . . A time to rend, and a time to sew. Ecclesiastes 3:1-7.

Those irritating little burrs! Some people call them stick-tights. You know the kind. Every time you return from a walk in a field of tall grass or from the woods, you must spend what seems like hours and hours removing the ugly little pests from your socks and pants legs—one at a time. Talk about a waste of nature's creative energy—right? What good can they possibly serve?

That's exactly how Swiss mountaineer George de Mestral felt when in 1948 he returned from an alpine climb only to find his lower pants legs coated with them. While yanking them from his trousers, he stopped long enough to study one. Just why had God created such a useless thing? Fascinated by the burr's hooklike structure, he wondered if the plant's construction could be used in producing a device that could fasten people's clothing. Buttons, snaps, hooks, zippers—could this tiny burr compete with such tried-and-true methods?

When he shared his discovery and subsequent idea with others, they all laughed—all except a French textile weaver. "Your idea just might work," the weaver told George.

First, the two men created two strips of cotton—one piece with hooks and the other of a velvet-like fabric. It worked, or at least almost. Unfortunately, every time they pulled the two strips apart, the tiny hooks broke. Experimenting with nylon thread, they discovered that by exposing the woven thread to infrared light, the nylon melted into tiny, almost-indestructible hooks. They named their new product Velcro—*vel* for velvet and *cro* for crochet, which in French means hook.

Today sneakers, jackets, sleeping bags—all sorts of products—use Velcro. As of 1959 the French-based company has manufactured and sold more than 60 million yards of Velcro—all made possible by a hike up a mountain and by George de Mestral's habit of observing Mother Nature's lessons. George discovered that even an irksome burr has a purpose to its existence—if you take the time to discover its strengths.

The past few days we've talked about the methods God uses to speak to us. Nature is one more way. Take a walk in the woods today, or if you're a city dweller, study the life of plants and creatures living in an empty lot or even in a crack in the sidewalk. If you take the time to look and listen, you may be surprised at what God, through Mother Nature, can teach you.

SEPTEMBER 8

AN EASIER WAY

I will listen to what God the Lord will say. Psalm 85:8, NIV.

Jody huddled herself into a tight little ball and hugged a bed pillow to her chest. Cory was at it again—screaming, crying, and throwing her stuffed animals against the wall.

"They're so mean. It's so unfair! I don't understand why Mom and Dad won't let me go with the gang tonight," Cory raged. "They insist upon treating me like a baby—'don't do this, don't do that.' If I listened to everything they said, I'd never have any fun! It's my life; I should be allowed to live it—my way!"

Jody knew better than to answer her older sister in the middle of a tirade. Cory was about to pick up her argument where she'd left off when they heard their mother's voice.

"Cory, one more word and you're grounded! Now get yourself down here and set the table for supper—you too, Jody."

"See," Cory hissed, "what did I tell you? Might as well be living in Communist China or something!"

Jody sighed. She'd seen and heard it all before. No matter what their parents did or said, Cory insisted they were being unfair and weren't allowing her to grow up and make her own decisions.

"I'm in high school now. It's time to let go! I'm not a dumb little kid anymore."

Jody grimaced. From where she sat, Cory acted dumber now than she had a few years ago.

"You wait until you get to be my age; you'll understand." Cory stormed from the room in a swirl of tousled blonde curls.

"Her age! As if being 18 months older makes her a mental giant of some kind!" Jody muttered to herself. It wasn't that Jody was a goody-goody or was afraid to think for herself. It was because she did think for herself that Jody could see just how foolish Cory could be. Long ago Jody learned to listen and watch her older sister, Cory, rush headfirst into trouble before she would follow after. This precaution had saved Jody much pain over the years—pain from spankings, from privileges denied, from groundings, from natural consequences of unwise decisions.

Just as Jody didn't need to jump off a bridge to learn that she'd only belly-flop on the water below, she didn't have to try all the foolish things Cory did to learn what might be harmful. Wise beyond her years, Jody chose to learn from, instead of blindly copying, her sister's mistakes. God spoke to Jody; Jody listened.

SEPTEMBER 9

WHEN PARENTS AREN'T THERE

Listen, my son, to your father's instruction and do not forsake your mother's teaching. They will be a garland to grace your head and a chain to adorn your neck. Proverbs 1:8, 9, NIV.

Good advice! God nurtures willing parents so they can wisely instruct and teach their children. After about six years or so, He adds teachers and pastors to the child's learning center. But what happens when no one is around to advise you? What can happen when Mom and Dad cannot give you the advice you need to save you from destruction? How does God speak to you then?

Let me tell you about Kelli and Rhonda, my two daughters. Our home at Blue Mountain Academy sat alongside a dirt road that wound through the woods, then back again. Throughout the summer the girls rode their bikes along the trails, then down the hill again to our house.

One morning in late autumn, I cautioned them not to ride up into the woods. "Deer hunting season opened this morning. Only ride up to the edge of the woods and back down again for the next few days." Every year hunters managed to ignore the "No Trespassing" signs posted on the school's property.

A half hour or so later I stepped to the back door to check on the girls and spied the neon yellow slickers of three hunters stalking through our woods. I stepped outside to warn the hunters that they were in a no-hunting area when I saw two of the men crouch down and level their rifles. I whipped about and looked in the direction of their aim, and my heart stopped.

Rhonda and Kelli—they were aiming at Rhonda and Kelli. Before I could react, I heard the whine of two rifle shots zing, and I saw my daughters fall flat on their faces on the ground. I shrieked and ran toward my daughters' attackers, screaming, "You crazy idiots! You shot my children."

(Story to be continued.)

SEPTEMBER 10

ANOTHER VOICE

My son [and daughter], pay attention to what I say; listen closely to my words. . . . Keep them within your heart; for they are life to those who find them and health to a man's [and a woman's] whole body. Proverbs 4:20-22, NIV.

The startled hunters took one look at the wild woman running toward them and the two children lying on the ground, then took off running into the woods. I dashed to my daughters, but not before they got to their feet and threw themselves into my arms.

Weeping uncontrollably, I squeezed them tightly. "Oh, my babies!" I wailed. "I thought you'd been shot."

"We would have been, Mommy," Rhonda said, her eyes round with fear, "if you hadn't yelled for us to lie down on the ground."

"But I"—I shook my head violently—"I didn't tell you to lie down."

"Yes, you did," Kelli interrupted. "I heard you."

"Yeah," Rhonda said, "you told us to lie on the ground."

"All I did was scream."

"It was your voice; I know it," Rhonda insisted.

Tears filled my eyes as I realized that God had saved the lives of my daughters by speaking to them in my clear soprano tones—not bass, not tenor, but high soprano.

Later, when my husband arrived home, he went out to see the spot where the girls had fallen. Taking a jackknife from his pocket, he dug a bullet out of the tree trunk right behind where the girls had fallen. The other slug he found in the next tree trunk—both at the level the girls' heads would have been while sitting on their bikes.

If Kelli and Rhonda hadn't been in the habit of knowing and obeying my voice, they wouldn't have been so quick to fall to the ground. God does speak to us through family and friends. And occasionally He speaks directly in the voice He knows will best grab our attention, thus saving us from danger and destruction. Our job is to be listening so we won't miss God's message, no matter which method of communication He might choose to use.

SEPTEMBER 11

FIVE-POINT FORMULA FOR SUCCESS

Whatever your hand finds to do, do it with all your might. Ecclesiastes 9:10, NIV.

Deciding what you want to be when you "grow up" is scary whether you're 10 years old or 40 years old. And too many people, parents and kids alike, think that choosing a career is an irrevocable decision: once a doctor, always a doctor; once a mechanic, always a mechanic; once a hair stylist—well, you get the picture. The average person changes careers at least five times during working years. So don't worry if you change your mind a lot. It's OK. Most people do.

Moses studied to be a pharaoh, but became a sheepherder, a rebel leader, a people mover, a judge, and a writer. Throw in a few incredible engineering feats, city planning, and becoming the country's health inspector, and you have a very busy man. Remember Paul the apostle, Paul the student, Paul the philosopher, Paul the tentmaker, Paul the preacher, and Paul the author? Paul and Moses had more than their writings in common—both men let God lead them, and they both did their very best at each task, probably the two most important lessons kids and adults can ever learn.

Another lesson too many people learn too late is "Open doors; don't close them." Often a person will slam a door shut too soon without considering the possibilities. Because of one lousy D in third grade arithmetic, a student may decide mathematics is too hard. Bang! There goes the door—slammed shut to more than 50 percent of the most interesting careers available. Convince yourself you hate reading? Bang! That door-slamming decision closes 30 to 40 percent of the fun jobs available! Slammed doors become mental blocks—barriers more difficult to overcome than the subject itself ever could be.

Learn new skills. Pursue new hobbies. Be open to new experiences. Don't be afraid to mess up. Sometimes you learn more from your mistakes than from your successes. These new experiences will increase your options considerably.

Whether you are 9 or 90, this five-point formula can make your life richer: 1. Identify your natural-born talents and think of creative ways to use them. 2. Don't close doors too soon. What might not appeal today might be great fun for you tomorrow—keep at it. 3. Open doors to skills you've never tried. 4. As today's text says, do your best. Never settle for a go-cart quality job when with a little more effort you can have Rolls Royce results. 5. Most important—let God lead you. He knows where you'll be the happiest.

SEPTEMBER 12

DREAM IT: DO IT

Children in whom was no blemish, but well favoured, and skilful in all wisdom, and cunning in knowledge, and understanding science, and such as had ability in them to stand in the king's palace, and whom they might teach the learning and the tongue of the Chaldeans. Daniel 1:4.

Wow! Talk about talent "coming out your ears"! Talk about having it all together. Exceptionally handsome, gifted, wise, clever, cool, and scientific whiz kids to boot! The list describes the Babylonian king's choice Israelite captives. Did you ever wonder what happened to all of the duds, the bozos, and the dweebs who were captured along with Daniel and his friends? The Bible doesn't tell us. And unfortunately, most of us would probably have been among those not mentioned—like my friend Ian. "I have no talents at all. I can't sing. I can't play the piano; I can't even play a kazoo,'' Ian wailed. ''My drawings look like nightmares come to life. I'm a klutz at basketball. And at softball I hold the world's record for the shortest time up to bat before striking out. You name it, and I can't do it!''

Perhaps like Ian you aren't gifted in those areas. Perhaps your musical ear is made of tin, and when you try to draw, your hand more closely resembles a bear claw than a human hand. Your lack of coordination makes you feel like a palsied centipede. And you've decided that your only option for a career choice is sorting recyclable trash—a very important task in the 1990s, I might add.

But wait! There's more to this talent business than sports, music, and art. Talents come in all shapes and sizes. For instance, if you enjoy putting jigsaw puzzles together, it could mean that you have a sharp eye, that you're a problem solver. Combine that ability with an interest in science, and you might be the one who solves the problem of acid rain or repairs the hole in the ozone layer. Combine problem solving with an interest in construction, and you'd make a terrific engineer or an architect or an interior designer. If you have a knack for saying just the right thing at the right time, you could become a U.S. ambassador, a diplomat, a congressman, a pastor, a disc jockey—even a stand-up comic. If you hurt when someone else is hurting, perhaps you should be a nurse, a lawyer, a social worker—the list is endless.

The combination of ordinary, everyday talents blended with a spark of creativity and a sense of adventure can turn you into a missionary to Argentina, a video producer, or the president of the United States. No matter how ho-hum your talents may seem or how wild and crazy your ideas can become, God can use those talents for His cause if you let Him. So go ahead and dream. Dream big dreams, little dreams, silly dreams, and scary dreams. If you can dream it, you can find a way to do it. The only real limit to your dreams is the limit you place on yourself. All God expects is your best.

SEPTEMBER 13

DR. E'S SAW

He gave to each one according to his ability. Matthew 25:15, TEV.

To me the truly scary side of this talent business is not what talents God gave me or continues to give me, but how I use the talents He gives. With talent, it's a matter of ''use it or lose it.'' The great conductor-pianist

Leonard Bernstein once said, "If I miss practicing for one day, I can tell the difference in my playing. If I miss for one week, my wife can tell the difference. If I fail to practice for a month, the entire world knows."

Tennis pros practice tennis. Gymnasts practice flips and splits. Swimmers practice doing the butterfly and the crawl. Even taste testers practice tasting. Use it or lose it.

It's true; if you're practicing to run a marathon, you might have to lighten up on your time on the basketball court. If you're studying for your final exams in math, you might have to stay away from your computer screen for a while.

Dr. E is an example of focusing on a skill while maintaining his other skills as well. While attending medical school and doing his resident studies, he had very little time for his second love—playing his saw. Now, God didn't expect Dr. E to become both a physician and a professional saw player. Yet Dr. E's interest in playing this humble instrument is a blessing to him and to the people around him. On Friday night Dr. E relaxes by reproducing the high, quivery melody of "Amazing Grace" on his saw. On Sabbath and at camp meetings Dr. E shares his talent with others. So while his energy must be focused on medicine and on his patients, he continues to use his ability to create music on his saw to bless others.

God has a purpose for each of your talents—no matter how small or how weak a particular talent might be. If you are willing to use each one of your talents for God, He will make them grow. Like the servants who doubled their talents and their master rewarded their efforts, so God will reward you by increasing your talents in both size and quantity.

SEPTEMBER 14

GENUINE PRIDE

Pride leads to destruction, and arrogance to downfall. It is better to be humble and stay poor than to be one of the arrogant and get a share of their loot. Proverbs 16:18, 19, TEV.

Go for the gold! Since this past January I've been encouraging you to go for the gold. You've watched the Olympics, you're watching the presidential campaign—all are saying "Go for the gold!" How do you go for the gold, work hard for excellence, and keep it from "going to your head"?

It's not easy. No discussion of talents would be complete without mentioning that ugly five-letter word—"pride." We've all read about the star who takes his publicity agent's hype seriously and becomes impossible to work with, or the musician who is too busy "living it up" to meet his appointments, or the writer who is annoyed by the "little people" who buy his books.

Today's text applies to more than just Robin Leach's *Lifestyles of the Rich and Famous*. On the local scene, the lead soprano in choir who knows absolutely everything there is to know about music, or the star basketball jock who swaggers about the school in his team jersey, or the class brain who never needs to study yet pulls straight A's—all suffer from the same malady.

Only by remembering the source of our talents can we keep from getting conceited in our successes. Two celebrity performers illustrate this point. On her hair coloring ad, the actress Cybill Shepherd admits that yes, she's pretty, but she didn't have anything to do with that—it came from her parents and grandparents. Yes, that's right, talents are inherited. Scientists have discovered that twins separated from each other and from their natural parents at birth will often share the same likes and dislikes and the same talents. God-given gifts.

The second, Barbara Mandrell, attributes her success in country-western music to the fact that yes, while many singers are better and have a greater talent than she, few are willing to work as hard or harder. Thomas Edison once said, "Genius is 1 percent inspiration and 99 percent perspiration."

The third and most important element in talent is God. First, God gives you the gift, a tiny spark of creativity. Then He fans it to a flame by giving you opportunities through which you can develop it—such as at school, church, Sabbath school, in your own community. And last, God gives you the health and the strength to enjoy perfecting your skill. So first, last, and always, your talents—and mine—come from God. What a Father! What a Creator! What a Friend! Of Him we can be genuinely proud.

SEPTEMBER 15

EXAMINE THE POSSIBILITIES

The disciples went and preached everywhere. Mark 16:20, TEV.

I have declared today to be Missionary Day. A fantastic event occurred on this date—September 15, 1874. John N. Andrews, his daughter, Mary, and his son, Charles, sailed from the United States for

Europe (Switzerland, to be exact), becoming the first foreign missionaries sent out by the Seventh-day Adventist Church. They were ordinary people exercising extraordinary faith! The hundreds of thousands of missionaries who followed the Andrews' example during the following 118 years have also been just ordinary people exercising extraordinary faith.

If you have ever spent spring break helping to build a grade school in Baja, Mexico, your two-week vacation smuggling Bibles into Cuba, a summer on the island of Guam working on the Adventist radio station, a year teaching English in Japan, or the rest of your life at a medical clinic in Malawi, Africa, this is your day to celebrate. If you have ever conducted a successful Investment project or saved your pennies for Thirteenth Sabbath, today you can party. Better yet, let's party all week. If you have ever imagined yourself going to Africa, India, China, Alaska—wherever—as a missionary, here are a few party ideas you might consider that will increase your awareness of mission service:

1. Invite a missionary to your school to share his or her experiences.
2. Read a book about missionaries.
3. Suggest a "lunch break" at school. Convince your friends to eat only a sandwich one day and give the money they would have spent on dessert, fruit, and peanuts to missions—either locally at the soup kitchen for the homeless or as a special offering for Thirteenth Sabbath.
4. Collect blankets from the local church members to give the shelter for the homeless.
5. Start a big brother/big sister tutoring program at school. Teach someone to read or to memorize the times tables.
6. Set up a "Santa's workshop." Collect used or new toys from your classmates, repair them, and give them to needy kids at Christmas.
7. Plan a "missionary party," in which everyone comes dressed in costumes native to other nationalities. Play games and music from other cultures. Ask members in your church who represent another nationality to bring samples of food, games, and music and then have them tell about daily life in their society.

Seven possibilities among thousands. "Hey," you say, "I can't do any of these things—I'm just an ordinary kid." Remember what I said about ordinary people with extraordinary faith? Oh really? Did you know that some kid your age successfully pulled off every idea I listed above—either through school, the Pathfinder Club, the church, or in some cases, all by himself or herself? Ordinary people, extraordinary faith, and God's blessing can do—and does—wonders.

NO DUMB MOOSE, PART 1

Do everything without complaining or arguing, so that you may become blameless and pure, children of God without fault in a crooked and depraved generation. Philippians 2:14, 15, NIV.

Buck, the Pathfinder director, sighed in exasperation at his 13-year-old charge. "Josh," Buck said, "can't you do anything without griping or arguing about it?"

Arms folded defiantly, the boy stared down at his untied sneakers and said nothing.

"Look," Buck continued, "either you carry your share of the gear back to camp or you're on KP duty for the rest of the weekend."

Back at camp the director turned the stubborn Josh over to Cookie, the camp chef, who kept the young man busy scrubbing pots and washing dishes long after the other boys had left for a moonlight hike down by the river.

As Josh slammed the last cast-iron pot on the storage shelf and straightened up, Cookie stepped up behind him. "We're not quite done yet."

Josh groaned. "You're kiddin'!"

A tiny grin teased the corners of Cookie's mouth. "Nope! Come on over to the fire and sit down. We still need to toast these marshmallows. Here's a great stick to toast them on."

Reluctantly, Josh dragged himself over to the biggest log next to the camp fire and accepted the forked branch from Cookie. Cookie spent the next few minutes instructing Josh on the fine art of marshmallow toasting. Josh slurped his first gooey marshmallow into his mouth and grinned at the grizzled old man.

"Got some goo on your upper lip," Cookie chuckled.

"Thanks." Josh wiped his lip clean with his sleeve.

Cookie smiled to himself and dropped another marshmallow into the boy's hand. "Wanna try it again?"

Minutes passed as the man and the boy sat side by side on the log, watching the fire and eating singed marshmallows. Finally, Cookie glanced at Josh. "You know, since we sat down here by the fire, you haven't used the word *no* once. It's been nice."

Josh reddened and stared into the fire.

"I'll bet you don't even know why you say no sometimes," Cookie added. "I'll bet it's more of a habit than a difference of an opinion. You're a neat kid when you give yourself half a chance."

(Story to be continued.)

SEPTEMBER 17

NO DUMB MOOSE, PART 2

Put away perversity from your mouth. Proverbs 4:24, NIV.

Flames flickered and gyrated in an intriguing dance as the darkness of the crisp autumn evening surrounded Josh and Cookie. They'd long since tired of the sicky, sweet marshmallows and had tossed their branches into the fire.

"Sitting here reminds me of my years working on the Trans-Canadian Railroad," Cookie began. "Many a night I sat high up in the Canadian Rockies, warming my hands and feet by a fire much like this one."

Cookie told one story after another, much to Josh's delight. Josh's eager face revealed his keen interest in what the old man had to say.

"Once," Cookie continued, "a moose wandered into what we called the Lower Spiral Tunnel and refused to come out. We workers knew that if the moose stayed in the tunnel, the train would be derailed, killing both the animal and a lot of innocent people. Old Jim Dominicis, a section man like me and armed with a lamp and iron nerve, volunteered to go in after the wild animal." Cookie paused, then pressed on. "Outside the tunnel where the rest of us stood, we could hear an approaching freight train. We stood helplessly by as the train entered the far end of the tunnel, then came out at our end of the tunnel. Right behind the caboose Jim strolled out of the tunnel hauling a very angry moose by one ear."

Josh laughed at the picture Cookie's words created in his mind.

"Crazy moose wasn't smart enough to realize that old Jim was trying to save his life. When Jim saw the train's headlight bobbing toward them, he realized neither of them would escape from the tunnel before the train reached them."

"So what did he do?" Josh asked.

"He flattened himself and the startled animal against the tunnel wall. The train cleared old Joe's jacket with less than six inches to spare. Even after such a scare, the stubborn old moose still refused to come out of the tunnel willingly."

"What a dumb moose!" Josh shook his head in disgust.

''Lots of people go through life acting just as dumb, and they eventually die because of their stubbornness. . . . Guess I'd better hide the evidence.'' Cookie picked up the half-empty marshmallow bag and took it back inside the cook tent.

The next day as Josh helped Cookie break camp, he said, ''Thanks for the moose story. I got your message.''

Cookie laughed and rustled Josh's blond hair. ''Hey, you're sure no dumb moose!''

SEPTEMBER 18

TWO FREEDOMS

If the Son sets you free, then you will be really free. John 8:36, TEV.

Lester Moreno Perez grew up in Cuba, an island 90 miles south of Florida. In Cuba people are not allowed the same privileges as we Americans enjoy. (A few months ago I told you about Noble Alexander, a young pastor in Cuba whom the Communist government threw into prison for preaching about Jesus Christ.)

At 17 Lester was required to become a Communist and serve in the Cuban Army. But Lester didn't believe in Communism. The only answer was to leave Cuba. The government certainly would not allow him to leave. They'd throw him in jail for trying. Yet he knew he must go, but just where would he go? And how would he get there?

Lester, a skilled wind surfer, decided to escape by sea on his sailboard. And he'd head for the United States.

One night about 8:00 he jumped on his sailboard and paddled out into the surf. Adjusting his sail to allow the winds to carry him north, he entered the deep-blue channel waters and held on as his craft carried him, without being detected by the Cuban Coast Guard, into international waters. He carried with him only some fresh water and a can of milk. A storm brewed, and the overcast sky made navigation impossible. The winds caught his sail, whipping him about and buffeting him first in one direction, then another. Off both port and starboard of his flimsy craft, he could see the angular fins of sharks circling about, biding their time until he either tired and lost his grip or the unusually high waves tossed him free of the board.

He had been sailing for 16 hours when he saw a large oceangoing vessel in the distance. Instantly he waved and shouted. Then a new thought came to him. *What if the ship is Cuban?* Yet he knew his strength was almost gone. He'd have to take the risk. The ship drew closer. Waving and shouting, Lester managed to attract someone's attention on board. It was an American Merchant Marine ship. They pulled him aboard. After hearing his story, the captain informed the windsurfer that he had traveled about 60 miles on his board. Lester says he loves living in the United States. He's busy learning English and wishes to teach surfboarding.

Whether he knows it or not, Lester needs two freedoms to be truly happy. The United States of America gave him the first—freedom from Communism. But only Jesus can give him the second—freedom from sin.

SEPTEMBER 19

GIFT OF LOVE

Trust in the Lord, and do good. Psalm 37:3.

Thousands of stories have come out of America's war in Vietnam—a different one for every soldier who served there. Hollywood has recreated hundreds of these sometimes tragic and often poignant stories. Pfc. Paul Hensler's story is unique. Instead of being a tale of blood and violence, it is one of loving and being loved.

Paul went straight from the high school basketball court to Vietnam, with only a very short stopover for training in a U.S. Army boot camp. The wanton destruction of war left him shell-shocked at first. Everywhere he looked he saw people suffering, especially the hundreds of orphaned children. He decided to do something to ease their pain. Within two months of his arrival, he had become "Uncle Paul" to 13 children. After two years his "family" had grown to 126. He became all things to the children whom he and two nuns fed, housed, and cared for. He brought them food, special treats, and toys of every kind. He became the orphanage maintenance man. Broken hearts or broken toilets—if it needed fixing, Paul fixed it. He roughhoused with the little boys during the day, and at night, when the sounds of the war kept frightened little girls awake, he rocked them to sleep with the words "Don't cry; it's only thunder."

When Paul's tour of duty ended, he went to the orphanage to say goodbye to his family. While there, he asked the officials of the orphanage what he might still do to help.

One of the nuns who had detested Paul because he was an American came up to him and said, "Do you remember when I said that I hated Americans?"

Paul answered, "Yes."

"Well, I've come to realize that it's not Americans I hate—it's all those people who choose war as a way to answer their questions. So if you want to help us, teach peace and happiness to the children you meet. Then maybe when they grow up, they will choose peace, not war."

Paul, along with the Catholic nun, silently watched the children playing for a moment, then he asked, "Do you think they'll remember the happiness we had here together?"

The nun replied, "Maybe not. The material things, your gifts, will be lost or broken. The food you brought will be eaten, and the toilets you fixed will become jammed again, I imagine. Your playing made them happy for a moment. But your love—that is the gift you gave. It is what they needed most and will always remember."

The memory of love given and received is the only true gift that lasts a lifetime.

SEPTEMBER 20

ETERNAL LOVE

Love never gives up; and its faith, hope, and patience never fail. 1 Corinthians 13:7, TEV.

A young man named Robert found a different kind of love in Vietnam. The 20-year-old hadn't been in Saigon long when he met Hao, a 15-year-old street vendor in Saigon. The two young men struck up a friendship after Robert, the son of a tuna fisherman from the Pacific Northwest, rescued Hao from a bunch of street thugs who'd been harassing the younger boy. To show his gratitude, Hao invited Robert to visit his home. And that's where Robert's love story begins.

When Robert visited Hao's home, the homesick boy fell in love with Hao's family—his father, his mother, his younger brother, and with Mai, Hao's 18-year-old sister. The family liked Robert as much as he liked them. Before long Robert was spending all his free time with his new adopted family—especially Mai. Robert and Mai's friendship blossomed into love.

One day Robert learned that he was being shipped home. He hurried to see Mai. As he gave her the news he realized he just couldn't go home without her. "I love you," he told Mai. "Marry me. Come to the United States with me."

"You know that is impossible," she reminded him. "With all the Vietnamese leaving the country and all the Americans leaving, we could never get the government to allow it."

"Let me try," Robert insisted.

In the days that followed, Robert visited every United States and South Vietnamese official in order to obtain the necessary papers that would allow Mai to accompany him to America. No one would help him. Finally he was forced to leave Mai behind with the promise that he would go home to the United States, make the necessary arrangements, then return for her.

After he arrived back in the States, Robert initiated a campaign to make Mai his wife. Unfortunately for the young couple, the Viet Cong invaded South Vietnam and cut off all communication with the United States. Although Mai's letters stopped, Robert never doubted her love for him. He continued to badger senators and representatives in Washington, along with officials in the State Department and anyone else who would listen.

Ten years after he left Vietnam, Robert decided to wait no longer. If caught, it could mean his death. Yet his love for Mai outweighed his fears. With the help of his parents and the money he'd saved, Robert flew to Manila, the capital of the Philippines, bought a small fishing boat, and sailed for Vietnam.

What similarities can you see between Robert's love for Mai and Christ's love for you?

(Story to be continued.)

SEPTEMBER 21

MAI'S STORY

[Love] always protects, always trusts, always hopes, always perseveres. Love never fails. 1 Corinthians 13:7, 8, NIV.

For 10 years Mai believed Robert's promise to return for her. At every possible opportunity she attempted to smuggle letters to him, hoping he would receive them. Yet she received no reply.

Whenever her parents encouraged her to become interested in one of the men in her community, she told them, "I know Robert's coming for me someday."

Though she was right about Robert, another year passed before Mai learned of Robert's voyage to Vietnam, that he had managed to reach within one mile of her home before the Vietnamese military police had arrested him and thrown him into jail.

One day two policemen appeared at her home.

"You will come with us," they demanded. Without a word of explanation, they took her to a Saigon hotel where Robert and a representative from the International Red Cross waited for her.

A cry of happiness burst from Mai as she threw herself into his arms. She ran her hands lovingly across his face, repeating again and again, "It can't be true. It can't be true."

The Red Cross representative explained the chain of events that finally reunited the young couple. When Robert didn't return after having been gone for a few months, his father contacted the United States government and the Red Cross. When newspapers around the world printed the "love story of the century," the Vietnamese government agreed to allow Mai to join Robert and for both to leave for the United States.

When I think of how much Robert loved Mai, I remember how much Jesus must love me to have risked leaving the throne of heaven to come to this earth to die for me. When I think of Mai's love for Robert, I look at my love for Jesus and pray that my love will never fail—no matter how long I must wait for Him to return. What about you?

SEPTEMBER 22

THE FACE OF GOD

But we know that when he appears, we shall be like him, for we shall see him as he is. 1 John 3:2, NIV.

Today let's try a little experiment. I want to give you a new way of looking at yourself. Close your eyes. Place one hand on your forehead. Bring it down the center of your face slowly. Feel the bridge of your nose and your eyes on each side of your nose. Run your fingers gently across your eyelashes and eyebrows. Come down farther and touch the two holes at the bottom of your nose. Feel the air passing in and out of your nose. Slowly trace your lips, your chin, and your neck. Now touch each of your ears. Describe how they feel. Would you recognize yourself by the way your face feels?

After you have explored your own face, ask your mom or dad to allow you, keeping your eyes closed, to do the same with their faces. Would you know them just by feeling their facial features?

This is how blind people "see" new friends. A visually impaired person can tell a lot about another human being by touching his or her face.

Have you ever seen the face of God? Of course not. Yet you and I read the Bible, go to church, have family worship, study our Sabbath school lessons, and pray in order to "see" the face of God. We can catch glimpses of God's image through the book of nature.

Pick an apple. Feel the smooth, shiny surface and the rough-textured stem. Cut it open and run your fingers across the moist fruit inside. Smell the apple's sweet fragrance. Taste and see how good it is. By inspecting God's handiwork, you gain a glimpse of what God is like.

No matter how hard we try, you and I are visually impaired when it comes to viewing God's face. We can see only a shadow of what God is truly like, as if we were looking through a smoky glass. One day, as the promise reminds us, the darkened glass will be removed, our eyesight will be healed, and we will see Him face-to-face.

For today, discover all you can about our Creator by looking, smelling, tasting, listening, and touching all the evidence He's given in order to help us "see" Him and love Him.

SEPTEMBER 23

MEASURE UP

"Love the Lord your God with all your heart, with all your soul, and with all your mind." This is the greatest and the most important commandment. The second most important commandment is like it: "Love your neighbor as you love yourself." Matthew 22:37-39, TEV.

In 1990 the Detroit Pistons trounced the Portland Trailblazers in the NBA basketball finals. The last play of the last game broke the Trailblazers' fans' hearts. While they were ahead, the Detroit Pistons lost the ball to the Trailblazers seconds before the end of the game. The buzzer announcing the end of the game sounded just as Gary Petrovich sent the ball into the basket, making it seem as though Portland had tied the game, sending it into overtime. If that were the case, then this would give the Portland team a chance to win and stay alive for a sixth and perhaps a seventh game with the Pistons. The crowd roared as the referees hesitated on the call. Had the ball left Gary's hand before the buzzer sounded, or after? Instant replay revealed the truth, and the Portland Trailblazers lost the NBA championship finals by a fraction of a second.

Measurements are important in sports and in most other areas of our lives. If I want to sew a dress, I must measure out the amount of fabric I will need. If I want to buy new tires for my car, I need to know the right size. If I want to build a boat in my garage, I'd better measure the garage door to be certain I can get the boat out of the garage once it's finished.

Once distances were measured using a cubit—about the length of one's forearm. Another measure was the hand—the height of a horse by the size of a man's hand. Since forearms and hands vary in size from person to person, the results were not always accurate. Today we use two more universal systems of measurement: the old English system and the metric system.

You've studied these in school.

Another measurement you learned in school, if you attend a Christian school, is the set of measurements for love that God gave to Moses—the Ten Commandments.

These measurements help us live happier, more productive lives. Jesus summed up the Ten Commandments in today's promise. Each of the two ways to measure love are vital, for if you love God, you will love your neighbor. And if you love your neighbor, you will find it easier to love your God. So how do you measure up this morning?

SEPTEMBER 24

MIRACLES

Everyone who is called by my name, whom I created for my glory, whom I formed and made. Isaiah 43:7, NIV.

If you could see me right now, you would be looking at a miracle. For that matter, look in the mirror and you'll come face-to-face with another miracle. The fact that you and I are alive today is nothing short of a miracle. Your life is a continuation of an unbroken genetic string reaching far back in your family tree—all the way to the first parents. How many times in the past has your cord of life almost been broken, perhaps during the Second World War or the Civil War or the bubonic plague? Shanghaied on an English slave ship? Great-grandparents crossing America's deserts and prairies in covered wagons? You are a survivor of survivors—a miracle. How many times during the 10, 11, or 12 years you've lived have you survived a dangerous situation? If you've ever contracted pneumonia, caught the flu, or been hit by a car, you have experienced some very real miracles.

You survived these crises for a reason. Somewhere beyond the world you and I see or understand is a reason that you are alive today. That makes you a walking miracle. Whether you're Black, Red, Yellow, or White; Brazilian, Czechoslovakian, Greek, or Kenyan; whether your mom attended Harvard, Oxford, or Winache Valley High School, or if she attended no school at all; whether your dad hobnobs with the Kennedys of

Massachusetts, the Trumps of New York, or the Joneses of Peoria, you are special. Just by being alive you are a winner, born to a line of winners.

God has given you a way not only to be a winner, but to double, or perhaps triple, your worth. When you give your life—the miracle of you—to Jesus, you multiply your value many times over by the price of Jesus' life. Jesus' death for you and your acceptance of His bid for your life make you precious beyond any price tag. I wonder what Donald Trump or Lee Iacocca would think of those odds? You want to be a winner? You want to see a miracle? Accept Jesus' offer today—and watch out! Dare to experience the great things He has planned for you.

SEPTEMBER 25

ONE MOTHER'S FAITH

Therefore I tell you, whatever you ask for in prayer, believe that you have received it, and it will be yours. Mark 11:24, NIV.

In northeast Portland, Oregon, 8-year-old Terry, hunched over a piece of paper, sat on his front porch. While the small boy couldn't read the strange words that had made his mother cry, he knew he was in trouble again.

"Dear Mrs. Johnson," the letter read, "we have tested your son, Terry, and have determined the boy to be mentally deficient, with little hope of improving . . ." Not only did the teacher declare Terry to be unteachable, but he had dyslexia, a reading problem in which one's brain reads letters and words backward and sometimes upside down. Often the letters themselves dance about the page in cartoon style. Terry also had a speech impediment—he couldn't speak clearly. "The best thing you can do for Terry is to place him in a hospital for mentally retarded children and allow the experts to deal with his problems."

Now, many mothers would have listened to the guidance counselor and reluctantly placed their son in an institution. Not Mrs. Johnson. "There's no way I'm going to accept this. Terry can learn. He's not hopeless!" Against her friends' and neighbors' advice, Mrs. Johnson switched Terry to a small Christian church school and worked with him at home until the boy could read, spell, and do math with the rest of them.

No matter how hard he tried, studying never came easy for Terry. All along he struggled just to pass his subjects. Somewhere during his high school years at Portland Adventist Academy, Terry decided that God wanted him to become a minister. A boy with a learning disability, a reading disorder, and a speech impediment?

Just being born Black and in the poorest section of the city would have been enough to discourage most young men, but not Terry—and not Terry's mother! During countless hours of studying algebra, English, geometry, physics, and U.S. history, Terry and his mother claimed the promise in Mark 11:24. Terry's mother reminded him that with God nothing is impossible—that the impossible just takes a little more effort and time. He did the impossible. He proved his elementary teacher wrong. He graduated from academy. God's promise came through for Terry Johnson, the boy who couldn't learn, speak or read, the boy who wanted to become a preacher.

(Story to be continued.)

SEPTEMBER 26

IN HIS HONOR

Trust in the Lord with all your heart. Never rely on what you think you know. Proverbs 3:5, TEV.

Terry had no idea where God wanted him to be, or even where he himself wished to be. He tried to find work, but none was available. He applied to college, but couldn't find a way of paying his tuition. Morning and evening Terry and his mother prayed for the Lord to show the young man which way to go.

"Maybe God has another way to answer your prayers about becoming a pastor," his mother comforted her discouraged son.

One day in mid-July, Terry went to Mall 205, a small shopping plaza near the academy. As he passed the Air Force recruiting office, he felt impressed to go inside and talk with the recruiter. "Now, you understand," Terry warned the military officer, "I am a Seventh-day Adventist. I do not work on Sabbath—under any circumstances! I would only be interested in joining if I can train to become an Air Force chaplain." The recruiter guaranteed Terry that such arrangements could be made. So Terry enlisted in the United States Air Force.

At basic training the drill sergeant took an instant dislike to the young man because of Terry's religious convictions. The officer made his life miserable in an effort to make Terry give up and go home. But Terry was accustomed to hard times. He stuck it out and witnessed to the rest of the guys in his unit as well. By the end of basic training, the sergeant gave Terry a special commendation for his behavior and performance.

Terry expected to go straight from basic training to chaplain school when a mix-up landed him at the military police academy. *Police academy*, he thought. *I can't do that. The military police carry guns.*

At each trial Terry turned to God. And at each trial God used Terry's problem to reach the other young men of his unit. Like Daniel and Joseph of the Bible, Terry couldn't understand why the Lord led him down such winding roads—until he reached the other end; then he knew. God knew best. Through what to a non-christian would have seemed a series of chance happenings, God propelled him higher and higher until Terry found himself a member of the most elite force in the United States—the president's honor guard.

During his four years in President Reagan's service, Terry shared Jesus with his fellow guards. God honored Terry's witness, and many were baptized as a result. His term of duty ended, and Terry enrolled at Oakwood College to prepare for the ministry.

If you don't understand how God is leading you, if people tell you that your dreams are impossible, remember Terry Johnson—the boy who couldn't, but with the help of God, did.

SEPTEMBER 27

THE LITTLE CORPORAL

For everyone who makes himself great will be humbled, and everyone who humbles himself will be made great. Luke 14:11, TEV.

During the Revolutionary War a tall soldier on horseback entered the gates of a frontier fort just as a group of soldiers were struggling to heave a bulky log into place along the wall. The horseman noted a little man strutting back and forth and shouting out orders at the men. Suddenly the log slipped, and the little boss screamed at the men.

"Perhaps another pair of strong arms would help," the man on horseback suggested.

The little man straightened his shoulders indignantly, then sneered at the stranger. "Sir," he said, "I am a corporal!"

"Oh, pardon me, Corporal, I had forgotten that." The man climbed off his horse, removed his coat, and joined the sweating men by putting his shoulder under the log. One heave and the log slipped into place.

The tall stranger put on his coat and mounted his horse. "Oh, Corporal," he turned to the pompous officer, "if you ever need any help again, just call your commander in chief. I'll be glad to help." The soldiers stood with their mouths gaping as General George Washington rode away.

I imagine the loudmouthed corporal never forgot his onetime encounter with the man who would become the first president of the United States. And most likely Washington never forgot the nasty little man who revealed just how "little" he really was—not physically, but where it really counts, on the inside.

Truly great people seldom need to advertise their greatness, while weak people often feel the need to convince others of their power or strength. Give a person a little power, put him in a position of leadership, and his greatness or his weakness will be revealed.

SEPTEMBER 28

NOT A COINCIDENCE

I am so happy I found the coin I lost. Let us celebrate. In the same way, I tell you, the angels of God rejoice over one sinner who repents. Luke 15:9, 10, TEV.

When Thomas Day turned 10, his father presented him with an 1858 fifty-cent piece because that was the year Thomas' father was born. On it the father had inscribed his initials, W.D., which stood for Waller Day. Thomas treasured his father's coin for many years, until in 1924 he gave it to his own son, Sam Waller Day, as a keepsake.

For many years Sam, who later became a grocer, carried the coin as a good luck piece in a small leather pouch in his pocket. But in 1949 Sam's luck ran out. While attending a grocers' picnic in Lincoln State Park about 30 miles from his home in Evansville, Illinois, the half dollar coin broke through the worn leather pouch, got mixed in with the other coins Sam carried in his pocket, and was accidentally spent at one of the concession stands.

Sick at heart, Sam tried to track down the coin that had been a family heirloom for more than 80 years, but he had no luck. In despair he returned to his grocery store. For the next few years Sam checked all the change that came through his cash register, but he never believed he'd actually find the lost coin.

Then in December of 1961, Sam reached into the till to pay Ace Weber, the baker, for a load of bread he'd delivered, and Ace noticed a very old coin. He called Sam's attention to the fact that the coin was very old—1858. Excited but almost afraid to believe it was possible, Sam turned over the coin—and there scratched into the coin's surface were the initials W.D. The coin had wandered for 13 years. Sam and his family and friends celebrated the coin's return "home."

That's an incredible story. Ask any mathematician what the probability of such a thing happening might be, and he or she would merely laugh.

Jesus talked about a woman who lost a coin, one of her family treasures. She searched and searched until she found it, then she called her friends to celebrate with her. Jesus compared the lost coin to people who were lost and didn't know they were lost. In the parable, Jesus described Himself as the woman searching for the coin and stated that all Heaven rejoiced when the coin was found. Incredible! Fantastic! Can you imagine the angels in heaven singing, "Hallelujah! Praise God for ________ [insert your own name]. ________ [again insert your own name] was lost but now has been found"?

I don't know if the angels sing a special song for each child of God who is saved. But I like to think that the song they sing for me is unique, written especially for me, and that the song they sing for you is all your own, too. That you and I might have our very own special composition to commemorate our birth into the family of God is much more credible than the chances of Sam's coin returning to his possession after so many years. Sam is only human, but our God is the Creator of all.

SEPTEMBER 29

THE GREAT DEBATE

Don't have anything to do with foolish and stupid arguments, because you know they produce quarrels. And the Lord's servant must not quarrel; instead, he must be kind to everyone, able to teach, not resentful. 2 Timothy 2:23, 24, NIV.

How many angels can dance on the head of a straight pin? What a silly question! Who cares? Yet during the Dark Ages, many church leaders defended their opinions on the subject for years. For that matter, debating unanswerable issues was their main source of entertainment. Sometimes I think my friend Bert would have enjoyed living back then.

Bert loves to argue—the more heated the disagreement grows, the more he enjoys himself, until the verbal battle becomes a physical one. If a friend says the sky is blue, Bert will describe it as being lavender. If a friend says it looks like rain, Bert will know better. He argues about which is the better car, Ford or Chevy; which is the best football team, baseball team, soccer team, ice hockey team—you name it, and he has an opinion. In spite of black eyes and bruises, Bert has never learned when to shut up and when to speak, when to stand for what is right and when to shrug and admit that it doesn't really matter. A favorite minister of mine would say that Bert needs to learn the "art of the committed chameleon."

While God wants loyal sons and daughters who stand up for what they believe, no matter who opposes them, He also expects us to get along with our neighbors—to live together peacefully. He said, "Love one another as I have loved you." He doesn't want us to go through life ready to fight at any moment.

In fact, the person who goes through life looking for trouble will find it. Tests done at Duke University during a 15-year-period revealed that people who are suspicious, argumentative, or quarrelsome have a 40 percent greater chance of dying earlier than people who are more relaxed and accepting of others. I feel sorry for all the Berts of this world. They aren't happy unless they're stirring up trouble, and they will miss the world to come if they don't ask Jesus to help them change their point of view.

SEPTEMBER 30

RETURN TO ME

"Return to me, and I will return to you," says the Lord Almighty. Malachi 3:7, NIV.

Robert Robinson, a poor orphan, wandered from place to place, never calling anywhere home until one night the Holy Spirit led him into a tent meeting. The preacher, the great evangelist George Whitefield, preached on the subject of Jesus' love for sinners.

Robert's heart was touched. He was baptized, enrolled in a ministerial college, and graduated as a Methodist minister. In 1758, at the age of 23, Robert wrote the words to the hymn "Come, Thou Fount of Every Blessing." The poem was published.

Years passed, and Robert drifted away from his calling as a minister and from his Saviour. One day he found himself traveling in a stagecoach with a Christian woman who insisted on talking with him about God. Feeling especially low, he tried to avoid speaking to her, but she persisted.

"You really should hear the words to this incredible poem I found." She read the poem to him, not realizing that he was the man who had written it years earlier.

When the woman had finished reading, Robert tried to change the subject. But the woman raved on about the poem and its beautiful message.

Finally in exasperation, Robert blurted out, "Madam, I know the words to the poem quite well. I am the poor, unhappy man who composed that hymn many years ago, and I would give a thousand worlds if I could enjoy the feelings I felt then."

Stunned by Robert's confession, the woman dared not speak again for the rest of the trip. By the time the stagecoach arrived at its destination, the Holy Spirit had "retuned" Robert's heart. Robert Robinson served his Lord from that day until his death in 1790.

Do you ever feel out of tune with Jesus? You will again and again until you finally discover that no matter what you do or how discouraged you may feel, God is standing by, eagerly waiting for you to return to Him once more.

When you have more time, read or sing the words to Robert's hymn. It's in the *Seventh-day Adventist Hymnal* (number 334). Ask your parents what the words to the hymn mean to them. Tell what the poem means to you. Put yourself in Robert Robinson's place in that stagecoach. Try to imagine how he felt when his own words returned to soften his heart.

OCTOBER 1

GOD'S PURPOSE: A PEEK AT THE BEAK

And God said, ". . . Let birds fly above the earth across the expanse of the sky." So God created . . . every winged bird according to its kind. Genesis 1:20, 21, NIV.

"According to its kind"—that's an interesting phrase. What does it mean? Did God sit down at a drawing board and sketch out each different kind of bird before He spoke it into being? Probably not. I would guess He visualized each one individually in His imagination. He needed to consider the purpose of each bird, from the scolding starling to the darting hummingbird. What equipment would each bird need in order to prosper, to survive, to eat? Which bird should have brightly colored feathers and which one would best survive in a wardrobe of brown?

God planned it all, right down to the tip of each bird's beak. That's right. If you want to know what a bird eats, take a peek at the beak. For instance, the spoonbill's beak allows it to dip into shallow water. By slowly walking forward, swinging his slightly open beak from side to side, Sam Spoonbill can catch small fish, crabs, tadpoles, and insects—his favorite delicacy.

Sally Skimmer's beak is both long and short at the same time. The top bill is short and the bottom one is long. Old Sally Skimmer flies just above the surface of the bay or ocean, plowing through the water with her lower beak to scoop up small fish or shrimp. As soon as she catches something, she clamps the top beak down on her prey, lifts the lower beak out of the water, and gulp—lunch alfresco.

Carey Crossbill's high-tech beak is curved and crossed at the tip—just right for prying open the scales of spruce, fir, and pine cones. After his bill gets the scales out of the way, he sticks his long tongue deep inside the cone and lifts out the tiny seeds hidden there.

And wouldn't you think Woody Woodpecker would have an Excedrin headache after drilling into the side of trees all day just to find his trail mix? He would if his bill and head were constructed like other birds'. Instead, God built into Woody strong neck muscles that allow his head to move at a rapid rate and muscles on his head that act as shock absorbers. Then when the hole is deep enough, he sticks his long, sticky, prickly tongue into the tree and drags out insects. All this high-tech equipment in one small bird. Talk about the engineering feat of all time!

While I might not be a bird enthusiast, I can appreciate the care the Creator put into designing each of His creations. It makes me want to praise Him. What about you?

(To be continued.)

OCTOBER 2

LEAN, MEAN MACHINES

Look at the birds of the air; they do not sow or reap or store away in barns, and yet your heavenly Father feeds them. Are you not much more valuable than they? Matthew 6:26, NIV.

The mean machine of the skies is the hawk. Herman Hawk keeps his hooked beak as sharp as a hunter's knife. This allows him to tear a freshly killed rabbit, rat, or sparrow into delicate bite-sized pieces. He disdains fast-food joints and enjoys a more elegant and slow form of dining.

Wendy Whippoorwill catches her food on the fly—the fast food junkie of the airways. Her beak acts like a net, catching moths, mosquitoes, and other night-flying insects—a true Ronald McDonald lover.

What Wendy Whippoorwill is to the airways, Cyril Shoveler is to the waterways. His wide, fat beak acts as a shovel. As he swims he snaps his beak open and closed in the water. Each time his beak opens, water filled with plants and insects flows in. When he closes his beak, the water drains out between tiny toothlike ridges, trapping his meal—buffet-style.

On the vegetarian side of birddom, Hattie Hummingbird sips flower nectar through her bill as smoothly as you sip 7 Up through a straw. And

Gary Grosbeak's short, fat bill allows this seed eater to crack the hard shell of a cherry pit as if it were a potato chip.

So who cares? you might ask. Well, for a start, the grosbeak, the hawk, and the hummingbird do. But so should you. If God took such care to design each creature in a specific manner, right down to the shape of its beak, how much more concern He had when He designed the beings that He would make in His own image—when He designed you! Whoever you are, wherever you live, whatever the size or shape of your "beak," you are specially and wonderfully made.

Another thought to consider this morning—if the Creator of the universe designed each bird's body so as to best suit the diet and eating style that it would need in order not only to survive but to thrive, do you think He might have done the same for you? Find out for yourself in God's Word just what foods will make your lean, mean, eating machine work best, and follow God's menu for happiness.

OCTOBER 3

HAPPY BIRTHDAY, CHARLIE BROWN

Come unto me, all of you who are tired from carrying heavy loads, and I will give you rest. Take my yoke and put it on you, and learn from me, because I am gentle and humble in spirit; and you will find rest. Matthew 11:28, 29, TEV.

Yesterday, October 2, Charlie Brown turned 42 years old. And Charlie Brown being Charlie Brown, we are wishing him a belated happy birthday. You know Charlie, everything goes wrong for poor old Charlie. He's always having problems. It would be his kind of luck for all his friends to wish him happy birthday a day late. Examples of Charlie's persistently bad luck can be found in many of his cartoon strips, including one of my favorites, in which Lucy is offering Charlie her unsolicited advice.

"Life," she says, "is like a deck chair. Some place it so they can see where they are going. Some place it so they can see where they have been. And some place it so they can see where they are at present."

Charlie Brown replies, "And I can't even get mine to open."

Every autumn, when football season comes around, Lucy suckers Charlie into kicking the ball while she holds it. And every year she snatches it away at the last minute, causing Charlie to fall on his head. He never learns. Over and over again for 42 years, he falls for the same practical joke.

Do you sometimes feel like Charlie? I do. Lots of people do. That's why he's been popular for so many years. But like Charlie, I seem to make the same mistakes over and over again. And no matter how sorry I am, I don't always learn from my pain. Often these mistakes are called sins; other times, merely stupidity.

Maybe it's these kinds of problems Jesus had in mind when He said, "Come unto me . . . learn from me . . . and you will find rest." It's certainly worth a try.

OCTOBER 4

C-Q DAY

Then call thou, and I will answer: or let me speak, and answer thou me. Job 13:22.

I have declared today to be C-Q Day, a day to recognize amateur radio operators everywhere. If you've ever listened while a ham friend talked on his or her radio, you know that the letters CQ are what ham operators say when they want to get another operator's attention. It sounds like this: "C-Q, C-Q, this is WB4UHN calling C-Q."

Another ham listening on the line who wishes to talk with WB4UHN will then answer the call. When they finish talking, they don't say goodbye; they say "10-4."

My husband is a ham operator. He talks with people all over the world. Usually I'm not interested at all in the ham radio—that is, I wasn't until the day I heard the voice of Tom Christian, one of the most popular ham operators in the entire world. Tom is the number one ham radio operator on Pitcairn Island and supplies the official link that the 55 islanders have with the rest of the world. The ham radio allows Tom to communicate with people from around the world and keeps him in touch with outside help should an emergency occur. And it provides ham radio operators all over the world the opportunity to make contact with one of the most remote radio stations in the world.

Pitcairn Island is a South Pacific Island more than 4,000 miles from North America. The island has no accessible harbor. Ships cannot dock. They must drop anchor a distance from shore and wait for the villagers to row out to them. In the beginning, this barrier was important, since Tom Christian's ancestors fled to the island in 1789 after instigating a mutiny on the English ship *Bounty*. Over the years, the once-drunken and violent islanders learned to love God and later began keeping the seventh-day Sabbath.

And thanks to Tom, his ham radio station, and the island's electrical generator, people in Japan, the United States, even France, can communicate with this isolated tropical paradise. When Tom calls, some ham operator somewhere in the world always answers. For that matter, if you have a ham friend who operates on Tom's radio frequency and knows the time the Adventist Ham Operators conduct their Bible Study Net, you can hear Tom check into the Net too.

As useful as the ham radio is to Tom and the rest of the islanders, he knows that it isn't his most important source of communication. Should the island generator break down, should a tropical storm blow down his radio antenna, he still can call out for help—not over his ham station, but through prayer. Tom knows that God is always listening and ready to help even when the rest of the world is thousands of miles away. And God never says "10-4."

OCTOBER 5

BECKY'S GOLDEN TRUMPET

Sing aloud unto God our strength: make a joyful noise unto the God of Jacob. Psalm 81:1.

Becky Wright curled her feet beneath her petticoats and shifted about on the rotting old stump in the front yard of the Wrights' homestead in the wilderness of western Ohio. She lifted her golden trumpet to her lips and played again, for what must have been the twentieth time, her favorite song, "Barbara Allen." Mottled patches of sunlight danced through the giant trees surrounding the small clearing.

The young girl brushed the stray blonde curls from her face and sighed, "I wish I could stop playing for a while." But Becky knew better. Pa and her three brothers depended on the sound of her trumpet to guide them home after a day of deer hunting.

At first, playing her beloved trumpet all day appealed to the girl, but after playing it all day, every day, for nearly two weeks, her fingers ached and her lips hurt. To make matters worse, the Bradleys, the nearest neighbors, who lived more than 10 miles away, asked Becky's mother to help deliver their newest baby, leaving Becky alone to keep house and make meals, as well as spend every free minute playing her trumpet for Pa and the boys.

The first few days, Becky enjoyed "playing house." By the fourth day, even this new adventure had worn thin. Becky grumbled as she shaped the bread dough into loaves and let them raise. Pa and her brothers helped with breakfast, then left her to do the morning dishes. By noon the aroma of freshly baked bread filled the cabin and drifted out to the stump where Becky sat playing "Yankee Doodle." Suddenly three Indians stepped out of the forest and into the clearing. She remembered Pa's worship text that morning about making a joyful noise unto the Lord.

"Oh, dear Jesus," she prayed silently, "what should I do?" *Maybe if I play louder, Pa will hear and come to my rescue*, she thought. Her light bouncy tone changed to a shrill and blaring noise.

It's not a joyful noise, dear Father, but I know that You can hear me and send someone to help me. The Indians seemed curious about the strange noise coming from her trumpet. Terrified, Becky raced through the song again, not knowing what else to do.

(Story to be continued.)

OCTOBER 6

BECKY'S GOLDEN BREAD

Cast your bread upon the waters, for after many days you will find it again. Ecclesiastes 11:1, NIV.

The three Indians listened to Becky's trumpet for a few seconds, then sniffed the sweet aroma of freshly baked bread. They sniffed their way into the cabin and over to the heavy oak table where Becky's mother's clean, linen tea towels covered the cooling loaves of bread. The leader grunted and pointed to the food."Oh," Becky gasped, "you're hungry." She hurried over to the sideboard and grabbed a long butcher knife. Startled, the Indians grasped the handles of their tomahawks. "No," she shook her head violently, "for the bread. I won't hurt you. I need to slice the bread."

Becky could feel the Indians' dark eyes following her every move as she sliced the bread, spread her mother's berry jam on each of the slices, and poured milk into four mugs. Then she turned and invited them to join her at the table. Looking about nervously, they sat down to the long table and ate the food. She nibbled at her slice of bread while the three hungry Indians finished off all the bread she'd baked for her father and brothers. Suddenly the leader of the group stood up, grunted a few strange sounds, and walked out of the cabin. The two others did the same. Before she could reach the door, her visitors had disappeared into the forest.

Immediately she ran to the stump, picked up her golden trumpet, and started blowing as loudly as she could. Someone had to hear and come to her rescue. Since no tunes came to her mind, she played scales—over and over again until she spied her father coming through the trees. She ran to his arms and babbled her frightening tale.

Becky never saw the Indians again. When neighboring settlers reported having animals stolen or fields burned by Indians, no one ever touched the Wrights' homestead. Years later, long after Becky and her family had moved farther west, the local Indian tribes told the tale of the kind yellow-haired girl who played a horrid-sounding horn and fed their chief and two braves. They told of the chief's decree that whoever dared attack the Wrights' home and lands would be attacking him and would be treated as such.

Becky's golden trumpet didn't save her on that day or on any other day; it was her kindness that saved her and her family for years to come. Becky learned that casting the bread of kindness upon the waters does come back to bless you.

OCTOBER 7

KICKING AND SCREAMING OR PRAISING GOD

Let every thing that hath breath praise the Lord. Praise ye the Lord. Psalm 150:6.

The other day right at the local Safeway market, I heard the most horrid sound coming from across the display of oranges and grapefruit. I peered over the top of the fruit to discover the source of the noise. I couldn't believe my eyes or my ears. There in the next aisle, an embarrassed woman struggled to keep a very angry and very vocal 2-year-old boy in the cart's child seat. I shook my head in amazement. How could such a tiny body create such a horrendous disturbance?

"Johnny needs a yum-yum! Johnny needs a yum-yum!" he shrieked.

"Johnny needs more than a yum-yum," I mumbled, certain no one could hear me over his cries.

An older woman standing nearby, glanced over and said, "Amen!"

Now, I love kids. I have two of my own and have provided a home for several others over the years, but this—this miniature tyrant caused the palms of my hands to itch. Just a light pop on his well-padded derriere would be enough to get his attention and would relieve my itch nicely.

As the child screamed and struggled to escape her hands, the harried woman cooed, "Johnny, now be a good little boy for Auntie June and sit still or you will go boom-boom on the floor."

I didn't know about the other shoppers, but at that moment I thought a sudden trip to the floor might be just what dear, sweet Johnny needed.

Instead, his tight little fists pummeled away at the aunt's head, face, and chest as she struggled to control him.

"If you keep it up," Auntie June continued, "we'll have to go home, and Johnny won't get his yum-yum."

I, along with a number of other shoppers, silently cheered as the thoroughly embarrassed Auntie June carried out her threat, taking her screaming nephew from the store.

Screaming Johnnys and wailing Jennys can be found wherever you go—and they're not all 2-years-old, either. I've seen 12-year-olds, 20-year-olds, 40-, 55-, and 70-year-olds kick and scream their way through life. In fact, I've kicked and screamed a time or two myself. However, I'm sure that your mom or dad soon taught you that kicking and screaming only increased your problems, never solved them.

Sons and daughters of the heavenly King must learn this lesson also. God wants grateful, happy, trusting children, not spoiled brats who kick and scream to get their own way. We do this by praising Him. And praising brings its own rewards by making us happier and healthier.

OCTOBER 8

GOD'S YUM-YUMS

I will extol the Lord at all times; his praise will always be on my lips. Psalm 34:1, NIV.

Wow! What a challenge! Can you imagine always being happy and always praising God? Can you do that 24 hours a day, 7 days a week, 52 weeks a year, round-the-clock for the rest of your life? Surely God expects you to gripe when a kid at school puts you down or tells lies about you.

And He would expect you to complain when you drop your bus money down a storm drain and have to walk the three miles home from school. He would certainly expect you to grumble when you've worked hard on a group science project only to have your friend, who goofed off the whole time, take the credit for it. By following the advice found in today's text, you wouldn't have much time left over to fuss. Hmm! I wonder if that's the whole idea?

Remember Johnny and the yum-yums he so desperately wanted but didn't deserve? When you and I praise instead of pout, God is eager to give us some of His very special yum-yums. (Some people call God's yum-yums blessings.) Here are a few that Ellen White mentions in her books:

1. Praise builds faith, hope, and courage (*Prophets and Kings*, p. 202).

2. Praise gives us power (*Christ's Object Lessons*, p. 300).
3. Praise makes us love God more (*Testimonies*, vol. 5, p. 317).
4. Praise begets greater blessings (*ibid.*).
5. Praise promotes good health (*Ministry of Healing*, p. 251).
6. Praise brings us closer to heaven (*Steps to Christ*, p. 104).

Courage, faith, hope, power, love, good health, and a preview of heaven—all this and so much more is yours and mine, not for the asking but for the receiving when our lips and our eyes turn upward toward our Father.

OCTOBER 9

DETERMINED TO WIN

Do you not know that in a race all the runners run, but only one gets the prize? Run in such a way as to get the prize. 1 Corinthians 9:24, NIV.

For Zola Budd, her dream of going for the gold in the 1984 Olympics in Los Angeles was second to the thrill of competing in the women's 3,000-meter race with her longtime hero and American role model, Mary Decker. The young farmgirl kept a poster of the beautiful and strong American runner on her bedroom wall. Zola's hero worship intensified when Zola discovered that she too had a talent for running—barefoot, as she preferred it.

From the start, the South African teenager had to fight for the right to compete. Because the country of South Africa practiced apartheid against the Blacks of their country, the South African teams were banned from participating in the Olympics. Zola, a White teenager from the Orange Free State of South Africa, continued to train even though she would not be allowed to participate in the Olympics if her country had no team.

"Pa," she announced one day, "my trainer thinks I stand a good chance of making it onto an Olympic team. He suggests I go to England and join the British team." Zola's father thought over his daughter's suggestion. "You know, you just might have something there. Your grandfather is British. You could change your citizenship."

On March 24 Zola left for Guildford Surrey in England, all expenses paid by her local newspaper, the *Daily Mail*. Upon arriving, the quiet little farmgirl suddenly found herself on the receiving end of intense hostility, first by the British running team, next by the *Daily Mail*'s rivals, and from the opponents of South Africa's racial policies.

Daunted by the pressures, she signed up for her first race in England on April 14 but later withdrew. On April 25, in tears, she crossed the finish line of the 1500-meter race after having been taunted throughout the race with nasty calls and with signs that read "White trash go home!"

This time Zola stuck it out and qualified for the British team by winning every race she entered. To do this she had to block out of her mind all the hateful words fired at her from the audience and all the mean things written about her in the papers, and concentrate on her running. She maintained her courage by keeping the image of her hero, Mary Decker, in mind.

You and I can learn from Zola's example. Golden crowns, not medals of gold or silver, are waiting for us. Some may tell you that running the race is not important. They may laugh at you and call you hurtful names like stupid, goody-goody, holy Joe, or dweeb.

Like Zola, we cannot let other people's words or opinions keep us from completing God's race. We have a much greater hero upon whom to concentrate, One who will never let us down—Jesus Christ.

(Story to be continued.)

OCTOBER 10

WHEN HEROES FALL

But you have turned from the way and by your teaching have caused many to stumble. Malachi 2:8, NIV.

On the other side of the world, Mary Decker had her problems. Muscle surgery, running accidents, and bad press about her temper outbursts haunted her. A change in scheduling of the 1500- and the 3,000-meter races forced her to choose to compete in only one of her two best heats at the upcoming Olympics. Mary decided to forgo running in the 1500-meter race and put all her energy into running the 3,000. Rumors of the barefoot runner from South Africa didn't disturb the American running star.

The day of the 3,000-meter race arrived. All went well during the first half of the race. At 1600 meters, Mary Decker and Wendy Sly, from Great Britain, led. At this point, Zola moved between them and took the lead on the turn along the outside edge of lane 1.

Mary, on the inside of lane 1, maintained her position and pace until the 1700-meter mark. While trying to pass Zola, Mary hit one of the South African girl's legs, throwing Zola off balance. Five strides later, they bumped again. Zola stumbled, her left leg shooting out in search of balance. Mary, running straight and hard, tripped on Zola's leg, her spikes cutting deeply into Zola's heel. Mary pitched forward onto the infield. Zola looked back in time to see her idol fall to the ground. Runners zipped by as Mary attempted to get up. She had pulled her left hip muscle.

Stunned, the crowd of 85,000 fell silent. Then the booing began. As the race continued, Zola Budd was booed at every turn. Bleeding and in tears because of the crowd's hateful reaction, she kept running, but her spirit was gone. Wendy Sly and Maricica Puica, of Romania, passed to take first and second place.

In the tunnel leading away from the track, Mary's fiancé, Richard Slaney, was comforting Mary when Zola approached.

"I'm sorry. I'm sorry. I'm sorry," the weeping teenager cried.

"Don't bother," Mary snarled. "I don't want to talk to you!"

As Zola stood crying, fifth-place winner Cornelia Burki, a Swiss runner, came to Zola's defense. "It's not her fault, Mary. It wasn't her fault."

"Yes it was," Mary screamed. "I know it was. It was!"

The video of the race proved Cornelia's words to be true. Later Mary told reporters, "I should have pushed her!"

Mary's physical injuries healed, allowing her to race again, but whether or not Zola recovered from the hurt her heart suffered that day, no one knows. Mary would never again be quite as lovely, quite as fantastic, or quite the hero in Zola's eyes that she once had been.

OCTOBER 11

A BLIND SPOT

Thy watchmen shall lift up the voice; with the voice together shall they sing: for they shall see eye to eye, when the Lord shall bring again Zion. Isaiah 52:8.

Did you know that even if you have 20/20 vision, you have a blind spot? That's right, your blind spot, where the optic nerve enters the eye, amounts to a flaw in your eye, because at this point there are no light-sensitive nerve endings. At that particular spot, you are blind. Test and see for yourself by drawing a cross (+) on a piece of paper. Place a dot exactly three inches from the cross. Now, close your left eye and hold the page in front of your right eye. Fix your gaze on the cross. Move the paper toward you and then away from you until you find the point where the dot completely disappears. This is the blind spot in your right eye. Do the same with your left eye to locate its blind spot.

It was no accident that God created this blind spot in your eye. And it is hardly an imperfection. On the contrary, you and I, and perhaps the entire world, would do well to develop blind spots. Think about the changes that would occur in South Africa if the men and women who govern the country would develop a blind spot to the color or shade of a person's skin. Or what would happen if every person who loves God chose to love each of His children as a brother or sister? And what about a person's weight? Some people I know actually judge a person's intelligence and value as a human being by the size of his or her waistline. They call overweight people cows, pigs, elephants, and whales. Karen Carpenter, a famous singer during the 1970s, is an example of how words can cut deep into the victim's soul and actually can kill in the form of anorexia and bulimia. Is your blind spot big enough to ignore this imperfection in a classmate or friend? Is it possible that while your friends make fun of the class klutz or joke about just how stupid the school "dummy" can be they are missing the pleasure of getting to know some truly fun people?

Remember the test I had you do to locate your blind spot. Think about it one more time. By staring at the cross, the dot disappeared. Hmm! Perhaps that test would help us develop our spiritual blind spot as well. Jesus demonstrated His love for each one of us—the klutz, the cool dude, the fatty, the nerd—at the cross. By keeping our attention on the cross and Jesus' love, we can develop a loving blind spot for God's other children. We can accept one another just as we are, and let God worry about the other guy's defect.

OCTOBER 12

IT'S NOT FAIR!

"I do not want anyone to die," says the Sovereign Lord. Ezekiel 18:32, TEV.

Sixteen-year-old Sylvia hugged her 7-year-old brother, Jeffrey, close to her side as they watched the ambulance, followed by her mother in the family station wagon, pull out of the driveway and disappear down the tree-lined street. "Come on, Jeff," she sniffed back her tears, "let's go inside. I'll make your favorite sandwich."

She hurried into the house. Jeff reluctantly followed her into the kitchen.

"If Dad's really . . . really gone, why did Mom have to go to the hospital with him?" Jeff whispered.

"She told you why before she left. She has papers to sign."

Jeff slumped into one of the kitchen chairs. "I don't understand why we couldn't go with her."

"Mom explained all this to you, Jeff. Grandma and Grandpa will be arriving at any time. She wants us to wait here for them."

"Well!" Jeff pounded his fist on the table. "I don't like it! It isn't fair!" Suddenly he leaped from the table and dashed out the back door.

"I don't like it either!" Sylvia shouted first at Jeff, then again at God. "It just isn't fair!"

Those who have lost someone they love can understand Sylvia's frustration and anger. Remember, death is Satan's idea, not God's. God hates death so much that He sent His Son, Jesus, to destroy death once and for all. And that's just what Jesus did on the cross. He destroyed death forever.

If that's so, why do people still die? The death Jesus destroyed is sometimes called the second death. This is the one the Bible talks about when it says, "The wages of sin is death; but the gift of God is eternal life" (Rom. 6:23). This is the death Jesus experienced.

Sylvia might very well ask, "So how does that help my dad? He's still dead. He can't play ball with Jeff or teach me to drive the car next year."

"In every way" would be my reply. "Your dad is gone, but only for a short time until Jesus comes back and calls him from the grave. Jesus will say, 'Arise, you that sleep in the dust—arise to everlasting life.' One day your dad will get to play ball with Jeff once again. And while he might not teach you to drive a car, you and he will discover all sorts of surprises together in God's perfect world."

(Story to be continued.)

OCTOBER 13

TAKING THE GOOD WITH THE BAD

He causes his sun to rise on the evil and the good, and sends rain on the righteous and the unrighteous. Matthew 5:45, NIV.

When Grandma and Grandpa Sherwood arrived at the house, Sylvia went to locate Jeff. She found him perched on a limb high in the apple tree.

"Jeff," she called, "come on down. Grandma and Grandpa are here."

"No," the boy shouted. "I can't."

"Are you stuck?"

"No, I just mean I can't come down—ever!"

"Jeff, get down here this instant!"

"No," the boy insisted. "This is my punishment for making dad die."

"What? You didn't make Dad die—cancer did!"

"No, it was my fault. I always gave Dad a rough time about taking out the garbage. Now God is punishing me by taking him away."

"Jeff, that's nonsense. God doesn't punish naughty little boys by killing their parents. Cancer is a disease that happens to good people and to bad people alike. It's not your fault."

After a few more minutes of coaxing, Jeff climbed down out of the tree. Together he and Sylvia returned to the house, where Grandma and Grandpa waited.

You and I might think Jeff's reasoning is silly, but the Bible relates many stories about people who came to the same conclusions about God. Like Job's friends, Jeff needed to realize that the rain and the sunshine fall on everyone. That's the way life is in a world where Satan and his devious little demons dominate. God never promised to keep us from experiencing troubles and pain. But He did promise to be with us and help us cope with these problems on this earth. And He promises to return and take us out of this world to a place where sin cannot trespass.

(Story to be continued.)

OCTOBER 14

OK TO CRY

Death has been swallowed up in victory. . . . Thanks be to God! 1 Corinthians 15:54-57, NIV.

Throughout her father's funeral and the graveside service, Sylvia bit her lip to keep from crying. She had to be strong for her mother and for her little brother, Jeff. A number of friends stopped by the house, bringing food and expressing compassion. But Sylvia wanted neither. How could she enjoy Mrs. Collins' great potato salad—Dad's favorite—now that her father would never get to taste it again? Eating seemed disloyal somehow. After the last of the visitors left, Mother and Grandma went upstairs, and Jeff disappeared out the back door. "He's probably up some tree," she mused as she stood by the kitchen window and rinsed the dishes in the sink.

Tears streamed down her cheeks as she cried aloud. "I just don't understand! I prayed! I believed God would heal him; I really did!"

Sylvia swiped at her tears when she heard footsteps approaching. Her usually jovial grandfather peered into the room.

“Who are you talking to, child?” he asked.

Sylvia’s face reddened at the thought of having been overheard.

Grandpa Sherwood walked over to the young girl and patted her shoulder. “I know. I prayed, too, that God would choose to spare my only son.”

“At first I didn’t want to believe it . . . when Dad got so sick . . .” Sylvia buried her face in her grandfather’s suit jacket. “I’m sorry, Grandpa. I want to be strong for Mom, and now I’m letting her down.”

“No, child, you’re not! It’s OK to cry,” he insisted. “If you broke an arm, you’d cry from the pain. Does a broken heart hurt any less? It will take time, lots of time, for your heart to heal. But you will heal,” he assured her. Mumbling more to himself than to Sylvia, he added, “You will heal . . .”

Grandpa Sherwood was right. With the help of family, friends, and a grief-recovery counselor, Sylvia learned to cope. She understood that tears and anger are part of the healing process, so are denial and making deals with God. By the end of the year, Sylvia reached the fifth and last stage—acceptance. While she still missed her father terribly, she could accept her loss for what it was—not God’s fault, but the consequences of living in a world of sin.

OCTOBER 15

DON’T TAKE CHANCES

Therefore, my brothers, be all the more eager to make your calling and election sure. For if you do . . . you will receive a rich welcome into the eternal kingdom of our Lord and Savior Jesus Christ. 2 Peter 1:10, 11, NIV.

What were the chances that in 1906 six babies would be born on board the German ship *Grosser Kurfurst*: one in first class, twins in second class, and triplets in third class? What were the chances of an employee of the Pepperidge Farm plant in Downingtown, Pennsylvania, being killed by falling into a vat of chocolate and his name would be Robert C. H. Hershey? And what were the chances, do you suppose, that Robert Todd Lincoln would be present at Ford’s Theater on April 14, 1865, when his father, Abraham Lincoln, was assassinated, that he would be at a Washington railroad station on July 2, 1881, when President James Garfield was shot, and that on September 6, 1901, he would be but a few feet away from President William McKinley at the Pan-American Exposition in Buffalo, New York, when McKinley was shot?

What were the chances that Suleyman Guresci would divorce his wife in a Turkish court in November of 1986 after a six-year battle and then, because he was lonely, turn to a computer service to find the ideal wife for himself and out of the 2,000 possible candidates be matched up with Nesrin Caglasas, his former wife? Believe it or not, it happened, and Suleyman married Nesrin with the comment "I decided to give her another try by being more tolerant toward her."

If a writer or a TV producer came up with such fantastic tales, he would be laughed at. Those coincidences are just too incredible to believe. But strange as it may seem, life plays some crazy games on us once in a while.

As incredible as the thought of living forever in a perfect world might be, it too is very, very true. However, heaven is not the result of a series of coincidences, and no one will be in God's kingdom because of chance or some bizarre accident. You and I must make a definite choice to follow Jesus. That's why Peter, the apostle and friend of Jesus, advises, "make your calling sure." Don't take chances on such an important thing as eternity. Don't leave your salvation to chance. Ask God today to teach you the way of salvation. He's even more eager to spend forever with you than you are to spend it with Him.

OCTOBER 16

DIRTY WORDS

Your words will be used to judge you—to declare you either innocent or guilty. Matthew 12:37, TEV.

Poor old Noah Webster never imagined when he compiled his first dictionary the number and the kinds of words that would one day be added. For better or worse, today is Noah Webster's birthday. I thought I would teach you some words that Noah never heard, saw, or uttered in his entire lifetime. He didn't know these words because they're new words that have been added to our vocabulary within the past 10 years, and they're dirty words—dirty words that you should have in your vocabulary.

Here goes—ready or not! *Exxon Valdez*, *Chernobyl*, *ozone*, *dioxin*, *acid rain*, *greenhouse effect*—a lexicon of losses! Each one stands for a mess we humans have created on Planet Earth. They break the rule you learned as a child—pick up after yourself.

Have you ever heard anyone say, "Why bother picking it up, somebody else is going to drop something else in the next few minutes anyway?'' or ''Why clean my room—it will only get messy again?'' Make sense? If you agree, then you are a part of earth's environmental problem and not a part of the cure.

''Hey! That's not fair!'' you say. ''I'm only 11 years old. I haven't been around long enough to be blamed for the earth's problems.''

You're partially right. No one can blame you for the nuclear reactor accident in Chernobyl, Russia. On the other hand, you are becoming the person you will become. Does that make sense? You are responsible from this point on for how you treat the earth's resources. As one commentator put it: ''We do not inherit the earth's resources from our parents and grandparents; we borrow them from our children and grandchildren.''

If, as today's text says, ''your words will be used to judge you,'' will God's judgment include the words we live as well as the words we speak? Interesting thought. *Air*, *sunshine*, *rain*, *rich soil*, and *cobalt blue waters* are more than just words. They are gifts from God that are worth far more than wealth, talent, or personality. You and I are responsible for those gifts—how we use them and how we abuse them.

OCTOBER 17

CLEAN IT AGAIN, SAM

God hath not called us unto uncleanness, but unto holiness. 1 Thessalonians 4:7.

I admire Sam. Sam lives beside a railroad underpass in Clackamas County, Oregon. Sometime in the past, teens in the neighborhood chose the walls of this overpass as the local graffiti board. While it started out bearing simple hearts and initials declaring undying love for one another, it recently turned ugly with hate words, satanic symbols, and obscenities spray painted on every inch of concrete.

The citizens of the neighborhood complained to the town authorities. ''We don't like it,'' they said. ''It's filthy and insulting to our community.''

''We don't know how to stop it,'' the Boring town officials replied. ''We don't have enough policemen to patrol your road as often as it would take to catch the offenders. You're in a better position to do that.''

No one took the town official serious except Sam. He decided he would do something. Taking money from his monthly pension, Sam purchased rollers, a roller pan, and gray paint at his local paint store. Then early the next Sunday morning Sam painted both concrete walls.

One day passed—the walls stayed unscarred. Two days, three. But on Thursday morning ugly red and yellow spray-painted words defaced his freshly painted wall. Without a word, Sam repainted the wall that day. By Sunday morning the vandals had scrawled more of their obscenities across the two surfaces.

By this point, the other people in the neighborhood asked Sam, "Why bother? They'll just come and mess it up again." And they were right. For weeks a battle raged. Sam repainted; the vandals desecrated—over and over again.

Again the neighbors asked, "Why keep trying, Sam?"

He replied, "For the same reason I bathe every day."

It worked, at least for one neighborhood in Clackamas County, Oregon. Today the bridge is clean. Sam didn't do it alone. Sam's neighbors caught his spirit and policed the bridge themselves. When they caught a vandal spray-painting graffiti on the concrete, they told him that either he could repaint the bridge's surface or they would turn him over to the sheriff and a judge who would fine the vandal or give him time in jail.

Two lessons today: One, what can you do to improve your environment, to change your personal world from one of uncleanness to holiness? And two, Sam and his paint can remind us of how often we get covered with the graffiti of sin and that God needs to clean us up—again and again.

OCTOBER 18

RICHES TO RAGS

Man does not live on bread alone. Luke 4:4, NIV.

Banana-nut ice cream. Howard wanted banana-nut ice cream! And since Howard was the richest man in the United States, whatever Howard wanted, Howard got. His chef kept a supply of banana-nut ice cream on hand at all times because Howard ate this rare flavor of ice cream three times a day for months.

One day Howard's chef ran in a panic to the rich man's chief aide. "The company that manufactures banana-nut ice cream has discontinued making that flavor! What will I do?"

"Do we have enough to meet Mr. Hughes' needs for the rest of the week, at least?"

"Yes, I think so," the chef replied.

"Then leave it to me. I'll see what I can do."

The chief aide called an emergency meeting of his staff. They solved the crisis by commissioning the ice-cream manufacturer to make up a special batch of 350 gallons of banana-nut ice cream. After paying a local food storage company to store the ice cream, the chief aide and Howard's chef breathed easier again.

The very next day after the shipment of banana-nut ice cream arrived, Howard finished his customary two scoops of banana-nut and said, "That's great ice cream, but it's time for a change. From now on, I want French vanilla."

Other strange obsessions that Howard developed included going for weeks eating only canned soup and for months eating only steak sandwiches. His worst obsession was with germs. He once wrote a three-page memo, one of hundreds of memos concerning hygiene, to his staff in which he detailed the nine steps he wanted taken in opening a can of fruit so that no germs would come in contact with its contents.

While Howard had money for the best of everything and could afford to satisfy such unusual whims, he died totally isolated from everyone who might have cared for him. He'd long since driven all of his friends away. At the end of his life, his wardrobe consisted of an old bathrobe, some pajamas, a Stetson hat, and several pairs of drawstring shorts. His blacked-out bedroom was never cleaned, his sheets rarely changed.

He seldom bathed, and never brushed his teeth. His fingernails and toenails grew inches long, and he took illegal drugs. His body was covered with oozing sores from sitting and sleeping in a lounge chair all day long. With an estimated fortune of $1.5-$2 billion, he died the richest and probably the loneliest man in the world.

Was he afraid of people trying to cheat him of his money? What changed the vibrant, powerful businessman into a haunted recluse? No one knows for sure. There are a lot of people in this world, with or without Howard's billions of dollars, who, like him, never ever learn that "man shall not live by bread alone"—that happiness doesn't come from acquiring wealth from other people but by giving love to others.

OCTOBER 19

APPLE DAY

Keep me as the apple of your eye; hide me in the shadow of your wings. Psalm 17:8, NIV.

In 1913 the governor of Indiana declared October 19 to be "Apple Day." To celebrate "Apple Day" residents of the state must eat at least one apple. "Apples keep you healthy," he said, instituting the phrase "An apple a day keeps the doctor away."

I love apples—apples of every kind. When I want to curl up on the couch with a good book, I need a crispy Mackintosh apple to keep me company. When I want to make an apple crisp, I use Granny Smith apples. Picnic apples must be Golden Delicious, straight from Washington State. Even the prickly crab apple makes great jelly. My history book tells me that originally the Baldwin apple was called a "pecker" apple because woodpeckers liked to nest in the trees.

When my family lived at Blue Mountain Academy in Pennsylvania, we had an apple tree in our yard that produced two kinds of apples—a Golden Delicious and a sour red apple. Someone in years past had grafted a branch from a tree that produced yellow apples onto the more bitter red apple tree. When I combined the two apples, I made the yummiest apple pies and most scrumptious applesauce for my family to eat all winter.

Apples vary in look, taste, and texture—just like people. Maybe that's why God instilled the wisdom into human beings to develop and produce so many varieties of apples. And like you and me, apple trees don't just grow and produce terrific fruit without care and training. The limbs of the trees must be pruned to rid them of suckers. Suckers are a specific kind of branch that robs the tree of the strength to produce a good crop of apples. Pests and insects must be destroyed. Birds must be shooed away in order to allow the apples to ripen without damage. The trees must sometimes be protected from violent storms and unexpected drops in temperature. All this takes the time and attention of a loving gardener.

I like knowing that I am the "apple of God's eye." If I am willing, He will remove the bad habits or suckers that sap my strength. He will protect me from dangerous pests that keep me from developing into the beautiful fruit He knows I can become. He is there to warm me and surround me with His love. And if a storm does break one of my limbs, my loving Gardener knows best how to repair the damage and restore me to good health once again.

Someone once put this text to music. When I'm down on myself, when I feel discouraged, I like to sing the catchy little tune to remind myself that I am, indeed, the "apple of God's eye." You are too, you know.

STRIKING THE ROCK

The secret things belong unto the Lord our God: but those things which are revealed belong unto us and to our children for ever, that we may do all the words of this law. Deuteronomy 29:29.

The blazing sun beats down on the robed man's shoulders as he leads his sheep nearer the rocks at the base of Mount Sinai. When he reaches the base of the mountain, he stops and studies the rocks for a few minutes, then lifts his rod high over his head and brings it down across the back of the rock with as much force as he can. And miracle of miracles, clean pure water gushes out of the rock—a cool refreshment for the dusty shepherd and his thirsty sheep. That's right, like his predecessor, Moses, the Bedouin shepherd of the Sinai desert knows that deep inside these granite rocks flow streams of living water.

Soft, porous limestone veins run through the rocks surrounding Mount Sinai. These limestone veins trap and hold the rainfall in the rainy season. The water seeps down through invisible arteries inside the rocks and collects in little pools or wells. The Bedouin's staff needs only to crack the side of a dry rock for water to gush out.

Obeying God's order to strike the rock would have been easy for Moses to follow. After all, Moses must have done the very same thing hundreds of times during his 40 years in the wilderness. He trusted and lived by the laws of nature. Each crack of his staff against the granite rocks required faith in the laws of nature—the same kind of faith it takes for you and me to flip a light switch to produce light or fly safely in an airplane.

Knowing and using the laws of nature is what God intended for us to do. How foolish it would be to know and understand the power of lightning, yet stand on a hilltop during an electrical storm. How stupid it would be to know and understand how the tiny connectors in the brain work, then destroy them with drugs! How utterly ridiculous it would be to know and understand how sin destroys your body, mind, and soul, then go on sinning anyway! Doesn't make sense, does it—to break the laws of nature when you know better?

(To be continued.)

OCTOBER 21

A BETTER WAY

Water will gush forth in the wilderness and streams in the desert. Isaiah 35:6, NIV.

When someone tells you how to do something, do you ever think you know a better way? If so, you're in good company. Moses thought he knew better. After wandering in the desert for some time, Moses and the people of Israel set up camp north of Mount Sinai at Kadesh.

"Our people are thirsty!" the tribal leaders complained. "Did God bring us and our cattle out here in the desert to die? Why have you made us come out of Egypt, to bring us to this evil place? There is no water to drink."

Moses and his brother Aaron prayed, and God ordered Moses to gather the people together in front of a specific rock, then speak to the rock, and water would burst forth. Can't you imagine hearing Moses say to God, "Excuse me? *Speak* to the rock? Don't You mean *strike* the rock?" After all, Moses had lived for 40 years in this desert. He knew the desert like the back of his hand. He knew the laws of nature. He knew a better way.

Now, Moses had had it up to his Adam's apple with the people's complaints. "Listen, you rebels!" Moses shouted. "Must we bring water out of this rock?"

Then he lifted his arm and struck the rock twice; and water gushed out. Oops! Moses goofed twice! First, he allowed his anger to overpower his judgment by taking part of the credit for God's miracle, then he disobeyed by striking the rock. Moses lost his self-control and his faith with one swoosh of his rod.

There are times when God directs us to do something, something that appears to conflict with the natural laws He created. That's where faith enters. That's when I, like Moses, either must choose to do as God says or "do it my own way."

If I trust Him despite "knowing a better way," God can turn my rocks into flowing streams, my impossible mountains into gold mines, my upsetting experiences into blessings. And if I will let Him, He can make "all things possible" (see Mark 9:23).

For me there is one more blessing to receive from this story—the evidence of God's love. God had a perfect right to ignore Moses after he disobeyed His direct orders. God could have embarrassed Moses royally by not producing water for the people. But He didn't. In spite of Moses' sin, God produced water upon demand and allowed Moses to save face. Don't imagine that Moses escaped payment for his error. Discover for yourself just what happened next.

While you and I and Moses must often pay the penalty for our sins, God is there to turn even sin's ugliest consequence into a blessing if we will only let Him.

OCTOBER 22

WHAT MAKES YOU YOU

I have been reminded of your sincere faith, which first lived in your grandmother Lois and in your mother Eunice and, I am persuaded, now lives in you also. 2 Timothy 1:5, NIV.

A brisk October breeze rustled Lucy's long brown curls as she climbed the hill beside her New Hampshire home. Lucy's father, William Miller, along with many other concerned people around the world had studied Bible prophecies for long hours and had decided that Jesus planned to return to earth on October 22, 1844. Learning of Christ's soon return, William traveled across New England preaching that Jesus would return—soon. Some people believed; others laughed and scorned the Advent preacher and his message. When the prophesied day arrived, he and his family ascended the hill to await the arrival of their Saviour.

Today, Lucy thought, t*oday, I will go home to live forever with Jesus*. Lucy remembered her grandmother and her baby sister, both resting in Jesus. *What will it be like—living in a perfect world where death and disease cannot exist?* A bramble caught the hem of Lucy's cambric crinoline and held it fast. Tugging it free, Lucy scowled, then smiled to herself. In heaven there would be no pesky thorns or brambles. She stopped and picked off the burrs accumulating on the sleeve of her dress—and no sticktights either!

Seconds, minutes, hours dragged by as God's people awaited the drama of all time to begin. They watched as the sun inched its way across the clear autumn sky, then sank beneath the western horizon. One by one the stars came out as the sky grew indigo. When the distant church clock struck midnight, they groaned in horror. The day had passed—and Jesus hadn't returned! Slowly, hearts filled with despair, they made their way back down the rocky hillside to their homes.

What did Lucy and her family do once October 22 passed? The same thing they'd done before October 22, 1844—they studied God's Word to discover just what it was God wanted of them. Of course they were disappointed when Jesus didn't return, wouldn't you be? But their faith told them that if a mistake had been made, it wasn't God's; it was theirs. Their faithfulness and Bible study became your heritage and mine. Because of that terribly discouraging day, real people dug deeply into God's Word to uncover the beautiful truths you and I believe—the very truths that make you and me Seventh-day Adventists.

OCTOBER 23

LUCY'S LEGACY

We do not want you to become lazy, but to imitate those who through faith and patience inherit what has been promised. Hebrews 6:12, NIV.

Yesterday we shared a very special day in the heritage of every Seventh-day Adventist. William Miller's family was only one of many who decided to study so they could find and correct their error. Ellen White did also. Can you think of others who experienced the disappointment of October 22, 1844, and who chose to study rather than give up?

Lucy grew up, married, became a mother. What do you think Lucy told her children about the day on the hillside as she waited for Jesus to return? Do you think she encouraged them to study for themselves? Can you hear Lucy speaking to her children, "I do not want you to become lazy, but to imitate those [your grandfather, your grandmother, your uncle John, etc.] who through faith and patience inherit the promises"? Lucy eventually died, inheriting the promise. That's right. Though it has been almost 150 years, God's promise was Lucy's the day she first believed it—not the day it will be fulfilled.

Today, you can visit the church where William Miller preached, and you can sit in the pew where Lucy sat as she listened to her father's message of hope. You can visit the cemetery where she sleeps until the day He calls her from the grave to immortality. Her salvation is secure. Yours can be too.

But first, it is important for you to discover just what salvation is all about. Just like William Miller, Ellen White, Joseph Bates, and so many others, you must discover the truths all over again for yourself. Do you know what truths these Adventist pioneers passed on to you as your inheritance? Do you know what makes you distinctly Seventh-day Adventist? Just what do you believe?

In the spaces below, can you list at least 10 truths that identify you as a Seventh-day Adventist Christian?

1.
2.
3.
4.
5.
6.
7.
8.
9.
10.

You and I cannot afford to be lazy about what we believe and about Jesus' return. Lucy Miller's legacy to us does not relieve us, who live in 1992, of the responsibility of studying for ourselves. On the contrary, in order to build faith in God's promises, you and I must discover for ourselves just what God expects of His children.

OCTOBER 24

SIMPLY WISE

Everything is possible for the person who has faith. Mark 9:23, TEV.

Today I want you to try an experiment. You will need two pieces of paper, both 18″ by 4″, and a roll of cellophane tape. Draw a black line the length of each strip of paper.

Take one of the strips of paper and tape the ends together, creating a loop. Take the second strip, give it a half-twist once (a twist of 180°), then join the ends together. The first strip has two edges and two surfaces—one inside the loop and one outside the loop, right? What about the second loop? Follow your black line around the loop, and you will discover that "both" surfaces have a continuous pencil line running around them, proving the band has only one surface. So what happened to the second surface and the second edge? Your second loop is called a Mobius strip, a strange phenomenon first described by August Ferdinand Mobius, a nineteenth-century German mathematician.

Now carefully cut your Mobius strip along the pencil line, and you would expect to have two bands, right? Instead, you now have one longer loop. How many twists does your new, longer band have? Now you no longer have a Mobius strip, for it again has two surfaces and two edges. Cut the band one more time down the middle, and you will have two interlocking Mobius bands. Impossible! Unbelievable! So how does it work? If I knew the answer to that question, I would go down in history as the one who discovered the "Rizzo Solution."

A Mobius strip reminds me of the Christian's faith in God. Remember when Jesus told the woman who touched His garment that her faith had made her whole? Now, I just can't understand how that happened. And I don't understand how exercising faith makes a person strong, gives him or her peace, and helps him or her survive. But you know what? I don't need to know how faith works; Jesus just expects me to believe that it works—that's all. It's so simple that the littlest child can possess it, and yet so complicated that the greatest minds of all time can't discover its secrets. No matter how many times you try it, the simple Mobius strip will work the same way. So faith in God and His promises work time and time again for the trusting child of God.

OCTOBER 25

BAD TRADES

Turn my eyes away from worthless things; preserve my life according to your word. Psalm 119:37, NIV.

One morning a Christian preacher walked along a beach in Hawaii. Up ahead he spotted two nationals standing in shallow surf. They were holding a screen between them—shaking it back and forth, sifting out the sand. As the sand filtered back into the water, a number of pretty shells remained, along with a small beetle. One of the islanders carefully picked off the beetle and placed it in a tin can, then tossed the shells back into the surf.

"What are you looking for?" the preacher asked. "You threw away some pretty shells."

The two Hawaiians laughed, then one replied, "You can't catch fish with shells. We must catch fish in order to feed our families."

The preacher watched the two men for a few more minutes, then continued his stroll. He thought about what the fisherman had said, "You can't catch fish with shells."

Although pretty shells are nice to collect, food is vital. The fishermen would have been foolish to waste their time and energy collecting the pretty shells while their children starved. Sometimes it is difficult to know what is important and what is just a pleasant distraction or trivia. I have a friend named Leo who has a fantastic memory. Leo can recite the number of runs, hits, and errors of every major league baseball player for the past 10 years. He can see an actor on TV or on a video and immediately identify him and tell you what other films or programs the actor has been in. Yet when it comes to Bible study, Leo has trouble remembering texts and recalling the who's and the what's of Bible times. Kind of sad—almost like starving for food while collecting pretty shells.

Don't misunderstand me. I enjoy trivia as much as anyone else. And knowing baseball statistics isn't any more evil than being a shell collector. If I have a limited amount of time and must make a choice in what I will spend my time learning, collecting baseball and TV trivia, or even pearly shells, is not as important to my survival as finding food. And that includes eating the Word of God—learning all I can about the Bible and His plan for my life.

Thank You, Father, for guiding me and giving me the freedom to choose. Help me not to make the mistake of losing a dollar in order to save a dime, of collecting pretty shells when I should be "eating" the bread of life.

OCTOBER 26

LEMONADE MAKERS

The Lord your God . . . turned the curse into a blessing for you, because the Lord your God loves you. Deuteronomy 23:5, NIV.

The first prison inmate to die in an electric chair was executed in New York in August 1890. When the emperor of Abyssinia (today's Ethiopia), Emperor Menelik II, heard about this great new technology, he decided his country needed to move into the twentieth century. Menelik immediately ordered three electric chairs from the U.S. manufacturers.

On the day the chairs arrived at the palace, Menelik invited the country's most important people to celebrate their arrival. But Menelik was in for a shock; no one had told him that the chairs needed an outside electrical source to work. Electricity hadn't yet arrived in the country of Abyssinia.

Undaunted by the disaster, Menelik saved face by ordering two of his strongest servants, "Remove my old throne from the royal reception room and replace it with one of these." He pointed to the electric chairs. The servants placed the other two chairs in storage against the day the first one wore out.

It took many years for the guests at Menelik's celebration that day to discover that the emperor's imperial throne was actually a chair invented for the purpose of execution.

A few years ago a book came out with the title *When Life Gives You Lemons, Make Lemonade*. The idea caught on—turn bad things into blessings. Bad things do happen, but they don't have to destroy us. It's all up to us. Either we can cry and complain about how unfair life can be or, like Emperor Menelik, we can turn bad things into good, make lemonade out of life's lemons, or make an imperial throne out of an electric chair.

God helped Daniel snatch victory out of the jaws of lions. With God's help, Esther transformed one man's prejudice into pride for her people, while Paul and Silas converted a prison cell into a concert hall of praise. God is famous for making blessings out of curses, good out of bad, and lemonade out of lemons—you and God together can do anything. Something to think about the next time tragedy strikes.

OCTOBER 27

PLANTING SPAGHETTI SEEDS

Do not be deceived: God cannot be mocked. A man reaps what he sows. . . . Let us not become weary in doing good, for at the proper time we will reap a harvest if we do not give up. Galatians 6:7-9, NIV.

On April Fool's Day in 1957, *Panorama*, a distinguished television current affairs program in England, carried an unusual news item. Richard Dimbleby, a highly regarded newscaster, reported on the annual spaghetti harvest in Ticino, a region on the border of Italy and Switzerland. Women were shown picking long strands of spaghetti from trees and laying them out to dry in the sun. Dimbleby closed his report with "There is nothing as delicious as eating freshly picked, homegrown spaghetti."

Now, you and I know spaghetti does not grow on trees. A mixture of wheat flour and other ingredients is run through a machine called a "pasta maker." Maybe your mother has one.

The people who heard Dimbleby's report responded in a variety of ways: some laughed at the humor, some complained that a serious news program like *Panorama* should not indulge in such absurd jokes, while a large number of others wrote to ask for further details on the festival in order to attend it.

Another practical joke that went far beyond the expected was played on Winston Norton, the son of Horace Norton, founder of Norton College in Chicago. In 1932 Winston delivered a speech at the Norton College reunion. In it he told the story of how in the 1860s Ulysses Simpson Grant gave Horace Norton a cigar. Recognizing the historical significance of a cigar once owned by the eighteenth president of the United States, Horace kept it as a family treasure.

His son, Winston, decided to light it at a Norton College gathering at the end of his speech.

"As I light this cigar with trembling hand," Winston Norton said, "it is not alone a tribute to him you call founder, but also to the titan among statesmen who was never too exalted to be a friend, who was—" *Bang!* The cigar exploded. It had been some 70 years, but President Grant finally got to play his joke.

We expect to laugh at practical jokes like the spaghetti crop and Grant's exploding cigar. A good laugh is the natural harvest of joke playing. But many things in life are not joking material, such as pranks that harm other people or their property, jokes that belittle a person's faith in God or make fun of spiritual matters. These kinds of jokes may get a laugh when told, but they will reap a harvest for both the teller and the listener—not of laughter but of tears. To destroy or weaken either your own faith or another person's faith in God is serious business. And while it make take many years to come to fruition, like Grant's joke on Norton, it will come. God will not be mocked—you can be sure of it.

OCTOBER 28

LET THERE BE LIGHT

The people walking in darkness have seen a great light. Isaiah 9:2, NIV.

Brisk October winds whipped down the channel, tossing the ferryboat like a toy boat floating in a 2-year-old's bathwater. Clutching the railing with one hand and my stomach with the other, I stared out at a misty world of somber gray. Whoever heard of anyone getting sick on the Staten Island ferry! *Will I survive?* I wondered. My next question was *Do I even care?*

In an effort to get my mind off the discomfort of seasickness, I tried to imagine the faces of the hundreds of thousands of people who rode in a similar ferry from Ellis Island, the holding island for immigrants wishing to become American citizens, to Manhattan Island and America. All their faces were as green as mine, at least in my imagination. I was still wallowing in my distress when my husband pointed into the air.

"See!" he said. "See the light!"

I looked up. All I could see through the heavy mist was the light from the torch of the Statue of Liberty. I couldn't see the spikes of Lady Liberty's crown or the open book in her hand or even the green folds of her gown—just the light.

At the sight of that flame of light piercing the gray, I forgot all about my upset stomach and my pounding head. I gulped back my tears and stared as the ferry inched past Liberty Island, the home of the statue of friendship and freedom that the French government donated to the people of the United States and which was dedicated on October 28, 1886.

To the thousands of immigrants who travel so far to see that light, it shines forth in freedom. To Americans who travel abroad, it says two of the most beautiful words in the English language—*Welcome home*.

Heaven will have a Statue of Liberty—not one made out of copper or mounted on marble, but a living, breathing statue who will welcome us home for all eternity—Jesus Christ. And to God's children He will say, "Welcome home." If my eyes tear every time I see this earth's symbol of freedom, I can only imagine the tears of happiness I will shed each time I see my Saviour. Jesus is one sight none of us will want to miss.

OCTOBER 29

BREAD, POTATOES, AND WATER

You will be safe; you will be as secure as if in a strong fortress. You will have food to eat and water to drink. Isaiah 33:16, TEV.

"The Panic of 1929;" "the stock market crash;" "the beginning of the Great Depression"—all are phrases that best describe this day in U.S. history. Although the majority of Americans didn't understand stocks and how the stock market worked, their lives were irrevocably changed because of the folly of a few hundred men in New York City.

For months stock prices had climbed at the New York Stock Exchange. Wealthy people had invested millions on the soaring stock until one day, October 29, 1929, the price of stocks plummeted so fast that the ticker-tape recorders couldn't keep pace with the disaster. Hundreds of individuals were financially ruined. And in the weeks that followed the crash, many once-wealthy people committed suicide.

To the plain, everyday dairy farmer near La Crosse, Wisconsin, or the coal miner in West Virginia, it seemed unimportant at first. But soon the entire country began to feel the effects of the crash. As the Depression intensified, people lost their jobs and factories closed. In the country, potato farmers ate potatoes three times a day for years. In the city, people waited in long lines to receive a bowl of soup or a loaf of bread. People traveled hundreds of miles from their homes in search of work. Many men, discouraged and embarrassed that they could no longer support their families, hopped trains and became hobos rather than return home as failures.

Even during this terrible time in our country's history, the people of God could trust His promises to watch over them. While they may have experienced hunger pains, they never starved to death. Although their shirts, their dresses, and their trousers faded and needed patching and they wore cardboard strips inside their holey shoes, they never went totally without.

Just as He sent ravens to feed Elijah and angels to care for Hagar, so God comes through for His people—and He always will. You can count on it.

OCTOBER 30

ON HALLOWEEN EVE

We have examined this, and it is true. So hear it and apply it to yourself. Job 5:27, NIV.

Today's lesson is one to think about, to mull over, to decide for yourself what it means to you. Allow the Holy Spirit to speak to you, to direct you. What will you do about Halloween this year? Let me share a few facts I uncovered at the local public library.

The "Gates of Hell" are said to be in Cranchan, Cannaught, England. And on Halloween, October 31, people throughout history have believed that Satan is allowed to open these gates to free his imps.

Remember the angels whom God cast out of heaven with Lucifer? According to legend, these imps take on the form of black cats, ravens, and black goats—all sacred symbols today to people who believe in witchcraft and are racing about the countryside to sacrifice farm animals and young children to their god—Satan. (Sound like anything you might have heard in the news regarding satanism today?) The imps amuse themselves by carrying off people's garden gates, ringing doorbells, and rapping on people's windows—hence today's "trick or treat."

Cut out of large turnips at first, then later out of pumpkins, jack-o'-lanterns with lighted candles inside were used to scare the devils from people's doors. People dressed in costumes so that the demons would not be able to recognize them. For the people of the Middle Ages, Halloween was not a game. It was serious—deadly serious.

Most Christians today know that Satan and his demons are real also. They also know that jack-o'-lanterns and weird costumes will not protect the child of God against the forces of evil. They know, too, that as strong as Satan's forces may be, Christ is stronger. Remember the promise in Romans 8:38-40—"Nothing can separate us from the love of Jesus . . ."?

You and I are the only ones who can keep us from Jesus. It is only as we, either for curiosity or for pleasure, toy with Satan's tricks or play his devious little games that we need to be afraid.

As you have already noticed, today is the day before Halloween—not Halloween itself. If you can't figure out why I chose to write about Halloween today, rather than tomorrow, think about today's text. Decide what you, a son or daughter of the royal courts of heaven, will do about Halloween this year.

OCTOBER 31

A THING OF BEAUTY

Do not consider his appearance or his height, for I have rejected him. The Lord does not look at the things man looks at. Man looks at the outward appearance, but the Lord looks at the heart. 1 Samuel 16:7, NIV.

"They say he's a madman at the keyboard," one concertgoer confided to another.

"Yes," the second replied. "I've heard that when his hands fly over the keys, it's as if he were in league with the devil."

"I say, what is his name again?"

"His name is Beethoven—Ludwig van Beethoven. Prince Lichnowsky brought him from Germany to Vienna to study with the masters. Haydn and Salieri will tone down his bombastic style," the man added knowingly as he seated himself and his guest inside his concert box.

The concert hall vibrated with anticipation as the house lights dimmed and the heavy brocade curtains parted. As the audience applauded, a short, swarthy fellow walked onto the stage and over to the piano. Whispers of shock swept through the audience as the ugly little creature placed his hands on the keyboard.

"This is the great Beethoven?"

"This is the madman of the keyboard?"

With confidence, Beethoven poised his hands over the piano keys. He seemed unconscious of the rest of the world. The muscles in his face seemed to swell; the veins on his forehead stood out; his wide eyes rolled about wildly; his mouth began to quiver.

"He is mad!" Wild speculation swept through the audience. "Look at his hairy little fingers. They can hardly stretch an octave!" And it was true; the backs of Beethoven's hands were densely covered with black hair. His fingers, broad at the tips, were so short they could barely reach more than an octave. But when the music started, the audience forgot the ugly little man and his stumplike fingers. Tears filled the eyes of his amazed audience. They sobbed loudly at the beauty of the man's music, completely forgetting the ugliness of the man himself. Critics of his time described his playing as "explosive"; "a titanic execution." The young musician from Germany became a hit in the courts of Vienna—not because of his beauty but because of the beauty he produced on the piano.

Another man, President Abraham Lincoln, as tall and homely as Beethoven was short and ugly, was once described by the mother of a soldier he'd just pardoned as the "handsomest man I've ever met."

Beauty goes far beyond the tilt of one's nose or the blue of one's eyes. Just as God looks beneath the pretty face or a handsome profile, so you and I must learn to look for the good in people beyond their outer beauty, their money, their great personality, to what is inside. The kid at your school whom you decide to shun might have the talents of a Beethoven or the compassion of a Lincoln, and might have what it takes to be the best friend you'll ever have.

NOVEMBER 1

A GOOD NAME

And [David's] name became well known. 1 Samuel 18:30, NIV.

My name is Kay Darlene Hancock Rizzo. It's a good name. I like it. Oh, once when I was a kid, I thought I might be happier or more popular if my name were Judy or Margie. But over the years I've grown into my name until it fits me just right. Once I looked my name up in a book and discovered that Kay means "rejoice" in Greek; Darlene means "dearly beloved" in Anglo-Saxon. My maiden name, Hancock, tells me that one of my ancestors ran a chicken ranch (hens, roosters). And my husband's last name originates from an Italian ancestor of his who had "brown hair."

What does your name mean? If you're curious, you can find out at your local library. You'll discover that, like Hancock, many last names originated with the bearer's occupation—names such as Butcher, Baker, Carpenter, Mason, Smith (or Schmidt in German and Kovac in Hungarian), Weaver, Fletcher (which means arrow in French), Archer, Calvert (or calf-herder), Collier (means a coal miner who burned wood to make charcoal), Cooper (maker of barrels), Harper, and Fiddler (musicians). Others came from titles—Pope, Bishop, Priest, King, Prince, and Knight.

But I imagine when Bible writers spoke of having a good name, they didn't mean how a name sounds or from whence it originated. They were talking about reputation.

In the old West one's reputation was worth protecting and fighting for—even to the point of a pistol. Even today a person's reputation follows him or her wherever he or she goes.

Look at the presidential primaries. A number of capable candidates were overlooked in the run for the presidency because of stains on their reputations. Fair or unfair, Senator Edward Kennedy's mistakes of the past probably cost him the presidency of the United States. A person's reputation sticks like glue.

The author of Ecclesiastes also talks about a good name. If he were to advise you today, I think he'd say, "If you have a good name, guard it—keep it that way—and it will surround you with the aroma of an expensive perfume."

NOVEMBER 2

A NEW NAME

The memory of the righteous will be a blessing, but the name of the wicked will rot. Proverbs 10:7, NIV.

When Richard, my husband-to-be, loaded his car for college, his father pulled him aside and said, "Son, I have but one piece of advice for you. The Rizzo name is clean and proud. Keep it that way." Richard's father didn't list all the no-no's of college life, such as "Don't flunk out of school" or "Don't get into trouble with the guys" or "Don't step out of line with the girls," yet in a way he did. Eleven words said it all.

That's great if you have a choice, but what happens when other people or events over which you have no control tarnish your name? Unfortunately that sometimes happens. When I was in academy I had a friend who lived in constant fear that someone would find out that her father was in prison for theft. Another friend lived in shame because her older sister got expelled from the academy during the first half of the school term.

Have you ever heard the phrase "Your name is mud"? Some people feel that the expression became popular after President Lincoln's assassination by the actor John Wilkes Booth. In his leap from the theater box to the stage, Booth broke his leg, but he escaped capture. Later that night Booth showed up at the door of a small-town doctor named, you guessed it, Dr. Samuel Mudd. Though the officials failed to catch the guilty actor, they did follow his trail to Mudd's door. Mudd was arrested for conspiracy to murder the president and sentenced to life imprisonment. In 1869 President Andrew Johnson pardoned the man, but Mudd never erased the bad connotation surrounding his name.

Another person who spent the rest of his days living down the tragedy of the day was the British actor Edward Booth, brother to John Wilkes Booth, the man who killed the president. You also need to know the rest of Edward's story. He proved that one can live above the past. He could have chosen to disappear into the countryside or change his name or become as much of a scoundrel as his brother, but he didn't. Instead, he went on to become a great Shakespearean actor in his own right. Whether or not other people forgot his brother's folly, Edward refused to allow past events to destroy him.

If you have been robbed of your good name, or perhaps one mistake has tarnished it, remember that Jesus understands. Satan has spent 6,000 years trying to destroy Jesus' good name. Best of all, you have a new name to look forward to in heaven—a name far more lovely, far more lasting, than the one you've been given on this earth.

NOVEMBER 3

A NAME NOT DESERVED

For we will all stand before God's judgment seat. It is written: "'As surely as I live,'" says the Lord, "'Every knee will bow before me, every tongue will confess to God.'" So then, each of us will give an account of himself to God. Romans 14:10-12, NIV.

Sometimes reputation works the other way. Sometimes people receive fame even when they don't deserve it. You know who I mean? The kid in your science project group who worked the least on the project yet brags about "his great idea" once the project earns an A. Or the phony who pretends to be a goody-goody but turns the air blue with bad language once all adults are out of hearing range.

I once asked one of my English classes what their biggest pet peeve was, expecting such answers as pop quizzes, curfews, etc. Instead, the overwhelming number of students answered, "Phonies"—people who pretend to be something they're not.

The scoundrel John Montague, the fourth earl of Sandwich, was like that. He seemed to be able to get away with horrid behavior and still retain enough respect to hold the office of first lord of the Admiralty and have Captain James Cooke name the Sandwich Islands after him. (Later they became the Hawaiian Islands.) A notoriously corrupt gambler who thought nothing of betraying family member or friend, Montague in 1762 spent 24 hours at the game table. During this marathon card game Montague's valet brought him sliced beef between bread, hence the first sandwich.

So while we might recognize today as the earl's 274th birthday, we don't recognize his character as one we'd admire or wish to copy. On the contrary, old "Monty" and all those like him are to be pitied for their sinful lives.

NOVEMBER 4

STRONGER THAN POPEYE

I do not have time to tell about Gideon, Barak, Samson, Jephthah, David, Samuel and the prophets, who through faith conquered kingdoms, administered justice, and gained what was promised; who shut the mouths of lions, quenched the fury of the flames, and escaped the edge of the sword; whose weakness was turned to strength; and who became powerful in battle and routed foreign armies. Hebrews 11:32-34, NIV.

Wow! That was a long one, huh? And every one of the people mentioned was a hero more powerful than Rambo, braver than Dick Tracy, and stronger than Batman. Do you know why? First, the people listed in today's text were real-live heroes, not make-believe characters taken from the pages of a comic book or from a scriptwriter's imagination.

Second, their hair-raising tales are true. If you want to curl your toes with excitement, read about Gideon's battles or David's adventures.

And third, being real-live humans, these men were weak like you and I, until God gave them the strength to win. While I may never spend the night with a pride of lions, I can still be assured that the same God who can shut lions' mouths can handle my frightening little skirmishes.

Another fictional hero, Popeye the sailorman, made his first appearance in the 1930s. He claimed to get his mighty strength and bulging muscles from the iron found in eating canned spinach. As a result, kids across America consumed 33 percent more spinach than they had in previous years.

However, the creator of Popeye got it all wrong because of a simple mathematical error—one you've probably made a time or two on your math papers. National researchers in the 1890s put a decimal point in the wrong place, thus giving spinach 10 times more iron than it actually contains. In actuality, spinach contains no more or no less iron than any of the other leafy green vegetables. However, a discovery in the 1940s helped redeem poor Popeye a bit. Nutritionists discovered that the folic acid in spinach does give strength. Maybe that's how Popeye got his muscles after all.

If you wish to develop bulging biceps or strong leg muscles, you must do more than eat spinach. You will need to spend hours exercising the appropriate muscles of your body. The same is true if you wish to possess the incredible spiritual strength of the Hebrew heroes. To build well-developed spiritual biceps and strong moral muscles you must exercise your faith in God and His promises.

NOVEMBER 5

AMBASSADORS FOR CHRIST

We are therefore Christ's ambassadors. 2 Corinthians 5:20, NIV.

I have a secret—a secret that guarantees success. I wish someone had shared this secret with me when I was your age. By the end of this reading you'll know my secret, but first let me tell you a story.

Emma grew up in a little backwater town in Arkansas. She felt more at home on her father's hay wagon than she did in a parlor. After Emma graduated from high school, she attended a college in Oklahoma, where she met and fell in love with Sam, a young law student. He looked beyond Emma's shyness to the kind and beautiful person inside.

Sam had high ambitions. He dreamed of entering politics. Within a few short years he had been appointed as a junior aide to the ambassador of France. That's when Emma found herself moving to Paris. The whirlwind of French social life frightened the timid woman. As the wife of a U.S. Embassy staff member, she too was an ambassador for her country. How would she survive at all those parties and dinners? What would she talk about? She had nothing worth saying.

That's when a very wise woman, the wife of a longtime U.S. senator, took Emma aside and said, "You're feeling uncomfortable, aren't you? I know how you feel. I remember."

Emma grinned shyly at the woman, though she didn't quite believe the celebrated hostess' words.

"The secret to being a good conversationalist, one who fits into any crowd and is guaranteed to be a social success wherever one goes, is to learn to listen. That's right—learn to listen. Most of the people here feel nervous and out of place."

Emma scanned the crowd of partyers and exclaimed, "You're kidding!"

"Search for people who look as uncomfortable as you feel, then get acquainted. Let them talk about themselves. Listen sincerely and ask them questions."

It worked. Before long the ambassador walked up to Sam and said, "What a wonderful conversationalist your lovely wife is."

All Emma did was show a true interest in other people.

When I find myself in uncomfortable situations, Emma's secret helps me too. What I do, what I say, and how I act is important because I am an official ambassador for the King of the universe. Emma's and my secret can help you become a more effective ambassador too.

NOVEMBER 6

TOOT YOUR OWN HORN DAY

Love your neighbor as you love yourself. Matthew 22:39, TEV.

Let's celebrate the birthday of Antoine-Joseph Sax, the inventor of the saxophone, by declaring today to be Toot Your Own Horn Day. I doubt he'd mind.

"All right, Mrs. R," I can almost hear you saying, "isn't it bragging to toot your own horn?"

It would be if you were to report your findings to your friends and classmates. But here in the family circle it will be a safe and healthy exercise, I promise. Now, are you ready to toot your horn? Remember, you must follow all the steps of the exercise to make it work for you.

1. Reread the text, putting the emphasis on the last three words—that's right, put the emphasis on "you love yourself." Who is speaking these words? Jesus proved your worth when He died for you at Calvary.

2. Admit that you are a designer original—made in the image of God. Repeat the following words aloud: "No one and nothing can make me feel inferior without my consent. God has a plan for my life." Jesus knew that you must be able to love and accept yourself first before you would have the courage to love others. You need to see in yourself what Jesus sees in you so that you may be able to see in others what He sees in them.

3. Make a list of five things you like about yourself. Share your list with your family. What steps can you take to strengthen those five positive traits?

4. Make a list of five things you'd like to change about yourself. Share the list with your family. What steps can you take to eliminate or

weaken those negative traits? If there are things you cannot change, how can you learn not only to accept them but also to turn them into blessings?

5. Make a list of five character traits you'd like to possess (for instance, to be kinder, happier, more honest, etc.). Find out what the Bible says about these traits of character.

6. Pray. Show Jesus the lists you've made. Ask Him to show you how you can use all of your character traits in order to help someone else today.

7. Do something for somebody today without being asked and without telling anyone that you did it. Report your findings to God. Tell Him how it felt to help someone else, how it made you feel inside. Thank Him for showing you how to obey His law of love today.

NOVEMBER 7

A PIECE OF MY MIND

Do you see a man who speaks in haste? There is more hope for a fool than for him. . . . An angry man stirs up dissension, and a hot-tempered one commits many sins. Proverbs 29:20-22, NIV.

Holly grinned with delight. *I can really get into this assignment,* she thought as she bounded down the hall to her bedroom. *Imagine Mama suggesting such a thing! Maybe she understands how angry I am after all.*

Holly's troubles started the day that both Holly and her best friend, Cheri, tried out for the lead role in the Christmas play. When Cheri got the part, Holly tried to be nice about it and hide her disappointment. As the only sixth grader chosen to be in the upper graders' play, Cheri was nervous that she might do something stupid. To make Cheri feel better, Holly volunteered to help her friend learn her lines.

At first all went well. But as the weeks passed, Cheri started hanging around the other cast members during recess and after school—one in particular, Greg. When Holly would suggest they walk home together after school or study together in the evening, Cheri always claimed to be too busy.

The breaking point for Holly came when she asked to sit at Cheri's table in the cafeteria.

"Oh," Cheri reddened, "I'm saving that seat for Greg."

Holly simmered all afternoon. In English class she didn't care about verb tenses. She felt tense enough on her own. By the time Holly got home, her hurt had turned to fury. And as usual, she poured out her frustrations on her mother.

Holly's mother listened carefully, then made a strange suggestion. "Well, I think you need to write Cheri a letter telling her what you just told me. Tell her exactly what you think of her."

Holly couldn't believe she'd heard her mother right. "You do?"

"Absolutely!"

Holly's face brightened into a smile. "All right! Boy, I'll tell her off. She'll be sorry she ever treated me that way."

Mother's advice sounds like a contradiction of today's text. Why would Mother suggest such a thing to her daughter? It doesn't sound too wise, does it? Think about the text and about Mother's instructions until tomorrow, when you'll learn the rest of the story; then you may decide whether or not Mother's advice was wise or foolish.

(Story to be continued.)

NOVEMBER 8

DIFFICULT ADVICE TO FOLLOW

Perfume and incense bring joy to the heart, and the pleasantness of one's friend springs from his earnest counsel. Proverbs 27:9, NIV.

Holly curled up on her bed and poured out all her anger on the paper. Pleased with her vicious masterpiece and feeling much better, she smiled to herself. *That will teach Cheri,* Holly thought. *She'll be sorry.* Holly leaped from the bed and rushed downstairs to find her mother.

"Wanna hear what I wrote?"

"Sure," her mother replied.

After reading the letter to her mother, Holly asked, "Well, what do you think?"

"Good! Great job! Now take the letter to the kitchen, tear it up, and throw it in the garbage."

"What?" Holly screeched. "But you told me to write it!"

"Yes, I did," Mother admitted. "And writing it made you feel better, didn't it? The letter served its purpose, so throw it away. It won't help the situation between you and Cheri to send the letter, will it?"

"No," Holly mumbled, "but I'll feel better."

"You already feel better just having written it," Mother reminded. "Cheri is acting a little stupid right now. A good friend will realize that Cheri's success is affecting her better judgment and will be patient with her. My guess is that in time she'll be your friend again."

"But what should I do about it?"

"Perhaps nothing at all for now. Be nice to her. Treat her with kindness," mother suggested. "But until Cheri discovers how foolish she's been, hang out with Karen and Meg or some of your other friends."

"What if she never . . ." Holly couldn't make herself say the awful words.

"Then I guess you'll have to admit to yourself that Cheri wasn't the great friend you thought she was. But knowing Cheri, I don't think that will happen."

Do you agree with Mother's advice to tear up the letter and to be patient with Cheri? Considering the message in today's text, what advice for Holly would you add?

(Story to be continued.)

NOVEMBER 9

THE THIRD LETTER

Friends always show their love. What are brothers [and sisters] for if not to share trouble? Proverbs 17:17, TEV.

On the evening of the Christmas program, Holly wrote a second letter and slipped it into Cheri's hand just before the play began. "Dear Cheri," the note said. "You're going to do a great job tonight. You've practiced and worked hard. I'm proud of you. Go out there and wow the audience for our class. I'm proud of you. Your best friend, Holly."

When Cheri walked out onto the stage, her gaze swept across the audience and stopped when she spotted Holly.

Holly grinned and gave her friend a thumbs up. Even from where Holly sat, she could see Cheri's eyes fill up with tears. Cheri paused for a moment, then spoke her opening lines.

Throughout the play, Holly sat mesmerized as her friend became the character she played. *Wow! Cheri's good,* Holly thought, *really good. I can see why Mr. Hanson gave her the part.*

The curtain fell to thunderous applause, and no one applauded louder than Holly.

By the time Holly reached backstage, a crowd had surrounded the sixth-grade star. "I guess I'll have to wait until tomorrow to congratulate her," Holly sighed and turned to leave. Suddenly a hand grabbed her shoulder and turned her about.

"Hey, wait a minute," Cheri giggled. "Where do you think you're going so fast?"

The two girls hugged each other and twirled about, both talking at the same time.

"I'm sorry I've been such a jerk these past few days," Cheri said.

"It's OK," Holly admitted. "I've done some dumb things in the past too. Hey, where's Greg? Are you two still . . . you know?"

"Are you kidding? Talk about jerks—he's the king of jerks. You wouldn't believe—wait till I tell you . . ."

How did Mom get to be so smart? Holly wondered. As she listened and laughed at Cheri's wild tales, Holly made a mental note to herself. "Dear Holly," the third letter said, "thank Mom for being so wise. And thank *you* for being my best friend."

NOVEMBER 10

THE WALL TUMBLED DOWN

With your help I can advance against a troop; with my God I can scale a wall. Psalm 18:29, NIV.

One of the most exciting events that has happened in your lifetime and mine occurred during this week three years ago. The Berlin Wall, built to keep people apart, came down. I remember watching on television as people from East Berlin scaled the wall and dropped to the other side. Family members who had not seen each other in years fell into one another's arms, crying with happiness. I watched individuals, tears streaming from their eyes, smash pickaxes and sledgehammers against the hated wall.

Just two weeks earlier an American tourist visited the wall. While there he asked a West German official if the wall would ever come down.

"Not in our lifetime," the official answered. No one would have guessed at that time how wrong the official was.

Within a few days after the fall of the wall, I visited a local curio shop in Portland, Oregon, and saw a sign that read "Buy a chunk of the Berlin Wall." As usual, someone had found a way to get rich off the event.

A German friend of mine visited Berlin a few weeks after the wall was taken down. He told of staring at the remaining rubble and thinking of family members, friends, and all the other brave people who over the years had tried to escape and had been cut down by Communist soldiers' bullets. And now the hated, bloodstained wall was gone.

It's easy to forget that the Communists are not the only people who build walls. You do; I do too. When we're afraid or lonely or insecure, we build protective little walls to keep other people at a safe distance. If we get to know someone too well, we might come to care for him or her and about his or her problems. That could get messy. On the other hand, if we keep people at a distance, they can't hurt us as much. If they get too close and begin to see our flaws, they might reject us.

What walls separate you from your friends, your mom and dad, your brothers or sisters, your teacher, your God? Will you ask Jesus to help you scale the walls that keep you from being totally free to love others? Or better yet, will you ask Him to help you tear them down?

NOVEMBER 11

IN MEMORY

The Lord is his memorial. Hosea 12:5.

Today many visitors will tour the monuments of Washington, D.C., in honor of all the people who served their country during war. They'll climb the steps to the top of the Washington Monument, which is dedicated to the memory of the first U.S. president. They'll read the Gettysburg Address at the Lincoln Memorial, where the greatest U.S. president is honored. And at the Jefferson Memorial—which honors the president who transcribed the concepts of freedom into words that could be read, memorized, and lived by—they'll speak in whispers and tiptoe as if touring a church.

The monument that never fails to bring tears to my eyes is the Tomb of the Unknowns, across the river from Washington, D.C., in Arlington National Cemetery. This memorial honors the men and women who died in America's wars but could not be identified.

It's a simple memorial, boxlike, with wreaths of flowers standing in front. An honor guard marches back and forth in front of this memorial. People come from around the nation and around the world to watch the changing of the guard and to pay their respects to the American soldiers whose identities are unknown but who died fighting for their country. Other countries, such as England, France, and the U.S.S.R., have similar memorials for their unknown soldiers.

Heaven too has a war memorial—not a memorial made of granite or marble to honor the dead, but a living, breathing memorial that honors the One who put an end to all wars—our first and greatest President, the One who put into action the words "love" and "sacrifice." In His hands and feet will be the scars, the memorials for all time, of earth's terrible war and

His great sacrifice. Heaven will have no monument dedicated to the unknown soldier, for every soldier of Christ will be living, breathing memorials to Jesus' great victory.

NOVEMBER 12

CURSES INTO BLESSINGS

"I called you to curse my enemies, but three times now you have blessed them instead." Numbers 24:10, TEV.

Blinded by her tears, Mindy dashed into the girls' restroom, straight into Miss Bell, the PE instructor.

"Hey there." Miss Bell steadied the girl with her hands. "What's the hurry?"

"I, ah . . ." Mindy caught her breath, then threw herself into the teacher's arms. "Oh, Miss Bell, I can't take it anymore. I'm leaving school."

"Why?" the surprised teacher asked.

At first Mindy refused to say. But after Miss Bell persisted, Mindy confessed. "It's Tess and her clique—they're at it again."

Miss Bell understood immediately. The teacher had been hearing rumors of how the tight little gang of girls had been terrorizing the other students.

"She's telling horrid lies about me all over school."

"I haven't heard—"

"You will. But by the time they reach the teaching staff, my reputation will be completely destroyed."

"Come on," Miss Bell said as she placed her arm about Mindy's shoulder. "Let's go to my office for a few minutes."

They talked through two class periods. But Mindy remained adamant—she was leaving school. Finally Miss Bell said, "Mindy, make a deal with me. Give me until the end of the week to check things out. In the meantime, go home and read the story of Balaam and how God turns curses into blessings."

Mindy agreed, since the story of the talking donkey was one of her favorites. When Friday came and she hadn't heard from Miss Bell, Mindy went straight to the principal's office to fill out her drop slip to leave school. She had three more forms to fill out when the bell rang for morning chapel. "You'll have to come back after chapel," the principal's secretary informed her.

Mindy slipped into the back of the auditorium just as the principal began the morning announcements. "Tess Williams has an announcement to make this morning."

Mindy groaned as Tess and her friends took the platform.

"I have an apology to make to a number of you today," Tess said. "I just learned that Mindy Harris is leaving school because of some stories I told about her. I'm sorry." Tess went through the entire list of people she'd picked on during the school term, apologizing to each one.

From that day on, it seemed to Mindy that "Tess the Terrible" worked terribly hard to become "Tess the Tolerable." *Whatever did Miss Bell do or say to cause such a change to occur?* Mindy wondered. Whenever Mindy asked Miss Bell about it, the woman just smiled and said, "Remember old Balaam? Our God turns curses into blessings."

NOVEMBER 13

A REASON FOR SINGING

Blessed are you when people insult you, persecute you and falsely say all kinds of evil against you because of me. Rejoice and be glad, because great is your reward in heaven, for in the same way they persecuted the prophets who were before you. Matthew 5:11, 12, NIV.

It would be nice if every time someone insulted you or lied about you, they would make a public apology like Tess did. But you and I know that rarely happens. More often we must either live with the pain or forgive. And forgiving is never easy.

At the turn of the century, Japan invaded, conquered, and occupied Korea. The conquerors committed inhumane crimes against the people of Korea, especially against the Christians. In addition to the individual persecution, the Japanese locked all Christians out of their churches. One pastor asked that his church be opened for one last service. Finally the local Japanese police chief agreed.

On the approved day, Korean families entered the church to praise God. They began their worship by singing. During a stanza of "At the Cross," Japanese soldiers barricaded all the exits and set fire to the church.

The helpless people outside the church listened and watched as the strains of music and the wails of children were swallowed by the roar of the flames. The fire died, but the flames of hate burned deep within the Koreans' hearts. When Japan was defeated it left Korea, but for Christian and non-Christian alike the hatred toward their conquerors grew with each passing year. The memorial the Koreans built on the spot where the church had once stood only reminded them of the disaster.

In 1971 a group of Japanese tourists traveling through Korea accidentally discovered the monument. When they read the names of the people who had been killed there and the details of the story, they were overcome with shame. They returned to Japan, committed themselves to try to right the wrong by raising 10 million yen ($25,000) to erect a new church—a small, white chapel on the site of the tragedy.

The Japanese sent a delegation to the dedication service. Speeches were made, details of the tragedy were recalled, and the dead honored, yet the hate that had festered for decades could be felt within the room. Something remarkable happened at the end of the service, when the Korean Christians and the Japanese Christians began singing the closing hymn, "At the Cross."

Tears flowed from the eyes of the normally stoic Japanese. They turned to their spiritual relatives and begged for forgiveness. The hate-filled hearts of the Koreans broke as they sang the chorus. "At the cross, at the cross, where I first saw the light, and the burden of my heart rolled away . . ."

One Korean turned to his Japanese brother, then another, until the floodgates of emotion could no longer be held back. Tears of repentance and forgiveness bathed the site of the bitterness and hatred, leaving only reconciliation and love in their place.

NOVEMBER 14

TEA AND POTPOURRI

Get rid of all bitterness, rage and anger, brawling and slander, along with every form of malice. Be kind and compassionate to one another, forgiving each other, just as in Christ God forgave you. Ephesians 4:31, 32, NIV.

I used to visit my grandmother in Pennsylvania when I was a kid. Grandma always kept a pot of tea brewing on the back burner of her gigantic black wrought-iron stove. Whenever I smell tea brewing, I travel back in my mind to the kitchen with the slanted floor in a little old rowhouse in Shinglehouse, Pennsylvania. So what do tea and back burners have to do with forgiveness? Imagine the following situations.

1. Your teacher accuses you of cheating off another student's paper when, in fact, he cheated off yours. Nothing you say changes your teacher's mind about you.

2. Hours before your tenth birthday party, your father goes to the corner store to buy an extra gallon of ice cream and never returns.

3. You make a terrible mistake, one that will embarrass you for the rest of your life. You make a second mistake by telling a friend about it. She in turn passed it on, until the entire school knows.

All these situations are true. They happened to friends of mine. Perhaps they have happened to you. We don't live in the world long before we experience some kind of hurt. Did your little brother break your favorite doll a few years ago and get away with it? Did your parents do or say something to you that still eats away at your peace? Did an aunt or an uncle or a teacher offend you and never acknowledge the mistake? And no matter how you try to forget, that hurt sits, like Grandma's old tea pot, on a back burner of your mind, waiting for the opportunity to come back and steal your joy.

Calvary was the place of forgiveness. Christ paid for these sins with outstretched arms; He paid for your sins and my sins in the same way.

It's only by forgiving—even before we are asked—and then letting go of the resentment that you can be forgiven. Just as potpourri does away with unwanted odors, so forgiveness allows the sweet fragrance of His forgiveness to rid you of all the noxious odors, stale injuries, and hurts that are simmering on the back burners of your mind. Let's turn off those back burners today.

NOVEMBER 15

AFRAID OF THE DARK

He who watches over you will not slumber; indeed, he who watches over Israel will neither slumber nor sleep. Psalm 121:3, 4, NIV.

Did you ever wake up in the night and feel scared? You have? Then you are very normal, no matter what your age may be. The creepiest place I ever lived was the girls' dormitory at Milo Adventist Academy—after it had emptied out for a vacation. During Thanksgiving vacation my husband and daughters were late getting back from doing some early Christmas shopping in Medford, Oregon. At the best of times, when the dormitory bulged with more than 160 teenage girls, the building made strange creaks and groans throughout the night. But now that it was empty, every sound echoed along the long, dark corridors.

One after another, the girls checked out for vacation, leaving only Peggy, one of my phone monitors, and me in the building. After eating supper together in my apartment, Peggy decided to put in a little time at the switchboard, since occasional calls were still coming in. I decided to stretch out on my sofa for a nap.

I don't know how long I'd been asleep when suddenly I heard someone running the length of the hall on third floor. Disoriented from sleep, I leaped up and rushed out into my office, across the hall, and into the phone monitor's booth.

"Did you hear that?" I sputtered. "I thought all the end doors were locked!"

"Yeiiiii!" Peggy's eyes bugged out of her head as she shot up from the easy chair where she'd been dozing and looked into my startled face. She screamed again; I screamed at her scream. We grabbed each other in terror.

By the time we settled down enough to look for our intruder, Peggy and I realized no one had been there in the first place—at least that's what we convinced ourselves rather than risk going up to third floor to check on the sounds I'd heard. We laughed at how terrified we looked as we screamed into each other's face—over nothing. Yet we stayed together in my apartment until Richard and the girls got home from shopping.

Even though Peggy and I felt we were all alone in that big old dormitory, we weren't—and we both knew it. God was with us the entire time, despite the fact that we scared each other silly. And He will be with you in the darkness and in the sunlight—just as He promised.

NOVEMBER 16

RIBBONS, MEDALS, AND TROPHIES

Everyone who competes in the games goes into strict training. They do it to get a crown that will not last; but we do it to get a crown that will last forever. 1 Corinthians 9:25, NIV.

In the year of the Olympics, we hear a lot about gold medal winners, silver medal winners, and bronze medal winners, yet every athlete at the Olympics was already a winner, even if he or she didn't take home any honors. Just making it through the tryouts made them all winners.

Special Olympics is another competition in which every participant is a winner. Any person who pushes himself or herself beyond what are believed to be physical or mental limitations becomes a winner, even before the games begin.

Every participant knows that it feels good to win—to push yourself to do your very best. Yet there's not one of the athletes, regardless of the event or the competition, who does not appreciate receiving recognition for his or her efforts. Even having your mom or dad or a teacher or friend say "Good job" brings warmth to your heart. Since Jesus made you, I think He knows and understands this need within you to be recognized for your efforts. That's why He's planning such a slam-bang victory celebration for us. The food will be scrumptious, the decorations unbelievable, the music out of this world! And all the "right" people will be there.

He will personally place a crown of pure gold on your head and give you a fabulous wardrobe designed especially for you. As host He will greet you with "Well done, good and faithful servant, come and share your Master's happiness!" That "well done" will be worth more than all the Olympic medals, all Hollywood's Oscars, all the Miss America trophies, all the president's certificates of achievement. And best of all, the "well done" will be for what He did, not for what you did. For you became a winner the day you gave your heart to Jesus. And you win every day thereafter by loving and serving Him.

NOVEMBER 17

WRITE YOUR OWN PSALM

Oh, give thanks to the Lord, for he is good; his lovingkindness continues forever. Give thanks to the God of gods, for his lovingkindness continues forever. Give thanks to the Lord of lords, for his lovingkindness continues forever. Praise him who alone does mighty miracles, for his lovingkindness continues forever. Psalm 136:1-4, TLB.

I sat beside the north end of Monterey Bay, watching the late afternoon sun dance on the incoming tide. My eyes focused on a small seal dining on its catch of the day. Its routine fascinated me. It would disappear into the surf, then surface, and turn over on its back. And from where I sat on the rocks, I could hear it crunching the bones in its mouth. When it finished the meal, the seal extended its flippers above the water line, and whack, whack, whack applauded the Creator. It was as if the seal were so delighted with its meal that it had to say Thank You. At least, that's how I interpreted what I saw. I started to laugh, not at the seal, but because I shared its joy of being alive.

Do you ever feel like the seal—so grateful for all that God has done for you that you can't help singing or shouting or applauding? I'm certain there is a perfectly scientific reason seals applaud with their flippers, but I like my interpretation so much better! I can just see the Creator smiling at my delight and enjoying the seal's antics just as much as I. For when we enjoy His creation, He enjoys it with us.

When David the boy shepherd wrote his psalms to God, he wrote about the things he saw and heard in the world around him. Picture with me David herding his sheep up a hillside. Then when he is certain that they are all content munching away on the green grass, he finds himself a large rock to sit on. He glances about at the sheep, the trees, the wild flowers, the blue sky, and his heart swells with happiness. He's just gotta sing. Then he reaches over his shoulder into his back pack and hauls out his harp—not a harp like you would see at the symphony, but a small, portable one about the size of a ukulele or banjo. And the results of David's joy? Psalm 23.

Let's create together a psalm today. Using the pattern of Psalm 136, take turns creating your own song of thanksgiving and praise. Read the verses at the beginning of today's lesson again, and then fill in the blanks with the things you are thankful for today. Finally, repeat the words "His love is eternal" in unison. Let's try it once. I'll go first.

"Give thanks to the Lord, *for seals and otters and dolphins that remind me of God's playfulness*."

(Together) "His love is eternal." (Now it's your turn.)

"Give thanks to the Lord, for ______________________________
____."

(Together) "His love is eternal."

Continue creating your own psalm until everyone has had a turn.

NOVEMBER 18

ACHOO

I will bring health and healing to it; I will heal my people. Jeremiah 33:6, NIV.

Achoo! Your head aches, your nose is stuffy, your throat burns, you ache all over—you have an old-fashioned cold. Or perhaps you have a new-fashioned cold. Researchers have just about given up on curing this pesky disease, because every time they are close to discovering a cure, the virus mutates into a new form until there are virtually hundreds of different types of cold viruses. But right now you feel utterly miserable, and you don't care whether the cold is old-fashioned or new-fashioned.

On your first sneeze, your mom will probably press the inside of her wrist against your forehead, take your temperature, shake her head sadly, and march you back to bed. She'll dose you with a pain medicine to relieve your symptoms and drown you with liquids. Moms are great to have around when you feel lousy. If Mom can't fix the problem, she'll take you to the doctor, and he'll prescribe stronger medicine.

Not all illnesses are like the flu or an ear infection or a sore throat. Sometimes they're problems such as worry, loneliness, and disappointment. For these problems you need more than a couple Tylenol tablets and a thermometer. And while Mom might comfort you in such situations, you need outside help—not from your family doctor, but from God, the heavenly physician. He is always ready to help, no matter what the problem, and He can supply you with the proper medicine if you'll only ask.

So next time your spirit goes "Achoo!" from an illness that thermometers, Tylenol, and Mom can't cure, remember to turn to God, who provides medicine for your greatest needs.

NOVEMBER 19

THREE FLOWERS

So then, just as you received Christ Jesus as Lord, continue to live in him, rooted and built up in him, strengthened in the faith as you were taught, and overflowing with thankfulness. Colossians 2:6, 7, NIV.

Picture three perfectly formed, deep purple African violets—one made of silk, one freshly picked, and the other still attached to the mother plant. If you were to be one of these three flowers, which would you choose?

The silk blossom with its plastic stem will stay beautiful indefinitely, but it is fake, phony. It lacks the delicate scent of real violets and the precious spark of life. It never feels pain. It never feels the warmth of the sun on its petals. It never feels anything. It appears to be a flower only by chance. The manufacturer could just as well have turned that scrap of fabric into a dust ruffle or a parachute.

The picked blossom gives off the appropriate scent and looks lovely in Mom's favorite crystal vase. In a few days, however, it will wither. The petals will turn brown and fall off. Why? Because it has been cut off from its roots. Once the blossom uses up the life forces within the stem and petals, it can no longer be nourished. Some people I know have chosen to be picked violets, cut off from what they know is right, free to do their own thing. And when they've used up their life forces, they'll wither and die—never to live again.

The third flower contains life and vitality. It will give off sweet perfume, grow to its full potential, and live out the life cycle designed for a violet.

The Bible tells us that if we want to be beautiful people and grow to our full potential, we must be rooted in Jesus. We must depend on Him for life itself. He supplies the strength to keep us from withering under the weight of our problems. He supplies the nutrients that keep us forever growing. That's what it means to be rooted in Jesus.

You and I have it far better than even the rooted violet blossom, because when we choose to be rooted in Jesus, we don't live out our life and disappear forever. God promises eternal life for those rooted in His Son. That means blossoming and growing forever.

NOVEMBER 20

A SPECIAL KIND OF DATE

He blessed the seventh day and set it apart as a special day. Genesis 2:3, TEV.

What is the Sabbath to you? Is it a day filled with "Don't do this" and "Don't do that"? Why did God set it apart as special at the end of Creation week? Did God make the Sabbath day because He needed a rest after working so hard creating the world? Or do you think that Adam was tired after being alive for only one day?

Adam might not have needed the rest on that first Sabbath, but 6,000 years of Sabbaths later, I sure do. My body and my mind just naturally begin to relax as the Friday afternoon sun disappears beyond the horizon. I don't feel guilty for sitting and listening to music or chatting with friends instead of working on the next chapter of my latest book or polishing my brass candlesticks or weeding the flower garden by my front door. Yet God had a whole lot more in mind when He blessed the seventh day.

When I was 11 years old, I eagerly looked forward to dating boys, even though I knew I had at least five more years to wait. I didn't realize then that in a way I had already begun dating. Each Sabbath I had a date with the King of the universe.

God knew that love takes time to grow—time spent together, time to get acquainted with one another. A boy and a girl who like each other might spend all day together, attending college classes. They might have biology lab, literature class, even band practice together. Yet if they like each other enough, they will choose to spend more time together outside their classes. They will date. And if they continue to do this, chances are they'll fall in love and marry. That's just the way it works, both for couples in love and for us as we learn to love God.

But there is one big difference. A man and a woman must learn to love each other. While with God, He already loves me with an everlasting love. I'm the one who needs the lessons in loving.

NOVEMBER 21

SABBATH TRADITIONS

And Jesus concluded, "The Sabbath was made for the good of man; man was not made for the Sabbath. So the Son of Man is Lord even of the Sabbath." Mark 2:27, 28, TEV.

Today I would like to invite you for Sabbath dinner. As you enter my house, you'll notice that the furniture shines a little brighter than it does any other day of the week, the carpets look a little smoother, the desk in my office is a little less cluttered. (At least the books and papers are stacked a little neater.) My husband will have already started playing a CD, perhaps by Sandi Patti or by Larnell Harris. Hopefully, the aroma of a baked casserole will be making your mouth water while I smooth out the tablecloth (any other day we'd be using place mats) and set the candle holders near the center of the table. Dinner will be served up with outbursts of laughter, good conversation, and an extra measure of love. These are just a few of the Sabbath traditions that make Sabbath special for us.

Every family establishes some sort of Sabbath traditions, since Sabbath is a pleasant break in the weekly routine. What are your family's Sabbath traditions? What do you do in your home that is special for your weekly day with Jesus Christ? Maybe you don't have Friday evening stew, but that's OK. Campbell's tomato soup can be as much a Sabbath tradition, especially when it is dished up with an added dash of love.

When my daughters grew up and went away to college, what they missed most was not the cat or the dog or even their parents, but the good times we had together on the Sabbath day. Sabbath is a time to remember those we love, and most of all, to remember the One who loves us and created us.

What traditions do you have in your home? Make a list of them. Which do you enjoy the most? What can you do to make the Sabbath more special in your home?

Sabbath is more than a day for memories. It's also a day of the future, a day to talk about heaven. The Bible tells us that each Sabbath we will worship at the throne of God with all of the beings of the universe. Wow!

What a choir! Song service will literally shake the golden rafters. I wonder what the subject of God's first sermon will be? I doubt anyone will fall asleep during that church service! And the potluck after—my mouth waters with anticipation!

Remember the list of family traditions you made? Which of those traditions will you continue in heaven? The ones that involve the people you love?

NOVEMBER 22

INTO ALL THE WORLD

And this gospel of the kingdom will be preached in the whole world as a testimony to all nations, and then the end will come. Matthew 24:14, NIV.

"So tell me, just how is running a Pathfinder club part of preaching the gospel; and just where in the world is Pohnpei?"

Of course, he'd be doing much more than just leading the Pathfinders during his year as a student missionary from Walla Walla College, but those were the questions Bruce Earhardt's friends most asked. And at times Bruce's own feelings about taking a year off from school to travel to a different part of the world seemed jumbled.

Life on Pohnpei, an island in the central Pacific, seven degrees north of the equator, proved to be full and exciting for the college sophomore. Before he and his fellow student missionaries realized it, the year was almost over. They would all be returning to the States and to their own respective college campuses—back to classes, middle-of-the-night pizza runs during test week, and night study sessions.

Tired at the end of the second day of a Pathfinder outing on one of the outer islands in the Ant Atoll chain, the Pathfinders were hot into a game of moonlight capture the flag when Bruce and his student missionary friends decided to take a short walk on the beach. Hundreds of hermit crabs scurried out of the way of the oncoming footsteps as the college students strolled across moonlit sand.

"Remember the time . . ." one of the counselors began, and the group started sharing their memories of the year together. Their laughter echoed out across the barrier reef that separated them from the main island of Pohnpei as they recalled adjusting to the island's strange customs. They talked about some of the wonderful Sabbaths they'd shared with the kids in their club, snorkeling and exploring the mysterious inlets about the islands.

Gazing out over the jagged reef, one of the student missionaries spotted the wrecked hull of a Japanese transport boat that had run aground on the reef during World War II. "Looks kind of spooky, huh?—that skeleton of a ship. Sure wouldn't want to be out there tonight."

"Yeah," another added. "On Friday a large fishing boat jammed its propeller into the coral between here and the open sea."

"And the sharks," one of the girls added. "Don't forget the sharks."

As if any of them could. No one living on the island for any length of time ever forgot the bloodthirsty sharks that circled in and out of the reef's inlets as they searched for food.

Bruce thought of all the people he'd met during his year on the island—the kids he'd scuba-dived with, sung with, prayed with. He thought of leaving in a few days. He'd be glad to get back to his studies. He'd treasure the memories he would take with him wherever he went—to Walla Walla, to his home in Idaho, and beyond into the unknown future. *There's a lot to this missionary stuff*, he decided. *And I'm not sure who gets the best of the deal—the people whose lives you touch, or the people who touch you.*

(Story to be continued.)

NOVEMBER 23

SURROUNDED BY SHARKS

Ask and it will be given to you; seek and you will find; knock and the door will be opened to you. Matthew 7:7, NIV.

The voices of the other student missionaries faded as Bruce studied the shadows of the dancing palm fronds lacing the beach. *Leaving this paradise will be difficult*, he thought again for what must have been the hundredth time over the weekend. Suddenly a scream broke through his thoughts. He turned to see one of the campers racing toward him.

"Takiyuki cut his foot," the young girl shrieked.

"How did it happen?" Bruce asked.

"He jumped over a sand dune and sliced his toe on a large broken clamshell."

Bruce sighed. *Another small crisis to deal with*, he thought. *Guess I'd better have a look.*

He followed the young girl to the cooking area of the camp and pushed his way through the mob of Pathfinders to reach the small boy.

One look and Bruce knew that Takiyuki's injury would need immediate medical attention—more than he or any of the staff could give. The top of the boy's toe from the tip of the knuckle to the bone was missing.

"Oh, no," Bruce groaned, "we'll have to take Takiyuki back to Pohnpei right away."

"The trip would be much safer in the daylight," one of the other counselors reminded.

Bruce grimaced at the thought of sailing for the main island through shark-infested waters. "Yes, but by morning, the foot may be seriously infected. No, we'll have to go tonight."

Dear God in heaven, Bruce prayed as he cleansed the wound as best he could, *help me to do the right thing for Takiyuki*. While he wrapped clean towels about the boy's foot, Bruce glanced out at the dark, foreboding waters. *Take us safely across the channel to Pohnpei*.

Miller, one of the Pohnpeian teachers and Pathfinder counselors, volunteered to go with Bruce and the owner of a 13-foot fishing boat across the treacherous channel waters to the main island. Together, he and Bruce carried the boy to the waiting boat and climbed aboard. Then Miller pushed off into the darkness of the lagoon. They skimmed across the water's smooth surface until they reached the open ocean.

Once the fishing boat edged out of the mouth of the lagoon and into the open sea, giant waves crashed against the side of the boat. *Only four miles*, Bruce reminded himself as he and Miller struggled to keep Takiyuki's leg suspended so as to absorb the shock from the pounding waves—*four miles and we'll make it to Pohnpei's inner lagoon and to safety*.

(Story to be continued.)

NOVEMBER 24

BEYOND THE REEF

Angels came and ministered unto him. Matthew 4:11.

Bruce panicked as he glanced about the small fishing boat. He thought about the shark-infested waters swirling and crashing about the tiny boat. He'd heard that sharks could pick up the scent of blood several miles away. With Takiyuki's injury . . . he refused to think about the results.

Oh, Father, give me courage; and give our driver the skill to navigate this tub, he prayed.

Bruce sighed with relief when he noticed that Takiyuki had fallen asleep. One hour after they left Ant, the boat entered the Pohnpei lagoon.

Yet the night's adventure was far from over. The reef inside the lagoon projected like jagged fingers out from the island in an irregular fashion. A sign had been cemented to the tip of each finger, warning boaters not to sail any closer to shore at that point.

Using a small flashlight, the boat's driver spotted the first few signs easily. The signs were spaced about a quarter of a mile apart. Then the flashlight died.

"Oh no!" Bruce groaned.

"Hey, I think I've got another flashlight here somewhere." Miller searched, then drew a small penlight from one of his pockets. The dim light did little to break through the blackness of the night.

"I can't see anything," the fisherman shouted.

"I'll climb up on the bow," Miller suggested. "Maybe I'll be able to make out the edges of the reef by the pattern of the waves."

Silence hung over the passengers as the little boat inched its way through the darkness.

Suddenly Miller shouted something in Pohnpeian. The driver had barely yanked the outboard out of the water when the momentum of the boat sent them crunching across the coral. Bruce cringed, certain that the saw-toothed coral had ripped a hole in the fiberglass hull. Then together the three men eased the boat off the reef and back into the channel. Again and again, for another hour, they repeated their daring dance with death, until they arrived at Kolonia, the only city on the island.

As the little boat docked, Bruce shook Takiyuki by the shoulder. "Wake up. We've reached Kolonian Harbor."

"We've reached Kolokian Harbor safely," Bruce whispered to himself, tears glistening in his eyes.

They rushed Takiyuki to the hospital, where the doctors performed a toe graft on the boy. Two weeks later Takiyuki walked from the hospital.

When Bruce arrived back at Walla Walla College, he assured his friends, "If you ever have a chance to go as a student missionary, take it. I'll never forget my year in Pohnpei. And more important, I'll never forget that my God protects His servants, even in the most remote parts of the world."

NOVEMBER 25

MAKE A LIST DAY

O give thanks unto the Lord; for he is good: for his mercy endureth for ever. Psalm 136:1.

Someone once said, "Being thankful is a choice, not a chance." I like that. That means, no matter what else is happening in my life, I can choose to be thankful. And I've discovered that when I am thankful, I am happy. Therefore, I can always choose to be happy. Make sense?

Today, on the day before Thanksgiving, I'm especially happy. I'll have a house full of company tomorrow. I need to scrub the bathtub, wash the kitchen floor, put clean sheets on the guest room bed, dust, vacuum—oh, the list is endless. With so much to do before my company arrives, it would be easy to become so busy getting ready for Thanksgiving that I forget to be thankful. So to prevent that from happening to you or to me, let's play a Day-Before-Thanksgiving-Day game around the breakfast table this morning.

Starting with the letter A, give one thing you are thankful for—for example, air, then tell why you're thankful for it. The person next to you gives one thing he's thankful for that begins with B and so on, until you run out of either time or blessings. My guess is that you'll run out of time first. You might want to continue the game during tonight's family worship, too. See who can come up with the most unusual blessing that God has given you.

Saying thank you is important. It helps us remember that the gifts God gives are just that—gifts. They aren't something we earn or even deserve, but come from the divine heart of love. We can never say thank You to God, or even to those we love, often enough.

So let's see. Today I am thankful for . . . uh . . . artichokes—because they taste so yummy with lemon-butter sauce. Now it's your turn.

NOVEMBER 26

GO AND ENJOY

Go and enjoy choice food and sweet drinks, and send some to those who have nothing prepared. This day is sacred to our Lord. Do not grieve, for the joy of the Lord is your strength. Nehemiah 8:10, NIV.

Every child born in the United States has heard the story of the first Thanksgiving. In school you probably drew pictures of turkeys or made headbands with different-colored feathers. Perhaps you cut out profiles of sober-faced Pilgrims with their tall black hats, gold belt buckles, and long-barreled guns. Your teacher probably told you stories about popcorn, wild turkeys, sailing ships, and Plymouth Rock.

But do you know how the official national Thanksgiving Day came about? Sara J. Hale, the editor of the popular women's magazine *Godey's Lady's Book* wrote a Thanksgiving Day editorial in the September 1863 issue of her magazine. Up until that time, there was no official National Thanksgiving Day. She centered her thoughts on being thankful around Nehemiah 8:10. When the issue came off the press, she sent a copy to President Lincoln.

At that time President Lincoln had bigger worries than establishing a day on which to be thankful. The country was in the middle of the Civil War. The Union armies had lost battles to the Confederates on many fronts. Many of his generals worried more about the cut of their uniforms than about the young men dying under their commands. Newspapers blasted the beleaguered president, no matter what he did or didn't do. Some members of the Cabinet made fun of him, called him names behind his back. The presidency of the United States of America seemed on the verge of crumbling, along with the country itself—not exactly a time to give thanks!

President Lincoln read Mrs. Hale's editorial. And despite his political and personal troubles, on October 3, 1863, he declared the last Thursday of every November to be a national Thanksgiving Day.

What a lesson for you and me. Lincoln didn't wait until the end of the war to be thankful. He declared his gratitude and praise at a time when it seemed he had the least for which to be thankful. The message of Nehemiah 8:10 is just that—the joy of giving thanks to the Lord is your strength. It's easy to say thank you when everything's terrific, but when things go bad, the true joy of thankfulness gives strength—"the joy of the Lord is your strength."

NOVEMBER 27

JUST WHO ARE YOU, ANYWAY?

Where were you when I laid the earth's foundation? Tell me, if you understand. . . . Who shut up the sea? . . . Have you ever given orders to the morning? . . . Does the rain have a father? . . . Can you loose the cords of Orion? . . . Do you send the lightning bolts on their way? . . . Do you hunt the prey for the lioness? . . . Who provides food for the raven? . . . Do you know when the mountain goats give birth? . . . Who let the wild donkey go free? . . . Will the wild ox consent to serve you? . . . Do you give the horse his strength? . . . Does the hawk take flight by your wisdom? . . . Does the eagle soar at your command? Job 38:4–39:27, NIV.

Job wanted answers. He hurt inside and out! Why was he suffering so? His house, his children, his money, his health—everything had been taken from him. "Why, God, why?" he demanded.

Imagine how the voice of God must have sounded as you read aloud today's text one more time. God needed to remind Job of his place in the process of living. "Who are you to be asking Me to explain My actions? You weren't around when I formed the skies, the sun, the stars. You weren't there when I placed the natural instincts in the animals' brains."

After a difficult day of juggling the country's problems, or after attending a party where everyone treated him like royalty, President Teddy Roosevelt would go out on the White House lawn and stare up at the star-studded sky. After locating and identifying his favorite constellations and other heavenly sights, including the barely visible Andromeda Nebula, he would say, "Now I think I am small enough. It's time to go to bed."

So who do you think you are? Do you sometimes feel too small, like you are totally unimportant and in the way? Consider all of God's creation, the wonderful things He has made. Then remember that you are the crown of His creation. When you are feeling too important, too good, too talented, or too anything more than other people, consider God's creation and be made small. And when troubles weigh you down and you want to ask why such things happen, consider God's creation and say, "You created all things, Lord, including me. Considering all the problems you solved just at Creation, I'm sure my problems are simple in comparison. So I leave them in your hands." A look at God's creation puts everything and everyone into perspective. Do you think that may be why Satan has tried so hard to make people doubt the truth of Creation as presented in the Bible?

NOVEMBER 28

PRAISE YE THE LORD

Before you assume somebody goofed, that the printers forgot today's Bible text, read on. This morning each person will need a copy of the King James Version of the Bible. If you have a tape deck and an empty cassette, record today's creative morning worship to play back later, or perhaps you may want to send it to a relative as part of a Christmas present—a great way to share your family's worship time with others. If you're all alone while reading this, you should still give it a try. You could possibly make your voice sound different for each group.

Open your Bibles to Psalm 150. Divide your family into two groups. You are going to function as a speech choir. One group will be Group A and the other, Group B. A third command will be All, which you read in unison. Adding the appropriate expression into your voice as you read will make it more interesting to the listener. Practice once before you begin the tape recorder.

Order of Service

All

(Sing "Alleluia" in unison.)

All

(verse 1) "Praise ye the Lord."

Group A

(verse 1) "Praise God in his sanctuary."

Group B

(verse 1) "Praise him in the firmament of his power."

Group A

(verse 2) "Praise him for his mighty acts."

Group B

(verse 2) "Praise him according to his excellent greatness."

Group A

(verse 3) "Praise him with the sound of the trumpet."

Group B

(verse 3) "Praise him with the psaltery and harp."

(Continue this pattern throughout the six verses.)

All

"Praise ye the Lord."

All

(Sing "Alleluia" in harmony.)

Choose someone to close your worship with a short prayer.

NOVEMBER 29

TRUSTWORTHY JOHNNY

My son, do not forget my teaching, but keep my commands in your heart, for they will prolong your life many years and bring you prosperity. Proverbs 3:1, 2, NIV.

Last night I heard a story I want to share with you. Johnny ran away from a bad foster-care home. Life on the streets was rough for the 13-year-old, but he didn't know how to go back. He'd run away from foster-care homes so often in the three years since his mother died that the county child services officer had threatened to place him in the state reform school should he run away one more time. Many nights Johnny huddled inside a partially filled dumpster to hide from violent street gangs or to get out of the rain.

Inside the dark, dirty, giant-sized garbage can, Johnny would think about his mother and the lessons she'd taught him, lessons in honesty, truthfulness, and dependability—lessons hard to live by on the streets of the city. "I'm trying, Mama," he would whisper in the darkness. "I'm trying."

One day Johnny saw a sign in the window of the red-brick newspaper building. "Wanted: newsboys." He got the job. Instead of delivering the morning paper to people's homes, he was assigned a street corner outside a large downtown office building. Before long, Johnny knew all the people working in the building by name. He liked one man in particular, who purchased a paper every morning—Mr. Hendricks, from the seventeenth floor.

One year passed; two years passed. Every morning Johnny greeted Mr. Hendricks with a friendly smile. When Mr. Hendricks was late getting to work, Johnny saved a morning paper for him. One day Mr. Hendricks stopped to talk with Johnny.

"Johnny," Mr. Hendricks said as he pulled a huge wad of bills from his pocket, "if I bought every one of your papers this morning, would you do me a favor?"

Johnny's eyes widened with disbelief. "Uh, sure, if I can."

"Oh, you can, son," Mr. Hendricks replied. "All you need to do is go to the corner and turn right. Walk five blocks. Make a left on Maple Street. Walk two more blocks until you come to a large red-brick house." Mr. Hendricks paused to be certain Johnny understood his instructions. "Ring the bell. A man in a black suit will answer the door. Say to him, 'John 3:16.'"

"'John 3:16?'"

"That's right, son. Can you do it?"

"Sure can, Mr. Hendricks. Sure can, but what's the catch? Why are you doing this?"

"For lots of reasons, which you will come to understand in time. Right now, all you need to know is that I've been watching you, and I know that I can trust you to follow my instructions."

Johnny shook his head in amazement and stuffed the money in his pocket. *Just as Mama promised,* he thought. *People notice and are pleased when one is honest and dependable.*

(Story to be continued.)

NOVEMBER 30

JOHN 3:16 JOHNNY

For God so loved the world that he gave his one and only Son, that whoever believes in him shall not perish but have eternal life. John 3:16, NIV.

Johnny carefully followed Mr. Hendricks' directions. After he rang the doorbell, a frowning man in a black suit answered the door, just as Mr. Hendricks said would happen.

"Uh, John 3:16?" Johnny gulped. He'd never seen a real live butler before.

Suddenly the man's face broke into a smile. He led the boy into the house, then looked Johnny over from shoes to baseball cap. Johnny hadn't had a decent bath since the first frost, because his only bathtub was the lake at the edge of town.

"Perhaps you would enjoy a bath?" the man suggested. "Please, follow me."

Johnny followed him up the stairs to the bathroom. When he first saw the massive tub, he couldn't believe his eyes. And after Johnny shed his clothes and sank into the hot, sudsy water, he couldn't believe his good luck. *Wow*, Johnny thought, *John 3:16 is great for getting a boy clean.*

After the bath, the butler brought Johnny a giant bowl of stew, homemade bread with peanut butter and jelly on top, a giant glass of cold milk, and a plate stacked with freshly baked oatmeal cookies. *Wow,* Johnny thought, *John 3:16 is great for a hungry boy.*

Johnny finished every crumb of bread and every drop of stew. The cookies and the milk disappeared equally as fast. Then the butler took Johnny to a large room with a king-size bed and suggested the boy sleep until the master returned home. *Wow,* Johnny thought as he bounced up and down on the springy mattress and crisp white sheets, *John 3:16 is terrific for a tired boy.*

He awoke when Mr. Hendricks entered the room. "Why have you brought me here," Johnny asked, "and why have you been so nice?"

Mr. Hendricks sat on the edge of the bed. "Last year my wife and 13-year-old son were killed in a car accident," he explained. "I've been so lonely since. And seeing you every day at the newspaper stand reminded me of my boy." Mr. Hendricks cleared his throat before continuing. "I did a little inquiring about you and found that you were alone in the world also. Maybe together we can both be a little less lonely. If you'll let me, I'd like to adopt you as my son."

Johnny readily agreed. The two talked long into the night. After all of Johnny's other questions were answered, Johnny said, "There's just one thing I don't understand, Mr. Hendricks—er, Dad. What does John 3:16 mean?"

"Well, son," Mr. Hendricks replied, "it was after reading John 3:16 that I came up with the plan I told you about tonight. If God loved me so much that He gave His only Son, Jesus, to die for me, the least I could do is reach out in love to someone else who needed me."

That night as Johnny prepared for bed, he thought, *John 3:16 is just what a lonely boy needs. Whether they are cold or hungry, tired or dirty, or as wealthy as Mr. Hendricks, John 3:16 is what every boy or girl, man or woman, in the entire world needs.*

DECEMBER 1

THROUGH RAIN AND SUNSHINE

But if it were I, I would appeal to God; I would lay my cause before him. He performs wonders that cannot be fathomed, miracles that cannot be counted. He bestows rain on the earth; he sends water upon the countryside. Job 5:8-10, NIV.

Remember the story of Elijah and the three-year drought? Later, on Mount Carmel, he and the God of the universe faced off against the heathen god Baal and his priests. And the rest is history, as they say. While droughts and floods, earthquakes and hurricanes, are a part of Mother Nature's bag of tricks, God can and does use weather patterns to occasionally carry out His plans.

A few weeks ago on national TV news I learned of people in a drought-ridden area of New Jersey who prayed for rain for seven days straight. At the end of the seven days, it rained. The people in that farming community did what children of God have done for thousands of years—they took the text in Job to heart, and God honored their faith. And when the rains came, millions of people across America heard about their simple prayer of faith.

God was with them. He saw their need and He blessed them. Let me ask you, if it hadn't rained, would that mean God wasn't with His children in New Jersey? Some people would have you think so. But those people are wrong—very, very wrong. While you and I may not understand the way God chooses to operate—why at one time He performs a miracle, and at another time He allows nature to take its course—we can always be confident that He is with us—in good times and bad, happy and sad, in times of discouragement and in times of confidence.

The United States Postal Service used to have a motto about delivering the mail in all kinds of weather—regardless of rain, sleet, snow, etc., the mails must go through. While they might be exaggerating a bit about their faithfulness, God isn't. Whether we have trouble or joy, He is still the one who is always there for us. In the end, when you and I look back over the rainstorms and tornadoes of troubles in our lives, we will say, "Yes, dear

Father, You were right all along. That's just how I would have done things."

DECEMBER 2

ON RAINMAKERS, TRUST, AND PEDESTALS

Don't put your trust in human leaders; no human being can save you. Psalm 146:3, TEV.

Throughout the years people have tried to control the weather—especially the rain. Men crisscrossed the country selling their magical services as "rainmakers" to desperate farmers and small communities. The customers didn't find out that many of these men were con artists, charlatans, phonies, until the "rainmaker" skipped town with the farmers' hard-earned money.

Not so with Charles Hatfield, the greatest rainmaker of all times. During a 30-year span, he won a name for himself by filling lakes, saving crops, and breaking droughts from Alaska's Yukon to Guatemala. His most spectacular production of rain occurred in San Diego, California. In December of 1915, Charles asked the San Diego City Council for $10,000 to fill the reservoir of Morena Dam. The deal was that if no rain fell, he would expect no pay—sounded like a safe bet for the city, since the reservoir was designed to hold 15 billion gallons but had never been more than a third filled.

One council member reminded the other members, "If this Hatfield guy succeeds in producing 10 billion gallons, his fee will amount to one cent per 10,000 gallons of water."

When the council agreed to his offer, Charles erected outside of town a wooden tower 20 feet high. He installed large galvanized trays containing a special moisture-attracting ingredient—his closely guarded secret. This would "coax and court nature."

Four days later, it began to rain. For nine days heavy, continuous rain fell. Then the downpour began in earnest and continued for 10 days. The town's citizens thought the rain would never end. By the end of the month, the rain fell at the rate of two inches per hour, filling the dam, within five inches of the top.

A dam farther up river, Nesaby Lower Oray Dam, broke and sent a wall of water 40 feet high plowing the 12 miles to the Pacific Ocean. Fifty people drowned, and 200 bridges and miles of track were destroyed, which halted the trains for 32 days.

When Charles went to claim his money, the council refused, maintaining the rains were "an act of God." He filed a lawsuit against the community, but finally gave up because he had made the mistake of trusting them with an oral agreement instead of signing a legal contract. Charles learned the hard way not to put his trust in human leaders, not even the San Diego City Council.

Have you ever put your trust in a person you perceived as famous or powerful and then been disappointed? I have a tendency to put people on pedestals, and that's not fair to them. Because whether it is your Sabbath school teacher or the president of the General Conference, he or she is just like you. He or she must turn to Jesus for strength, for forgiveness, for salvation. The only one who warrants our complete trust is Jesus Christ.

It would have been nice if the San Diego City Council had honored their word, but I would imagine Charles Hatfield was a much wiser man in the future. By the way, Charles didn't lose out entirely when the city council refused to pay him, because news of the event spread across the country and established his reputation as "King of the Cloud Compellers." And the next time the council hired a rainmaker, they took out an insurance policy.

DECEMBER 3

THE SNOWSTORM

Brethren, pray for us. 1 Thessalonians 5:25.

Yesterday I warned you against putting your trust in human leaders. Sounds kind of cynical, huh? It would be if I didn't follow through with today's story.

Traveling in Canada during midwinter can be hazardous to one's safety, especially during a blizzard. That's where I found myself and my two daughters one cold midwinter day—stranded at a truck stop in London, Ontario, in the middle of the worst blizzard to hit Ontario in 50 years—at least that's what the natives were saying.

The freak blizzard had taken many people by surprise. People who had been out for a Sunday drive were stranded without cash or a change of clothing for 48 hours at the truck stop, along with the rest of us. The crowded facility allowed standing room only. In one corner, a group of college kids sang hippie protest songs, while in another corner businessmen argued politics. From one's waist up, the air was blue from cigarette and cigar smoke. At mealtimes people took turns sitting at the counter in the restaurant and ordering whatever food the restaurant proprietors hadn't run out of. Even the prime minister of Ontario had to wait out the storm.

So that I wouldn't have to watch Rhonda and Kelli every minute, I brought in the sleeping bags we kept in the trunk of our car and stretched them out under the sinks in the ladies' room, where the smoke wasn't quite so thick. There the girls could scramble back and forth without getting in the way or getting stepped on.

Though we women tried to stretch out on the tiled floors to sleep, it was too cold, so we talked. On the morning of the third day the snowstorm had stopped, and the road crews were busy clearing the highways. I decided to make a phone call.

I called the local Seventh-day Adventist pastor and told him about my predicament, that I was the wife of an academy teacher at Wisconsin Academy, and that I needed a place to sleep for a few hours before continuing my journey home—could he help me? He said he'd call me back.

Fifteen minutes later the pastor arrived to take me and my daughters to a local elder's home. Excited with the prospects of getting a few hours of much-needed sleep, I rushed into the ladies' room to collect the girls and our belongings. When I told the women in the restroom what the pastor was doing for me, they shook their heads in amazement.

"I can't believe it!" one woman sputtered. "The day my priest drives down the block for me, let alone 10 miles in the snow . . ."

I tried to explain how God's family works, but I knew she couldn't begin to understand. Though he never knew, that Canadian Seventh-day Adventist pastor preached a sermon in the ladies' room that day, and it will be remembered for a long, long time.

So while Jesus is the only one in whom we can place all our trust, our leaders deserve our respect and our prayers. They are God-ordained humans struggling to perform the superhuman task of leading God's children to the Promised Land.

DECEMBER 4

SAYING THANK YOU

It is a good thing to give thanks unto the Lord. Psalm 92:1.

Saying thank you is so easy. Those two words can make all the difference in another person's entire day. Maybe you remember to say thanks from day to day to your mom and dad for clean clothes, good food, and for being there when you need them. Maybe you tell the pastor thanks for a sermon well done or express appreciation to your teacher for the extra-special things she or he plans for you and your classmates. Maybe you even remember to write to your grandparents to say thank you for the beautiful, interesting, or downright ugly hat they brought back for you from their vacation in the Caribbean.

But are there people to whom you may not have said thank you but whom you really appreciate for their good example, for their faithfulness, for the time and effort they give to make your life a little more comfortable—like the deacon who arrives at church a half hour early to be certain the sanctuary is warm when you arrive, or the Sabbath school secretary who collects the offering and sees that it is counted and goes where it should go, or the janitor who picks up the abandoned church bulletins from the pews each week, along with your crumpled Kleenex tissues, gum wrappers, and bulletin inserts? All these people serve God just as much as the pastor who delivers the sermon or the musician who sings an anthem on Sabbath morning.

Yesterday I told you about my Canadian adventure and the church pastor. He took me to the local elder's home, where the elder's wife baby-sat my daughters while I slept. When I awoke, she had a bowl of hot, homemade stew ready for me before my daughters and I finished our trek home to Wisconsin. Although I wrote a letter of thanks to both her and the pastor upon arriving safely at home, I wish I could remember their names now. I wish I could tell them today, 20 years later, just how much their kindness still means to me. There are other people, too, I'd like to thank. To some I can write letters; others, I'll have to wait until I get to heaven.

I know I enjoy receiving thank-you's from former students or from people who read and enjoy my stories. I save them in a box I call my "rainy day" box—a box I open when I'm feeling down, when my heart is full of rain showers.

Being thankful is a great habit to develop. What about the people in your life who deserve your thanks? Make a list of people you can thank. Thank God for each one of the people on your list. Then decide to write one thank-you note a day until you complete your list. Chances are your list will grow, and you'll never come to the end.

DECEMBER 5

SING, GOD, SING

The Lord your God is with you, he is mighty to save. He will take great delight in you, he will quiet you with his love, he will rejoice over you with singing. Zephaniah 3:17, NIV.

Don't you love that picture of God? Sometimes you and I might have trouble understanding God the Father. We grew up loving the gentle Jesus and are fascinated by the Holy Spirit living inside us, helping us do what is right. But God the Father? He's the one who will judge us on the judgment day. He's the one who zapped the guy who touched the ark, who trapped Jonah in a whale's belly, who caused the walls of Jericho to tumble down on hundreds of unsuspecting heads. That kind of power and strength creates fear! And even though parents, teachers, and pastors try to convince us that God the Father, God the Son, and God the Holy Spirit all love us equally, we find it difficult to picture this all-powerful Being as loving.

That's why I like today's thought so much. First, "God is with me" in good times and bad—when I drive to the grocery store, when I'm stuck in rush-hour traffic, when I visit the dentist. Knowing He's with me gives me strength. I like that.

Second, "God will take great delight in me." Delight in me? Does that mean He likes my silly laugh? That He appreciates my weird sense of humor? That He enjoys my sometimes rambling conversations with Him while I scrub the tub in the bathroom? Incredible!

Third, "God rejoices over me with singing"—not rejoices with me, but over me. When I do something right, when I refuse a temptation, when I'm just being me, God rejoices over me. The specialness, the uniqueness, of me makes Him burst into song. I wonder what song He sings? Do angels accompany Him on harps or guitars or with trumpets? Or does He just break out in singing like I do when I see a beautiful rainbow or watch the sun go down at the end of the day? Does the heavenly choir sing backup, or does He do His own harmony? I wonder—I wonder. But this one thing I know—I want to give Him a reason to sing every day I live. What about you?

DECEMBER 6

OUT OF FOCUS

I have learned that everything has limits; but your commandment is perfect. . . . Your commandment is with me all the time and makes me wiser than my enemies. Psalm 119:96-98, TEV.

A few months ago I wrote about the remarkable Hubble telescope that would reveal the mysteries of outer space to us. Since you are reading this book two years after the telescope was propelled into space, you already know that the project was not the huge success that everyone had hoped it would be. But do you know why?

When the scientists first used the gigantic telescope, they discovered that it could not focus properly. They soon discovered that the curvature of the main mirror was 1.3 millimeters off. As the experts traced the telescope back to its roots, they discovered that one of the devices used in shaping the mirror had been used backward, which then resulted in the tiny error. The imperfection went unnoticed before the telescope was hurtled into outer space. But once there, the distortion rendered out-of-focus images. Scientists decided that they could correct some of the distortion by computer enhancement, but that works only for the brighter images. A multimillion-dollar mistake caused by an error of less than two millimeters.

Living your life by either your own ideas of right and wrong or by another human being's can be even more costly. It can cost you eternity. God knew that people would become more and more flawed the further we strayed from Creation. So He gave us the Ten Commandments. By measuring ourselves against these laws, we see our flaws. Then, if we ask Him, God will adjust our lives to a perfect measure, not to a distorted measure that will make us useless in God's beautifully planned universe.

DECEMBER 7

PEACE AND SAFETY

While people are saying, "Peace and safety," destruction will come on them suddenly, . . . and they will not escape. 1 Thessalonians 5:3, NIV.

Early Sunday morning, December 7, 1941, an enlisted man in one of the United States services in Honolulu, Hawaii, was practicing with the radar equipment, hoping to learn the system well enough to qualify to operate it. As he watched the screen, he detected incoming planes 132 miles away to the west of the islands. When he reported his observations to his superior officers, the officers laughed at the young man's overactive imagination. There was no threat in that area of the world. Adolf Hitler was busy battling all of Europe, thousands of miles away. And the Japanese? Why, at that very moment, a Japanese envoy was in the midst of negotiations with the president of the United States in Washington, D.C.

By 8:00 a.m. the people of the United States of America knew the meaning of today's text. The surprise attack by Japanese bombers sank more than 15 U.S. ships, destroyed more than 150 planes, and killed or wounded 3,000 people. The war in the Pacific had begun.

In less than a week, America went from a quiet sense of safety to one of total involvement. On December 8 the United States declared war on Japan. And on December 11 President Roosevelt and Congress officially declared war on Germany and Italy as well.

Peace and safety have not been part of the world's history since sin entered. There is never a time when the threat of war has been totally erased. If Iraq isn't rattling sabers, Cuba is. If Qaddafi isn't terrorizing someone, Northern Ireland is. And Satan, the father of violence, sits back and laughs. This is Satan's personality. He is so filled with sin that he isn't happy until he's instigating pain and destruction. And after 6,000 years of mayhem and destruction, his character won't change now.

Imagine, before Jesus cast Satan and his sympathizers from heaven, Lucifer had a chance to repent. He could have come clean. But he sealed his fate and later killed the Son of God. And now you and I and the millions of people trapped on this planet suffer the consequences.

It would be easy to get "down" about the horrid things happening in the world today and throughout history. It would be easy to give up hope. But we have God's solid gold promise of perfect peace, and in His arms we can be totally secure.

Despite mad dictators and kings, renegade rulers and despots, unbelievable crime and violence, all Satan's forces can never take the security of God's promises and His presence from us. I like that, don't you?

DECEMBER 8

EVEN AS A CHILD

The wicked man flees though no one pursues, but the righteous are as bold as a lion. Proverbs 28:1, NIV.

When a bully picks on a younger kid at school or when someone gets blamed unfairly, do you have the courage to speak out, to defend this person against the wrong? Or are you afraid your friends will make fun of you or turn against you? Let me introduce you to one of my all-time heroes.

One day Anne and two of her friends were playing on the lawn in front of her friends' home when they heard someone crying.

Anne stopped and listened. "Who's crying?" she asked.

One of her friends pointed to a 5-year-old boy across the street. "That bigger boy took his toy sailboat away from him."

Anne leaped to her feet. "He had no right to do that! I'm going to make him give it back!"

"Oh, you can't," one of the friends cried. "He'll hurt you."

But Anne didn't answer. Her friends stared in horror as Anne marched across the street and up to the older boy. While they couldn't hear what she said, it obviously worked, for suddenly the older boy shoved the sailboat into the crying child's hands and stormed down the street.

Sounds like a simple little tale, one that could happen anywhere, anytime. Actually, it occurred more than 375 years ago. The courageous little Anne grew into the brave adult Anne Marbury Hutchinson, a woman who helped establish the idea of religious liberty in the American colonies.

Because Anne dared to hold prayer meetings with the women in her neighborhood and to tell them that God was a loving God, not a vengeful God, the leaders of the Massachusetts Bay Colony forced an already sick Anne, her husband, and her children to leave the colony in the middle of a snowy New England winter.

The Hutchinsons didn't know where to go. After praying about it, God sent Roger Williams, another man who believed in religious liberty and who had founded a colony in Rhode Island, to save Anne's and her family's lives. They had to fight snowstorms and icy road conditions, but Anne and her family arrived safely at Roger Williams' colony, where they could worship God as they thought best and where Anne could share her faith with others.

I like the story of Anne Hutchinson because it reminds me that heroic adults were once brave children. People like Daniel, Esther, Peter, Ellen Harmon, Joseph Bates, and Anne developed a habit of courage, a habit of choosing to do what is right long before they grew into adults and had to stand out in public for what they knew to be right. If you want to grow up to be as bold as a lion, start today while you're still a cub, and you'll develop the "muscles" you need when the big tests come.

DECEMBER 9

MATHEMATICAL CHRISTIANS

He determines the number of the stars. Psalm 147:4, NIV.

Ian tapped the keys on his calculator: 1 + 1 =. Instantly a 2 appeared on the screen. He tried it again: 2 + 2 = . . . and up popped a 4. *Let's try, 6 − 4 = . . . 2. Wow, this is cool*, he thought.

Ian carried his magical machine everywhere and demonstrated his fabulous discoveries to everyone he met. Whenever Ian met someone who didn't know how to use his marvelous machine, who added 2 + 2 = 4 with paper and pencil, he insisted that he or she discard the old-fashioned methods of adding and subtracting and learn how to use his marvelous machine.

One day Alex, a friend of Ian's, asked what some of the other buttons on the machine were for. Ian just shrugged. "Who cares?" he said. "They're not important. I know how to add, subtract, multiply, and divide—that's what counts. See?"

Occasionally one of Ian's friends would try to show him how to use the rest of the buttons on the machine.

"Look," a friend tried to explain, "this button allows you to figure percentages, and this one will give you radical numbers. And look! These buttons can tell you the sine, cosine, and tangent of a number."

Ian sniffed indignantly. "I don't need to know those things."

"But, as terrific as arithmetic may be, it's only the beginning."

Poor Ian never learned just how marvelous his machine really was, because he refused to go beyond the basics of arithmetic. An entire world of advanced mathematics, calculus, and trigonometry lies forever beyond his ability. While Ian can add, subtract, multiply, and divide well enough to pay for his groceries, he will never be able to build a skyscraper that can withstand earthquakes or explore the outer regions of the Milky Way by using only simple arithmetic.

Like Ian and his simple arithmetic, a new Christian misses out on the great spiritual truths of the Bible if he or she stops studying and growing. Remember today's text regarding the innumerable thoughts of God, the Creator? Like the grains of sand on a California beach, there is no limit to the incredible truths about God that you and I can learn if we continue to dig deeper in His Word. We can discover the mathematics of prophecy, the calculus of Christian love, and the trigonometry of eternity, which will enable us to develop Christian characters strong enough to withstand the greatest earthquake of all time and will take us far beyond the wispy fringes of the Milky Way.

DECEMBER 10

JUST REWARDS

For the living know that they will die, but the dead know nothing; they have no further reward, and even the memory of

them is forgotten. Their love, their hate and their jealousy have long since vanished. Ecclesiastes 9:5, 6, NIV.

This is the anniversary of the day Alfred died.

"Alfred?" you ask. "So who's Alfred?"

Few people remember that the Swedish chemist and engineer, Alfred Nobel, invented dynamite. Instead of being world renowned for what he created during his lifetime, Alfred is remembered for the program he funded after his death. Alfred Nobel established the prestigious Nobel prize awards in his will. These awards honor people who have made the most significant advancements for the survival of humanity in areas such as science, literature, and politics during a year's time. The most famous of these is the Nobel Peace Prize.

None of the prize winners can say thank you to Alfred for his gift or for being chosen to receive the award. He never gets to attend the banquet or see his picture in the newspaper, for Alfred is dead. Television programs and Hollywood movies would have you and me believe that the dead watch and enjoy what is happening to those they love still living on Planet Earth. While that fantasy may appeal to some people, it is not God's plan.

One of the greatest Olympic athletes of all time, James Francis Thorpe, lost the medals and titles he won for playing minor league baseball in North Carolina before entering the 1912 Olympics. The $25 a week that he had earned disqualified him as an amateur.

In 1982 the International Olympic Committee voted to lift the ban against Thorpe and return his name to the Olympic record books. On January 18, 1983, his gold medals were presented to his children, which made Jim neither happy nor sad, for he had long since died a broken man—in 1953. He sleeps in a grave in the town of Mauch Chunk, Pennsylvania, which later changed its name to Jim Thorpe, in his honor.

A third man, Avery Brundage, president of the International Olympic Committee from 1952-1972, blocked Jim Thorpe's reinstatement until his own death. Why? While the answer to that question lies safely in the books of heaven, it is interesting to note that he was one of the men Jim defeated in the 1912 Olympic pentathlon and decathlon events at Stockholm. Avery came in sixth in the first event and failed to qualify in the second. Did Avery withhold Thorpe's honors for all those years because of jealousy? No one really knows.

Alfred cannot enjoy the good his awards do. Avery's anger can no longer hurt Jim. And Jim's disappointment has long since vanished.

Wrongs righted, honors bestowed, jealousies revealed, and victories won cannot touch the lives of Jim Thorpe, Avery Brundage, or Alfred Nobel now.

However, a day will come when good deeds will be rewarded and evil deeds made right. On that day all questions will be answered, all mysteries solved. And Alfred, Avery, and Jim will be there, right alongside you and me, to receive their just rewards.

DECEMBER 11

TO ALL THE WORLD

We have seen and tell others that the Father sent his Son to be the Savior of the world. 1 John 4:14, TEV.

Have you ever wondered why Jesus was born in Bethlehem of Judea instead of somewhere like New York City of New York, or Rome of Italy, or Tokyo of Japan, or even Cape Town of South Africa? In today's world these cities are important hubs of commerce for their nations, and, in some cases, for the world. Well, part of the reason was that in Jesus' day the center of the then-known world was Judea. More people traveled in and out of this country on their way to other places than any other. Another more important reason was that God made a promise to the Jewish people that He would send them the Messiah. He had to keep His word. That didn't mean Jesus was the property of the Jewish people so they could do with Him as they pleased. Christ's mission was to the entire world. When the Jewish people as a nation failed to carry out their part of the deal, God opened up the invitation to individuals no matter what color their skin might be or what language they might speak or where they might call home.

One popular Christmas carol illustrates how international Christ's birth really was. "O Come, All Ye Faithful" was written by an Englishman named John Francis Wade, who wrote the words to the carol in Latin while living in France. He took the music from an ancient Portuguese hymn. The carol was later translated into 120 languages. There have been more than 140 English translations alone. The one we sing was translated from the Latin in 1852 by Frederick Oakeley. Statesmen such as Robert E. Lee and President Teddy Roosevelt claimed it as their favorite hymn.

GFTG-12

Each time you sing or hear the carol "O Come, All Ye Faithful" during this holiday season, try to picture the children in El Salvador, in Australia, in Thailand, in Brazil, in Egypt, in Zimbabwe, and in Romania singing with you.

DECEMBER 12

OUT OF THE MOUTH OF A CHILD

Inasmuch as ye have done it unto one of the least of these my brethren, ye have done it unto me. Matthew 25:40.

The year Janey learned to read, she was allowed to distribute the family Christmas gifts on Christmas morning. According to the family custom, the person distributing the gifts could open the first package. Eagerly Janey removed the wrapping paper and squealed with delight upon seeing a beautiful porcelain doll with long blonde curls and blue eyes that opened and closed.

"Come on," Janey's older brother, Jeffrey, urged. "The rest of us want to see our presents too."

Reluctantly Janey put the doll aside and handed her brother his first gift. "Ah, a race car. Thanks, Dad."

One after another, Janey read the tags on the presents and passed out the gifts. One after another, family members oohed and aahed over their presents. In a short time, Janey read the tag on the last present beneath the tree. "To Dad, love Jeff." While her father opened the package, Janey searched through the branches for more presents. Finally, she stood and cocked her head to one side. A troubled frown creased her forehead.

"What's the matter Janey," her father asked. "Didn't you get enough presents?"

"Oh, yes, I got plenty."

"Then what are you looking for?"

The little girl's frown deepened as she said, "I thought Christmas was Jesus' birthday, and I was just wondering where His present is. I guess everyone forgot, huh?"

Janey's wise observation should make moms and dads, as well as kids and grandmas, stop and think for a moment. While you and I may not be able to hand-knit a soft, blue woolen sweater for Jesus to wear or construct a birdhouse for His backyard, there are things we can do during the holiday season and all year-round to wish Him a happy birthday.

Jesus Himself said that when His children do kind things for others, they are doing those kind things for Him. Make a list. Discuss the possibilities with your parents, then choose one or two activities that you might do to say Happy Birthday to Jesus during this holiday season.

I've begun the list for you:

1. Give the family's extra blankets or your outgrown winter jackets and coats to the shelter for the homeless.

2. Go Christmas caroling to your neighbors—without asking for a donation.

3. On Christmas Eve, take colorfully wrapped packages of Christmas cookies as gifts to gas station attendants, firemen, hospital employees, policemen, and others who have to work instead of being able to be home with their families.

4. Adopt a grandparent. In the weeks before Christmas, go to a nursing home and adopt a grandparent for Christmas. Talk with him or her, listen to his or her stories, have your parents arrange to invite him or her to your home for the day if he or she is well enough to come. If your adopted grandparent can't enjoy Christmas in your home, visit him or her in the nursing home on Christmas afternoon. Don't forget to take along some goodies to share.

5.

6.

7.

DECEMBER 13

O CHRISTMAS TREE

Your word, O Lord, is eternal; it stands firm in the heavens. Your faithfulness continues through all generations. Psalm 119:89, 90, NIV.

The moment I move into a new house, whether the move occurs in March or July, I choose the perfect spot where I will place our family's Christmas tree when the appropriate time comes. I can hardly wait until it's time to put up our tree. While America's pioneers and those hardier families of today might head out into the high country to cut down their own trees, I am perfectly happy to drive to the vacant lot next to the market and choose a precut version. Then we bring it home, and the ceremony begins. My husband starts the Christmas carols on the CD player, while I remove the first decoration from its box. After the last trinket or doll has been placed on the limbs and the Nativity set holds its honored place beneath the tree, we turn off the table lamps, light the lights, and enjoy the smells, sights, and sounds of Christmas.

History credits Martin Luther of Germany for establishing the tradition of bringing an evergreen into the house to decorate during the Christmas season. The Luthers and their neighbors decorated their holiday tree with small white candles. It wasn't until 1840 that Princess Helena of Mecklenburg introduced the custom to England. Soon after, German immigrants brought the custom to America. German friends of mine still illuminate their trees with white candles each year. However, the invention of the electric light bulb and the fear of fire caused people to abandon the candle for the safer string of lights.

How appropriate it is for the symbol of Christmas to be an evergreen tree! While apple trees stand bare against the winter sky and the maple's brilliant change of clothing falls to the forest floor, the stately evergreen remains full and green year-round. Like Jesus—always the same, from generation to generation.

This Christmas season, as you help decorate the family tree, take time to think about the symbol of the Christmas tree and its promise of eternity.

DECEMBER 14

GREETINGS IN JESUS

All who are with me send you greetings. Give our greetings to our friends in the faith. God's grace be with you all. Titus 3:15, TEV.

In 1843 Sir Henry Cole had a novel idea. The more he considered his plan, the more determined he became to carry it through. Taking his plan to a local London artist named John C. Horsley, he paid the artist to lithograph, then color by hand, the first Christmas cards (1,000 of them), which he sent to his friends. Within 20 years several British companies were manufacturing Christmas cards for the general public to purchase. Now, of course, sending Christmas cards has become a social custom.

Along the way, probably after the invention of the first copy machine, some thrifty person must have decided, "If I have to pay so much to mail out a card that says so little, why not insert a letter in with it?" And so began the Christmas letter.

Exchanging cards and letters with friends and family members who live too far away to see every now and then keeps us in touch with one another. The apostle Paul spent his days in a Roman prison writing letters to his friends and to his Christian family. The New Testament contains some of those letters. Imagine what it must have been like for Mr. Titus when he received a special letter from Paul addressed to him. I imagine that he read it through many times, probably until he had the message memorized. Take some time today to read Paul's short letter to Mr. Titus. In it you will find encouragement and instruction on establishing the new church. At the end of the letter, Paul gave Titus an assignment. "Tell our friends in the faith we said hi, and may God be with you." Sounds like the typical message you or I might add at the end of a card or letter, doesn't it?

An ingenious friend of mine has combined the creativity of Sir Henry Cole with the apostle Paul's witnessing technique. Ann never just sends an ordinary card or letter. She turns every letter into a special Christmas letter and every card into a Christmas card by stuffing the envelope with little poems and other appropriate messages of cheer that she's collected and photocopied for her friends. Kind of like a modern-day Paul, Ann builds up the receiver with encouragement and instruction. It's her own special ministry.

A good idea, huh? What a creative way to share the love of Jesus and the good news of salvation with distant family and friends. If you're looking for an interesting and unusual way to witness to those you love, perhaps Ann's ministry can be your ministry during this holiday season and on into 1993.

DECEMBER 15

A NEW SONG

He put a new song in my mouth, a hymn of praise to our God. Psalm 40:3, NIV.

It had been snowing for 24 hours in the tiny alpine village of Oberndorf, near Salzburg, Austria, as the village schoolmaster, Franz Gruber, made his way to the church parsonage. "Father Josef," Franz cried, "the church organ is broken, and I don't know how to fix it in time for the Christmas program tonight. The children's choir can never sing the ancient carols without the organ to back them up."

"If they can't sing the old carols without the organ," the cheerful young priest suggested, "let's teach them a new song. Why, just this afternoon as I stood watching the snowflakes falling, these words came to me and I wrote them down." The priest placed a copy of his poem in the schoolmaster's hands.

"Silent Night, holy night, All is calm, all is bright;
Round yon virgin mother and Child!
Holy Infant, so tender and mild,
Sleep in heavenly peace."

Silently, Franz read the words. ''Father Josef, the words sing themselves. I am going home right away and write down the melody before it slips away.''

That evening Franz Gruber, Father Josef Mohr, and the choir sang what would one day become the world's best-loved Christmas carol, ''Silent Night.'' If the church organ in Oberndorf hadn't broken down on that snowy Christmas Eve in 1818, that simple yet elegant carol would never have been written, and generations of Christians would have missed the blessing.

God has promised to give each of us a new song to sing. Sometimes, as with Franz Gruber and Josef Mohr, it takes an apparent tragedy before we are prepared to listen to and appreciate that song.

DECEMBER 16

A SPECIAL CHRISTMAS STORY

Love does no harm to its neighbor. Therefore love is the fulfillment of the law. Romans 13:10, NIV.

It happened in the French countryside during World War I. The fierce fighting between the French and the German soldiers subsided as the two armies dug in for the night on the night before Christmas. As the soldiers stood guard, a full moon plated every bush and tree with its silvery light. The beauty of the scene only intensified the German soldiers' homesickness.

Although no one spoke of home and family that night, each soldier envisioned his loved ones celebrating Christmas Eve around the family tree. Forgetting where he was, one soldier started humming his favorite carol, ''Silent Night.'' The next soldier down the trench line added his voice to the tune. Then another and another joined in until the tender melody could be heard from one end of the encampment to the other. When they'd hummed through it once, one particularly brave soldier began singing the words. Again, one after another, the other German soldiers joined in, unaware that the music traveled across to the opposite side of the field, where no man dared enter the French Army's trench.

What a perfect opportunity for the French soldiers to aim their cannons in the direction from which the sound came and blow their enemy to bits! But on the far side of the field, young French soldiers also saw the silver-gilded field and felt the same loneliness for family and friends. So instead of firing their cannons and rifles, the soldiers joined in singing the old German carol. Beautiful harmony filled the crisp night air.

When the song ended, a French officer finally realized what a great opportunity it was to completely destroy the German forces. He ordered his men to fire on the Germans. They refused. How could they kill the Germans after having just sung of sleeping in heavenly peace? The German officers experienced the same reluctance from their men to fire on the enemy. The next day the soldiers on both sides still felt the same about killing one another. The only solution to the problem was to transfer all the soldiers to new posts, where they wouldn't be shooting at anyone they knew.

That's quite a lesson, isn't it? Is there someone you don't like? Try getting to know him or her as a real person. Laugh with him, cry with her, share good times and bad, maybe even sing with him or her—show Christian love. And before you know it, you'll discover that you understand that person a little better. For love sabotages hate and prejudice.

DECEMBER 17

SING HALLELUJAH

May all the kings of the earth praise you, O Lord, when they hear the words of your mouth. May they sing of the ways of the Lord, for the glory of the Lord is great. Psalm 138:4, 5, NIV.

The loftiest of London's titled society, along with the wealthiest of England's social climbers, filled the Covent Garden Theatre on that night in 1743, not only because the famous composer Handel would be presenting his latest oratorio, *The Messiah*, but because King George II would be in attendance.

Backstage the orchestra members, along with the vocalist, anxiously waited for the curtain to rise. Would the king like the oratorio? His stamp of approval could make or break careers. While the audiences of Ireland had loved *The Messiah*, there were no guarantees regarding London's acceptance. And that rested entirely on the whims of one man, King George II.

The curtains opened and the concert began. Throughout the first half of the performance, audience and performer alike could not read the king's reactions to the music. But at the close of Part II of the oratorio, when the first magnificent chords of the "Hallelujah Chorus" began, there was little question as to his reaction. Together the entire assembly, with King George II taking the lead, rose to their feet and remained standing until the end of the anthem.

As one person in attendance later described the experience, "Before such majesty and power, earthly kings and social rulers faded into insignificance."

Since that time, each year during the Christmas season, kings and commoners, presidents and paupers around the world, attend performances of Handel's *Messiah.* And with the opening notes of the "Hallelujah Chorus," they rise to honor the King of kings and Lord of lords.

Mrs. Laetitia Hawkins, the daughter of a famous historian of music, reported that Handel, when asked about writing the "Hallelujah Chorus," replied, "I did think I did see all heaven before me—and the great God Himself."

What will God's children sing as they approach the gates of heaven for the first time? What will the angels sing as a welcome home? Imagine what the song will be like as we stand before God's throne and sing our praise and thanksgiving to Him. When I listen to or sing Handel's "Hallelujah Chorus," I feel like I'm there already. . . . I wish that feeling would never have to end.

DECEMBER 18

MICKI'S MISSIONARY CHRISTMAS

Everyone who has left houses or brothers or sisters or father or mother or children or fields for my sake, will receive a hundred times more and will be given eternal life. Matthew 19:29, TEV.

Micki stared out her bedroom window at the flowering shrubs and tall, willowy palm trees lining the walkway to the mission hospital. No matter how she tried, she couldn't make the warm sand on the beach look like the December snows back home in Vermont. When Mom and Dad first announced that the family was moving to the tropical island of Puerto Rico, 10-year-old Micki had shrieked with delight.

Her friends at school envied Micki's move to the beautiful tropical island. And during the first few weeks on the island, Micki enjoyed exploring the hospital grounds and taking daily trips to the beach, where she swam in the surf and built sand castles. But as the months passed, she grew homesick for her grandparents and friends. When Grandma wrote telling Micki about the beautiful autumn they were having in Vermont, and when Micki's best friend, Susan, wrote about the great time she had at school raking leaves and then jumping into the giant mound of leaves,

Micki felt the first twinges of homesickness. Her illness became critical with the arrival of the Christmas season.

On Christmas Day, Mom and Dad phoned Grandma to wish her a Merry Christmas. They talked some time before Grandma mentioned, "We had our first snowfall last night."

"Snow?" Micki whimpered. "O-o-h-h, I miss having a real Christmas, with snow and all."

"Micki," Grandma reminded, "don't you know that Christmas in Puerto Rico more closely resembles the first Christmas in Palestine than does a Christmas in Vermont? The sand, the palm trees, the warmer weather—isn't that what Jesus would have experienced that first Christmas Day?"

"Yeah, I guess," Micki admitted. "But I miss you and Grandpa so much."

"I miss you too, little one. But I know you're right where God wants you to be, and that makes me happy. After all," Grandma added, "it's that kind of love that sent Jesus here in the first place. And it's that kind of love that will bind us together as a family for all eternity."

Micki choked back her tears as she realized how right her grandmother was. Being a missionary was a lot more than trips to the beach or building sand castles—it meant being happy to be where God wanted you to be, even if you had to miss Christmas in Vermont.

DECEMBER 19

BUILDING GOOD MEMORIES

He [Jesus of Nazareth] went around doing good. Acts 10:38, NIV.

By the time the last flake of a heavy snowstorm had fallen, the fire in the fireplace was hardly more than embers. Jack's mom was decorating Christmas cookies in the kitchen. Lounging half on the couch and half off, 12-year-old Jack stared at the re-run talk show on late night TV. Mom and Dad had relaxed the early-to-bed rules once Christmas vacation had begun. Jack's only problem was that he couldn't find anything worth staying awake for until his dad came in from shoveling snow off the driveway.

"Interesting program?" Jack's dad asked as he stomped the snow from his boots.

"Naw, not really," Jack drawled amid a gigantic yawn.

"Wanna' do something fun with me that you'll remember 10 years from now?"

Jack straightened up. "At this hour?" Dad was usually in bed hours ago.

"Yeah, at this hour."

"Sure." Jack jumped to his feet. "What do you want to do?"

"Let's go shovel the Sorensons' front walk and driveway," Dad suggested.

"Shovel snow?" Jack groaned. He didn't even like grumpy old Mr. Sorenson and his equally grouchy wife.

"Come on," Dad coaxed. "You'll be glad you did."

Reluctantly Jack slipped into his jacket and boots, then followed his dad out of the house. Within a few minutes, they had the sidewalk and the driveway clear of snow without the Sorensons ever discovering who did it.

Years later, whenever Jack and his wife and children would visit his folks for the Christmas holidays, he and his dad would talk about the time they shoveled snow at midnight—a good memory that would last a lifetime.

Whenever you and I go out of our way to do something good for someone else, a much greater blessing becomes ours to keep. True happiness always comes from helping others. First, we feel good about what we've done, and later, we have the memory to enjoy for years to come.

Most important, though, is when we do something good for another person, we are living the way Jesus lived when He was here on earth. Wherever He went, He helped people. He went about doing good. And there's no better example to follow.

DECEMBER 20

ONE SOLITARY LIFE

For if, by the trespass of the one man, death reigned through that one man, how much more will those who receive God's abundant provision of grace and of the gift of righteousness reign in life through the one man, Jesus Christ. Romans 5:17, NIV.

Have you ever wondered what the world would be like if Jesus Christ hadn't come as a baby to Bethlehem to become our Saviour? There would be no Christmas, of course. But also there would be no churches, no Christian hymns, no Christian missionaries, no Christian doctors or nurses, no Christian hospitals, no Sabbath—can you add to the list of advantages we have because of Jesus' birth?

No one knows who wrote the following familiar essay, but the Christmas season is the perfect time to reread it and to think about how different everything would have been if Jesus hadn't been born.

"He was born in an obscure village, the child of a peasant woman. He grew up in another village. He worked in a carpenter's shop until He was 30, and then for three years was an itinerant preacher. He never wrote a book. He never held an office. He never owned a home. He never traveled 200 miles from the place where He was born. He never did one of the things that usually accompany greatness. He had no credentials but Himself.

"Although He walked the land over, curing the sick, giving sight to the blind, healing the lame, and raising people from the dead, the top established religious leaders turned against Him. His friends ran away. He was turned over to His enemies. He went through the mockery of a trial. He was spat upon, flogged, and ridiculed. He was nailed to a cross between two thieves. While He was dying, the executioners gambled for the only piece of property He had on earth, and that was His robe. When He was dead, He was laid in a borrowed grave through the pity of a friend.

"Nineteen wide centuries have come and gone, and today He is the central figure of the human race and the leader of the column of progress.

"All the armies that ever marched, and all the navies that were ever built, and all the parliaments that ever sat, and all the kings that ever reigned, put together, have not affected the life of man upon this earth as has that One Solitary Life."

DECEMBER 21

THE SPIRIT OF GIVING

For the wages of sin is death, but the gift of God is eternal life in Christ Jesus our Lord. Romans 6:23, NIV.

"Why in the world did you spend your money on a mustache cup?" Mel snarled at his cringing 7-year-old son, Mickey. "I don't even have a mustache!"

The boy's eyes filled with tears as he slunk away. He hadn't known the ceramic mug had anything to do with mustaches. He just thought the funny-faced old man on the ceramic cup would make his stern, no-nonsense father smile. And Mickey would do almost anything for a smile from his dad.

Mickey's mother frowned, then reached out to console her son when Mel defended, "Money doesn't grow on trees. The kid needs to learn to spend what he has more wisely."

Horrified, I watched and listened as Mel unwrapped and found fault with each of his gifts. The tie his wife gave him was the wrong color. He didn't need the robe his mother gave, since his old one was in fine condition. He was allergic to the bottle of cologne; his new sweater didn't fit quite right. And the white dress shirt didn't have a button-down collar. I don't remember what he said about the book I got him, since I tuned him out long before. I didn't particularly want him to spoil my Christmas, too.

Later, after I had time to subdue my anger, I realized that I not only felt sorry for Mickey, but I had more pity for his father. Poor Mel! No gift will ever be good enough or expensive enough to please him.

Mel has lots of company in the world today. When Jesus promises the gift of eternal life to all who love Him, Mel and others like him gripe and find fault. They want eternal life, but with no strings attached. They want to live a selfish, sinful life here, and instead of receiving the wages they deserve, they want God to grant them the gift of eternal life so they can go on sinning forever and ever.

Of course I pray that Mel will give his heart to Jesus and find the contentment and satisfaction he so desperately needs. But I'm also glad the population of heaven will not include selfish people, greedy people, hateful people, complaining people, cruel people, scheming people—the list goes on. I'm glad that Jesus can change selfish hearts into generous ones; greedy hearts into giving ones; hateful into loving; complaining into praising; cruel into kind; and scheming hearts into trusting hearts. Wherever I fit in that list of sinners, I'm glad I don't have to stay there. For, most of all, I am glad He can change me.

DECEMBER 22

THE PERFECT CHRISTMAS GIFT

It is more blessed to give than to receive. Acts 20:35, NIV.

Carl wanted to buy the perfect Christmas gift for his mother. She deserved the best. During the year since his father had died, she had worked very hard to keep adequate food on the table and clothes on him and his three sisters. In September Carl spotted the perfect gift in the window of Anderson's Jewelry Store in the mall—an antique clock from Holland. The price tag attached to the clock read $75, a hefty sum for any 12-year-old boy to manage. From that moment on, Carl schemed and saved every spare cent he could manage on his paper route. Whenever old Mr. Cooper gave him a tip for delivering the paper straight to the door, Carl stuck it in his treasure box.

Carl was doing well until Betsy's feet hit a growing spurt and the little girl needed new shoes. Mother asked Carl to take his youngest sister shopping. That's when Carl gave Betsy the extra $10 needed to help buy the more expensive shoes that she wanted so badly.

Then at Thanksgiving time, when Mama didn't have enough money for the family's traditional meal, Carl spent $20 on the necessary groceries and left them on the doorstep, rang the bell, and ran.

Three days before Christmas, Carl took out his treasure box and counted his money—$55! And he still didn't have gifts for his sisters. He didn't know what to do. *Maybe if I talk with Mr. Anderson, he will sell the clock cheaper or something,* Carl thought.

Carl went to talk with the jeweler. He explained how things had been during the past year for his mother and how much she'd love the clock. He told the jeweler about Betsy's shoes and about the Thanksgiving food. Then he asked the man, "Would you consider selling the clock for $45?"

Mr. Anderson shook his head no.

"Well, if you change your mind . . ." Carl wrote out his name and address on a piece of paper, handed it to the shopkeeper, and walked out of the store. *Oh, well, I might as well spend the money on some toys for the girls and, maybe, a new scarf for Mama.*

On Christmas morning, as Carl's mother removed the wrapping paper from the pink nylon scarf her son had chosen for her, Carl blurted out the story of the clock. "I'm sorry, Mama. I tried so hard to save up enough money to get you that clock. It would have been such a perfect gift for you."

Carl's mother swept her son into her arms, and with tears in her eyes, she said, "Son, you have already given me the perfect Christmas gift. You have given yourself. No mother could ask for more."

DECEMBER 23

THE REAL THING

There is a friend who sticks closer than a brother. Proverbs 18:24, NIV.

When I was a preschooler, my parents took me to the county fair. On the way my father asked me what I wanted to do most when we arrived. I replied, "I want to ride a real pony."

Since the pony rides were near the parking lot, my father suggested we go there first. As I clutched his hand and stumbled across the dirt clods, I kept repeating my request, "I'm going to ride a pony. I'm going to ride a pony."

Before I realized what was happening, my father had paid the attendant for my ride and was lifting me onto the back of a shaggy, fierce-looking horse. I screamed in terror. "Let me off. Let me off!"

"Kay," my father scolded, "you said you wanted to ride on a real pony."

"No, no," I sobbed. "I want to ride a real pony!"

Lifting me off the saddle, he said, "OK, show me the real pony you wish to ride."

"Over there," I pointed toward the carnival rides. "Over there."

After allowing me to pull him through the crowds, he discovered that my "real pony" was a painted wooden horse on the merry-go-round.

Like me and my "real pony," many adults and children confuse their ideas about God with the fictional character of Santa Claus. Some people who once believed that Santa Claus was real, that he lives at the North Pole with his elves and his reindeer, later find it difficult to believe that a true God exists, that He lives in heaven with the angels, and that He loves them.

God is the real thing, and He's no Santa Claus. While He loves to demonstrate His love for His children, He is not a bearded old man in a red flannel suit who can be bribed to bring gifts to good little boys and girls. He is a whole lot more. He is our Friend, our Father, the Creator, and the King of the universe. What other titles can you name for God? Your Bible concordance will help you. Most of all, God the Father is a real, live being who loves us and wants us to love Him in return, not for what He can give us but for what He has already given—His Son, Jesus.

DECEMBER 24

A MESSAGE FROM OUTER SPACE

And God said, Let the waters under the heaven be gathered together unto one place, and let the dry land appear: and it was so. And God called the dry land Earth; and the gathering together of the waters called he Seas: and God saw that it was good. Genesis 1:9, 10.

Early in the morning on December 24, 1968, a hundred people squeezed into a space meant for no more than 74 in a NASA viewing room to watch the big screen and see the same scene that the three astronauts

Frank Borman, James Lovell, Jr., and William Anders were seeing out the *Apollo 8* windows. Although it would not land, the *Apollo 8* craft would circle the moon for the first time.

Suddenly the familiar map of the earth vanished from the big screen, and in its place the map of the moon appeared. One reporter said his heart literally stopped beating from the excitement of the moment. A lighted sign above the screen flashed "Quiet Please," as if any of the people assembled was making a sound as they absorbed the moment.

Through the intercom, they could hear the captain of communications at NASA say, "*Apollo 8*, you are riding the best bird we can find."

Jim Lovell, aboard *Apollo* replied, "Thanks a lot, troops. We'll see you on the other side [of the moon]."

One of the viewers in the room whispered, "Jim, I hope so. I hope so."

At NASA the controllers counted the minutes until the spacecraft reappeared around the edge of the moon. The technicians in the control room and the people in the viewing room stood ominously still. The craft reappeared within seconds of its predicted time.

Once communication had been reestablished, to the surprise of the controllers and the millions of people watching on television, the three crew members took turns reading from Genesis about the creation of the earth. The effect was overpowering as Frank Borman, the commander of *Apollo 8*, read the last verses, which are today's text. When he finished reading, "and God said that it was good," he paused, then concluded, "And from the crew of *Apollo 8*, we close with good night, good luck, a Merry Christmas, and God bless all of you—all of you on the good earth."

As one NASA technician explained: "There were only six days left in the sad and chaotic year of 1968. Martin Luther King, Jr., and Robert Kennedy had been killed. The nation's cities were being torn apart by burnings, and the country was bitterly divided over the Vietnam War. Yet at that moment, I was standing on God's good earth and I was proud to be an American."

Frank Borman's message that Christmas Eve became the second most important message ever to reach us from outer space. Tomorrow we will read together the most important message ever delivered from outer space to people on Planet Earth.

THE ANGELS' SONG

And there were in the same country shepherds abiding in the field, keeping watch over their flock by night. Luke 2:8.

Stars shone in the clear night sky like diamonds scattered on black velvet as the shepherds herded their sheep onto the grassy slope overlooking Bethlehem. A long night stretched out ahead of them before dawn would break and they could go home to their wives and children, a long night of stargazing and good conversation with old friends.

Picture yourself as one of the shepherds on the hillside that night. Imagine the wind blowing through your hair. Listen as the older shepherds cluster together, first sharing the local town gossip, then moving on to meatier topics such as the coming of the Promised One. See the outlines of two or three of the youngest shepherds guarding the outer fringes of the flock and rounding up any strays. Join one of the groups of younger shepherds dotting the hillside. Listen while they talk about their dreams, about the prettiest young women in the village, then about the latest run-in with the hated Romans, and of the promised King who will set them free.

Suddenly a bright light fills the sky. An angel, straight from the throne of God, delivers the most important message ever sent from outer space to Planet Earth: "Christ, the Messiah, is born!" Hear the angel chorus sing, "Glory to God in the highest, and on earth peace, good will toward men."

Now for a special Christmas treat, take your favorite version of the Bible and read Luke 2:9-20 as a dramatic reading. Assign each person in the family a role to play. You will need at least one narrator, or two people could alternately read the verses; the angel Gabriel; and an angel choir. If you have a Nativity set, have one of the younger members of the family move the characters about as the story progresses.

What must it have been like for God the Father, God the Holy Spirit, and the rest of heaven's angels to watch the night's proceedings? What questions do you imagine the angels might have asked the Father? Satan and his demons also watched in shock and horror. Do you think they were surprised that the Son of God actually went through with the plan as promised? And the rest of the inhabitants of the universe—what do you imagine they were thinking?

And last, imagine the majority of the people of the world who did not even notice the wonderful event. The very ones for whom the event transpired cared the least.

AS A THIEF

Wake up! . . . Remember, therefore, what you have received and heard; obey it, and repent. But if you do not wake up, I will come like a thief, and you will not know at what time I will come to you. Revelation 3:2, 3, NIV.

The Hessian soldiers in the British army stationed at Trenton, New Jersey, continued their 1776 Christmas celebrations of feasting and drinking well into the evening. Colonel Rall, the Hessian commander, knew his encampment was safe from General Washington and his ragtag army on the other side of the Delaware. Rall felt so secure that he placed a token guard at the borders of the camp without even bothering to order his men to set up the cannons.

After the common soldiers staggered off to their quarters to sleep off the effects of the night's partying, Rall and his fellow officers gathered around a table at headquarters, not to plan battle strategy but to drink and play cards. Sometime during the night, one of the guards brought a message to headquarters and gave it to the corporal on duty. "A Loyalist just asked me to deliver this note to Colonel Rall," the guard reported.

The corporal took the note and entered the room where the officers were playing. When the corporal tried to explain his mission to Rall, Rall was in the middle of a winning streak and didn't want to be bothered. So instead of reading the note, Rall slipped the note into his vest pocket and waved the corporal away.

The message on the note was from a farmer who lived alongside the Delaware River near the town that is today called Taylorsville. From his bedroom window, the farmer had spotted the first of the flat-bottomed boats carrying General George Washington's 2,400 men across the river in preparation for an attack on the British position at Trenton. Washington and his troops reached the picket line before they were discovered, completely taking the British encampment by surprise in a 25-minute battle. More than 1,000 prisoners were taken. Colonel Rall defeated himself. He probably died without ever discovering that the note in his vest pocket could have saved his life and possibly have won the war.

Jesus is coming back a second time—not as a baby in a manger, but as the King of kings and Lord of lords. He has warned you and me to be prepared for His return. To those who are not prepared, those who are not watching and longing for His coming, it will be like Washington and his troops swooping down on Rall and his Hessian soldiers. They will have defeated themselves, for they knew all along but did nothing to prepare for it.

DECEMBER 27

THE FESTIVAL OF LIGHTS

You are like light for the whole world. . . . Your light must shine before people, so that they will see the good things you do and praise your Father in heaven. Matthew 5:14-16, TEV.

In my husband's classroom hangs a photograph of the United States taken from a U.S. satellite in outer space—at night. The east coast is ablaze with light. The individual lights of cars, homes, and shopping malls run together from one city to the next to form large blotches of light. Tiny lights, bright lights, soft lights, glaring lights, all contribute to the festival of lights. The size of the blotches parallels the size of the city or the number of people living in that region.

However, the spots of light across the country diminish in quantity and brilliance as you move west until you reach the Pacific Ocean. Patches of lights string north from San Diego to Los Angeles, and up the Sacramento Valley and the San Francisco Bay area. From there they leap to Portland and up to Seattle. In the vast southwestern region, it is easy to identify cities like Albuquerque, Tucson, and Oklahoma City.

God commissioned you and me to be lights to the world. If God took a similar picture of the earth from outer space, except that it would be of the lights shining from His children, would the light distribution be the same as it is on my husband's classroom poster? Would New York City be brighter than Boise, Idaho? Would Boston, Massachusetts, outshine Omaha, Nebraska? Would He see a festival of lights identifying your town, your school, your home?

Remember, though, that God didn't say, "Check to be certain your brother's light is shining or your sister's light is bright enough." He just said, "Let *your* light so shine . . ." You don't have to worry about anyone's light, but your own. And size doesn't matter either; whether your light illuminates the Astrodome in Texas or a closet in a home in St. Louis, you are equally important to God, for you are faithfully fulfilling His command to you to be a light to the world. So how's your light today? Is your light visible on God's giant photograph, or is there a splotch of darkness in the place where you live?

HOUSES BUILT ON ROCK

So then, anyone who hears these words of mine and obeys them is like a wise man who built his house on a rock. . . . But anyone who hears these words of mine and does not obey them is like a foolish man who built his house on the sand. Matthew 7:24-26, TEV.

In the middle of writing this book, I moved with my husband to Santa Cruz, California, a small beach town a few miles from the epicenter of the 1989 San Francisco earthquake. Before we moved, I listened as my husband asked his new employer about the quake damage.

"Oh," the principal said, "there was some damage, of course. The school's library books fell off the shelves, for instance, but nothing big like the shopping mall downtown. The mall was reduced to rubble, and four people were killed."

"But the mall is less than two miles away."

"True, but remember, the school is built on rock, whereas the downtown section of Santa Cruz is built on a plate of sand. None of the buildings built on the rocky surface suffered any real damage."

Hmm, I thought. *Some truths never change.* Almost 2,000 years ago Jesus told His disciples about the wisdom of building one's house on the rock. Cradle roll and kindergarten children sing about the wise man and the foolish man and the walls that come tumbling down.

Do you remember the third verse to that song—the part about building your life on the Lord Jesus Christ? Without that verse, the song is nothing more than a ditty, and the wisdom of building on rock or sand must make good sense. Adding the third verse turns a simple ditty and common sense into a heavenly truth.

Yesterday we talked about shining as lights in this dark world—lights to shine for Jesus. If you forget that the basics of being a Christian means building your life on Jesus Christ and His love, you will never shine as God wants you to—and you'll be no wiser than the foolish man who built his house on sand.

DECEMBER 29

A HEARTBEAT AWAY

Blessed are the pure in heart, for they will see God. Matthew 5:8, NIV.

During the past few years people have become concerned about blood cholesterol levels and maintaining healthy hearts—and for good reason. A damaged heart cannot sustain life for long. After all, this relatively simple machine works hard to keep you alive.

For instance, how many times does your heart beat in one year's time? While your heartbeat is by no means constant and the rate can vary from minute to minute, depending on stress and body temperature, a rate of 72-80 beats per minute is considered normal for a healthy heart at rest. And since a solar year contains 525,948 minutes and 48 seconds, at the rate of 80 beats per minute, your heart beats an average of 42,075,904 beats in one year's time, give or take a million. In one average lifetime of 70 years, a human heart beats some 3 billion times.

We keep our physical hearts pure, healthy, and thumping happily within our rib cages by exercising every day and by eating foods that keep the veins and arteries unclogged. While modern medicine has discovered a way to replace one human heart with that of another, it is a painful and expensive operation, and not always successful. If possible, it is an operation to avoid—just ask my friend Wesley Merrill, the first heart-transplant recipient in the Pacific Northwest.

When we come to Jesus, He performs a spiritual heart transplant by giving us a pure, brand-new, perfect heart. It enables us to live a healthy spiritual life. We keep our spiritual hearts operating in much the same way as our physical hearts. Feasting on the Word of God instead of junk food keeps the veins that enter the spiritual heart clear and clean. Exercising our faith in God and our love for one another each day keeps the arteries in good working order.

However, when our new heart gets clogged with sin, Jesus, the great physician, is ready and willing to replace our broken-down hearts once again. And one day He will take all of those whose hearts He has purified home with Him, where we will live together with God the Father for all eternity.

DECEMBER 30

IMAGINATION PRAYER

Today, on the 365th day of 1992, we are going to take a trip in our imaginations. First, choose one person to read today's lesson while everyone else closes his or her eyes and completely relaxes. As you picture the scenes described, remember to use all five senses—touch, taste, smell, sight, and hearing. You will share your answers at the end of the journey.

1. Picture yourself in your favorite room of any home you've lived in. What does the room look like? What are you wearing?

2. Imagine yourself sitting in your favorite chair in that room. Describe the chair. There's a knock at the door. You go to open it. Jesus is standing there.

3. What does He look like? What is He wearing? What does He say to you? You ask Him in and invite Him to sit in your favorite chair.

4. Where do you sit? What do you talk about? What three questions do you ask Him?

5. How does He answer your questions? After you talk a while, you invite Him to dinner.

6. What food do you prepare for Him to eat? When you both finish the meal, He invites you to go with Him to His home. You take Him up on the invitation.

7. Describe the journey. You enter the gates of the Holy City, and an angel takes you to the throne of God.

8. What does the actual throne look like? Jesus is sitting there.

9. What does He look like now? How is He dressed?

10. What other people from earth are standing at the foot of the throne? Jesus beckons you to come up and sit beside Him on the throne of the universe. You obey.

11. What does it feel like to sit next to Jesus on His favorite chair?

Now read today's text.

Here I am! I stand at the door and knock. If anyone hears my voice and opens the door, I will come in and eat with him, and he with me. To him who overcomes, I will give the right to sit with me on my throne, just as I overcame and sat down with my Father on his throne. Revelation 3:20, 21, NIV.

Ask everyone to open his or her eyes. Reread the questions, giving each participant time to share his or her sights and impressions. When you finish all 11 questions, continue on to the final question.

12. What did it feel like to open your eyes after your imaginary journey? For me, I felt kind of sad, having to return to earth. After God gave Ellen White visions of heaven, she described returning to earth as an overwhelming "darkness."

While today's journey was totally imaginary, it won't always be so. One day soon you and I, along with all of God's children throughout the ages, will make just such a trip from Planet Earth to heaven—not in our imaginations, but "in the flesh." God's promise to take us home with Him forever is as real as the air we breathe and the food we eat and the paper it took to make this book.

That golden promise is worth any price. Go for the gold!

DECEMBER 31

A QUANTUM LEAP

By my God have I leaped over a wall. 2 Samuel 22:30.

Three years ago the award-winning television show *Quantum Leap* first aired. The program's theme was based on a scientist who had discovered a way to leap back and forth through time. But something went wrong with his calculations. He couldn't control the leap. With each leap, he faced a new problem and new fears.

You might not have thought about it, but tonight at midnight you will make the quantum leap from 1992 to 1993. Are you sometimes a little afraid of what the new year will bring? While you are eager to have the freedoms of a grown-up, do you occasionally wish you could stay a child? Maybe with all the physical changes taking place inside you, you feel as if your body is betraying you, forcing you to leap into a different person—and that's scary. Perhaps in 1993 you will move to a new home and to a new school or be forced to adjust to new members of your family or the loss of old members. And you wonder just how you'll manage to make such a gigantic change, a leap into the unknown.

Most of us are stronger than we think we are. We possess an inner strength when trouble threatens. The will is more important than the skill. For instance, two men are working on a car. While one man is underneath, the jack slips and the car falls. His companion finds himself picking up the car and rescuing his friend from death. Where did his strength come from?

You may be aware of your everyday strengths and weaknesses, such as how high you can jump, how fast you can run, or how brave you feel. Yet there are times when you don't feel strong. You're scared, you're lonely, and any inner strength you might have had has evaporated. That's when you actually have the most power, and that's when Jesus can do the most for you—when you feel the weakest.

When you call on His strength, no walls are impossible for you to scale, no problems are too big for you to solve, and no enemy is too strong for you to defeat. With Jesus at your side, any goal is possible, any dream can come true, and any fear can be overcome. So don't be afraid of the future. Bring on the new year. Get ready to leap into the exciting world of tomorrow! Nothing can stop you and Jesus. Go on, give it your all. Go for the gold!

SCRIPTURE INDEX